CLINICAL
ASSESSMENT
FOR SOCIAL WORKERS

Related books of interest

Research Methods for Social Workers: A Practice-Based Approach, Second Edition
Samuel S. Faulkner and Cynthia A. Faulkner

**Mixed Methods Research for Social Work:
Integrating Methodologies to Strengthen Practice and Policy**
Wendy L. Haight and Laurel N. Bidwell

Social Work Evaluation: Enhancing What We Do, Second Edition
James R. Dudley

**Evidence-Based Practices for Social Workers:
An Interdisciplinary Approach, Second Edition**
Thomas O'Hare

**Essential Skills of Social Work Practice:
Assessment, Intervention, and Evaluation, Second Edition**
Thomas O'Hare

Interviewing for the Helping Professions: A Relational Approach
Fred R. McKenzie

Social Work Practice with Families: A Resiliency-Based Approach, Second Edition
Mary Patricia Van Hook

Best Practices in Community Mental Health: A Pocket Guide
Vikki L. Vandiver

CLINICAL ASSESSMENT

FOR SOCIAL WORKERS

Quantitative and Qualitative Methods

Edited by

CATHELEEN JORDAN
University of Texas, Arlington

CYNTHIA FRANKLIN
University of Texas, Austin

OXFORD
UNIVERSITY PRESS

OXFORD
UNIVERSITY PRESS

Oxford University Press is a department of the University of Oxford.
It furthers the University's objective of excellence in research, scholarship,
and education by publishing worldwide.

Oxford   New York
Auckland   Cape Town   Dar es Salaam   Hong Kong   Karachi
Kuala Lumpur   Madrid   Melbourne   Mexico City   Nairobi
New Delhi   Shanghai   Taipei   Toronto

With offices in
Argentina   Austria   Brazil   Chile   Czech Republic   France   Greece
Guatemala   Hungary   Italy   Japan   Poland   Portugal   Singapore
South Korea   Switzerland   Thailand   Turkey   Ukraine   Vietnam

Oxford is a registered trade mark of Oxford University Press
in the UK and certain other countries.

Published in the United States of America by
Oxford University Press
198 Madison Avenue, New York, NY 10016

Library of Congress Cataloging-in-Publication Data

    Clinical assessment for social workers : quantitative and qualitative methods /
edited by Catheleen Jordan, Cynthia Franklin.—Fourth edition.
       pages cm
    Includes bibliographical references.
    ISBN 978-0-19-065643-0 (pbk.: alk. paper)
    1. Psychodiagnostics. 2. Psychiatric social work. 3. Needs assessment.
4. Behavioral assessment. 5. Family assessment. I. Jordan, Catheleen, 1947–
editor. II. Franklin, Cynthia, editor.
    RC469.J67 2016
    616.89′075—dc23
                                                        2015026153I

ISBN 978-0-19-065643-0

Dedication

For my children and grandchildren—Kate, Cormac, Chris, Melody, Kaydence, Leah, Breana, Kayne—for filling our family life with joy!—Catheleen Jordan

To Jim and Christina, who continue to be my inspiration—Cynthia Franklin

Contents

APPENDIXES

List of Tables, Figures, and Boxes

TABLES

FIGURES

BOXES

Preface

Clinical Assessment for Social Workers: Quantitative and Qualitative Methods, fourth edition, is designed for graduate and undergraduate social work students, as well as for social work practitioners and other related helping professionals—licensed professional counselors, marriage and family counselors, and psychologists. This book has always advocated the use of a scientific orientation to practice, so in keeping with the goals of the text, this new fourth edition emphasizes evidence-based assessment and provides new examples of standardized measures and other approaches to assessment that can be used in clinical practice. The fourth edition of *Clinical Assessment*, like earlier editions of this text, continues to show how to combine practice wisdom and evidence-based methods when formulating assessments and intervention plans. This new edition also emphasizes the biopsychosocial-spiritual framework and the importance of the strengths perspective in assessment, including updates on neuroscience. Additionally, every chapter in this fourth edition includes new updated information that covers approaches to assessment, and how to assess various client populations including clients from multistressed and diverse ethnic backgrounds. Additional measurement instruments are also covered in each chapter; new examples of measures, including measures from the public domain that can be used for pedagogy and clinical practice, have been added to the chapters.

Clinical Assessment for Social Workers, fourth edition, also updates clinical practitioners on recent changes in the *Diagnostic and Statistical Manual of Mental Disorders*, fifth edition (DSM-5) and adds new diagnostic approaches and assessment measures from the DSM-5 to each chapter. While acknowledging the importance of the DSM-5, *Clinical Assessment for Social Workers* also goes much farther by defining the differences between assessment and diagnosis and provides critiques to the DSM-5 while at the same time illustrating how the DSM-5 can be used in a broader approach that takes into account the person-in-environment assessment and the context of the client.

Similar to previous editions, the current book reviews several assessment methods from different theoretical models, and shows different assessment methods such as interview questions and measurement instruments as they apply to various populations. Even though we cover assessment methods from various theoretical perspectives, we do not assume that the reader adheres to a particular theoretical orientation or epistemology. Instead, we advocate for multiple methods and believe that information can be collected using a variety of different ways. Having a repertoire of methods and measurement instruments for performing assessment, derived from different perspectives, allows professionals more creativity and flexibility in information gathering and intervention planning. For example, some clients might readily provide information by filling out a standardized questionnaire, whereas other clients might be happier sharing information through a genogram, ecological map, or interview.

This revision of the *Clinical Assessment* text provides new case material and clinical examples of different assessment methods, and resources that will help clinicians find and evaluate measurement instruments. Chapter 1 offers a brief overview of the clinical assessment process, including a definition of assessment and an overview of several different approaches for assessing, monitoring, and evaluating a client's progress over time. Chapters 2 and 3 provide a complementary understanding of quantitative and qualitative assessment methods with new examples; chapter 3 also updates information on how to find and evaluate standardized measures. Each chapter further shows specific examples of assessment methods. Chapters 4 to 9 provide case studies that integrate the results of measurement instruments into intervention plans. Chapters 4 to 9 have further been thoroughly updated with new measures and case materials that will help practitioners understand DSM-5 diagnoses for different client populations, as well as ways to understand and assess client groups. Chapter 8 also offers new measures on assessing stress and caregiving and focuses more attention on cultural sensitivity and the importance of assessing high-risk behaviors. Chapter 9 specifically focuses on how to assess different ethnic groups; it was updated to show how to use the DSM-5 cultural assessment tools. Chapter 10 has been updated to help practitioners plan interventions and evaluate their own practices; it includes additional resources for finding evidence-based practices (EBPs). Every chapter also emphasizes the centrality of clinical decision-making and client preferences in assessment.

We thank the reviewers for their insightful and helpful reviews of the manuscript, the chapter contributors, and the social workers who have used this book into its fourth edition. We also thank Anao Zhang for his helpful comments and editorial work on the manuscript and our publisher, David Follmer, for his continued support of our work. Finally, we thank our families and friends for their tolerance, support, and sense of humor during the development of this text.

PART I

Introduction to Clinical Assessment

Assessment in social work is an ongoing process that begins with problem (and strength) identification using both quantitative and qualitative approaches to gathering information. This fourth edition text continues to emphasize the use of multiple methods for assessment and adhering to the evidence-based approach, which the early chapters of the book introduce. Part I sets the stage for the remaining chapters by defining the process of clinical assessment and illustrating a range of assessment methods that social workers can use in practice. Part I, chapter 1, "Assessment Process and Methods," introduces the reader to the complex case conceptualization and practice skills involved in assessment and provides an integrative assessment framework using several theoretical perspectives that are used in social work, such as psychosocial, cognitive-behavioral, and strengths-based, solution-focused brief therapy. Diagnostic approaches like the *Diagnostic and Statistical Manual of Mental Disorders*, fifth edition (DSM-5) and *International Classification of Diseases*, tenth revision (ICD-10; World Health Organization, 2010) and specific methods for determining the selection of measurement instruments are also covered along with the importance of clinical decision-making. Chapter 1 shows how assessment information is intricately interwoven with the development of intervention plans including outcome measurement, further setting the stage for information in subsequent chapters.

CHAPTER 1

Assessment Process and Methods

Cynthia Franklin and Catheleen Jordan

The content in chapter 1 provides the background and underlying philosophy necessary to navigate through the rest of the book. In this chapter, we provide a definition of social work assessment and a framework for understanding how to conduct a comprehensive social work assessment. We briefly describe many facets of social work assessment, concepts that are subsequently elaborated on and applied to populations in other chapters of this book. We also discuss ways that students and practitioners use theory to guide practice, and common practice skills that are needed for being able to do assessment, particularly clinical decision making, problem specification, problem monitoring, and treatment planning. This chapter and the chapters to follow show practitioners how to use evidence-based knowledge to guide their assessments with clients. In particular, this chapter highlights the importance of using evidence in assessment and describes criteria for evaluating assessments. Finally, chapter 1 highlights an integrative, technical-eclectic approach for choosing which elements go into a comprehensive assessment; this approach is supported through the review of several social work practice models. We use technical eclecticism to integrate assessment information across the models reviewed into the Integrative Skills Assessment Protocol, which practitioners can use to guide assessment. In addition, we show how assessment in an ongoing clinical process that involves moving from assessment to intervention improves intervention outcomes.

DEFINITION OF SOCIAL WORK ASSESSMENT

Social work assessment requires a complex set of practice skills that range from interviewing skills and making accurate judgments based on practice theory(s), to using the best methods available to obtain information, and to competently using various sources of information to make valid and reliable decisions concerning client care. Barker (2003) defines social work assessment as "the process of determining the

nature, cause, progression, and prognosis of a problem and the personalities and situations involved therein; the social work function of
acquiring an understanding of a problem, what causes it, and what can
be changed to minimize or resolve it" (p. 30). This definition suggests
that assessment involves looking into people and their social environments and ascertaining problems, causes of problems, and plans for
changing those problems. Austiran (2009) describes assessment as an
ongoing process involving five steps:

1. Exploration through multiple methods, such as listening, observing, and other means of data collection;

2. Inferential thinking, which leads to clinical judgments that are
   grounded in empirical knowledge and guide the decision making
   about a case;

3. Evaluation of the capacity of a client's functioning and skills, as
   well as of the stressors of social environments that may impede a
   client's optimal functioning;

4. Well-defined problem definitions that are agreed on by client and
   social worker; and

5. Intervention planning with the client, which leads to more effective outcomes.

Chapters in this book flesh out this definition with clinical examples
and cover these five steps in some detail, demonstrating many methods
and techniques that social workers can use in conducting clinical assessments. A person-in-environment, systems approach to examining clients
and their concerns guides assessment in social work. Diverse methods are
used in an assessment to identify and measure specific problem behaviors
and protective and resilience factors, and to determine when treatment is
necessary and which treatment(s) might work best in a given situation.
When conducting an assessment, social workers usually gather information from a variety of sources (e.g., the client, family members, case
records, observation, rapid assessment measures, genograms). Types of
assessment include biopsychosocial history taking, multiple-dimension
crisis assessment, symptom checklists, functional analysis, and mental
status exams (Levine, 2008).

The methods of assessment illustrated within this book are multidimensional and include face-to-face interviews with people (for twelve
essential questions to ask in these interviews, see box 1.1), behavioral
observations, reviews of written documents, and the use of standardized
measurement instruments. As suggested in the five steps mentioned earlier, assessment also refers to ongoing analysis and synthesis of information about the client and his or her social environment for the purpose of
compiling a case formulation, diagnosis, and coherent intervention plan

Box 1.1
Twelve Essential Questions to Be Asked in a
Brief Assessment Interview

1. Why is the client entering therapy now?
2. Are there any signs of psychosis, delusions, or thought disorders that would indicate that the client needs immediate medical and/or psychiatric treatment?
3. Are there signs of illness indicating the need for neurological or other medical treatment?
4. Is there evidence of depression or suicidal or homicidal ideations?
5. What are the presenting complaints?
6. What are the important antecedent factors of the client's problem?
7. Who or what is maintaining the problem?
8. What does the client wish to derive from therapy?
9. What is the client's preference for therapy style? How can you match that style?
10. Are there clear indications for a specific modality of treatment based on a person-in-environment assessment?
11. Can a therapeutic alliance be maintained or should the client be referred?
12. What are the client's positive attributes and strengths?

SOURCE: Adapted from Franklin, C., & Jordan, C. (1999). The clinical utility of models and methods of assessment in managed care. In B. S. Compton & B. Galaway (Eds.), Social work processes (p. 289). Pacific Grove, CA: Brooks/Cole.

to help the client. Particular elements of an assessment are usually guided by practice theories and a case construction process, which involves the cognitive appraisal of information, use of diverse theories and clinical judgment, and the incorporation of that information into a written psychosocial study or report. Underlying this approach is an evidence-based philosophy and guidelines for selecting the best practices.

Using Evidence-Based Practice in Assessment

Evidence-based practice (EBP) is a scientific paradigm that encompasses clinician expertise, client characteristics, and client values and preferences. Evidence-based assessment has been defined as "the use of research and theory to inform the selection of targets, the methods and measures used in the assessment, and the assessment process itself" (Hunsley & Mash, 2007, p. 29). The primary focus of evidence-based assessment is on locating the best evidence regarding the most effective assessment instruments and protocols that fit best with a client's situation, culture, values, and preferences. Four major factors to consider when engaging in assessment underlie this broad definition:

1. Psychometric adequacy of standardized instruments or assessment protocols (reliability and validity)
2. Diversity issues and individual client characteristics, and the fit of various assessment instruments or protocols with these characteristics
3. Issues of comorbidity
4. Clinical utility of standardized instruments or assessment protocols

Chapter 3 defines and covers specific issues of validity, reliability, and clinical utility of measures in much more detail. Other chapters provide illustrations of how assessment methods are used to address diversity and comorbity issues. Social workers should remember that when they select measures based on evidence, those measures become one source of information in an ongoing process of decision making between social workers and clients, and that all methods of assessment are subject to limitations in the information that may be collected at any point in time (Hunsley & Mash, 2012).

As we progress in our knowledge about evidence-based assessments, certain reviews emerge about the best assessment methods for certain populations and problem areas. The American Psychological Association has been a leader in evaluating specific measurement instruments that can be used in practice (e.g., American Psychological Association, 2015). This means that specific measures are evaluated with a critical eye so that we can make more-informed judgments about measures that have been thoroughly researched and may be most useful in clinical practice. Practitioners that follow evidence-based assessment may consult lists or choices for the best measures to use like those provided by the American Psychological Association and other groups, and those guidelines may enhance the work of clinical assessment. This text, however, does not create lists of evidence-based measures for assessing different populations or problem areas but serves as a foundation text for learning about different assessment methods that social work practitioners can use. Furthermore, it teaches the steps of EBP that social workers can follow in identifying and formulating the best assessment methods for their individual cases. Although we agree that reviews of evidence-based assessment measures can guide practitioners toward the best assessment practices, we believe that the most relevant approaches to assessment will draw on the guidelines provided and individualize those methods to each client situation. As mentioned, this is not purely a prescriptive practice but also requires creativity and clinical decision making in the process of continuous collection of assessment information.

Searching for the Best Evidence-Based Assessment Method

Chapter 3 provides a list of sources for finding assessments based on the best scientific evidence. It is also important to know how to search for the best assessment methods. Leff and Conley (2006) provide a review of how to best search for evidence-based mental health information, and this also applies to instruments and protocols to follow in an evidence-based assessment. Three basic sources of information that lead to rapid reviews of the information are

1. Narrative reviews, which review the literature but do not include any quantitative analysis;
2. Systematic reviews, such as meta-analysis, which include a secondary statistical analysis of studies; and
3. Registries developed by federal agencies and independent groups that provide reviews and ratings of different programs and interventions, including assessment instruments (e.g., the What Works Clearinghouse, kept by the Institute of Educational Sciences at the Department of Education; the Cochrane Collaboration). For a description of how registries work and how practitioners can use them, see Kim, Trepper, Smock, McCollum, and Franklin (2010).

Each of these sources has strengths and weaknesses. Leff and Conley (2006) recommend that practitioners combine the sources to make use of the best information. This text also advocates the use of multiple methods to improve information collected about clients. Franklin and Kelly (2009) further discuss the need for training on methods used once the practitioner discovers evidence-based guidelines and the importance of working as a team with other professionals in making the decisions on which EBPs to use.

DIAGNOSTIC AND NOSOLOGICAL SYSTEMS

Clinical assessment may entail determining a diagnosis for a client. This is particularly true when social workers are employed in health or mental health care or private practice because billing requires diagnostic codes in order for the provider to receive payment for the services rendered. The very definition of a clinical social worker suggests an individual that is competent to diagnose, assess, and treat mental disorders, suggesting the importance of both diagnostic and broader assessment skills in practice. Diagnostic labels also influence the way clinicians interact and intervene with clients, making it essential for practitioners to understand mental and behavioral health diagnoses and their nosological systems. It should be noted that diagnosis is different from client assessment.

Diagnoses are made using nosological systems for mental illnesses based on a set of prescriptive and descriptive medical criteria that may be based on categories or dimensions for various illnesses, but assessments are made in a broader approach to understanding clients in the larger context of their relationships and environment. The purpose of this book is to cover clinical assessment, but because diagnostic classifications are also important for clinical social work practice, this chapter will summarize the most frequently used nosological system in clinical social work, the *Diagnostic and Statistical Manual of Mental Disorders*, fifth edition (DSM-5) (American Psychiatric Association [APA], 2013) and the *International Classification of Diseases*, tenth revision (ICD-10; World Health Organization, 2010). Both the DSM-5 and ICD-10 are important for clinical social work practice, and the ICD-10 is becoming even more important because billing codes are used. At this time, however, the DSM-5 remains one of the most frequently used approaches to diagnostic assessment and for this reason other chapters in this book will elaborate on the DSM-5 assessment for various population groups.

DSM-5

The DSM-5 (APA, 2013) is only one source of information to be considered in an assessment and the corresponding intervention plan, but determining a diagnosis requires social workers to evaluate many dimensions of client functioning using DSM-5 criteria. Central to these criteria are clinically significant distress of the client and difficulties in functioning across settings.

The DSM-5 uses a dimensional approach that also takes into account internalizing (e.g., depression, anxiety, somatic symptoms) and externalizing dimensions of disorders (e.g., antisocial behavior, substance use), life cycle development, and cultural factors, among other considerations. Diagnoses are also often made based on certain numbers of symptoms and behaviors, but the DSM-5 also encourages evaluation of clients in their contexts using a much broader perspective for the clients' psychosocial functioning such as dimensions like culture and gender.

One of the goals of the DSM-5 task force was to make the DSM more of a guide for clinical practice and to make it something that clinicians could use as a source of information in their case conceptualizations. For this reason the manual provides important information on client risk factors, prognosis, suicide risk, and comorbidity for different disorders. New to the DSM-5 are several crosscutting measures that may be of use in clinical practice. These measures provide assessment of client symptoms such as depression and provide assessment tools for diagnosis of children and adults. Consistent with the case conceptualization approach, this text will infuse the DSM-5 diagnosis and appropriate assessment measures into different chapters to show examples of how to include the DSM-5 diagnoses in case reports.

ICD-10

Another important classification system besides the DSM-5 is the ICD-10 that has been developed by the World Health Organization (2010) and is standard for use across all health-care practice in the United States. ICD-10 is used by 95 percent of the health-care professionals in the world (Goodheart, 2014). In fact, the ICD-10 and its recent release the ICD-10-CM—standing for clinical modification—are also used by the federal government and by the Centers for Medicare and Medicaid. Over the years the developers of the DSM have focused on making the DSM classifications more closely resemble the ICD descriptions of various mental disorders. The new DSM-5 actually lists the ICD codes along with DSM-5 codes. Insurance and billing sources frequently require the ICD codes and this increases the importance of social workers and other mental health professionals knowing more about the ICD-10 and the ICD-11 (ICD eleventh revision) that is scheduled for release in 2017 (World Health Organization, in press).

Consistent with the parity of the DSM-5 with the ICD is an increased emphasis on medical, neurological, and genetic reasons for mental illnesses and a renewed commitment to make progress in research on the brain sciences. It is anticipated that brain research will lead to better diagnostic tools than the DSM-5. For this reason, this text has also included more information on the neurobiological understandings of human behavior. In sum, considerable research is being conducted on nosological systems for mental disorders that may lead to new and improved ways to diagnose mental illnesses. However this work exists in the world of academic researchers and has not yet been developed into assessment methods that can be used in clinical practice. At this time, the DSM-5 remains the main nosological system that is utilized by social workers; we will cover the DSM-5 in the chapters of this text.

Next we will visit some of the practice models that guide assessment. We adhere to a technically eclectic model of assessment and intervention—that is, we blend compatible approaches into an integrated model of assessment and practice. Our belief is that no single model alone can explain the vast inter- and intrapersonal behavior that we aspire to understand.

PRACTICE MODELS GUIDING ASSESSMENT

The social workers' practice model dictates the type of information they gather and how they think about that information and synthesize it into a conclusion. In this way all practice models offer, to a greater or lesser degree, their own case construction processes. The next section describes several models of social work intervention from the perspective of their unique contribution to social work assessment and their utility for performing assessments. Although the models are distinct, it is common for practitioners to combine or integrate features from different models into their own unique way of thinking about client problems.

Psychosocial Assessment Model

Some of the major contributors to the psychosocial approach were Hollis and Wood (1981) and Woods and Robinson (1996). The goal of the psychosocial approach, sometimes called the "diagnostic approach," is to determine a psychosocial diagnosis for the client, taking into account factors such as the conscious and unconscious minds, client history, and the developmental process in making this diagnosis and in implementing the change efforts. The term "person-in-environment" originated with the thinking of this model and is thus important to our conceptualization of the client in the context of his or her multiple roles and environments. All of the models in the book share this person-in-environment perspective; in fact, it is what makes social work unique among other similar helping professions! Ego psychology is the major theoretical basis of the psychosocial assessment framework, but appreciation for the interplay of biopsychosocial, and spiritual processes is an inherent part of the model, as well as an orientation toward environmental modification. (For an overview of the areas of assessment to cover when following a comprehensive biopsychosocial-spiritual framework, see figure 1.1.) The reader may also be interested in reviewing other ego approaches that use ego psychology in social work, such as Berzoff, Flanagan, and Hertz (2011); Blanck and Blanck (1974); Brandell (2008); Gitterman, Goldstein, and Rose (1988); Goldstein (1986, 2002); Maluccio (1981); and Parad and Miller (1963).

Over the years, the psychosocial model has adapted to variations of other models, such as aspects of the shorter-term functional casework model, which deemphasizes history and focuses on solving problems in the here and now through the use of agency resources. Some of the outcomes of these adaptations include shortening the amount of history taken in a diagnostic interview and working more collaboratively with the client to solve problems. In one of the most recent explications of the psychosocial approach, Goldstein (2002) explains that, compared to the classical psychoanalytical thought that dominated early social work practice, ego psychology presents a more optimistic and sociocultural view of human behavior. Ego psychology concepts were used to refocus the study and assessment process on (a) the client's person-in-environment transactions in the here and now, particularly the degree to which he or she copes effectively with major life roles and tasks; (b) the client's

Figure 1.1   Areas for Assessment Using Biopsychosocial-
Spiritual Framework

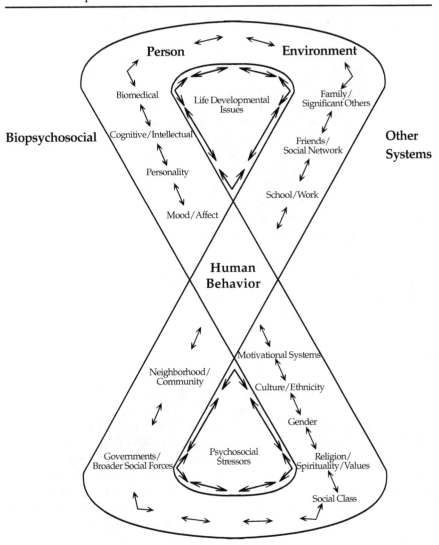

adaptive, autonomous, and conflict-free areas of ego functioning, as well as ego deficits and maladaptive defenses and patterns; (c) the key developmental issues affecting the client's current reactions; and (d) the degree to which the external environment creates obstacles to successful coping.

Unique Methods in Psychosocial Assessment.   Turner (2005) suggests that psychosocial assessment and treatment is an ongoing process of identifying and labeling problems, as well as recognizing client strengths; labeling problems and recognizing strengths are the main contributions of this approach and why we include it. Detailed psychosocial interviewing has become a key component of assessment in the psychosocial model. Specific assessment techniques include classical psychiatric interviewing for the purpose of making a diagnosis, use of standardized and projective testing to aid accurate diagnosis, psychosocial and developmental study to identify problem patterns, observations and interpretations of the client–social worker relationship to help clients understand their problem patterns and to provide a corrective emotional experience, use of standardized interviews to obtain an accurate mental health diagnosis, and further monitoring of symptoms to make sure they are changed in intervention plans.

The person-in-environment perspective offered by the psychosocial model is perhaps one of the most popular ways to understand clients in social work practice. It has also influenced many other important social work models, such as the problem-solving and task-centered models. Despite its popularity, the model actually has little research support other than some links to the medically based, biopsychosocial, and spiritual perspectives. More research on the contributions of the person-in-environment perspective is definitely needed.

Problem-Solving Assessment Model

In the 1950s at the University of Chicago, Helen Harris Perlman attempted to integrate the two prominent models of the day, the diagnostic and the functional perspectives, into a framework known as the "problem-solving social casework model." The diagnostic model integrated psycho-analytic theory into social casework, whereas the functional model, based on the work of the psychologist Otto Rank, focused on growth and realization of potential and the agency function. Perlman (1957) stated that the problem-solving model was an eclectic construct. Johnson (1981) later suggested that the problem-solving approach was theoretically eclectic, drawing on ego psychology, symbolic interactionism, role theory, and John Dewey's rational problem solving.

Unique Methods in Problem-Solving Assessment.   The unique contribution of this approach is the goal of problem-solving assessment to help the client cope by identifying the problem in the context of relevant intrapersonal issues (Johnson, 1981). Perlman (1957) suggested using the four Ps—person or personality, problem, place or agency, and process—as a way to collect and organize assessment data from clients. Others have added further assessment criteria. Doremus (1976) added the four Rs: roles, reactions, relationships, and resources. Sheafor, Horejsi, and Horejsi (1988) added the four Ms: motivation, meanings, management, and mon-

itoring. The authors suggest the following questions that practitioners can ask clients when collecting data on the four Ps, four Rs, and four Ms:

Four Ps

- Person or personality: What personality characteristics are important to understanding the problem? What is the interaction between the client's personality and other people or the environment?

- Problem: What is the definition of the problem? Is the client's perception of the problem the same or different from others' perception of it? What are the specifics of the problem (e.g., frequency, magnitude)? Is the situation a crisis? What other solutions have been attempted and with what outcomes?

- Place or agency: What concerns and fears does the client have about being in contact with this particular agency? Is this agency setting the most helpful setting for this client with this particular problem? What barriers to helping the client can be attributed to the agency?

- Process: What type of helping process is best for this particular client? What are the consequences of the helping process for the client and his or her significant others?

Four Rs

- Roles: What roles must the client perform, and how well does he or she perform them? What do significant others report about the client's role performance?

- Reactions: What are the client's psychological, emotional, behavioral, and physical reactions to the problem?

- Relationships: Who are the client's significant others, and what is their relationship to the problem? What are the consequences of the problem for them?

- Resources: What resources does the client already have that may be used in this situation, and what resources need to be developed?

Four Ms

- Motivation: How motivated is the client to change, and does discomfort or optimism motivate that change?

- Meanings: What is the client's perception of the problem, or what meaning does he or she attribute to the problem? What client beliefs and values are important in order for the practitioner to understand the problem?

- Management: How will the practitioner structure casework activity to work with the client?

- Monitoring: How will the practitioner monitor the problem and evaluate the outcome? Who is available to help collect data?

Cognitive Behavioral Assessment Models

Cognitive behavioral therapy focuses on clients' present functioning and attributes clients' problem behavior to learning processes, the formation of maladaptive cognitive schemas, errors in information processing, and proactive cognitive structures or meaning systems (Beck, 2011). Social workers who have integrated cognitive and behavioral techniques into social work practice include Berlin (1996); Brower and Nurius (1993); Gambrill (1983); Gambrill, Thomas, and Carter (1971); Gitterman et al. (1988); Granvold (1996); Mattaini (1990); Rose (1977); Shorkey and Sutton-Simon (1983); Stuart (2003); and Thyer (1983, 1987, 1988). Social work academics Cormier, Nurius, and Osborne (2008) integrate the cognitive behavioral perspective into their practice text.

The cognitive behavioral model is complex and includes numerous schools of therapy and practice models. For this reason, cognitive behavioral therapy has become more of a school of thought than a unitary theory or set of practices; it ranked as the most popular type of therapy model used by psychotherapists in a survey conducted by Dr. Joan Cook at Columbia University (Psychotherapy Networker, 2007), however, thus its inclusion here. It is also an evidence-based approach. It has been influenced by diverse theoretical and philosophical positions, ranging from psychoanalytic and behavioral to constructivist and experiential therapies. Cognitive approaches have been associated most with behavior therapies, which has resulted in the term "cognitive behavior therapy." Newer approaches integrate mindfulness and offer different understandings of cognitive processing than previous models (e.g., Herbert, Gershkovich, & Forman [2014]; Segal, Williams, & Teasdale [2012]).

Unique Methods in Cognitive Behavioral Assessment.   The goal of cognitive behavioral assessment is to specify the behavior (thoughts, feelings, or overt behavior) to be changed, along with its antecedents, consequences, and underlying cognitive mechanisms. From Gambrill et al.'s (1971) nine-step behavioral assessment, behavioral assessment has evolved into a multidimensional contextual model (Barth, 1986; Gambrill, 1983; Mattaini, 1990; Whittaker & Tracy, 1989). Gambrill (1983) identified sources of influence on clients' behavior, including the actions of others, thoughts, emotions, physiological factors, setting, events, physical characteristics of the environment, ethnic and cultural factors, material and community resources, past history, societal factors, and developmental factors. Other influences include obstacles and opportunities, consequences of attempted solutions, environmental deficiencies, and motivations and/or inhibitions, as well as behavioral deficits inherent to the individual. Specific assessment approaches used in the cognitive behavioral model include behavioral analysis theory, interviewing, identification of underlying cognitive schemas, logs, self-anchored scales, and standardized measures (Bellack & Hersen, 1988; Hudson, 1982; Kanfer &

Schefft, 1988; Shorkey & Sutton-Simon, 1983). Chapter 2 summarizes and illustrates these methods.

In assessment systems, cognitive behaviorists have focused on theoretically and experimentally based approaches to identifying and tracking specific behaviors and cognitions that need to be changed. Now there is an increasing focus on understanding people in their social contexts and on understanding how clients' developmental history and attachment relationships have influenced their current schemas and automatic thoughts. Also, in this type of assessment, it is important to collect data on the frequency and duration of cognitions and behaviors to observe the difficulties that clients experience and to monitor their changes. Among the popular earlier models was the ABC model, which focused on tracking antecedents (A), self-talk or automatic thoughts or beliefs (B), and behaviors and consequences of particular problems (C). The identification of automatic thoughts and their underlying schemas and the assessment of behavioral deficits and excesses are at the center of current models.

In general, cognitive behavior therapists have been forerunners in advocating valid and reliable methods for client assessment. Beck and Beck (2002), for example, developed measures for depression and suicidal ideation. (For a discussion of the measures, see Perelman School of Medicine, n.d.)

It is impossible to describe a full spectrum of cognitive behavioral approaches to assessment because of the increasing numbers of specific models and their unique features. One comprehensive assessment framework developed from the cognitive behavioral approach is multimodal assessment (Lazarus, 1989), and we describe that model here.

Multimodal Assessment

Using the multimodal assessment framework, practitioners evaluate client problems in great depth and detail across different modalities, including behavior, affect, sensation, imagery, cognitions, interpersonal relationships, and physiological factors of client functioning—and the interactive effects of all of these (Lazarus, 2006b). Lazarus (1991) developed a multimodal life-history inventory to help practitioners gain information about different modalities. Lazarus uses the acronym BASIC ID to describe the components that go into a comprehensive behavioral assessment: behavior, affect, sensation, imagery, cognition, interpersonal, and drugs. This multidimensional assessment blends well with our integrative perspective.

The multimodal model helps practitioners formulate a brief but comprehensive assessment by developing a modality profile. A modality profile organizes information according to the BASIC ID assessment. Using BASIC ID, the practitioner is able to make differential decisions about effective treatments. It is also possible to scale the modality preferences to see in which areas a client may show a more favorable response to treatment (Lazarus, 2006b). For example, some clients may experience difficulties in behavior, whereas others may experience difficulties with affects or interpersonal relationships. Even a client with a presenting problem such as anxiety (an affect) may experience the problem in a way that responds to treatments that focus on another modality. For example, one of us had a client who experienced anxiety attacks mainly as physiological sensations (rapid pulse and tight muscles). The modality profile indicated that a treatment that focused on the sensation modality should be used as the first approach. As it turned out, teaching the client progressive muscle-relaxation exercises helped him. Using BASIC ID, it is possible for a practitioner to systematically plan interventions based on the client's assessment profile.

Life-Model Assessment

Germain and Gitterman (2008), of the Columbia University School of Social Work, developed the life model of social work practice. The authors suggest that an ecology metaphor best describes their approach. The underlying theory is ecological, concerned with interactions between people and their environments, thus an extension of the person-in-environment perspective described earlier. Important concepts include stress, coping, and adaptation, as well as competence, autonomy, social networks, and organizations. Germain and Gitterman explain assessment as being concerned with "the interplay of dynamic forces within the life space, including the influence of the agency as a presence in the client's ecological context" (p. 633). The primary goal of assessment is to determine problems by examining three areas of the life space: life transitions, environmental pressures, and maladaptive interpersonal processes (Germain & Gitterman, 2008).

Gitterman identified five major aims of the life model (Gitterman et al., 1988). The first aim is to develop a perspective to give equal attention to people and to the environment. The second aim is to develop a model of practice to build bridges among the traditional specializations of casework, administration and planning, and family therapy. This third aim is for the model to mirror life processes closely so that social workers fit in with clients; clients should not be required to fit in with social workers' theoretical orientations. The fourth aim is to build on people's strengths rather than on their pathologies; labeling is viewed as blaming clients for their problems. The fifth and final aim is to build bridges between treatment and social reform.

Unique Methods in Life-Model Assessment.   Life-model assessment techniques include interviewing and ecomaps or social network mapping and standardized social support assessment instruments. The ecomap is one of the most important assessment tools to have evolved from this model (see figure 1.2).

Ecobehavioral Assessment Model

The work of Mattaini and Lowery (2007) focuses on combining the ecological assessment model with specific, targeted interventions from the more empirical behavioral practice. Using an ecological systems framework is an important step in assessment: the model provides practitioners with

Figure 1.2   Ecomap

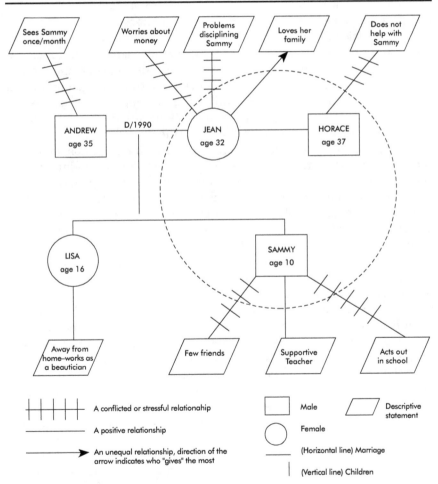

useful computerized assessment tools for generating ecomaps and other graphics-based assessments. This model's main contribution is to combine ecological systems theories with contemporary behavioral practice from behavioral analysis traditions. There has been ongoing criticism from behavioral researchers and theorists that clinicians practicing behavioral therapies have not updated their knowledge about newer learning theories and thus have not keep abreast of the empirical and theoretical work going on in experimental psychology. The ecobehavioral model, however, does make use of knowledge from newer learning theories. Contemporary behavioral practice addresses overt behaviors and private experiences such as cognition and emotion, and it focuses on the social environment and major systems that shape humans (Mattaini, Lowery, & Meyer, 2002). The model also considers the structure and function of language (verbal behavior). Another contribution is the use of computerized assessment that provides utility and convenience to the assessment process.

Three major developments guide the new behaviorism. First is the questioning of a mechanistic view of clients: mechanistic stimulus and response, simple contingency analysis (i.e., antecedents and conse-quences), and mediation models have been determined to be limited in explaining human behavior. Second is the development of contextual behavioral models that argue in favor of holism and a full contextual analysis for understanding of behavior: contextual behaviorists believe that no type of human response (e.g., overt behavior, cognition, emotion) can be separated from its contexts. This includes all forms of interaction, such as thinking, feeling, doing, and verbal behavior (rule governed), and the environmental contexts in which the behaviors take place. Contextual behaviorism rejects simple cause-and-effect relations because one area of observation, such as behavior or cognition, cannot explain psychological events; they must be analyzed in their full context, which includes all domains of responding. This is a systemic view, and contextual behav-iorists are interested in the functions of behavior across contexts and in why a behavior is occurring. This means that they see both the history of the client and his or her current situation as important. Third is research on human verbal behavior (rule governed) and how humans derive bidi-rectional relations in learning. This research has led to an understanding of the importance of indirect contingencies for behavior. Experiments have shown, for example, that once humans learn one set of assumptions or a distinct pattern, they can transfer that pattern to another similar pat-tern without any further direct learning.

Humans may also learn through observation and verbal associations instead of direct experience. This means that they can learn by watching others and can talk themselves into responding a certain way in the pres-ent on the basis of a past association. Indirect contingencies often mediate more-direct contingencies. This means that the internal meanings and expectations dictate responses to current experiences. So, what is aversive to one person may not be to another person who responds differently. Psychological problems such as phobias are usually learned indirectly through rule-governed behavior and not through direct experiences. Research on rule-governed, verbal behavior has led contemporary behaviorists to use more-covert psychological events, such as valued element (the potency of private reinforcers), different expectations (rules), and different meanings (equivalence relations), to understand the functional analysis of a behavior (Mattaini, 1999).

As with most contemporary behavioral models, the ecobehavioral model has broadened behaviorism as it was originally conceived. It shares features with other models. For example, it shares many features with the cognitive-ecological model of Brower and Nurius (1993), the life model, and the psychosocial model. The ecobehavioral model also incorporates knowledge and research from culture-analytic theory to help practitioners better assess and plan interventions with groups of people such as families. Using culture-analytic theory, the practitioner becomes acquainted with how culture shapes reinforcers, or rules for behavior, and sets the stage for individuals to form different meanings from their experiences (Mattaini, 1999).

Unique Methods in Ecobehavioral Assessment. The ecobehavioral model assumes that human behavior is complex and highly interconnected, and that the best way to understand human behavior is to assess it using an ecological framework. Assessment is understood as the process of defining the difference between a client's current state and his or her goal state. This method is similar to that used in solution-focused therapy (to be reviewed later in this chapter) in that the focus is on change, goals, and new behavior, and not on past pathology. The assessment process involves engaging, determining the difference in the goal state and the current state, envisioning how the client wants a situation to change, and planning the intervention. Assessment is completed in a framework of collaboration or shared power between the client and the practitioner (Mattaini, 1999). The ecobehavioral model is useful with individuals, families, groups, communities, and organizations, but it is better developed for micro practice than for macro practice.

In ecobehavioral assessment, the ecomap is an essential tool, along with other graphic methods that allow practitioners to map the context and relations of behavior. Mattaini (1992) provides detailed instructions and computer-based tools for graphing, as well as a framework and outline for conducting assessment following the ecobehavioral model (see box 1.2).

Box 1.2
Ecobehavioral Assessment

I. Ecobehavioral Scan

I'd like to ask you a few questions so that we can develop a clear picture of your situation together and so that I can be sure I understand your life as it is now. (The social worker may wish to draw a transactional ecomap with the family during this stage.)

a. Let's start with what is going right. What areas of your family life are currently going the best?
b. What about connections you have outside the immediate family? How much contact do you have with relatives or extended family? On a scale of 0 (not at all) to 5 (a lot), how much satisfaction do you get from those contacts? Are there any struggles with those folks? On a scale of 0 to 5, how much pain do those struggles cause? (Use a similar scale with each of the following areas that appears particularly relevant.)
c. Do you have many friends? How often do you see friends? How are those relationships going? Anyone else?
d. What about work and school? What is going well there? So on our 0 to 5 scale, are there things that aren't going so well? About a ___ on our scale?
e. Tell me a little about where you live. How satisfied are you with your home and neighborhood?
f. Any religious or church affiliation? Are you active?
g. Is anyone in the family active in other groups or organizations?
h. Any legal involvement?
i. How is everyone's health? Any problems there?
j. How much alcohol do people in the family use? Anyone take medication or drugs?
k. Now let's turn to your family itself. What is going right in the family? Who gets along best with whom? Who has more struggles getting along? (Elaborate and quantify as necessary to explore the relationships within the family.)
l. Does anyone else live in your home? How do you all get along? (Explore both positive and negative exchanges, and quantify if possible.)
m. What would you like to do more of in your family? What would you like to do less of? (Suggest self-monitoring or observational measures to expand data.)

II. Identification of Focal Issues

(Remember that focal issues may involve the behavior of only one person; however, to the extent possible, try to shift toward transactional definitions. Also, remember that focal issues need not involve only family members, but may involve transactions with other people or systems.)

a. So, out of all of this, where would you like to begin? What is most important to you?
b. I notice that you seemed to struggle a bit with _____. Is that one thing we should pay attention to?

Box 1.2 *Continued*

c. What do you think would be a realistic goal here? (Expand with specifics, but build on the envisioning that occurred earlier.)
d. Do you think that there is anything else we should work on at this point?
e. So, specifically, one of our goals right now is _____. (Explicate in behavioral terms.)

III. Contextual Analysis of Focal Issues

Now, let's see if we can get a really clear picture of our first goal (or focal issue), which is _____. (The general flow is from current undesirable situation to goal state; this kind of analysis should occur for each identified focal issue, although they might not all be done at the same time. Focal issues left aside for later should be clearly stated and written down, however, so that the family knows they will be addressed later.)

a. As near as you can tell, how did this problem start?
b. When was that?
c. Does this problem behavior ever pay off in any way for anyone? Does it ever produce any advantages for anybody?
d. Who else acts a little like this sometimes?
e. Who or what supports the current pattern?
f. What are the costs? What other problems does it cause?
g. What seems to trigger the problem? Are there times when it does not happen? (Identify occasions.)
h. Are there some times when this is not a problem? Tell me about those times. When is the problem most likely to come up? (Search for motivating antecedents.)
i. What do you think it would take to get from where you are to where you want to be? (Explore resources, including tangible, personal, and social.)
j. Who would be willing to help you achieve this goal or resolve this problem?
k. Who or what might stand in the way?
l. How important is this to you? Why? How will reaching this goal enrich your lives? How quickly do you think that will happen? (Build motivation.)

IV. Identification of Interventive Tasks

(This part of the assessment process needs to flow from the information provided in earlier stages, and it should emphasize tasks that will address the areas identified in the contextual analysis. It should explore interventive options for mobilizing the resources and addressing the obstacles discussed in that analysis. Identify approaches with the best empirical support in the context of the family situation. Careful specification of the multiple steps required to work toward the goal may be required. Explore possible reinforcers to be used along the way as well.)

SOURCE: Mattaini, M. (1999). Intervention with families. Washington, DC: National Association of Social Workers Press.

Behavioral principles are used as analytical tools to map the exchanges between individuals, families, and their environment. For example, in the ecobehavioral model practitioners use graphic tools or maps to help them understand the ecoscan (i.e., a mini-psychosocial history). This involves identifying focal issues and using contingency analysis to understand the consequences of overt and covert behavior that may reinforce a behavior. The practitioner also seeks to determine who is involved in the issues and the motivating antecedents that may trigger a behavior. The final goal is to carry out the desired intervention tasks.

Family Systems Assessment Model

Over the past forty years, the family therapy field has developed many methods for assessing families as a system. Family systems assessment focuses on the systemic or relational network characteristics of family functioning and associated presenting problems. Systemic functioning specifically refers to the circular, patterned way in which family groups are believed to behave. To effectively assess family systems, clinicians must use assessment methods that focus on the interactive sequences, communication, and relational network characteristics of the entire family. In this view, assessment serves a dual function: it is a way to discover how a family system is functioning and a method for intervening in the patterns of a family system. The processes of assessment and change interventions are not distinct but interactive and circular, which allows for assessment methods to contribute to information-gathering strategies and interventive methods. Viewing assessment as intervention blurs the boundaries between methods that are for the purposes of assessment and those that are for the purposes of change. Family systems models have no distinct assessment phase; instead, they combine assessment with intervention, showing how assessment is an ongoing process of formulating client behavior and intervening into that behavior.

Unique Methods in Family Systems Assessment. In a family assessment, practitioners use special questioning techniques to gather information and to introduce information into a family system. Techniques include circular questions; conversational or therapeutic questions; hypothesizing, circularity, and neutrality; tracking problems, solutions, or exceptions to problems; and pretherapy change assessment. Graphic tools such as genograms are also used to assess longitudinal emotional and behavioral patterns in families (see figure 1.3). Finally, family assessment uses empirically derived assessment models and standardized measures, which derive from research on the classification and assessment of family systems functioning. (Chapter 7 reviews and illustrates several family systems assessment methods.)

Figure 1.3 Family Genogram

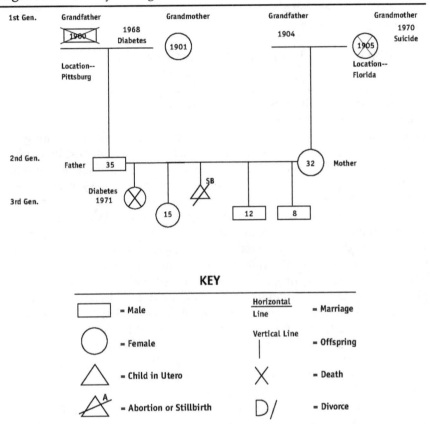

SOURCE: Foley, V. (1989). Family therapy. In R. Corsini & D. Wedding (Eds.), *Current Psychotherapies* (4th ed.). Itasca, IL: Peacock.

Task-Centered Assessment Model

The task-centered model was developed in the 1960s from a psychoana-lytically oriented short-term model (Reid, 1988, 1992, 2000). Today, it is more akin to cognitive behavioral practice than to the psychosocial model. The model's focus is on specific problems that clients want to resolve. This approach has been used worldwide with many different types of social work clients (Fortune, Reid, & Reyome, 2009). The theo-retical base of task-centered casework was designed to be open to inte-grating various theoretical and technical orientations (Reid, 1988). Ideas important to the original model were that casework is a problem-solving process (Perlman, 1957) and that the client's task is the focus (Studt, 1968). Theory and techniques were borrowed from crisis-intervention literature. More recently, theory and techniques from behavioral theory, cognitive and learning theory, and structural family therapy have been integrated into the task-centered model.

Unique Methods in Task-Centered Assessment. The goal of assessment is to specify target problems and their desired outcomes. Reid and Epstein (1972) and Reid (1988, 2000) explain the assessment and task-planning process. The first activity is initial problem formulation. The clients' perception of the problem is important, though it has been recognized that clients may need help expressing or even acknowledging the full range of a problem. Practitioners may help in this process by exploring, clarifying, and specifying a problem. In the case of clients who are required to seek services (e.g., in the case of child abuse), practitioners begin with the problem that brought the clients to the service provider. After formulating the problem, the practitioner then places it in the context in which it occurs, including conditions that perpetuate the problem, resources, and interpersonal and intrapersonal systems. The practitioner may use standardized instruments. Assessment continues into intervention and monitoring of case progress. In summary, the task-centered process includes task planning, implementation, and review (Reid, 1988).

The task-centered approach is useful for ensuring that assessment moves into specific intervention planning. The model has been shown to be helpful for both voluntary and nonvoluntary clients. It has been used in case management and clinical services with much success (Reid & Fortune, 2008). Task-centered assessment is prescriptive, in that specification of tasks and problems leads to specific intervention plans. The client and the clinician usually define tasks through a collaborative process in a face-to-face interview. Specific forms and contractual agreements signed by both parties may be used to write down the problems, tasks, and goals. Task-centered assessment offers a tremendous amount of specificity on the desired outcomes of assessment, as the resulting service contract illustrates. It is, however, unclear which specific tasks work best with which clients and client problems. The link between assessment and intervention appears to be left up to the collaborative process of the interview and to the practitioner's own clinical judgment.

The Strengths Perspective in Assessment

Dennis Saleebey (1997, 2013) pioneered the strengths perspective in social work practice. The essence of this model is the heart of social work's unique philosophical viewpoints on helping. Practicing from a strengths perspective incorporates a value system that encompasses belief in the dignity and worth of individuals, their self-determination, and the transformative power of humans and human relationships. Regardless of the model used, practicing with clients from a strengths perspective means viewing them through a humanistic lens that assumes that all clients can grow and change (Early & GlenMaye, 2000).

The strengths-oriented practitioner empowers clients, treating them as equals in a collaborative relationship. He or she looks beyond the individual and the oppressive systems that marginalize and define realities, toward the larger community and cultural contexts that help the practitioner understand clients and their life circumstances. The practitioner also moves away from pathologizing language and diagnostic schemes, such as mental health classifications systems like the DSM-5 in favor of broader, person-in-environment assessment for understanding client functioning. Saleebey (1997) argues that social work practice gives only lip service to strengths and that our continued practice within pathologizing, medical models has obliterated any strengths orientation. The importance of client strengths, however, can be traced to earlier models in social work, such as the functional, psychosocial, cognitive behavioral, and systems perspectives.

Unique Methods in Strengths Assessment.   As a practice model, the strengths perspective is more of a philosophical stance than a set of assessment and intervention skills. However, some important skills do emerge in the literature. These assessment and intervention skills mostly relate to the values and the therapeutic and helping stance of the practitioner. It is important in assessment, for example, for the practitioner to give preeminence to clients' viewpoints of the problem and their subjective interpretations and experiences. It is equally important for the practitioner to establish a collaborative helping relationship with clients as a part of a dialogic, ongoing assessment. As a part of assessment, clients participate in defining their problems, goals, and ways of being helped. The practitioner uses the words and language of the client to establish rapport and mutual understanding. The practitioner avoids simplistic, black-and-white thinking and/or simple cause-effect relationships in favor of longer narratives and complex explanations that are laden with situational and contextual meanings.

Finally, the practitioner focuses on assessing and defining competencies and uniqueness while avoiding blaming, pejorative labels, and debilitating diagnoses, all of which serve to disable clients (Cowger & Snively, 2008). In this manner, many social work practitioners practicing from the strengths perspective steer away from prescriptive and normative approaches to assessment, such as exclusively relying on the DSM-5 and approaches using standardized measures. These approaches are believed to be contrived and to produce limited options in their outcomes. Other practitioners, however, seek ways to integrate measurement approaches with the strengths perspective. The type of context-driven and open-ended assessment that strengths practitioners most value is consistent with qualitative and naturalistic approaches, which chapter 3 describes in some detail.

Strengths-Based, Solution-Focused Brief Therapy Assessment

Solution-focused brief therapy is a strengths-based therapy model developed by two social work practitioners, Steve de Shazer and Insoo Kim Berg, and their associates at the Brief Family Therapy Center in Milwaukee, Wisconsin. De Shazer and Berg are deceased and the center has shut down, but the Solution-Focused Brief Therapy Association (http://www .sfbta.org) has continued the training and is a repository for information and resources. Solution-focused brief therapy has been compared to motivational interviewing. The two are conceptually similar and have some overlapping techniques, but solution-focused brief therapy is a unique approach to social work practice. The treatment manual for solution-focused therapy (http://www.sfbta.org) has also been published in book form (Franklin, Trepper, McCollum, & Gingerich, 2012). The book highlights research on solution-focused brief therapy reviewing studies from helping professionals in different countries that have found it to be an effective approach, as well as strengths-based measures that may be used in practice. Solution-focused brief therapy is being practiced in many different countries in mental health, health care, schools, and children's services. Prominent social workers who conduct research, practice, and training on solution-focused brief therapy include De Jong and Berg (2008); Gingerich and Peterson (2013); Kelly, Kim, and Franklin (2008); Kim (2008); and Kim and Franklin (2009). Peter Lehman (Lehman & Patton, 2012) has developed a fidelity measure for solution-focused therapy and offers a certificate training program for solution-focused brief therapy at the University of Texas at Arlington. Franklin (2015) offers an update on the research and practice of solution-focused brief therapy for social workers.

Unique Methods in Solution-Focused Brief Therapy Assessment. Much like the family systems models described earlier, the solution-focused model does not separate assessment and intervention; assessment is part of the intervention process. A unique feature of this model is that practitioners assess in each particular case who is motivated to change. This assessment is guided by a case construction process that helps practitioners think about who in the case is the customer, complainant, or visitor. The customer is the person who is willing to make a commitment to the change process. The complainant is the person who is complaining about a problem and must be satisfied that a change has occurred—the complainant usually does not view him- or herself as part of the problem. The visitor is not very invested in the change process but is willing to be peripherally involved and may provide needed information. Solution-focused therapists use this assessment to develop goals and intervention strategies for a particular case. The solution-focused model also suggests that not all clients are customers and should not be treated in that manner by practitioners. The solution-focused model offers a wealth of information for assessing and working with mandated, or involuntary, clients who are required to seek services by other agencies, such as the child protection system, schools, and legal authorities (De Jong & Berg, 2001).

In working with a mandated client, practitioners are advised to change their relationship stance toward the client. For example, to begin the change process or to form a contract for the purposes of working with the client, it is not always necessary for practitioners to engage in a completely mutual, trusting relationship. Instead, practitioners may follow these principles for assessment and practice with mandated clients, summarized here by Franklin (2002, pp. 39–46):

1. Use nonjudgmental acceptance to investigate the client's problem. Use reflective listening skills and hear the client's version of the story. Let the client tell you how others view him or her. Listen to the explanation for how the client was referred. Empathize with the client's perceptions.

2. Increase motivational congruence by making the fit between what the client genuinely wants and the services you, the practitioner, provides as congruent as possible. Thus, find out what the client wants and to define roles in accordance with that purpose. For example, if the client wishes to have his or her children returned from child protective services, then discuss with the client ways that treatment can help that happen. Use reframing to help the client view his or her motivations and the system's or referral sources' motivation as similar. For example, say, "You and child protective services both want to get your child back home as soon as possible."

3. Emphasize the client's choices when possible. Mandated clients often feel forced and helpless, like they have no choice but to come to see you. Emphasize that clients do have choices and point out areas in which such choices exist. For example, clients do not have to come to sessions; they can choose to take the consequences.

4. Educate clients about what to expect during intervention. Clients who are mandated may not know what to expect and may be very fearful of the situation. Their angry responses may be exacerbated by their fears. Practitioners should take care to inform clients about what to expect and to teach novice clients about the social services and legal systems.

5. Develop specific contracts and goals with the client. A contract can and should be different from the one developed with other systems. You can define what others expect differently than you define what you expect. The contract should involve your role and what the client agrees on with you.

6. Define for the client what is nonnegotiable from the standpoint of referring agencies. Offer or point out incentives for the client to comply with behavioral demands with which he or she does not agree. For example: "When Charles insults you, hitting Charles is not acceptable to the school. They want you to go to this dumb conflict resolution person instead. You do not agree with that idea and neither does your dad. You think it is a dumb practice that does not fit into being a man or staying alive in your neighborhood. However, if you go to the conflict person, you can keep from being sent to the alternative school. Right? You said that you do not want to go to that place because you do not get to play basketball or leave school early. So, perhaps it is worth doing something dumb to avoid being sent to the alternative school. Anyway, I guess you have a choice on which way to go."

7. Use the client's goal of getting the system off his or her back as a way to gain compliance. For example: "As you see it, your teachers have it in for you, and it is difficult to get them to see you any differently. However, you have got to find a way to get them off your back so that they do not continue to call your mom every other day. So, are you willing to work on a few things they want just so you can get them off your back?"

Solution-focused brief therapy also offers a wealth of questioning techniques that can help facilitate client assessment and change. Solution-focused therapists are interested in clients' perspectives of their lives and in facilitating and coconstructing solution-building conversations with clients (De Jong & Berg, 2001). Practitioners therefore focus on exceptions to problems, strengths, and competencies of clients instead of on their weaknesses and pathologies. In particular, practitioners work with clients to coconstruct specific goals that can move them in small steps toward their solutions. Box 1.3 briefly describes some of the questioning techniques used in solution-focused assessment.

Box 1.3
Questions Used in a Solution-Focused Assessment

Tracking Solution Behaviors or Exceptions to the Problem.   The therapist identifies times when the problem does not occur, effective coping responses, and the contexts for the absence of the problem. The therapist says something such as, "Even though this is a very bad problem, in my experience people's lives do not always stay the same. I bet that there are times when the problem of being sent to the principal's office is not happening or at least is not as bad. Describe those times. What is different? How did you get that to happen?" The therapist gathers as many exceptions

Box 1.3 *Continued*

to the problem pattern as possible by repeatedly asking the client, "What else . . . ? What other times . . . ?" Once an exception has been identified by the client, the therapist uses prompts such as, "Tell me more about that," to help the client describe the exceptions in detail. The therapist also uses his or her own affects, tone, and intense attention to the client's story to communicate to the client that he or she is very interested in those exceptions. Such nonverbal gestures as nodding, smiling, leaning forward, and looking surprised are used. The therapist also may say something such as, "How about that!," "I'm amazed," or "Wow!" as social reinforcement to the client. This encourages the client to talk on and to develop in more detail the exceptions story.

Scaling the Problem.   This approach uses scaling questions to assess the problem and to track progress toward problem resolutions. The therapist says, "On a scale of 1 to 10, with 1 being that you are getting in trouble every day in class, picking on Johnny and Susi, getting out of your seat and being scolded by your teacher, and 10 being that instead of fighting with Johnny and Susi you are doing your work, and that you ask permission to get out of your seat, and your teacher says something nice to you, where would you be on that scale now?" With children, smiley and sad faces are often used to anchor the two ends of the scale.

Other uses of the scaling technique in the therapy process include the following: (a) asking questions about where the client is on the scale in relationship to solving the problem; (b) using the scaling experience to find exceptions to problems, such as saying "How did you get to the 3?" or "What are you doing so you are not a 1?"; (c) employing scales to construct so-called miracles or to identify solution behaviors. For example, the therapist inquires as to where the client is on the scale (with 1 representing low and 10 representing high). The therapist then proceeds to ask the client how he or she will get from a 1 to a 3. Or, the therapist inquires how the client managed to move from a 4 rating to a 5 rating, for example by asking, "How did you get that to happen? What new behaviors did you try? What was different in your life that made the changes happen?" Solution-focused therapists may also express surprise that the problem is not worse on the scale as a way of complimenting the client's coping behavior or as a way to use language to change the client's perception of the intractable nature of the problem.

Using Coping and Motivation Questions.   This is a variation on the scaling question that helps the therapist assess the client's motivation for solving the problem as well as how well the client perceives that he or she is coping with the problem. The therapist says something like, "On a scale of 1 to 10, with 10 being that you would do anything to solve this problem, and 1 being that you do not care so much about solving it, where would you say you are right now?" Or the therapist may say, "On a scale of 1 to 10 with

Box 1.3 *Continued*

1 being that you are ready to throw in the towel and give up ever doing well in school, and 10 being that you are ready to keep on trying, where would you rate yourself right now?" After asking coping and motivation questions, the therapist should be able to determine the following:

1. If the problem that has been defined is overwhelming for the client. If the problem is overwhelming, then the problem needs to be broken down into smaller steps and redefined for the client.

2. How much self-efficacy and hope the client possesses toward the problem resolution. If the client does not believe the problem can be solved, steps must be taken to change this belief. Here, the exception questions can be empowering.

3. The client's degree of commitment to work on the problem. If the client is not interested in committing to work on the problem, then client and therapist must work together to redefine the problem to achieve client commitment.

4. If the problem that has been defined is the one that really interests the client and if it is a priority for him or her.

   Asking the Miracle Question.   The so-called miracle question seeks to assess the client's priorities and to develop solutions. The therapist says, for example, "Let's suppose that an overnight miracle happened and your problem disappeared; but you were sleeping and did not know it. When you woke up the next day, what would be the first thing that you would notice?" The therapist proceeds to help the client envision how things could be different. An extreme amount of detail is elicited to help develop a set of solution behaviors that are concrete and behaviorally specific. The miracle question helps the therapist to assess a detailed description of the client's perception of what life would be like without the problem. It also helps the therapist coconstruct with the client's input a specific set of behaviors, thoughts, and feelings that can be substituted for problem patterns. Ultimately, the therapist can assess what is most important to the client and others concerning which changes the client believes will solve the problem.

SOURCE: Franklin, C., & Moore, K. (1999). Solution-focused therapy. In C. Franklin & C. Jordan, Family practice: Brief systems methods for social work. Pacific Grove, CA: Brooks/Cole.

COMMON FEATURES OF SOCIAL WORK ASSESSMENT MODELS

Assessment information and social work practice models reviewed in this chapter share the following features concerning how assessment works:

- Social work assessment emphasizes both individuals and their social environments: viewing clients in their contexts of families, groups, and communities is the preferred approach to assessment.
- Social work assessments are evidence based, combining the best scientific methods available for assessment with clinical judgment, client values, and preferences; and ongoing clinical decision making about what is in the best interest of clients.
- Social work assessment includes the strengths and resilience of clients: it is as important to assess competencies and strengths as it is to address problem areas and pathologies. The goals of most approaches include increasing the self-efficacy of clients, restoring or supporting their inherent problem-solving capacities, and returning clients to their best adaptive functioning.
- Most social work assessment models are integrative and rely on more than one underlying theory: the theory base of social work practice is eclectic. Social work models combine multiple theories in their assessment and practice focuses. Social work is interprofessional by nature, and social workers usually are employed in host settings such as hospitals, schools, and primary care settings. Social work assessment also integrates knowledge from several fields and work with other professionals on interprofessional teams in formulating assessments.
- Assessments in social work deemphasize long history taking, even in models that traditionally focused on this information (e.g., psychosocial). Instead, only relevant history is used strategically to understand presenting problems and needed interventions.
- Assessments are organized around task-centered planning or goal orientations: the purpose of assessment across models is to resolve presenting problems or to move clients toward desired goals. Assessments across social work models focus mostly on the present context and future behaviors that clients desire.
- Social work assessments share common types of information: even though different methods are used across models to gather information from clients, social work models value information similarly, including definitions, identified strengths, specific goals, intervention planning or solution building, and outcome monitoring.
- Social work assessments use a collaborative process between client and practitioner: All models prefer collaborative work with clients in gathering information and goal construction. Shared power and client-centered perspectives are important to the clinical assessment process, in contrast to more authoritative approaches in which the practitioner is considered the only expert on the client and his or her problems.

- Assessments in social work emphasize brief, time-limited perspectives. All models reviewed here prefer brevity and short-term assessments, perhaps because of the realities of practice environments and the applied problem-solving nature of social work practice.

INTEGRATING THE COMPONENTS OF PRACTICE MODELS FOR SOCIAL WORK ASSESSMENT

This text takes an integrative approach to assessment. The integration of theory is a common approach to assessment and intervention in social work practice, as can be seen from the diverse practice models reviewed. We agree with Lazarus's (1981) technical eclecticism, which assumes that practice methods from different underlying theoretical models can be used together. Lazarus believes that it is not necessary to embrace the theory in borrowing techniques compatible with one's own theoretical and practice approach. Rather than choosing techniques based on one's theoretical philosophy, choice is based on research support for the technique or the best available practice wisdom. Although there are some limitations to a pragmatic approach like technical eclecticism, such as the lack of overarching or defining theory to guide practice, technical eclecticism allows for a more experimental and problem-solving approach that tests different assessment methods without being limited to one school of thought or set of practice methods. It is also important for the practitioner to evaluate assessment techniques with practice evaluation methods. Box 1.4 integrates the major assessment issues covered in each model reviewed and shows the elements that can be used in a comprehensive social work assessment.

Box 1.4
Integrative Skills Assessment Protocol

    I. Identifying Information
       A. Name
       B. Address
       C. Home phone number
       D. Work phone number
       E. Date of birth
       F. Family members living at home
          1. Name
          2. Age
          3. Relationship
       G. Occupation
       H. Income
       I. Gender
       J. Race
       K. Religious affiliation
       L. Brief description of the presenting problem or symptom(s)

Box 1.4 *Continued*

II. Nature of Presenting Problem(s)
   A. Problems identified by the client and/or practitioner
      1. Create a list of problems.
         a. What is the specific problem(s)?
   B. Specification of problem(s)
      1. Develop a history.
         a. When did the problem first occur?
         b. Is this a long-standing, unresolved problem or a recently emerged problem?
      2. Determine the duration of the problem(s).
         a. How long has the problem been going on?
      3. Determine the frequency of the problem(s).
         a. How often does the problem occur?
      4. Determine the magnitude of the problem(s).
         a. What is the intensity of the problem?
      5. Determine the antecedents of the problem(s).
         a. What happens immediately before the problem occurs?
      6. Determine the consequences of the problem(s).
         a. What happens immediately after the problem occurs?
      7. Determine the exceptions to the problem(s).
         a. What exceptions to the problem exist?
         b. How often have exceptions occurred?
         c. When was the last time an exception happened?
         d. What was different in the situation in which the exception occurred from situations in which the problem happened?
         e. Who was involved in making the exception happen?
      8. Determine the client's reason for seeking help.
         a. What makes the client seek help now and not before?
      9. Determine prior efforts to solve the problem(s).
         a. How has the client sought to solve the problem previously, including other therapy?
         b. What were the results of those efforts?
    10. Determine client motivation.
         a. What is the level of your motivation for solving the problem?
         b. On a scale of 1 to 10 with 10 being you would do anything to solve this problem and 1 being that you do not care much about solving it, where would you say you are right now? (Use scaling question to identify client motivation.)
    11. Determine client resources/strengths.
         a. What are the client resources available for solving the problem?
         b. On a scale of 1 to 10, with 1 being that you are ready to throw in the towel and give up and 10 being that you are ready to keep on trying, where would you rate yourself right now? (Use scaling question to assess coping.)
    12. Other.
         a. Do you have other difficulties associated with or in addition to the problem?
   C. Prioritization of problems and goals
      1. Through negotiations with the client, prioritize problems in terms of severity.

Box 1.4 *Continued*

2. Determine what the client's goals are. Goals should be something he or she is motivated to accomplish.
3. Identify a small, obtainable goal. Determine what the client can do toward the goal immediately and before the next session.
4. Determine what, when, how, and with whom the behavior is to happen.
5. Determine what the client will do instead of the problem behavior.
6. Ask yourself if the client understands that the goal is the first step and not the end to solving the problem.
7. Determine if the goal is something the client can do in the context of his or her life.
8. Ask yourself if the client understands that the goal is hard work and that effort must be put forth, and if the client is committed to doing so.
9. Use the miracle question to prompt the client to set a goal or to envision a solution to the problem. Guide the client in discussing what life would be like without the problem.
   a. Let's suppose that an overnight miracle happened and the problem you are having disappeared, but you were sleeping and did not know it. When you woke up the next morning, what would be the first thing you would notice?

III. Client
   A. Intrapersonal issues
      1. Determine the client's cognitive functioning.
         a. What is your perception of the problem and its solution?
         b. What are your most common upsetting thoughts?
         c. What underlying beliefs and schemas support your upsetting thoughts and subsequent emotions and behaviors? (Identify maladaptive cognitive schemas as the central focus of intervention.)
   B. Maladaptive schemas around autonomy
      1. Determine the client's dependence (on others for support, fear one cannot take care of self).
      2. Determine the client's subjugation (sacrifice of one's own needs to satisfy others' needs).
      3. Determine the client's vulnerability to harm or illness (fear of disasters).
      4. Determine the client's fear of losing self-control (over own mind, behavior, impulses, body, etc.).
   C. Maladaptive schemas around connectedness
      1. Determine the client's emotional deprivation (expectation that his or her own needs will not be met).
      2. Determine the client's abandonment/loss (fear of losing significant others and of being isolated forever).
      3. Determine the client's mistrust (expectation others will hurt, abuse, cheat, lie, manipulate, or take advantage).
      4. Determine the client's social isolation/alienation (feels different from others, not part of the community).
   D. Maladaptive schemas around worthiness
      1. Determine the client's defectiveness/unlovability (feels inwardly defective, flawed, unlovable).
      2. Determine the client's social undesirability (feels outwardly undesirable, ugly, of low status, dull).

Box 1.4   *Continued*

   3. Determine the client's incompetence/failure (believes self cannot perform).
   4. Determine the client's guilt/punishment (believes self morally or ethically bad and deserving of punishment or harsh criticism).
   5. Determine the client's shame/embarrassment (believes one's inadequacies are totally unacceptable to others).
   E. Maladaptive schemas around limits and standards
   1. Determine any unrelenting standards (relentless striving to meet extremely high expectations of oneself at the expense of happiness, pleasure, health, satisfying relationships).
      a. What are the antecedents, beliefs, and consequences of your upsetting thoughts and behaviors?
      b. What are the hot cognitions, or those cognitions that are related to underlying emotions and schemas?
      c. What is your view of self, others, and the world?
      d. What evidence is there for your own problem-solving capacity?
      e. In what ways have you solved problems in the past?
   2. Determine any evidence of rational vs. irrational thoughts.
   F. Emotional functioning
   1. Describe the client's affect and mood.
   2. Determine if the client can express a range of emotions.
   3. Search for evidence of appropriate vs. inappropriate emotions such as extreme anger, elation, or depression.
   4. Search for evidence that the client's cultural group or primary reference group views the client's affect or mood as being outside the norm.
   G. Behavioral functioning
   1. Describe the client's physical appearance.
   2. Describe the client's mannerisms.
   3. Describe the client's speech.
   4. Describe the client's abilities and disabilities.
   5. Describe the client's antisocial or acting-out behavior.
   6. Describe behavioral deficits or excesses such as lack of social skills or addictions.
   H. Physiological functioning
   1. Determine if the client has been seen medically during the past year.
   2. If so, what were the results?
   3. Is there any evidence of drug and alcohol usage?
   4. Does the client take any medications?
   5. Describe diet, caffeine, alcohol, and drug usage.
   I. Client mental status
   1. Describe disturbances in appearance, dress, posture, etc.
   2. Describe disturbances in thoughts (hallucinations, delusions, etc.).
   3. Describe disturbances in level of awareness (memory, attention, etc.).
   4. Describe disturbances in thought processes (logic, intelligibility, coherence).
   5. Describe disturbances in emotional tone (deviations in affect or discrepancies in verbal reports of mood and client affect).
   6. Describe degree to which the client seems aware of the nature of the problem and the need for treatment.

Box 1.4 *Continued*

J. Ethnic/cultural/gender considerations
   1. What is the client's ethnic group?
   2. What is the degree of acculturation?
   3. What is the client's perception of how ethnic/cultural/gender group identification has helped or not helped?
   4. Are the sources of conflict related to ethnic/cultural/gender issues?
K. Motivation
   1. What stage of change is the client in?
   2. Is the client unaware of a need for change?
   3. Is the client currently contemplating a need to change without making a full commitment to the change process?
   4. Has the client fully embraced the idea of change, and is he or she ready to move forward?
   5. Has the client already made some recent changes and does he or she need help maintaining those changes?
   6. Has the client changed the problem behavior in the past but since relapsed?
   7. What are factors that may contribute to client motivation, either causing client discomfort or causing client to have hope for the future?
L. Client roles and role performance
   1. What roles does the client perform (wife, mother, etc.)?
   2. What are the client's issues related to role performance?
   3. What are the client's issues related to satisfaction or dissatisfaction?
   4. What are the client's gender issues?
   5. Are there any social and economic injustices?
M. Developmental considerations
   1. Trace the birth and developmental history of the client (the mother's pregnancy, developmental milestones, illness, trauma, etc.).
   2. Is there an identified patient? If so, who is it?
   3. What is each family member's perspective of the problem(s)?
N. Marital status
   1. What is the client's sexual dating and/or marital history?
   2. What is the quality of the client's intimate relationships?
   3. How long has the client been married (if married)?
   4. How many times has the client been married?
O. Interpersonal: Family structure
   1. Describe the quality of the client's family interactions.
   2. Describe the family boundaries.
   3. Describe the family alliances.
   4. Describe the family power structure.
   5. Describe the family communication patterns.
   6. Describe family and narratives.
   7. Describe the family strengths.
P. Interpersonal: Work or school
   1. Describe the client's occupation or grade in school.
   2. Describe the client's satisfaction with work/school.
   3. Are there indicators of successful achievement in work/school?

Box 1.4 *Continued*

　　　4. What are issues related to the client's grades, pay, promotions, etc.?
　　　　a. Describe relationships with your colleagues/peers.
　　　5. Effect of problem(s) on work/school
　　　　a. Does the problem(s) occur in this setting? If so, how do you get along with peers, teachers/bosses, other authority figures?
　　　　b. What is your academic/work history?
　　　6. Is there any evidence of antisocial behavior?
　Q. Interpersonal: Peers
　　　1. Determine if the client is satisfied with number of peers/friends.
　　　2. Who are the client's friends and what is the quality of these relationships?
IV. Context and Social Support Networks
　A. Agency considerations
　　　1. Does the agency setting have an effect on the problem/client: Does the client have negative feelings about seeking services at this agency? Is the agency located too far away to be accessible to the client? Does the agency have the resources to deal with the client's problem in terms of worker time, interest, etc.?
　　　2. Would referral be best for the client, and if so, what is the best referral source?
　B. Client's environmental context
　　　1. What environmental resources does the client have (e.g., adequate housing, transportation, food/clothing, recreation, social supports, educational opportunities, etc.)?
　　　2. What environmental resources exist that the client is not currently utilizing (access to family or peer support, support from agencies in the neighborhood, etc.)?
　　　3. What environmental resources do not exist and need to be developed? What gaps in resources exist for this client?
V. Measurement (use global and/or rapid assessment instruments)
　A. Family functioning
　B. Marital (or significant other) functioning
　C. Individual functioning
　D. Social supports
　E. Strengths, resources, and protective factors
VI. Summary
　A. Practitioner impressions
　　　1. Summarize areas for presentation to the client. List concerns of highest priority to the client. What is the goal? Generate a list of exceptions to the problem and a list of client strengths. Obtain client feedback.
　　　2. Establish a DSM diagnosis.
　　　3. Articulate problem(s) or solutions to be targeted for immediate intervention.
　B. To be negotiated with client and prioritized
　　　1. What are some progress indicators?
　　　2. What are desired outcomes?
　　　3. What is the baseline?
　　　4. What are the results of either pretest or repeated measurement of targeted problems and strengths?

Box 1.4   *Continued*

VII. Treatment Plan
    A. Problem(s):
        1.
        2.
    B. Definition(s):
        1.
        2.
    C. Goal(s):
        1.
        2.
    D. Objective(s) (measurement):
        1.
        2.
        3.
        4.
    E. Intervention(s):
        1.
        2.
        3.
        4.

Moving from Assessment to Intervention Planning

This final section describes how assessment is an integral part of forming intervention plans. Clinical decision-making, problem monitoring, and treatment planning are a part of the social worker's assessment skills and are discussed here.

Clinical Decision Making

What happens in the assessment phase of treatment affects interventions selected at later stages of treatment? The information collected during assessment helps the practitioner focus on specific problems to be targeted for intervention and to specify the type of intervention that will be of most help for those problems. Various treatment-planning manuals guide practitioners in selecting appropriate interventions (see, e.g., Jordan, Franklin, & Johnson, 2015; Reid, 2000). To meet this end, the social worker must make three important decisions during assessment: how much and which data to collect, which assessment tools to use, and the specific problem to target. Each chapter in this book offers information to help practitioners make these decisions.

    The following five steps that are associated with EBP give further guidance on selecting and evaluating assessment practices (adapted from Sackett, Straus, Richardson, Rosenberg, & Haynes, 2000; see also figure 1.4). The steps assume a collaborative approach with clients.

Figure 1.4   Evidence-Informed Behavioral Practice

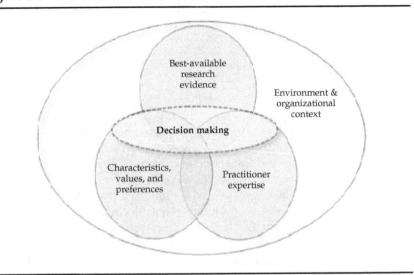

SOURCE: Spring, B., & Hitchcock, K. (2009). Evidence-based practice in psychology. In I. B. Weiner & W. E. Craighead (Eds.), *Corsini's Encyclopedia of Psychology* (4th ed., pp. 603–607). New York: Wiley. Used with permission.

Step 1: Convert information needs into a relevant question for practice in a community and/or organizational context. Determine what data you need to collect.

Step 2: Track down with maximum efficiency the best evidence to answer the question. When applying this step to the assessment process, determine what types of assessment tools are best to use.

Step 3: Critically appraise the evidence for its validity and usefulness. In this step, it is important to determine how effective and efficient the assessment tools are and to determine how much confidence we have in the information we have obtained from them.

Step 4: Provide clients with appropriate information about the efficacy of different interventions and collaborate with them in making the final decision on the best practice. This means sharing the results of our assessments with clients, including their limitations, and verifying information we have obtained with clients.

Step 5: Apply the results of this appraisal in making policy and practice decisions that affect organizational, community, or client change. Use the results of the assessment and client feedback to choose an intervention.

Step 6: Assess the fidelity of implementing the micro or macro practice intervention. Use ongoing assessments of the client to monitor the intervention and make sure it is delivered as planned.

Step 7: Evaluate service outcomes from implementing the best practice. Measure the outcomes of the intervention to determine whether it is working and then make any adaptations to ensure the best results.

Collecting Data

We recommend performing assessment from a multidimensional perspective and across systems to gain the big picture of a client's issues; it also is important, however, to know how to propose limits to data collection in assessment. Gambrill (1983) suggests that a thorough assessment should consider inter- and intrapersonal issues related to client functioning and that the assessment data collected should be relevant. In limiting the information to collect, consider who requested the assessment and for what purpose. For instance, if a judge requests child protective services to perform an assessment and provide a report to a court, the judge may require a thorough assessment that includes a report of every detail of the child's life and environmental situation. However, if the assessment is performed in a managed care setting and the client requests time-limited help with a child management problem, it is possible that only information pertinent to the parent-child relationship would be relevant.

The Integrative Skills Assessment Protocol covers the big systems picture about what might be relevant for a multidimensional perspective and covers details across the client's life to ask about (see box 1.4). In a comprehensive psychosocial assessment, it might be important to learn as much as possible about each area, but not all the information on the protocol is necessary for every case. Box 1.5 provides a checklist to guide

---

Box 1.5
Checklist for Brief Assessment with the
Integrative Skills Assessment Protocol

Instructions: 1. Check off the sections below as they apply to the client and/or the client's problem(s). (Note: Sections required for all clients are checked.)
2. Next, go to the Integrative Skills Assessment Protocol and complete only the sections checked.

I. Identifying Information

_____ 1.–12.

II. Nature of Presenting Problem

_____ 13.a. List all problems.
_____ 14.a.–k. Provide specification of specific, discrete problem(s) behavior(s).
_____ 15.a. Prioritize problem(s).

Box 1.5 *Continued*

III. Client

_____ 16.a.–i. List intrapersonal issue(s).
_____ 17.a.–d. List interpersonal: family.
_____ 18.a.–b. List interpersonal: work or school.
_____ 19.a. List interpersonal: peers.

IV. Context and Social Support Networks

_____ 20.a.–b. List agency considerations.
_____ 21.a.–c. Describe client's environmental context.

V. Assessment Measures

_____ 22. Describe family functioning.
_____ 23. Describe marital (or significant other) functioning.
_____ 24. Describe individual functioning.
_____ 25. Describe social supports.

VI. Strengths and Resources

_____ 26. Identify client strengths.
_____ 27. Identify environmental strengths.

VII. Assessment Summary and Treatment Recommendations

_____ 28.a. Describe baseline.
_____ 29.a. Describe practitioner impressions.
_____ 30. Make a DSM-IV-(R) diagnosis.
_____ 31.a. Describe problem(s) targeted for intervention.
_____ 32.a.–b. Describe recommended treatment alternatives.

VIII. Methods Used in Assessment

_____ 33. Standardized interview
_____ 34. Ethnographic interview
_____ 35. Nonstandardized interview
_____ 36. Background information sheets and questionnaires
_____ 37. Standardized assessment measures
_____ 38. Behavioral observations
_____ 39. Projective measures
_____ 40. Self-anchored or self-rating scales
_____ 41. Client logs or diaries
_____ 42. Graphs or maps
_____ 43. Experiential and task assignments
_____ 44. Information from collateral sources
_____ 45. Previous treatment or other social service records
_____ 46. Other (*please specify*)

---

practitioners in selecting relevant information. Use of the checklist requires clinical judgment and decision making based on what is most relevant to each individual case. Note that the checklist asks the practitioner to consider the various areas that might be included in the assessment, such as client intrapersonal issues, family issues, or work issues. The practitioner should check off only the areas pertinent to the client; the Integrative Skills Assessment Protocol addresses only the checked-off areas.

Specifying Problems

Problem definition follows from this assessment process and requires operationalizing the problems that are to be the focus of the intervention. Problems might be overt or covert behaviors, including thoughts and feelings; problems also might be conceptualized at the environmental level, such as lack of needed resources. Measurement of the problems targeted for intervention requires the use of quantitative measures to ascertain the existence, extent, severity, duration, and so forth of the problems. These quantitative measures can be standardized measures, behavioral observations, self-anchored scales, and so on. Other qualitative measures may also be used to gather other information about the problems or to provide a more in-depth perspective. Chapters 2 and 4 provide more information on both quantitative and qualitative methods for problem specification.

Problem Monitoring

After the assessment reveals problems targeted for change, the issue is to monitor the problems over the course of the therapeutic process. Quantitative data such as measures and specific monitoring of client behaviors provides the clinician not only with information to determine the extent and severity of the problem during assessment, but also with information to use in evaluations over the course of the assessment and treatment. The recommended monitoring system for evaluating practice activities is single-subject design; this approach is covered in detail in chapter 10. This evaluation design is different from the traditional group research design, which compares pre- and postintervention information. Rather than measuring the client's problems at only two points in time (pre- and postintervention), single-subject methodology requires repeated measurement of the problem over the course of assessment and treatment. This gives the practitioner a more in-depth look at the client's progress throughout the case activity. Single-subject data allow for changes to be made at any point during treatment if necessary. For example, if the data reveal that behavioral therapy is not making the anticipated difference in a client's level of depression, the practitioner might decide to change to an intervention such as cognitive therapy.

Bloom, Fischer, and Orme (2009) described the stages involved in single-subject design:

1. The measures are administered repeatedly, usually weekly or daily. The client, significant others, the practitioner, or a combination of interested parties can collect the data.

2. The data are collected systematically over the course of the treatment, using the same measurement instruments at all phases of the case.

3. The baseline phase of the case refers to the time before the formal intervention is begun when measurements are made.

4. The design of single-subject evaluation involves various phases, typically baseline, intervention, and follow-up. Comparisons are made between the phases to judge the success or failure of the treatment being implemented.

5. This approach requires a clear definition of intervention. Because the single-subject methodology relies on a comparison of phases—most importantly, the baseline and intervention phases—it is important for the practitioner to operationalize the selected intervention. To judge the effectiveness of a treatment, it is important to know when the intervention is being applied and when it is not.

6. Finally, the therapist analyzes the data. Single-subject data are often analyzed simply by eyeballing or observing the level, trend, and stability of the data in the different phases. However, there are some simple tools to use when the data are confusing to the eye. The Shewhart chart and celebration line (Bloom, Fischer, & Orme, 2009) are two examples of such tools.

The single-subject design is advantageous to clients, practitioners, and agency administrators. Clients may become more self-aware, and practitioners and administrators may benefit from increased practitioner accountability and improved agency performance. (For more detail on the single-subject design, see chapter 10.)

CASE STUDY: TREATMENT PLANNING

Treatments should follow logically from and be related to the problems targeted for change, as the following case illustrates. Jordan and Cobb (1993) first discussed the case of Tom and Julie in *101 Interventions in Family Therapy*. Tom and Julie are a dual-career couple, committed to both their jobs and to their family life. In treatment they presented difficulties about how to balance those two very demanding worlds. As a way to show the link between assessment and intervention, we next present a summary of the assessment on Tom and Julie. Following the assessment summary is a list of problems targeted for intervention, measurements to be used for case monitoring, and a brief discussion of the interventions selected.

Assessment Summary

Tom and Julie are dual-career spouses, each with a promising career, in banking and merchandising, respectively. In addition to a commitment to their jobs and to each other, they have an eighteen-month-old daughter, CeCe. They came to therapy to resolve issues related to their busy lifestyle. Julie reported that Tom disagrees with her about who should be responsible for household chores, which results in yelling and screaming matches between them. Arguments also occur about who should be the primary caretaker for CeCe. CeCe is enrolled in a day school, but Tom and Julie disagree about who should drop her off and pick her up from school and about who should take her to the doctor and other appointments that occur during the day. Both Tom and Julie reported feeling "stressed out" most of the time. They feel that their relationship is suffering from their lack of time to complete their many jobs.

Problem Selection

The practitioner identified the following problems as areas of concern: poor communication and stress.

Problem Definition

The practitioner defined Tom and Julie's problems as follows:

- Poor communication: Communication style defined by angry arguments with yelling and screaming; disagreements remain unresolved.
- Stress: Feelings of tension from inability to get jobs done; no time for important activities.

The practitioner presented the results of the assessment and the targeted problems to Tom and Julie and asked the couple for feedback. Both Tom and Julie agreed that communication and stress were the two major problems for them; they expressed a desire to continue in treatment to work on both problems.

Goals

Goals for the treatment were to improve the couple's communication and to reduce the couple's stress.

Objectives

During the assessment phase, the practitioner used three measures to assess the extent and severity of Tom and Julie's problems and to describe the objectives (note that the practitioner continued to collect data from Tom and Julie using these same measures over the course of treatment as a way to monitor outcomes):

1. The Primary Communication Inventory (Navran, 1967). Improvement on the inventory shows improved communication.
2. The Stress Arousal Checklist (Mackay, Cox, Burrows, & Lazzerini, 1978). This checklist is used to measure reduced stress.

Interventions Selected

The practitioner offered two types of intervention approaches to Tom and Julie: family therapy using a human validation process model, and skills training. After hearing a brief description of each intervention, the couple chose the skills-training approach, which involved two components: communication training and stress management training.

For communication training, the therapist focused on teaching the couple both verbal and nonverbal skills of effective communicating, including use of "I" statements to communicate needs, active listening, correct timing of message delivery, expression of feelings, and editing of unproductive communications. Nonverbal techniques included appropriate facial expressions to match verbal content, posture, voice, physical proximity to partner, and other voice qualities. In addition, anger control techniques the practitioner also taught to the couple included recognition of escalating anger, taking a time-out, admitting one's own part in the argument, and problem solving.

In stress management training, the practitioner helped both partners identify and analyze the stressors in their lives. In analyzing stress, Tom and Julie considered whether it came from lack of organization or from overwhelming responsibilities. The practitioner then designated four components of stress management as appropriate interventions for Tom and Julie: self-monitoring, daily relaxation exercises, cognitive restructuring of unproductive irrational beliefs contributing to stress, and environmental alteration.

SUMMARY

This chapter provided a definition of social work assessment, differentiated from diagnosis, and a framework for understanding how to conduct a comprehensive social work assessment. We reviewed many facets of social work assessment in this chapter, including the ways that students and practitioners can construct information in a case and use theory to guide practice. This chapter and the chapters that follow guide practitioners to use evidence-based knowledge to guide their assessments with clients. The chapter highlighted the importance of using evidence in assessment and DSM-5 and ICD-10 diagnostic approaches, and described criteria for evaluating assessments. The chapter further emphasized an integrative, technical-eclectic approach for the elements that go into a comprehensive assessment, and supported that approach with the review of several social work practice models. We also described common features for current-day assessment and the convergent elements found in the diverse practice models. We used technical eclecticism to integrate assessment information across the models into an Integrative Skills Assessment Protocol that practitioners can use to guide assessment. The final section of this chapter moved readers from assessment to treatment, introducing clinical decision making, problem monitoring, and treatment planning.

A final word: in writing this book and in our practice activities, we assume a broad approach to assessment and intervention planning. We believe that theoretical narrowness—limiting ourselves to only one method of collecting information about clients—does a disservice to our clients and to ourselves. We believe that broadening our approach by learning a variety of creative ways to obtain client information, both of a quantitative and a qualitative nature, helps us know and be sensitive to our clients. We encourage practitioners to use the techniques presented in this book while always thinking about the client's needs, style, and willingness to participate. It is when we put the client first and foremost in our practice that we can be the most help.

STUDY QUESTIONS

1. What are the major issues covered in social work assessment?

2. Describe the features of practice context, clients served, and practice model, and explain how those features affect social work assessment.

3. Describe the common assessment features that are found across social work practice models. What impacts do these features have on our work with clients?

4. How are the DSM-5 and ICD-10 relevant to social work practice?

5. Practice using the protocol by interviewing a friend.

6. What are the steps that can be used to select and evaluate an intervention using an evidence-based approach? Apply these to a specific problem.

7. How does single-subject design inform assessment and treatment? Describe the steps of single-subject design.

8. How has the prevalence of managed care affected assessment and treatment?

9. How would you time the movement from assessment to intervention? How would you choose the appropriate intervention?

10. Use a case study from the text and design a treatment plan.

REFERENCES

American Psychiatric Association (APA). (2013). *Diagnostic and statistical manual of mental disorders* (5th ed.; DSM-5). Washington, DC: Author.

American Psychological Association. (2015). *Evidence-based assessment resources.* Retrieved from http://www.apadivisions.org/division-54/evidence-based/assessment-resources.aspx

Austiran, S. G. (2009). *Mental disorders, medications, and clinical social work* (3rd ed.). New York: Columbia Press.

Barker, R. (2003). *Social workers dictionary.* Washington, DC: National Association of Social Workers Press.

Barth, R. (1986). *Social and cognitive treatment of children and adolescents.* San Francisco: Jossey-Bass.

Beck, J. S. (2011). *Cognitive behavior therapy: Basics and beyond.* New York: Guilford Press.

Beck, J. S., & Beck, A. T. (2002). *Beck youth inventories of emotional and social impairment.* San Antonio, TX: Psychological Corporation.

Bellack, A. S., & Hersen, M. (1988). *Behavioral assessment: A practical handbook* (3rd ed.). Elmsford, NY: Pergamon Press.

Berlin, S. B. (1996). Constructivism and the environment: A cognitive-integrative perspective for social work practice. *Families in Society, 77,* 326–335.

Berzoff, J., Flanagan, L. M., & Hertz, P. (Eds.). (2011). *Inside out and outside in: Psychodynamic clinical theory and psychopathology in contemporary multicultural contexts* (3rd ed.). Lanham, MD: Rowman & Littlefield.

Blanck, G., & Blanck, R. (1974). *Ego psychology in theory and practice.* New York: Columbia University Press.

Bloom, M., Fischer, J., & Orme, J. (2009). *Evaluating practice: Guidelines for the accountable professional* (6th ed.). Englewood Cliffs, NJ: Prentice Hall.

Brandell, J. (2008). Using self psychology in clinical social work. In A. R. Roberts (Ed.), *Social workers' desk reference* (2nd ed., pp. 311–317). New York: Oxford University Press.

Brower, A. M., & Nurius, P. S. (1993). *Social cognition and individual change: Current theory and counseling guidelines.* Newbury Park, CA: Sage.

Cormier, S., Nurius, P. S., & Osborn, C. J. (2008). *Interviewing and change strategies for helpers: Fundamental skills and cognitive behavioral interventions* (6th ed.). Pacific Grove, CA: Brooks/Cole–Thompson Learning.

Cowger, C. D., & Snively, C. A. (2008). Assessing client strengths. In A. R. Roberts & G. J. Greene (Eds.), *Social workers' desk reference* (pp. 221–225). New York: Oxford University Press.

De Jong, P., & Berg, I. K. (2001). Co-constructing cooperation with mandated clients. *Social Work, 46,* 361–374.

De Jong, P., & Berg, I. K. (2008). *Interviewing for solutions* (3rd ed.). Pacific Grove, CA: Cengage Learning.

Doremus, B. (1976). The four Rs: Social diagnosis in health care. *Health and Social Work, 1,* 121–139.

Early, T., & GlenMaye, L. F. (2000). Valuing families: Social work practice with families from a strengths perspective. *Social Work, 45,* 118–130.

Fortune, A. E., Reid, W. J., & Reyome, D. P. (2009). Task-centered practice. In A. R. Roberts (Ed.), *Social workers' desk reference* (2nd ed., pp. 226–230). New York: Oxford University Press.

Franklin, C. (2002, March/April). Becoming a strengths fact finder. *Family Therapy Magazine, 1*(2), 30–33.

Franklin, C. (2015). An up-date on strengths-based, solution-focused brief therapy. *Health and Social Work, 40*(2): 73–76. doi:10.1093/hsw/hlv022

Franklin, C., & Jordan, C. (1999). The clinical utility of models and methods of assessment in managed care. In B. S. Compton & B. Galaway (Eds.), *Social work processes.* Pacific Grove, CA: Brooks/Cole.

Franklin, C., & Kelly, M. (2009). Implementation of evidence-based practice in the real world of schools. *Children and Schools, 31,* 46–56.

Franklin, C., & Moore, K. (1999). Solution-focused therapy. In C. Franklin & C. Jordan, *Family practice: Brief systems methods for social work* (pp. 105–142). Pacific Grove, CA: Brooks/Cole.

Franklin, C., Trepper, T., McCollum, E., & Gingerich, W. (2012). *Solution-focused brief therapy.* New York: Oxford University Press.

Gambrill, E. (1983). *Casework: A competency based approach.* Englewood Cliffs, NJ: Prentice Hall.

Gambrill, E., Thomas, E., & Carter, R. (1971). Procedure for sociobehavioral practice in open settings. *Social Work, 16,* 51–62.

Germain, C., & Gitterman, A. (2008). *The life model approach to social work practice: Advances in theory and practice* (3rd ed.). New York: Columbia University Press.

Gingerich, W. J., & Peterson, L. T. (2013). Effectiveness of solution-focused brief therapy: A systematic qualitative review of controlled outcome studies. *Research on Social Work Practice, 23*(3), 266–283.

Gitterman, A., Goldstein, E. G., & Rose, S. (1988, March). *Alternative practice explanatory frameworks: A debate.* Presentation at the annual program meeting, Council on Social Work Education, Atlanta, GA.

Goldstein, E. G. (1986). Ego psychology. In F. J. Turner (Ed.), *Social work treatment* (3rd ed., pp. 375–405). New York: Free Press.

Goldstein, E. G. (2002). *Object relations theory and self-psychology in social work.* New York: Free Press.

Goodheart, C. D. (2014). *A primer for ICD-10-CM users.* Washington DC: American Psychological Association.

Granvold, D. K. (1996). Constructivist psychotherapy. *Families in Society, 77*(6), 345–357.

Herbert, J. D., Gershkovich, M., & Forman, E. M. (2014). Acceptance and mindfulness-based therapies for social anxiety disorder: Current findings and future directions. In *Wiley Blackwell Handbook of Social Anxiety Disorder* (pp. 588–607). Hoboken, NJ: Wiley-Blackwell.

Hollis, F., & Wood, M. E. (1981). *Social casework: A psychosocial therapy* (3rd ed.). New York: Random House.

Hudson, W. W. (1982). *The clinical measurement package.* Homewood, IL: Dorsey Press.

Hunsley, J., & Mash, E. J. (2007). Evidence-based assessment. *Annual Review of Clinical Psychology, 3,* 29–51.

Hunsley, J., & Mash, E. J. (2012). Evidence-based assessment. In D. H. Barlow (Ed.), *Oxford handbook of clinical psychology* (Online). Oxford, UK: Oxford University Press. doi: 10.1093/oxfordhb/9780195366884.013.0005

Johnson, L. (1981). *Social work practice: A generalist approach.* Boston: Allyn and Bacon.

Jordan, C., & Cobb, N. (1993). Treating dual career couples. In T. Nelson & T. Trepper (Eds.), *101 interventions in family therapy* (pp. 108–112). New York: Haworth Press.

Jordan, C., Franklin, C., & Johnson, S. (2015). Treatment planning with families. In Corcoran, K. & A. Roberts (Eds.), *The social workers' desk reference* (3rd ed.; chap. 55, pp. 433–437). New York: Oxford University Press.

Kanfer, F. H., & Schefft, B. K. (1988). *Guiding the process of therapeutic change.* Champaign, IL: Research Press.

Kelly, M., Kim, J. S., & Franklin, C. (2008). *Solution-focused brief therapy in schools.* New York: Oxford University Press.

Kim, J. S. (2008). Examining the effectiveness of solution-focused brief therapy: A meta-analysis. *Research on Social Work Practice, 18,* 107–116.

Kim, J., & Franklin, C. (2009). Solution-focused, brief therapy in schools: A review of the outcome literature. *Children and Youth Services Review, 31,* 461–470.

Kim, J. S., Trepper, T., Smock, S., McCollum, E., & Franklin, C. (2010). Is solution-focused brief therapy evidence-based? *Families in Society, 91,* 300–306.

Lazarus, A. (1989). Multimodal therapy. In R. Corsini & D. Wedding (Eds.), *Current psychotherapies* (4th ed., pp. 503–544). Itasca, IL: Peacock.

Lazarus, A. (1991). *The multi-modal life history inventory.* Champaign, IL: Research Press.

Lazarus, A. (2006a). *Brief but comprehensive psychotherapy: The multimodal way.* New York: Springer.

Lazarus, A. (2006b). Multimodal therapy: A seven-point integration. In G. Stricker & J. Gold (Eds.), *A casebook of psychotherapy integration* (pp. 17–28). Washington, DC: American Psychological Association.

Leff, H. S., & Conley, J. A. (2006). Desired attributes of evidence assessments for evidence-based practices. *Administration and Policy in Mental Health, 33,* 648–658.

Lehman, P., & Patton, J. (2012). The development of a solution-focused fidelity instrument. In C. Franklin, T. Trepper, E. McCollum, & W. Gingerich (Eds.), *Solution-focused brief therapy* (pp. 39–54). New York: Oxford University Press.

Levine, E. R. (2008). Glossary. In A. R. Roberts (Ed.), *Social workers' desk reference* (2nd ed., pp. 829–849). New York: Oxford University Press.

Mackay, C., Cox, T., Burrows, G., & Lazzerini, T. (1978). An inventory for the measurement of self-reported stress and arousal. *British Journal of Social and Clinical Psychology, 17,* 283–284.

Maluccio, A. N. (Ed.). (1981). *Promoting competence in clients: A new/old approach to social work practice.* New York: Free Press.

Mattaini, M. A. (1990). Contextual behavioral analysis in the assessment process. *Families in Society, 7,* 236–245.

Mattaini, M. A. (1992). *More than a thousand words: Graphics for clinical practice.* Washington, DC: National Association of Social Workers Press.

Mattaini, M. A. (1993). Misdiagnosing assessment. *Social Work, 38,* 231–233.

Mattaini, M. A. (1999). *Intervention with families.* Washington, DC: National Association of Social Workers Press.

Mattaini, M. A., & Lowery, C. T. (2007). *Foundations of social work practice* (4th ed.). Washington, DC: National Association of Social Workers Press.

Mattaini, M. A., Lowery, C. T., & Meyer, C. H. (2002). *Foundations of social work practice* (3rd ed.). Washington, DC: National Association of Social Workers Press.

Navran, L. (1967). Communication and adjustment in marriage. *Family Process, 6,* 173–184.

Parad, H. J., & Miller, R. (Eds.). (1963). *Ego-oriented casework.* New York: Family Service Association of America.

Perlman, H. (1957). *Social casework: A problem solving process.* Chicago: University of Chicago Press.

Perelman School of Medicine. (n.d.). *Beck scales and inventories.* Retrieved from http://www.med.upenn.edu/suicide/beck/scales.html

Psychotherapy Networker. (2007). Ten most influential therapists. Retrieved from http://www.psychotherapynetworker.org/component/content/article/81-2007-marchapril/898-ten-most-influential-therapists

Reid, W. J. (1988). Brief task-centered treatment. In R. A. Dorfman (Ed.), *Paradigms of clinical social work* (pp. 196–219). New York: Brunner/Mazel.

Reid, W. J. (1992). *Task strategies: An empirical approach to clinical social work.* New York: Columbia University Press.

Reid, W. J. (2000). *The task planner.* New York: Columbia University Press.

Reid, W. J., & Epstein, L. (1972). *Task-centered casework.* New York: Columbia University Press.

Reid, W. J., & Fortune, A. E. (2008). The task-centered model. In A. R. Roberts & G. J. Greene (Eds.), *Social workers' desk reference* (pp. 101–104). New York: Oxford University Press.

Rose, S. (1977). *Group therapy: A behavioral approach.* Englewood Cliffs, NJ: Prentice Hall.

Sackett, D., Straus, S. E., Richardson, W., Rosenberg, W., & Haynes, R. (2000). *Evidence-based medicine: How to practice and teach EBM* (2nd ed.). New York: Churchill Livingstone.

Saleebey, D. (1997). *The strengths perspective in social work practice* (2nd ed.). New York: Longman.

Saleebey, D. (2013). *The strengths perspective in social work practice* (6th ed.). (Advancing core competencies series). New York: Pearson.

Segal, Z. V., Williams, J. M. G., & Teasdale, J. D. (2012). *Mindfulness-based cognitive therapy for depression.* New York: Guilford Press.

Sheafor, B., Horejsi, C., & Horejsi, G. (1988). *Techniques and guidelines for social work practice.* Boston: Allyn and Bacon.

Shorkey, C. T., & Sutton-Simon, K. (1983). Reliability and validity of the Rational Behavior Inventory with a clinical population. *Journal of Clinical Psychology, 39,* 34–38.

Spring, B., & Hitchcock, K. (2009). Evidence-based practice in psychology. In I. B. Weiner & W. E. Craighead (Eds.), *Corsini's encyclopedia of psychology* (4th ed., pp. 603–607). New York: John Wiley & Sons.

Stuart, R. (2003). *Helping couples change: A social learning approach to marital therapy.* New York: Guilford Press.

Studt, E. (1968). *C-unit, search for community in prison.* New York: Russell Sage Foundation.

Thyer, B. A. (1983). Review of *Behavior Modification in Social Work Practice. Behavior Therapist, 8,* 161–162.

Thyer, B. A. (1987). Contingency analysis: Toward a unified theory for social work practice. *Social Work, 32,* 150–157.

Thyer, B. A. (1988). Radical behaviorism and clinical social work. In R. Dorfman (Ed.), *Paradigms of clinical social work* (pp. 123–148). New York: Brunner/Mazel.

Turner, F. (2005). *Social work diagnosis in contemporary practice.* New York: Oxford University Press.

Whittaker, J., & Tracy, E. (1989). *Social treatment: An introduction to interpersonal helping in social work practice* (2nd ed.). New York: Aldine de Gruyter.

Woods, M. E., & Robinson, H. (1996). Psychosocial theory and social work treatment. In F. J. Turner (Ed.), *Social work treatment* (4th ed., pp. 555–580). New York: Free Press.

World Health Organization. (2010). *International classification of diseases* (10th rev.; ICD-10). Retrieved from http://www.who.int/classifications/icd/en/

World Health Organization. (In press). *International classification of diseases* (11th rev.; ICD-11).

PART II

Clinical Assessment Methods

Part II introduces quantitative and qualitative methods of assessment and shows how both ways of assessing are equally important and contribute different information. Part II also shows how to select sound approaches to assessment so that practitioners can pay close attention to the research basis of an assessment method and its clinical applicability. Chapter 2, "Quantitative Clinical Assessment Methods," provides a rationale for the inclusion of quantitative assessment methods in social work and summarizes the most frequently used types of measurement approaches for assessing client behavior. Chapter 3, "Standardized Assessment Measures and Computer-Assisted Assessment," helps practitioners become informed consumers in the selection, use, and interpretation of standardized measurement instruments. Finally, chapter 4, "Qualitative Assessment Methods," explains the unique contributions of qualitative assessment methods. Together, the three chapters aim to present a complete picture of various assessment methods so that practitioners can be well equipped to assess different clients.

CHAPTER 2

Quantitative Clinical Assessment Methods

Cynthia Franklin and Anao Zhang

INTRODUCTION

Quantitative clinical assessment involves measurement that includes categorizing client characteristics, assigning diagnostic labels, developing behavior profiles, and systematically tracking problem behaviors, to observe change over the course of treatment and afterward. Measurements contribute to the practitioner's subjective and intuitive information (practice wisdom) and add specificity and concreteness. In this chapter, readers will learn about evidence-based assessment and how to conduct assessment so that measurement of client behaviors is part of the assessment process. Measurement not only assists practitioners in defining client problems and attributes, and in observing them over the course of treatment, as chapters 1 and 10 discuss, but also may help practitioners define the client's environmental context by ascertaining situation-specific behaviors across settings. Examples include the rate of disruptive behavior in the school, home, and community; the functioning of social systems (e.g., families, friends); the quality of interpersonal interactions (e.g., peer relationships, classroom behaviors); the availability of resources (e.g., finances, special assistance programs); and the availability of support networks (e.g., clubs, kin groups, close friends).

The main focus of this chapter is on providing a rationale for the inclusion of quantitative assessment methods in social work and on illustrating several different methods for assessing clients, including the following:

- Client self-reporting and monitoring
- Self-anchored and rating scales
- Questionnaires
- Direct behavioral observations
- Role-play and analog situations
- Behavioral by-products
- Psychophysiological measures

- Goal attainment scaling
- Standardized measures
- Projective measures

Assessment methods discussed and illustrated here are also relevant to evaluating client change and effective intervention planning. Finally, because there will be times when practitioners simply cannot find a quantitative assessment tool that is right for their client's circumstances, this chapter provides guidelines for developing self-anchored and rating scales.

RATIONALE FOR INCLUDING QUANTITATIVE MEASURES IN ASSESSMENT

Clinical assessment is designed to provide a portrayal of client functioning that is as complete as possible. The complexity of the client's biopsychosocial and spiritual functioning and the immediate situations in which the presenting problems arise are gathered into a clinical understanding or case conceptualization that facilitates the social work intervention. As part of an assessment, social work practitioners usually develop a narrative psychosocial assessment, often based on a clinical interview that summarizes the client's history and current functioning. The report defines the presenting problem, tells the client's story, summarizes the major strengths and weaknesses of the client, and provides a formulation for treatment. Quantitative assessment can enhance and add to the case formulation and narrative report by providing additional methods for assessing the client's strengths, problem, behavior, and attributes.

Although essential to social work assessments, the narrative assessment uses the judgments and opinions of both practitioners and clients; however, these views may be subject to bias and to misformulations of client problems. Including additional assessment methods such as quantitative measures in addition to interviews and narrative assessment helps practitioners and clients clarify and verify their opinions, and provides multiple sources of data to consider in the assessment process. The use of multiple sources of information is particularly important in obtaining accurate assessments (O'Hare, 2009). For example, in the case of a child with school problems, practitioners can interview the client (i.e., the child), the parents, and the child's teachers, and they can collect quantitative information from the parents and school using a questionnaire. It might be useful in some circumstances for the practitioner to observe the child in the classroom using a child behavior rating scale.

Measurement provides us with tools that we can incorporate into the assessment process and use as objective indicators of client problems and progress during the course of treatment (Barlow, Nock, & Hersen, 2008). In fact, clients may actually prefer the use of systematic data collection.

Holosko, Dulmus, and Sowers (2012) found that the use of standardized scales and single-subject designs was associated with improved outcomes for clients. Social workers who used empirical clinical practice techniques showed significantly greater reductions in the severity of client problems. The use of such techniques may also affect client outcomes beyond the effect of the intervention alone (Faul, McMurtry, & Hudson, 2001).The objective assessment of client problems with measures improves treatment, for example by increasing the accuracy of the practitioner's understanding of client problems and by providing feedback for the practitioner during treatment. Monitoring client progress with measures allows the practitioner to change treatment if progress is not being made. Several studies have shown that this monitoring improves treatment outcomes; in particular the outcomes improve when the feedback from clinical measures are given to therapists (Kelley & Bickman, 2009; Whipple & Lambert, 2011).

There is no doubt that objective measures provide an integral link between research and practice, which makes it easier for practitioners to evaluate the outcomes of their own practice. Practice evaluation is essential to good service provision in today's practice environment. Funding sources, such as federal agencies and insurance companies, demand that practitioners provide evidence of their accountability and effectiveness with clients. The federal government and other companies and agencies, for example, hire their own professional experts who require social workers to monitor the progress of intervention.

QUANTITATIVE ASSESSMENT METHODS

We have been discussing reasons for including quantitative measures as part of social work assessment practice evaluation. The remainder of this chapter summarizes several assessment methods for measuring client problems, behaviors, and goals. It also suggests guidelines for developing a measurement tool.

Client Self-Recording and Self-Monitoring

Client self-recording and self-monitoring are the most common methods of observing clients. The practitioner asks the client to record his or her thoughts, feelings, and behaviors. With self-recording, the practitioner asks the client to collect the observations and report the information in a retrospective fashion (e.g., for the client to record the number of times he or she thought about leaving a spouse in the previous week). In contrast, with self-monitoring, the practitioner asks the client to collect the observations every time the behavior occurs (e.g., for the client to record each time he or she thinks of leaving a spouse over the coming week). Methods of self-recording and self-monitoring vary and include such techniques as client logs, diaries, journals, and structured activities and behaviors.

Client self-recording and monitoring are useful clinical assessment tools that enable practitioners to obtain baseline measures of client problems. When baseline data show that the client is similar to a clinical sample or noticeably different from the general population, the measures tend to evidence the necessity of treatment (Corcoran & Boyer-Quick, 2008). Such information is particularly useful because it helps with the demands for accountability (Tuttle & Woods, 2013). For example, the practitioner may ask the client to record the number of episodes of depression he or she experiences and to report the specific nature of the episodes in a log (see table 2.1). Social work practitioners may use such a

Table 2.1   Client Self-Recording, Self-Monitoring

	Time	Duration	Situation	Nature of Depression
Sunday	8:00 A.M.	1 hours	alone eating breakfast	I am such a loser. Still eating breakfast by myself at this age. I wish I was never born to this world.
	6:00 P.M.	3 hours	walking by a shopping mall	Felt sad and wanted to cry. I should stay at home and never come out. All those dresses are beautiful but I can't afford them.
Monday				Nothing in particular happened today. I laid in bed for the whole day and did not feel like getting up.
Tuesday	9:15 P.M.	1.5 hours		Received phone call from my son. We only talked for 30 minutes and he did not say "I love you" to me by the end. He will leave me very soon, too.
Friday	6:00 P.M.	2 hours	Did not make the food right. Having dinner by myself alone.	I thought I had the worst luck ever and I would never be free from all the bad luck that I am in right now.
Saturday	8:00 A.M.	3 hours	alone at home	same
	9:45 P.M.	30 minutes	Had a disagreement earlier today with friends.	Sad, frustrated, and having trouble falling asleep.

log to explore the seriousness or magnitude of clients' depression and to monitor any increase or decrease in the frequency or magnitude of depressed mood over the course of treatment. Figure 2.1 shows an anger diary of incidents of arguments between a client and spouse. Table 2.2 is a structured form for observations in clients' recurring irrational thoughts that led to anxious mood. Practitioners ask clients to monitor their irrational beliefs according to Beck and Haigh's (2014) generic cognitive model, which uses cognitive restructuring as a primary vehicle for facilitating client change.

Figure 2.1   Anger Diary

Name: _____   Date: _____

How many arguments did you have this week? _____

How do you rate (0–10) your:

      Verbal: _____   Anger _____
                            Partner's Anger _____
                            Fear _____
      Physical _____   Anger _____
                            Partner's Anger _____
                            Fear _____

What were your internal signals when trouble began?

What signals came from your partner?

How many times did you call for time-out? _____

How many times did your partner call time? _____

Which steps did you use? (Answer Yes or No)

T sign _____   Exercise _____

Return of T _____   Error admitted _____

Leave quietly _____   Partner error _____

How long did you stay apart in time-out? _____

What happened afterward?

What other anger-control methods did you use?

	Practiced	Used in Real Life
Relaxation	_____	_____
Cognitive realignment	_____	_____
3-part assertion	_____	_____
Reflective listening	_____	_____
Diplomatic correction	_____	_____

Rate your happiness with this relationship if things go on just as they are (0–10):

Household responsibilities ____	General happiness ____	Spouse's independence ____
Rearing of children ____	Communication ____	Occupational progress ____
Money ____	Social life ____	Sex ____

Table 2.2 Daily Record of Thoughts

Client Name: _ John S. D. Parker Jr. _

Self-Identified Concerns: ___ Anxiety Disorders / Anxious Mood ___

Directions: When you notice your mood getting worse, ask yourself, What is going through my mind right now? Jot down the thought or mental image in the automatic thought column.

Date/Time: (When thought occurs)	Trigger/Situation: 1. Actual event leading to unpleasant emotion. 2. Distressing physical sensations.	Automatic Thoughts 1. Write down your thoughts that preceded your feelings 2. Rate how strong you believe in your thought(s) 0–100%	Feelings Describe: 1. specify your emotions 2. rate degree of emotions 0–100%	Challenge Your Thoughts Describe: If you were to think about this differently, how would you reevaluate your situation?	New Emotions Describe: How do you feel now? Any difference? 0–100%
Sunday (morning)	On my way to see my therapist, a man is begging and he looks scary Increased heart beat and shortened breath. Want to vomit.	He is going to beg money from me and he is probably dangerous. If I don't give him money, he will probably rob me. 90% sure	Anxious Nervous Worried 85% strong	The beggar does not ask for money from everyone, so he might not beg from me. If I say no, it also seems unlikely that he is going to rob me so early in the morning. The beggar has been here for a while and no robbery has been reported.	I feel less anxious and worried. 60% strong I am still nervous thinking about what could happen. 80% strong.
Tuesday (afternoon)	After my math class, I am discussing a project with other three of my classmates. Talking jittery and sweating a lot.	I must show the best side of me so that my classmates will not look down on me. 100%	Burdened Self-doubt Nervous 80% strong	It is a team work. It is not about how good I am but more about how well I can collaborate with other members of the team.	Less worried and nervous. 40% strong

Although client self-recording and self-monitoring are not terribly rigorous scientific forms of quantitative measurement, they are appropriate tools for clinical observations for a client's thoughts, feelings, and behaviors. Clinicians can improve the accuracy of client reports that result from self-monitoring by encouraging clients to collect the information in real time instead of retrospectively, as when one keeps a log and writes things down as they occur or better yet makes immediate telephone calls to the practitioner to report when a behaviors happens. Thompson and McCabe (2012) found, for example, that including client-identified goals in treatment results in significant improvements on clients' adherence. Self-recording and self-monitoring are a supplement to, never a substitute for, clinical judgment. They are compatible with other, more-rigorous measurement tools, such as standardized scales, and they provide useful validation information. Chapter 3 covers standardized measures in detail.

Self-Anchored and Rating Scales

Self-anchored scales are used as a measurement approach to client problems and are tools that the social worker and client construct together. Use of such scales is often necessary when a standardized instrument is not available or when a particular subtlety of the client's problem or goal needs to be part of the assessment. These "do-it-yourself scales," as they are sometimes called (Bloom, Fischer, & Orme, 2005), allow for the development of an assessment tool that represents the client's specific problem or concern. For example, a self-anchored rating scale may be constructed that measures a client's particular experience of postpartum depression that started six weeks after the birth of the baby and has been recurrent since then. The dimensions of the scale range from the maximum severity of postpartum depression (e.g., feeling overwhelmed, guilty of not being good enough, feeling angry) to maximum improvement in postpartum depression (e.g., feeling energetic, feeling alive and relieved). These two extremes are anchors, and they are used to describe the ends of a self-anchored rating scale. Practitioners ask clients to complete the self-anchored scale regularly—say, weekly or every other day or so (see figure 2.2). Scores on the self-anchored rating scale can be used to assess the client's depression and monitor its change over the course of treatment. Scale scores are practical and relevant because they are additional referents of the client's experience. By constructing a self-anchored rating scale, practitioners help clients define the problems by identifying the extremes. They construct the scale by identifying the extreme of the least magnitude as 1 and the extreme of the greatest magnitude as 7, which is an ideal scale range. The range of scale is ideal because it captures sufficient deviations to reflect the client's experience and, meanwhile, the

Figure 2.2   Self-Anchored Scale

Instructions: Circle the number that applies every day before 8:00 P.M.

Feeling overwhelmed	1	2	3	4	5	6	7	Feeling energetic
Feeling guilty of not being good enough	1	2	3	4	5	6	7	Feeling alive
Feeling angry	1	2	3	4	5	6	7	Feeling relieved

intervals are meaningful (Jordan, Franklin, & Corcoran, 2011). It is recommended to restrict the range of a self-anchored rating scale to five or seven intervals.

Self-anchored scales can be constructed for virtually any practice problem. They provide a systematic way for clients to observe their thoughts, feelings, and behaviors. Rating scales are similar to self-anchored scales in that the client and social worker co-construct them to reflect the client's presenting problem. However, someone other than the client completes a rating scale (see figure 2.3).

Figure 2.3 provides an example of a rating scale developed to assess the level of conflict avoidance of a couple in therapy. Rating scales allow the practitioner to obtain observations of client behavior from an outside observer, such as a spouse, a social worker, a teacher, or a member of a therapy group. These observations are helpful in that clients do not always observe themselves accurately; rating scales broaden the perspective on client functioning and substantiate progress in treatment.

Practitioners can use rating scales and self-anchored scales together as measures of client problems and behavior for even a broader scope and more accurate input. Self-anchored and rating scales also provide opportunities for the practitioner and client to quantify the presenting problem in ways that are clinically meaningful to both. Also not rigorous, scientifically valid, or reliable, like a client self-recording method, self-anchored and rating scales are useful only as a self-referenced comparison of the client's performance relative to the same client's previous performance.

Figure 2.3   Rating Scale for Conflict Avoidance

Changes the subject	1	2	3	4	5	6	7	Stay on topic
Leave the room and refuses to talk about conflictual issues	1	2	3	4	5	6	7	Stays in the room and discusses conflictual issues

Questionnaires

Questionnaires are another useful way to collect assessment information about clients. They provide clients with opportunities to report a large repertoire of behaviors and background information. Questionnaires are flexible; many are designed to solicit both specific, detailed information from the client and more global, comprehensive material. Although many questionnaires are available through commercial publishers and in the professional literature, the social work practitioner can also design them to meet the demands of a particular practice situation. An example of a standardized and well-researched commercial measure developed by a social work researcher is the Multi-Problem Screening Inventory (Hudson & McMurtry, 1997) that assesses clients on twenty-seven different areas of personal and social functioning. This instrument provides comprehensive assessment data to spot problems in areas that otherwise might not be investigated. Appendix 2A provides a sample questionnaire, the Patient Health Questionnaire-9 (Kroenke, Spitzer, & Williams, 2001), designed for measuring depression in primary health-care settings. This measure is available from Walmyr publishing and the scales of the measure can be viewed through their Web site (www.walmyr.com/mpsi.html).

The chief advantage of questionnaires is that they are useful background and screening tools for providing assessment information on clients in a simplified manner that does not require long interviews. Social workers need to consider carefully the advantages and purposes of using specific questionnaires. Many questionnaires are not particularly useful for monitoring clinical change, for example, but they are helpful in gathering history or background information and formulating treatment plans, and they may guide our diagnosis and referral decisions. Of course, there are many exceptional questionnaires, some of which gather information and are useful for monitoring outcomes; an example is the Multi-Problem Screening Inventory measure mentioned above.

Direct Behavioral Observation

Behavioral observation is one of the most direct and effective measures of client behavior. Behavior is observed in terms of its frequency, duration, or both (i.e., interval) (Bloom et al., 2005). To gauge frequency of behavior, it is first necessary to operationalize the behavior to be observed and to decide whether it is to be observed constantly (continuous recording) or on different occasions (time-sampling recording). Observers must be trained in the behavior to look for and in how to recognize it when it occurs.

Use of more than one observer at a time makes it possible to establish interobserver agreement; that is, the occurrences of observed behaviors between the observers can be compared to determine whether both are recording the same behavior. Interobserver agreement allows for calculation of a reliability statistic for observations to determine whether the ratings are consistent. It is also viewed as a very effective measurement strategy and has been used frequently in research on clinical practice (Nock & Kurtz, 2005). Agreement of 80 percent or greater is believed to be acceptable for most clinical situations.

In practice, direct behavioral observation is easiest to use in residential settings and in schools, where numerous professionals can comprehensively observe behavior in a natural context. For example, in a hospital setting a mental health aide and a nursing staff member can be trained to observe a client behavior such as withdrawal into the patient's room. Both staff may independently record the time the patient stays in his or her room for a work shift (duration measure). The two observers' recordings can then be compared to establish with greater confidence the actual occurrence of the behavior. Once we have established the frequency of behavior, we can continue to count the number of times the patient withdraws during a hospital stay to determine whether the patient's hospital stay is improving his or her social interaction.

Sometimes it is possible to use only one observer, either the social worker or a significant other of the client who is trained to observe the behavior. For example, the practitioner may ask a parent to record the amount of time a student studies during the week (duration measure). Behavioral observation with one rater lacks the scientific reliability of observation with two or more raters, but it remains an important measurement indicator in clinical assessments because it provides observations of the client's behavior in natural settings.

It is not always necessary to count every occurrence of a certain behavior to gain a sense of its frequency. Interval recording simplifies behavioral observations, which makes this measurement strategy more adaptable to clinical practice. In interval recording, the practitioner chooses a period of observation (e.g., twenty minutes) and divides it into equal (ten- to twenty-second) blocks (intervals). The social worker simply observes whether the client is performing the behavior (e.g., being off task in the classroom) during the interval. The practitioner records the behavior only once for that time interval no matter how many times it actually occurs (Bloom et al., 2005).

Interval recording is flexible in that almost any type of behavior can be recorded. It is also adaptable to clinical situations because it allows for observation of more than one behavior at a time. Interval recording is particularly useful for behaviors that are difficult to record using other methods (e.g., high-frequency behavior, behaviors of extended duration) (Bloom et al., 2005). Practitioners can also easily convert interval recording into percentages by dividing the number of intervals during which the behavior occurs by the total number of intervals observed and then multiplying by one hundred. Figure 2.4 provides an example of an interval

Figure 2.4   Interval Recording Form

Observer: _____ *School Social Worker* _____	Date: _____ *2/11/1997* _____
Reliability observer: _____ *paraprofessional* _____	DD/MM/YY
Teacher: _____ *Mrs. Jones (3rd Grade Reading)* _____	
School: _____ *Walnut Elementary* _____	Time stop: _____ *11:23* _____
Subject area: _____ *Reading-Seatwork* _____	Time start: _____ *11:05* _____
Referred pupil (R): _____ *Charles* _____	Total time: _____ *18 mins* _____
Comparison pupil (C): _____ *Kevin* _____	
Class size: _____ *34* _____ Class type: *Regular*	

Grouping Situation	*Teacher Reaction Code: (T)*	*Observation Recording Method*
R = student	T = teacher	(circle one)
C = student	AA = attention to all	(a) interval: size _____ 30″ _____
X = behavior occurs	A+ = positive attention to	(b) time sample: _____
O = behavior does	pupil	(c) event count
not occur	A– = negative attention	(d) duration for "out of
(circle one)	to pupil	seat"
L = large group	A0 = no attention to pupil	(e) latency
S = small group	An = neutral attention to	
O = one-to-one	pupil	
I = independent	= _____	
F = free time	= _____	
= _____	= _____	

Explicit classroom rules in effect during observation: *1. Work quietly 2. Sit at desks 3. Raise hand to ask question.*

recording form used to monitor a child's behavior. Direct behavioral observation of clients is one of the most effective tools for measuring client behavior; when used with two or more observers, it is considered scientifically rigorous. When following specific observational procedures, clinicians can effectively identify, define, and assess target behaviors that can serve as a guide to intervention (Nock & Kurtz, 2005). This makes direct behavioral observation a useful tool for both practice and research.

Role-Play and Analog Situations

Practitioners frequently use role-playing and other analog situations to assess clients' performance of various behaviors. These allow clients to demonstrate certain behaviors in the social worker's office. Social workers create role-plays or behavioral rehearsals in which clients demonstrate a behavior and the social worker observes. For example, a social worker might act as the client's "lazy" husband and engage in conversation with her. The observation serves as an assessment of potential skill and therapeutic feedback to facilitate goal attainment. In this example, the role-play allows the social worker to assess the client's pattern of communication with her husband and provides information the social worker can use to coach the client to improve. Observing this role-play on several occasions over a period makes it possible for the social worker to monitor improvement. The social worker can devise a plan for documenting this improvement, such as providing a rating scale of client performance or recording the client's improvements in a log, thus combining measurement strategies. The social worker can also document improvements through analog methods such as videotaping or audiotaping the role-plays, which helps clients understand their own behavior. Videotapes and audiotapes also are used in therapy and clinical supervision and serve as an analog measure of behavior for direct observation by the social worker and others. Reasonably priced recording equipment can greatly enhance routine clinical practice.

Another analog measure is the use of vignettes and other contrived behavioral situations. Vignettes are more structured than role-plays in that they usually provide the client with a set of questions to which he or she is to respond. The social worker asks clients to respond to a series of vignettes that approximate various behavioral situations. For example, a social worker can assess, at least hypothetically, an adolescent's problem-solving behavior by presenting the adolescent with a series of problem-solving vignettes or situations and asking him or her to respond. As with role-plays, the practitioner can use this information to help the adolescent improve his or her problem-solving skills.

Behavioral By-Products

Behavioral by-products are specific items or evidences that can be collected or accumulated as indicators of client behaviors. For example, cigarette butts can be collected to assess clients in a smoking cessation program. Similarly, weight gained or lost may serve as an indicator of client health functioning. A scale can verify the client's weight, and the scale readings are a measurement of the behavioral by-product. As another example, clients who are agoraphobic (afraid to go into public places) may be asked to keep theater ticket stubs and other paraphernalia indicating their attendance at social or recreational events.

Behavioral by-products are objective indicators of client behaviors. They are naturally associated with and represent the behavior the client wants to change. Collecting behavioral by-products is also easier for some clients than keeping a log or other written assignment.

Psychophysiological Measures

Psychophysiological measures are represented by mechanical and technological indexes of client behaviors. These measures assess the client's physiological performance because it relates to behavior. Several devices of clinical significance are used in clinical practice. Psychophysiological measures are frequently used in three categories of disorders: psychophysiological disorders (e.g., high blood pressure), anxiety disorders (e.g., stress symptoms, panic attacks), and sexual disorders (e.g., pedophilia, other deviant arousal syndromes) (Barlow et al., 2008). Examples of psychophysiological measures for each category follow.

Psychophysiological Disorder. The sphygmomanometer, an instrument that measures blood pressure, is frequently used to measure psychophysiological disorders. Various clinical biofeedback measures such as the electromyographic activity, a measure of tension or muscular contraction, and galvanic skin response, a measure of skin conductance, are also used.

Anxiety Disorder. Neurofeedback, as well as neurobiofeedback or electroencephalography biofeedback, is used to assess clients' anxiety and stress. Technology has increased the sophistication of electroencephalography biofeedback measures for clinical practice. For example, a quantitative electronencephalogram brain map is an assessment tool to objectively and scientifically evaluate a person's brainwave function. This sixty- to seventy-five-minute program consists of placing a snug cap on the client's head, a cap that contains small electrodes to measure the electrical activity coming from the brain (Hammond, 2011). The brainwave data are then statistically compared to a normative database and allows the professional to determine whether a client's brainwave patterns are significantly different from normal, and if so, how and where they differ. Thatcher (2010) verified the reliability of quantitative electronencephalogram, and the American Psychological Association has endorsed it.

Sexual Disorders. The most common psychophysiological measure used to assess and treat sexual disorders is the penile plethysmograph, a direct measure of blood flow that increases penile circumference. In the clinical setting, males with sexual deviations (e.g., pedophilia) are exposed to both appropriate and inappropriate sexual stimuli, and measures of penile arousal are obtained in conjunction with self-reports of sexual arousal. The plethysmograph makes it possible to measure deviant sexual arousal and aids the assessment and treatment of clients with sexual disorders (Barlow et al., 2008; Ward, Laws, & Hudson, 2003).

Psychophysiological measures are important indexes of client behaviors. Technological and mechanical devices greatly increase our ability to make scientifically valid and reliable assessments of client functioning in this domain. These measures, therefore, have significance for both clinical practice and research.

Goal Attainment Scaling Measures

Goal attainment scaling (GAS) is a method used to measure change in client problems according to clients' treatment goals (Kiresuk, Smith, & Cardillo, 2014) and thus to evaluate practice. Social workers have used GAS primarily to evaluate specific client or program outcomes. GAS is useful to ongoing assessment and monitoring because it allows practitioners and clients to operationalize and determine different levels of progress toward treatment goals. Outcomes or progress indicators range from most unfavorable to best anticipated. Table 2.3 shows a template of GAS developed based on the literature (e.g., Kiresuk et al., 2014; Ruble, McGrew, & Toland, 2012; Vu & Law, 2012). Measurable goals are operationalized mutually between the clients and practitioners, and the GASs are used throughout the course of treatment.

GAS is an effective method for assessing clinical change in clients and is a relevant and adaptable form of measurement that has proved successful in measuring client change across diverse clinical settings.

Standardized Measures

Standardized measures are ready-made instruments with proven records, in that their statistical and psychometric properties have been researched. Standardization refers to uniformity of procedures in scoring and administering the measure. In general, social work practitioners can have confidence in these measures and in their ability to assess the client behaviors for which they were developed. Even with excellent psychometric development, however, practitioners have to be aware of underlying flaws that may exist in scale properties and their clinical utility, which

Table 2.3   Goal Attainment Scaling Template

Check whether the scale has been mutually negotiated. Yes ☐ No ☐			
Check whether the goals have been mutually negotiated. Yes ☐ No ☐			
Level of Attainment	(Behavioral) Goal 1	(Behavioral) Goal 2	(Behavioral) Goal 3
Most unfavorable treatment outcome thought likely (–2)			
Less expected success with treatment (–1)			
Expected level of treatment success (0)			
More than expected success with treatment (+1)			
Best anticipated success with treatment (+2)			

might lessen their usefulness for clinical practice. Chapter 3 describes these issues in detail in relationship to the use of standardized measures in clinical assessment.

Standardized assessment measures assess a broad spectrum of client behaviors, such as personality, intelligence, marital satisfaction, self-esteem, and just about all aspects of human behavior (Fischer & Corcoran, 2007a, 2007b). Some standardized measures assess global behaviors such as personality (e.g., the Personality Inventory for Children; Lachar, 1982), and others assess specific behaviors such as level of dysphoric mood (e.g., the Beck Depression Inventory II, in Beck, Steer, & Brown, 1996; Center for Epidemiologic Studies Depression Scale–Revised [CESD-R], in Eaton, Smith, Ybarra, Muntaner, & Tien, 2004).

Self-report standardized measures exist, as do measures that others—such as parents, teachers, or some other informed individual—can complete. Both rapid assessment instruments and lengthy, comprehensive measures are available. For an example of a rapid assessment instrument, see the CESD-R (Eaton et al., 2004) and figure 2.5 (scoring instructions can

Figure 2.5 Center for Epidemiologic Studies Depression Scale–Revised

Please circle the numbers to tell me how often you have felt this way in the past week or so.	< 1 days	1–2 days	3–4 days	5–7 days	Every day
1. My appetite was poor.	0	1	2	3	4
2. I could not shake off the blues.	0	1	2	3	4
3. I had trouble keeping my mind on what I was doing.	0	1	2	3	4
4. I felt depressed.	0	1	2	3	4
5. My sleep was restless.	0	1	2	3	4
6. I felt sad.	0	1	2	3	4
7. I could not get going.	0	1	2	3	4
8. Nothing made me happy.	0	1	2	3	4
9. I felt like a bad person.	0	1	2	3	4
10. I lost interest in my usual activities.	0	1	2	3	4
11. I slept much more than usual.	0	1	2	3	4
12. I felt like I was moving too slowly.	0	1	2	3	4
13. I felt fidgety.	0	1	2	3	4
14. I wished I were dead.	0	1	2	3	4
15. I wanted to hurt myself.	0	1	2	3	4
16. I was tired all the time.	0	1	2	3	4
17. I did not like myself.	0	1	2	3	4
18. I lost a lot of weight without trying to.	0	1	2	3	4
19. I had a lot of trouble getting to sleep.	0	1	2	3	4
20. I could not focus on the important things.	0	1	2	3	4

SOURCE: http://cesd-r.com/
NOTE: CESD-R is available only for online testing. The book translated the content into the format as in figure 2.5.

be found in box 2.1). It should be noted that CESD-R has been used primarily in research settings and correlates significantly well with other clinical rating of depression (Hann, Winter, & Jacobsen, 1999).

Another example of a standardized outcome measure developed for guiding practice with children and adolescents is the Youth Outcome

---

Box 2.1
Score Interpretation for Center for Epidemiologic Studies Depression Scale–Revised

---

The Total CESD-R score is calculated as a sum of responses to all twenty questions. In order to make the revised CESD-R have the same range as the original version (i.e., the CESD style score), the values for the top two responses are given the same value:

- Not at all or less than 1 day = 0
- 1 to 2 days = 1
- 3 to 4 days = 2
- 5 to 7 days = 3
- Nearly every day for 2 weeks = 3

As in the original CESD the range of possible scores is between 0 (for those who reply "not at all or less than 1 day" to all twenty questions) and 60 (for those who reply "5 to 7 days" or "nearly every day for 2 weeks" for all twenty questions).

Determining Categories

The determination of possible depressive symptom category is based on an algorithm with the following logic:

- Meets criteria for major depressive episode: Anhedonia or dysphoria nearly every day for the past two weeks, plus symptoms in an additional four *Diagnostic and Statistical Manual of Mental Disorders* (DSM) symptom groups noted as occurring nearly every day for the past two weeks
- Probable major depressive episode: Anhedonia or dysphoria nearly every day for the past two weeks, plus symptoms in an additional three DSM symptom groups reported as occurring either nearly every day for the past two weeks, or five to seven days in the past week
- Possible major depressive episode: Anhedonia or dysphoria nearly every day for the past two weeks, plus symptoms in an additional two DSM symptom groups reported as occurring either nearly every day for the past two weeks, or five to seven days in the past week
- Subthreshhold depression symptoms: People who have a CESD-style score of at least sixteen but do not meet above criteria
- No clinical significance: People who have a total CESD-style score less than sixteen across all twenty questions.

Questionnaire (YOQ), which was designed to bridge the gap between traditional diagnostic measures and measures specifically designed to track outcomes (Burlingame et al., 2001; Wells, Burlingame, Lambert, Hoag, & Hope, 1996). A reliable and valid measure that can document and track treatment outcomes, clinicians, researchers, and managed-care administrators cooperatively designed the YOQ to meet the needs of all three. Its sensitivity to change in the client over time makes the YOQ an ideal instrument for evaluating client outcomes for evidence-based practice (EBP). Appendix 2B provides a sample clinician report from the YOQ generated by Carepaths; the appendix provides several scores, documenting client change over time.

Standardized measures generally make use of two points of reference that aid in their interpretation: criterion referenced and norm referenced. These methods may be combined, however. Criterion-referenced measures interpret specific content to be mastered. Clients' scores are interpreted on the basis of clients' ability to master a certain number of items on the measure (Urbina, 2011). For example, criterion-referenced standardized measures are used frequently in education to measure educational achievement. Norm-referenced measures are used to interpret outcomes on a particular measure for a specific population. Client scores on the measure are compared with the scores from a normative group of persons who have completed the measure. Norm-referenced standardized measures are generally used in clinical situations to assess the normative characteristics of clients. However, both types of measures can be used in clinical situations.

Standardized Measures and the DSM-5

The recently published the DSM-5 (American Psychiatric Association [APA], 2013), for example, contains various components of instruments to facilitate patient assessment and to aid in developing a comprehensive case formulation. During the development of the DSM-5 the work groups proposed or considered including standardized measures. The DSM-5 Mood Disorder Work Group, for example, considered using the Patient Health Questionnaire–9 for diagnosing major depressive disorder (Jones, 2012, p. 483). Even though this proposal was not accepted, the current DSM (DSM-5) has moved to provide a variety of self-report and rating scales called "crosscutting symptom measures." The DSM-5 designated a whole section on emerging measures and models, namely the crosscutting assessments. Crosscutting assessments are not specific to any particular disorder but evaluate symptoms of high importance to nearly all clients in most clinical settings (Jones, 2012). The crosscutting assessment consists of two levels: Level 1 assessments are self-report measures that evaluate major clinical domains including depressed mood, anxiety, suicide risk, and others. If any Level 1 domain is screened with clinical significance, a Level 2 clinician-rated follow-up measure is available to provide a more detailed assessment of the specific symptoms endorsed on the Level 1 measure. The Level 1 measure has separate versions for both adults and children (APA, 2013). A copy of the crosscutting measurement tools is available online, along with other DSM-5 measures (APA, 2015).

Crosscutting measures also support a more dimensional and scaled approach to assessment, recognizing that disorders exist on a spectrum that can be rated. To overcome problems rooted in the basic design of the previous DSM classification, the concept of a dimensional approach to diagnosis was also added to the DSM-5 (APA, 2013). The dimensional approach to diagnosis overcomes the downside of a "yes–no" categorical model, and more similar to standardized instruments uses three or more ordered categories to measure severity, intensity, frequency, as well as other clinical parameters for the symptoms observed (Regier, Narrow, Kuhl, & Kupfer, 2009). The dimensional diagnosis approach further views disorders within dimensions of internalizing and externalizing disorders, drawing on concepts from the measurement literature that show important factors for describing different types of psychopathology. The proposed dimensional approach adds valuable clinical information for practitioners to determine the best therapeutic plan, and the crosscutting symptom measures provide clinical tools that are easily accessed and can be used in clinical practice.

Box 2.2 provides a list of reference sources that practitioners can use to explore and review standardized measures. Because of their importance to clinical assessment, chapter 3 is devoted to norm-referenced standardized measurement instruments.

Projective Measures

Projective measures, used widely in clinical practice, are less structured than the other quantitative assessment tools we have discussed in this chapter. Projective measures typically assign a task that allows for an unlimited variety of responses. For example, a practitioner gives a client a partially completed sentence to finish or asks the client to describe what is happening in a picture. The most famous projective measure is the Rorschach test (Exner, 2003). Most projective measures are designed to assess global personality functioning and to uncover hidden or unconscious personality processes. Moreover, most of the measures are based on psychoanalytic concepts, and researchers have widely criticized them for their clinical inadequacies and lack of psychometric properties, such as reliability and validity (Kine, 2013; Weiner & Greene, 2011). From this

Box 2.2
Resources for the Review of Standardized Measures

Books

Baer, L., & Blais, M. A. (2010). *Handbook of clinical rating scales and assessment in psychiatry and mental health.* New York: Humana Press.

Carlson, J. F., Geisinger, K. F., & Jonson, J. L. (2003). *The nineteenth mental measurements year book.* Lincoln, NE: Buros Institute of Mental Measurement.

Corcoran, K., & Fischer, J. (Eds.). (2013a). *Measures for clinical practice and research:* Vol. 1. *Couples, families, and children.* New York: Oxford University Press.

Corcoran, K., & Fischer, J. (Eds.). (2013b). *Measures for clinical practice and research.* Vol. 2. *Adults.* New York: Oxford University Press.

Groth-Marnat, G. (2009). *Handbook of psychological assessment.* Hoboken, NJ: John Wiley & Sons.

Murphy, L. L., Plake, B. S., Impara, J. C., & Spies, R. A. (2002). *Tests in print VI.* Lincoln, NE: Buros Institute of Mental Measurement.

Sajatovic, M., & Ramirez, L. F. (2012). *Rating scales in mental health.* Baltimore: JHU Press.

Simmons, C., & Lehmann, P. (2012). *Tools for strengths-based assessment and evaluation.* New York: Springer.

Suzuki, L. A., & Ponterotto, J. G. (Eds.). (2008). *Handbook of multicultural assessment: Clinical, psychological, and educational applications.* New York: John Wiley & Sons.

Thornicroft, G., & Tansella, M. (Eds.). (2010). *Mental health outcome measures.* London: RCPsych Publication.

Online Location Services and Reviews of Tests and Measures

All the Tests.Com: http://www.allthetests.com (all kinds of test and measures located and reviewed)

American Psychological Association: http://www.apa.org/science/faq-findtests.html (review psychological tests)

Barbarians On-line (test page with measures and reviews of fun measures)

Buros Institute http://www.unl.edu/buros (comprehensive list and critical reviews of most commercially available tests and measures available online)

ERIC Test Locator: http://www.ericae.net/test-%20col.htm (review tests)

Learning Styles Inventory measure: http://www.wizardrealm.com/tests/index.html (take the Learning Styles Inventory measure and have it scored online)

American Psychiatric Association (APA). (2015). *Online assessment measures (DSM-5).* http://www.psychiatry.org/practice/dsm/dsm5/online-assessment-measures

Open Psych Assessment: http://www.openpsychassessment.org/

SAMHSA-HRSA: http://www.integration.samhsa.gov/clinical-practice/screening-tools (comprehensive list for screen tools and resources for assessment in integrated health care)

perspective, they may not be quantitative measures at all in the psycho-metric sense (on psychometric properties, see chapter 3). Furthermore, with the exception of certain psychoanalytic constructs such as defense mechanisms, projective measures are not useful in tracking client progress in treatment.

Despite these criticisms, however, projective measures continue to be a favorite clinical assessment and measurement tool of clinicians (Shemmings, 2004; Viglione & Hilsenroth, 2001). Their continued popularity may be because of their viability as a clinical technique for unraveling the intricacies and subtleties of client functioning. Clinicians prefer projective measures because they reach for latent or broad aspects of client functioning; these measures allow clinicians to make interpretations that are more global than narrow approaches to assessment, such as rapid assessment instruments, allow. In this sense, projective measures are similar to the clinical interview because they rely on the interpretations and judgments of the interviewer. Although projective measures have several quantitative weaknesses, they can be useful in a comprehensive assessment to generate global hypotheses about client characteristics such as personality or intelligence. Because they are vastly popular as a clinical technique and as a measure of client attributes, we describe a few commonly used projective measures here.

Incomplete sentence forms are a common group of projective measures. In this measure, the practitioner presents incomplete sentences to the client. This measure allows for almost-unlimited completions (e.g., "My mother never . . . ," "What worries me is . . . ," "My father . . . "). The practitioner uses incomplete sentences to solicit clinical themes and relevant personality and affective characteristics of the client.

The Draw-A-Person (DAP) test, or the Goodenough-Harris Drawing test (Harris, 1963, Short, DeOrnellas, & Walrath, 2011) is one frequently used projective measure. Originally developed by Florence Goodenough in 1926, the DAP test was later revised and extended by Dr. Dale B. Harris in his book *Children's Drawings as Measures of Intellectual Maturity* (1963). In this measure, the practitioner instructs the child to draw the best picture he or she can of him- or herself and a woman. Credit is given for the inclusion of individual body parts, clothing details, proportion, perspective, and similar features. A level of intellectual maturity score can be determined on the basis of a standard score, with a mean of one hundred and a standard deviation of fifteen, which demonstrates the quantitative aspect of the measure (Harris, 1963; for a discussion of standard scores, see chapter 3). The DAP test has also been used to infer personality characteristics. There is some support for the use of the measure in assessing intellectual maturity (Harris, 1963; Williams, Fall, Eaves, & Woods-Groves, 2006). However, it has been widely criticized as a personality measure (e.g., Imuta, Scarf, Pharo, & Hayne, 2013).

Other popular types of projective measures include the inkblot test known as the "Rorschach test" (Rorschach, 1921/1942) and the picture-story technique known as the "Thematic Apperception Test" (Murray, 1938). Resources for further readings on the two measures include Darity (2008, pp. 284–285) for the Rorschach test; Walrath (2011) for the Thematic Apperception Test; and Exner (2003) for the interpretive system for the Rorschach test.

Projective measures are widely used in clinical practice and have become an entrenched part of clinical assessment. Research indicates that projective measures as a quantitative measurement instrument have several weaknesses, but as a clinical technique they may be extremely valuable in generating global hypotheses about a client. Social workers should be skeptical, however, about what they can determine with these instruments, and they should make interpretations with extreme caution. Among all measures, projective assessment tools are the weakest of all psychological measures. Regardless of their validity or reliability, however, they will continue to be used.

GUIDELINES FOR USING MEASURES IN CLIENT ASSESSMENT

Thus far, we have discussed the need for using quantitative measurement as a part of social work assessment. We have also summarized ten methods of measuring client behaviors that practitioners can use. Table 2.4 presents a conceptual representation of these methods. With so many different methods available for measuring client behaviors, it can be difficult for social work practitioners to decide which methods to use in their

Table 2.4   Measurement Method Summary

Ask and Interpret	Watch	Ask
Interpretive Report	Observe and/or obtain objective indicators from other sources	Self-report and/or obtain objective indicators from the client
Projective Measures	Direct behavioral observation (frequency, duration, and interval), rating scales, goal attainment scaling, standardized measures, psychophysiological measures, role plays/analogue situations, behavioral by-products	Logs, journals, diaries, structured behavioral report forms, goal attainment scaling, standardized measures, role plays/analogue situations, behavioral by-products

assessment. This section offers guidelines to help practitioners develop a measurement system for client assessments. Specific suggestions for developing an assessment plan follow general guidelines.

When possible, practitioners should determine the best evidence-based approaches (i.e., determined through research studies) for their particular populations or problem areas to make their assessments more effective and efficient. Evidence-based assessment helps clinical assessment tools to be more precise and may lessen the number of tools a practitioner needs to develop a good assessment.

Chapter 3 further discusses measures and the process of evidence-based assessment and the advantages and disadvantages of using standardized measures in social work assessment. In using evidence-based assessment, researchers and practitioners seek to learn the best ways to assess different problems and populations. As mentioned in chapter 1, as the field learns more about the best assessment tools for different populations, assessment protocols or guides to assessment for various populations or mental health disorders are becoming available. It is always a good idea to use multiple methods to measure client behaviors and to seek out the best measures available that can most efficiently provide an assessment. Keeping in mind the suggestions in this chapter about adding measurement tools to narrative assessments, we provide three guidelines for developing a social work assessment.

First, develop baseline indicators of client functioning. Baseline data that are considerably different from data on a general population can evidence treatment necessity. Alternatively, scores at the baseline that are similar to those of a clinical sample suggest the need for treatment. All measures should be given at least on a pretest and a posttest basis. Follow-ups are also desirable.

Second, use at least one repeated measure. This ensures that practitioners measure client behavior on several occasions to monitor progress over the course of treatment. This approach is consistent with the single-subject design approach (see chapter 10); it provides feedback on the practitioner's interaction with the client, and it may improve treatment through that feedback.

Third, include specific and global measures of client problems. Doing so increases the likelihood of capturing changes in client behaviors.

Following these general guidelines, an ideal measurement system for client assessment might include the following:

- A standardized measure or a client log or self-anchored scale (self-report)
- A behavioral observation (self-report)
- A standardized or do-it-yourself rating scale (significant other report)

Ideally, in any assessment situation the practitioner should use at a minimum both a client self-report and a report from another rater to help decrease bias of any one perspective. For example, a practitioner can administer the Beck Depression Inventory, a self-report, or standardized measure to a client reporting depression; the practitioner might also ask for a report from a relative on the client's specific behavioral symptoms of depression (e.g., crying, isolation, not going to work). In developing a measurement approach to aid assessment, it is important to consider whether the measure really captures client change in the real world and is sensitive to what the practitioner is asking of the client (e.g., in filling out forms and measures). It is important, for example, not to overwhelm the client with too many assessment tools and measures—more is not necessarily better. On some occasions, only one measure may be enough. For example, even though there are many good ways to assess attention deficit/hyperactivity disorder in children, Evans and Baird (2006) suggest that the behavioral rating system called the "daily report card," which teachers fill out, is one of the best evidence-based assessments and captures the behaviors of the child that need to be monitored and changed. Good measurement, like good practice, requires knowledge, creativity, and flexibility of the practitioner. As are other practice skills, clinical measurement is as much art as science. A clinical assessment and measurement approach should therefore be as unique as clients and their situations dictate.

SUMMARY

Quantitative measurement requires practitioners to devise or use methods to assign numerical indicators to behaviors, emotions, or other attributes. Including measures as part of assessment provides quantitative sources of data and helps practitioners and clients verify and clarify their opinions and judgments concerning client functioning. This chapter discussed ten methods of measurement that practitioners can use: client self-reporting and self-monitoring, self-anchored and rating scales, questionnaires, direct behavioral observation, role-play and analog situations, behavioral by-products, psychophysiological measures, goal attainment scaling, standardized measures, and projective measures. The chapter also provided examples of these measurements and guidelines for their use. Four important guidelines are the following: use of multiple methods (at a minimum a self-report and another report), development of baseline indicators of client functioning, use of repeated measures, and use of both global and specific measures. Thus, this chapter has provided a broad overview of quantitative assessment methods that social workers can use in assessment, client evaluation, and intervention plans.

REFERENCES

American Psychiatric Association (APA). (2013). *Diagnostic and statistical manual of mental disorders* (5th ed.; DSM-5). Washington, DC: Author.

American Psychiatric Association (APA). (2015). *Online assessment measures (DSM-5).* Retrieved from http://www.psychiatry.org/practice/dsm/dsm5/online-assessment-measures

Barlow, D. H., Nock, M. K., & Hersen, M. (2008). *Single case experimental designs: Strategies for studying behavior change* (3rd ed.). Boston: Allyn and Bacon.

Beck, A. T., & Haigh, E. A. P. (2014). Advances in cognitive theory and therapy: The generic cognitive model. *Annual Review of Clinical Psychology, 10,* 1–24.

Beck, A. T., Steer, R. A., & Brown, G. K. (1996). *Manual for the Beck Depression Inventory: II.* San Antonio, TX: Psychological Corporation.

Bloom, M. J., Fischer, J., & Orme, J. G. (2005). *Evaluating practice: Guidelines for the accountable professional* (5th ed.). Boston: Allyn and Bacon.

Burlingame, G. M., Mosier, J. I., Wells, M. G., Atkin, Q. G., Lambert, M. J., Whoolery, M., & Latkowski, M. (2001). Tracking the influence of mental health treatment: The development of the Youth Outcome Questionnaire. *Clinical Psychology and Psychotherapy, 8,* 361–379.

Corcoran, K., & Boyer-Quick, J. (2008). How clinicians can effectively use assessment tools to establish treatment necessity and throughout the treatment process. In A. R. Roberts & G. Greene (Eds.), *Social workers' desk reference* (pp. 317–322). New York: Oxford University Press.

Darity, W. A. (Ed.). (2008). Rorschach test. *International Encyclopedia of the Social Sciences, 7*(2), 284–285. Detroit: Macmillan Reference.

Eaton, W. W., Smith, C., Ybarra, M., Muntaner, C., & Tien, A. (2004). *Center for Epidemiologic Studies Depression Scale: Review and revision* (CESD and CESD-R). Retrieved from http://cesd-r.com/

Evans, S. W., & Baird, A. V. (2006). Evidence-based assessment of ADHD: Measuring outcomes. *Journal of the American Academy of Child and Adolescent Psychiatry, 9,* 1132–1137.

Exner, J. E. (2003). *The Rorschach: A comprehensive system* (4th ed.). New York: John Wiley & Sons.

Faul, A. C., McMurtry, S. L., & Hudson, W. W. (2001). Can empirical clinical practice techniques improve social work outcomes? *Research on Social Work Practice, 11,* 277–299.

Fischer, J., & Corcoran, K. (2007a). *Measures for clinical practice and research: A sourcebook: Vol. 1. Couples, families and children* (4th ed.). New York: Oxford University Press.

Fischer, J., & Corcoran, K. (2007b). *Measures for clinical practice and research: A sourcebook: Vol. 2. Adults* (4th ed.). New York: Oxford University Press.

Hammond, D. C. (2011). What is neurofeedback: An update. Journal of Neurotherapy: Investigations in Neuromodulation. *Neurofeedback and Applied Neuroscience, 15*(4), 305–336. doi: 10.1080/10874208.2011.623090

Hann, D., Winter, K., & Jacobsen, P. (1999). Measurement of depressive symptoms in cancer patients: Evaluation of the Center For Epidemiological Studies Depression Scale (CESD). *Journal of Psychosomatic Research, 46*(5), 437–443.

Harris, D. B. (1963). *Children's drawings as measures of intellectual maturity: A revision and extension of the Goodenough Draw-a-Person test*. New York: Harcourt Brace Jovanovich.

Holosko, M. J., Dulmus, C. N., & Sowers, K. M. (2012). *Social work practice with individuals and families: Evidence-informed assessments and interventions*. Hoboken, NJ: John Wiley & Sons.

Hudson, W. W., & McMurtry, S. L. (1997). Comprehensive assessment in social work practice: The Multi-Problem Screening Inventory. *Research on Social Work Practice, 7*(1), 79–98.

Imuta, K., Scarf, D., Pharo, H., & Hayne, H. (2013). Drawing a close to the use of human figure drawings as a projective measure of intelligence. *PloS One, 8*(3), e58991.

Jones, K. D. (2012). Dimensional and crosscutting assessment in the DSM-5. *Journal of Counseling & Development, 90*(4), 481–487.

Jordan, C., Franklin, C., & Corcoran, K. (2011). Standardized measures. In R. M. Grinnell Jr. (Ed.), *Social work research and evaluation* (6th ed., pp. 198–209). Itasca, IL: Peacock.

Kelley, S. D., & Bickman, L. (2009). Beyond outcomes monitoring: Measurement feedback systems (MFS) in child and adolescent clinical practice. *Current Opinion in Psychiatry, 22*(4), 363–368.

Kine, P. (2013). *Personality: The psychometric view*. New York: Routledge.

Kiresuk, T. J., Smith, A., & Cardillo, J. E. (Eds.). (2014). *Goal attainment scaling: Applications, theory, and measurement*. New York: Psychology Press.

Kroenke, K., Spitzer, R. L., & Williams, J. B. (2001). The PHQ-9. *Journal of General Internal Medicine, 16*(9), 606–613.

Lachar, D. (1982). *Personality inventory for children (PIC) revised format manual supplement*. Los Angeles: Western Psychological Services.

Murray, H. (1938). *Explorations in personality*. New York: Oxford.

Nock, M. K., & Kurtz, S. M. S. (2005). Direct behavioral observation in school settings: Bringing science to practice. *Cognitive and Behavioral Practice, 12*, 359–370.

O'Hare, T. (2009). *Essential skills of social work practice: Assessment, intervention, evaluation*. Chicago: Lyceum Books.

Regier, D., Narrow, W., Kuhl, E., & Kupfer, D. (2009). The conceptual development of DSM-V. *American Journal of Psychiatry, 166*(6), 645–650.

Rorschach, H. (1927). *Rorschach test–Psychodiagnostic plates*. Cambridge, MA: Hogrefe.

Ruble, L., McGrew, J. H., & Toland, M. D. (2012). Goal attainment scaling as an outcome measure in randomized controlled trials of psychosocial interventions in autism. *Journal of Autism and Developmental Disorders, 42*(9), 1974–1983. doi: 10.1007/s10803-012-1446-7

Shemmings, D. (2004). Researching relationships from an attachment perspective: The use of behavioural, interview, self-report and projective measures. *Journal of Social Work Practice, 18,* 299–314.

Short, C., DeOrnellas, K., & Walrath, R. (2011). Draw-A-Person test. In S. Goldstein & J. A. Naglieri (Eds.), *Encyclopedia of child behavior and development* (pp. 523–524). New York: Springer.

Thatcher, R. W. (2010). Validity and reliability of quantitative electroencephalography (qEEG). *Journal of Neurotherapy, 14,* 122–152.

Thompson, L., & McCabe, R. (2012). The effect of clinician-patient alliance and communication on treatment adherence in mental health care: A systematic review. *BioMed Central Psychiatry, 12*(1), 87.

Tuttle, G. M., & Woods, D. R. (2013). *The managed care answer book.* Bristol, PA: Routledge.

Urbina, S. (2011). *Essentials of psychological testing.* Hoboken, NJ: John Wiley & Sons.

Viglione, D. J., & Hilsenroth, M. J. (2001). The Rorschach: Facts, fictions, and future. *Psychological Assessment, 13,* 452–471.

Vu, M., & Law, A. V. (2012). Goal-attainment scaling: A review and applications to pharmacy practice. *Research in Social and Administrative Pharmacy, 8*(2), 102–121.

Walrath, R. (2011). Thematic Appreciation Test. In S. Goldstein & J. Naglieri (Eds.), *Encyclopedia of child behavior and development* (pp. 1481–1482). New York: Springer.

Ward, T., Laws, D. R., & Hudson, S. M. (2003). *Sexual deviance: Issues and controversies.* Thousand Oaks, CA: Sage.

Weiner, I. B., & Greene, R. L. (2011). *Handbook of personality assessment.* Hoboken, NJ: John Wiley & Sons.

Wells, M. G., Burlingame, G. M., Lambert, M. J., Hoag, M. J., & Hope, C. A. (1996). Conceptualization and measurement of patient change during psychotherapy: Development of the Outcome Questionnaire and Youth Outcome Questionnaire. *Psychotherapy, 33,* 275–283.

Whipple, J. L., & Lambert, M. J. (2011). Outcome measures for practice. *Annual Review of Clinical Psychology, 7,* 87–111.

Williams, T. O., Fall, A. M., Eaves, R. C., & Woods-Groves, S. (2006). The reliability of scores for the Human figure drawing intellectual ability test for children, adolescents, and adults. *Journal of Psychoeducational Assessment, 24,* 137–144. doi: 10.1177/0734282905285249

CHAPTER 3

Standardized Assessment Measures and Computer-Assisted Assessment

Danielle E. Parrish, David W. Springer, and
Cynthia Franklin

INTRODUCTION

The goal of this chapter is to help social work practitioners become informed consumers in the selection, use, and interpretation of standardized measurement instruments. The chapter explores major issues in the development, evaluation, and interpretation of standardized measures, as well as applications of standardized assessment systems that use computer technologies. This chapter further defines what is meant by the term "evidence-based assessment" and shows how standardized measures can be an important part of conducting an evidence-based social work assessment.

EVIDENCE-BASED PRACTICE PROCESS AND ASSESSMENT

Previous chapters have discussed the seminal definition of evidence-based practice (EBP); this definition originated in medicine and focuses on EBP as a process. As a matter of review, Sackett, Straus, Richardson, Rosenberg, and Haynes (2000) originally coined the term "evidence-based practice" as the "integration of the best available research evidence with clinical expertise and [client] values" (p. 1). This process involves the following steps:

1. Convert the need for information into an EBP question (e.g., about prevention, diagnosis, assessment, intervention, risk factors, cultural sensitivity).
2. Search for the best research evidence with which to answer that question (most often using Web-based resources).
3. Critically appraise that evidence for its validity and applicability.
4. Integrate the critical appraisal with clinical expertise and the client's unique characteristics, values, and circumstances.

5. Evaluate therapy effectiveness and efficiency in implementing the practice decision and the EBP process. (Adapted from Straus, Richardson, Glasziou, & Haynes, 2005)

To date, the primary focus and application of the EBP process has been on the selection of the most effective interventions, with little attention paid to the import of this process to guide evidence-based assessment (EBA) (Hunsley & Mash, 2005, 2007; Mash & Hunsley, 2005). To address this concern, a handful of journal special issues on the topic of EBA have emerged in the psychology literature; the collective sentiment is perhaps best reflected in a comment by Achenbach (2005), who likens the use of EBP without EBA to "a magnificent house with no foundation" (p. 547).

Definition of Evidence-Based Assessment

As chapter 1 mentioned, EBA has been defined as "the use of research and theory to inform the selection of targets, the methods and measures used in the assessment, and the assessment process itself" (Hunsley & Mash, 2007, p. 29). The primary focus of EBA is to locate the best evidence regarding the most effective assessment instruments and protocols that fit best with a client's situation, culture, values, and preferences. This chapter further defines and describes what is beneath this broad definition. Four major factors to consider when engaging in EBA are the following:

1. Psychometric adequacy of standardized instruments or assessment protocols (reliability and validity)
2. Diversity issues and individual client characteristics and the fit of various assessment instruments or protocols with those characteristics
3. Issues of comorbidity
4. Clinical utility of standardized instruments or assessment protocols

Although the consideration of these factors is not new, the explicit, thoughtful, and concurrent integration of such factors has come out of recent writings on EBA and is thought to increase the probability that assessment procedures selected will be the most effective and relevant to each individual client. The bulk of this chapter focuses on those four factors and their relation to EBA.

PSYCHOMETRIC ADEQUACY

Once thought to be the domain of psychologists, standardized measures and computer-assisted assessment technologies continue to gain popularity with social work practitioners and other counselors (Beidas et al., 2015; Bloom, Fischer, & Orme, 2008; Corcoran & Fischer, 2013). Practitioners from cognitive-behavioral and empirical practice orientations have long used standardized assessment measures. As we discussed in chapters 1 and 2, practitioners trained in the empirical practice models value scientific practice and single-case designs as important parts of the assessment process, which is why more empirically trained practitioners use standardized measures more often. Unfortunately, many social workers have not been thoroughly trained in standardized assessment methodologies, so we have devoted this chapter to their uses in clinical assessment.

Standardized measures encompass a wide range of assessment tools, including but not limited to personality assessment instruments, behavior-rating scales, social attitude scales, measures of couple and family functioning, achievement tests, measures of cognitive functioning, and aptitude measures (Corcoran & Fischer, 2013). Computerized assessment technologies have been developed for many standardized measures, and computers are increasingly being used to aid practitioners in making clinical judgments (Garb, 2000; Garg et al., 2005).

Standardization is essential to the development of useful measures for clinical practice; several authors define it differently, but most definitions are related (Jordan, Franklin, & Corcoran, 2005; Kaplan & Succuzzo, 2009). All definitions share two characteristics that distinguish a standardized measure from a nonstandardized measure.

First, standardized measures have uniform administration and scoring procedures. Measurement conditions and outcomes are clearly and completely specified to ensure comparability of the results. The development of the measure provides detailed directions about how the measure is to be given, to whom it is to be given, and the exact meanings of the results. Detailed directions include such information as materials to be used, oral instructions to be given while administering the measure, preliminary demonstrations, exact ways to score the measure, and meanings of the scores. These directions are often reported in a measurement manual that accompanies the measure at its purchase. All directions in the manual must be followed precisely to reduce or eliminate the influence of factors extraneous to the characteristic(s) of the client being assessed.

Second, standardization entails a process of establishing norms for a measure. A measure is thought to be standardized if it has gone through technical development involving a standardization sample (a large representative sample of people) used to establish its normalization (statistical properties). The establishment of norms is essential to the scoring and interpretation of the measure. Norms make the measure comparable across client groups and empirically define the limits and practicalities of the measure. For example, norms establish such relevant information as the average score on the measure, the deviations necessary to fall outside the average, and the client groups for which the measure is appropriate.

For a measure to be standardized, it must go through a rigorous process of research and development aimed to empirically verify the measure's characteristics and usefulness. The level of research and development for different standardized measures varies greatly from minimal, crude standardization (e.g., testing on a small group of college freshmen) to state-of-the-art development (e.g., testing on a large, representative national sample). As a rule, practitioners should incorporate only the best and most technically developed standardized measures into practice situations.

The remaining sections summarize important considerations for evaluating the psychometric properties of standardized measures. First, we discuss the assessment of reliability of measures. Second, we examine methods for determining measurement validity. Third, we described types of validity. Fourth, we summarize norms, scoring, and interpretation of standardized measures, as well as explain frequently used standard scoring systems. Fifth, we discuss the use of standardized instruments for assessing treatment outcome. Sixth, we summarize and illustrate the availability of computer-assisted assessment technologies. Finally, we present the limitations of standardized instruments.

DETERMINING RELIABILITY

Reliability refers both to the consistency of a measure and to its dependability and stability. A tool is reliable to the extent that it performs consistently over repeated uses. Reliability is understood by examining the reliability coefficient or by using the standard error of measurement. A measure cannot be trusted if its reliability coefficient is low. Reliability coefficients indicate the degree of consistency in the measurement of test scores, and they range from 1.00 (perfect reliability) to 0.00 (no reliability). High reliability is especially important for measures incorporated into practice that will be used to guide clinical decision making. As the reliability of a measure decreases, so should our faith in it.

From available measures, social workers should try to choose the assessment tools with the highest reliability. Four prominent types of reliability of measures are described in the following sections: test-retest, alternate-form, split-half, and internal consistency.

Test-Retest Reliability

Test-retest reliability is an index of a measure's stability. The same test is given to the same client groups (subjects) on two different occasions, usually within a relatively short time (one week to a month or two). The Pearson product-moment correlation (Pearson's r), which indicates the relationship between two interval or ratio variables, is applied to the scores. This correlation coefficient indicates how consistently the measure performs over time. To the extent that both sets of responses correlate with each other, test-retest reliability is established.

A challenge of establishing this type of reliability is that too much time between administrations of the measure allows for real change to take place in the group of clients, whereas too little time raises the possibility that the responses in the second set are based on memory of the first administration. In either case, the obtained correlation coefficients will be misleading. This type of reliability may be difficult to establish and accurately interpret for scales that measure highly variable emotional and interpersonal traits (e.g., depression, anxiety). For this reason, test-retest reliability is not as useful as is sometimes implied (Springer, Abell, & Hudson, 2002).

Alternate-Form Reliability

Also called "equivalent" or "parallel-form reliability," alternate-form reliability is obtained by giving two different but equivalent forms of the same measure to the same group of clients. The two sets of scores are then compared by computing a correlation coefficient (e.g., Pearson's r). If there is no measurement error, clients should score the same on both measures, which thus yields a high correlation coefficient. This type of reliability is most commonly encountered when a scale developer wishes to establish a shorter version of a scale, say, from twenty-five items to ten items, so that it is less time-consuming for clients to complete. A correlation coefficient of roughly 0.90 is needed to comfortably argue for the presence of alternate-form reliability (Springer et al., 2002).

Split-Half Reliability

Split-half reliability is obtained by dividing a measure into two equivalent halves. In essence, the split-half method consists of administering one form of a scale to a group of subjects. The developer then uses half the items to compute one total score and the other half to compute a second total score. The developer then computes a correlation between the two sets of scores. To the extent that the two halves correlate, split-half reliability is established. To use this method, all items must measure the same construct.

There is a limitation to this method of establishing reliability. The developer must decide how to divide the items. For example, on a thirty-item scale, one could create one set by taking the first fifteen items to create one score and the second set of fifteen items to create a second score.

A more common practice is to create two sets of scores by using all of the odd-numbered items and even-numbered items to create two scores. The possibilities are almost infinite. In fact, for a thirty-item instrument, there are 77 million estimates for split-half reliability (Hudson, 1999). Rather than choosing one of these estimates to determine the internal consistency of a new measure, the next approach allows us to effectively compute the average of all 77 million estimates.

Internal-Consistency Reliability

The coefficient alpha (Cronbach, 1951; Guttman, 1945) computes the mean of all possible split-half reliabilities. It is a measure of the internal consistency of a measure and is based on the positive intercorrelations of the scale's items (Kuder & Richardson, 1937). Computing the internal consistency of a measure allows one to estimate how consistently respondents performed or responded across items of a measure assessing the same construct. The internal consistency of a measure also lends support for evidence of its content validity.

Cronbach's (1951) alpha is appropriate for use with equal-appearing interval-level data (e.g., Likert-type responses). For measures with a dichotomous (e.g., yes–no) item response format, the Kuder-Richardson Formula 20 (an equivalent procedure) should be computed.

Reliability Standards

A satisfactory degree of reliability depends on how a measure is intended to be used. Group research is typically concerned with mean differences among groups of subjects (e.g., experimental versus comparison groups). Given the field's advancement in its ability to establish psychometrically sound scales, we should not accept anything as credible for use in nomothetic research with a reliability coefficient below .70 (Abell, Springer, & Kamata, 2009). However, in clinical work a higher reliability coefficient is needed for scales that will be used to help guide clinical decision making with individual clients. The reason for this standard is that, when working with an individual, there is no opportunity to average the inevitable measurement error contained in the scale, as there is in group research. A general rule of thumb is that a reliability coefficient of .80 is considered good and acceptable when working with individual clients, and anything greater than .90 is considered excellent.

These reliability standards can help social workers make decisions about a scale's degree of reliability. The greater the seriousness of the problem being measured (e.g., suicidal risk), and the graver the consequences of being wrong, the higher the standard should be held.

Reliability is a necessary but not sufficient condition for ensuring that a scale has solid psychometric properties. If an instrument measures something consistently (indicating reliability) but not accurately (indicating validity), then the measure lacks clinical utility.

DETERMINING VALIDITY

Validity is concerned with the target and method of measurement of a particular measurement tool—that is, a tool is valid to the extent that it measures what it purports to measure. Any information gathered as part of the process of developing or using a measure becomes relevant to its validity. No one type of validity is appropriate for every measurement situation. Validity must be verified with reference to the specific intended use of a measure. So, regarding a measurement tool, social workers must continually ask, "What and for whom is it valid?" The answers to these questions can be determined only by examining the validity studies of a particular measure. All procedures for establishing measurement validity are concerned with the relationship between performance on the measure and other independent empirical criteria. Four types of measurement validity are described here: content validity, criterion validity (concurrent and predictive), construct validity (convergent and discriminant), and factorial analysis.

Content Validity

Content validity refers to the evaluation of items on a measure to determine whether the content contained in the items relates to and is representative of the domain that the measure seeks to examine. For example, to select a measure that assesses behavioral disorders in children, it is necessary to examine the item universe (total number of items) of the measure to determine whether the items on the measure include representative samples of the behavior of children. If the items relate only to depression, (e.g., "I feel sad"), the measure does not reflect the representative behavior domain of children. Although depression may be one dimension of that behavior domain, such a measure could not be said to have content validity.

A measure reflecting representative samples of behavior for assessing behavior disorders in children is necessarily multidimensional (measuring several different traits or behaviors) rather than unidimensional (measuring one trait or behavior). For instance, the measure would include items covering hyperactive behavior, antisocial behavior, and anxious behavior, as well as depression. Several measures of this caliber have been developed, including the Revised Behavior Problem Checklist

(Quay, 1987), the Achenbach Child Behavior Checklist (Achenbach & Edelbrock, 1983), the Child and Adolescent Functional Assessment Scale (Hodges, 2000). Such measures are said to have good content validity because they reflect the domain of interest (behavior disorders of children) and include questions that reflect representative samples of the types of behavior to be measured (e.g., hyperactivity: fidgets in seat; antisocial: fights with other children).

To ensure the representativeness of a measure and its subsequent content validity, items to be included in the measure must be chosen carefully. According to Hudson (1982), developing the content of an item is the single most important step in developing a measure or selecting one for use. Items should represent the specific characteristics one wishes to measure. Hudson has proposed two rules for determining content validity of a measure: "A clear and unambiguous definition of the variable or construct to be measured should be available," and "Each item should represent some aspect of the variable or construct being measured" (p. 142). Hudson suggests that social workers examine the items of the measure and use the best possible wisdom, training, experience, insight, and intuition in determining whether a measure has content validity.

Criterion Validity

Criterion validity relates to the scores on the measure in relationship to some type of criterion. Procedures for criterion validity help establish a measure's accuracy in identifying client characteristics or predicting client performance on specific activities. The results are checked against an empirical criterion and must be measurable, free from bias, and relevant to the purposes of the measure. Research is done to establish the correlations (relationships) between scores on the measure and the outcomes of these independent, empirical criteria. If appropriate relationships are found, then social work practitioners can be confident that the measure is a useful tool for categorizing or predicting behavior.

Confidence is based on the measure's ability to produce the same results as the independent, objective criterion. For example, if a team of mental health professionals evaluates the clients, and a psychiatric assessment measure constantly assigns the same diagnosis for clients, the measure is said to have good criterion validity. The criterion that is used to validate the measure may be obtained at approximately the same time as the measure is given or at some future point. Authors often differentiate between concurrent and predictive criterion validity by these time relations (Kaplan & Succuzzo, 2009; Rubin & Babbie, 2013).

Concurrent validity is based on a current criterion or on a criterion existing at the same time the measure is given; it is useful for measures involved in diagnosis or assigning existing status. The example given previously concerning a measure's ability to formulate a consistent psychiatric diagnosis in relationship to an independent criterion (diagnosis by mental health team) illustrates concurrent validity of a measure. There are two primary types of concurrent criterion validity: known-instruments validity and known-groups validity.

Known-instruments validity is established to the extent that one's new measure correlates highly with a preexisting instrument that measures the same construct of interest. For example, a newly developed scale to measure clinical depression could be compared with an existing scale that measured depression. If the scores from the two scales correlated, then there exists known-instruments validity. To the extent that this new depression measure can distinguish between groups of people that one would expect to be clinically depressed from those that one would not expect to be depressed, known-groups validity is established; that is, a scale's ability to distinguish between groups of people who possess the construct being measured from those who do not demonstrates known-groups validity for that scale.

Predictive validity is based on a future, after-the-fact criterion and is necessary if a measure will be involved in specialized selection or classification. For instance, college entrance exams are assumed to have a certain degree of predictive validity. To establish predictive validity, the scores on the measures are compared with a person's later college grade point average or other performance criteria. High correlations between scores on the measure and subsequent behavior indicate that the measures have good predictive validity.

Construct Validity

Construct validity ensures that we are measuring the client behaviors under assessment. This type of validity is concerned with the degree of measurement of a theoretical construct or trait. A construct is a concept that has been invented for the purpose of inquiry. It is a variable that can be studied or measured and is believed to be important to the development of theories. Constructs derive from theories and are developed to explain and organize observed responses. Many measures are developed to assess various constructs. A measure that demonstrates construct validity is well developed and may be confidently used in practice situations as an indicator of the client characteristics under consideration.

Factorial Analysis

The purposes of factorial analysis are to examine the interrelationships of behavioral data such as scale items, to group items, and to make it possible to identify the underlying dimension or trait for a set of items. Simply stated, data can be simplified by reducing the number of items from many to the most relevant ones that best capture the construct of interest.

To illustrate, we will use the Adolescent Concerns Evaluation (ACE; Springer, 1998). The ACE is a forty-item instrument that measures the degree to which a youth is at risk of running away from home. It consists of four separate but interdependent domains: family, school, peer, and individual. The family domain includes twelve items, each of which clusters (correlates) more strongly with the family domain than with the other domains; that is, together they create a domain of items that captures how an adolescent perceives his or her family life. In contrast, suppose items that were intended to measure school functioning loaded more strongly on the peer domain; this would call into question the factorial structure of both the school and the peer domains. However, for the ACE, the family domain (twelve items), school domain (nine items), peer domain (seven items), and individual domain (twelve items) load on to (correlate with) the domain for which they were intended. Thus, there is evidence for the factorial validity of the ACE. In addition, because the items load onto the factors for which they were intended, there is also support for the ACE's content and construct validity.

A detailed description of factorial analysis and its uses in measurement construction are beyond the scope of this chapter. For a more detailed exposition on this topic, see additional resources (e.g., Abell et al., 2009; Kaplan & Succuzzo, 2009; Kurpius & Stafford, 2006).

Validity Standards

A rule that has been proposed to interpret validity coefficients is to consider coefficients in the range of 0.40 to 0.60 as acceptable (see Downie & Heath, 1974). However, Springer, Abell, and Nugent (2002) caution against using a strict criterion to interpret validity coefficients. Validity coefficients for one scale must be viewed in the context of similar validity coefficients for other measures that measure the same construct and are intended for similar uses (e.g., clinical decision making with clients, research studies).

INCREMENTAL VALIDITY

Incremental validity is a method of comparing standardized measures to determine whether data from one assessment instrument better predicts a criterion beyond what can be accomplished with other assessment efforts or instruments (Hunsley & Mash, 2003, 2007). The practical relevance of incremental validity for practice, in general, is to offer additional information (e.g., whether use of assessment procedure leads to better assessment and/or treatment outcomes) that helps practitioners decide among the large number of assessment instruments that are often available for the same purpose and population. According to Hunsley and Mash (2007), there are several questions related to incremental validity that play an essential role in guiding EBA and the development of EBA protocols. These questions ask whether it is worth it in terms of time and money to use a standardized measure, to obtain data on the same target using multiple methods, to collect parallel information from multiple informants, and to collect assessment data beyond information related to diagnostic status, as most evidence-based interventions are targeted at a diagnosis.

When research has sufficiently answered all these questions, the sum of this information should provide a protocol for the most effective and clinically useful assessment procedures with certain problems and populations. Efforts to establish incremental validity of assessment measures have increased substantially, as evidenced by the many articles published across varied standardized assessment efforts in recent years. As this literature continues to develop, and as the EBA movement grows and practitioners and researchers become more invested in identifying cost-effective assessment protocols or processes for working with disparate populations, it is likely that incremental validity will become the gold standard of validity.

NORMS, SCORING, AND INTERPRETATION OF MEASURES

Understanding normative measurement and its related scoring systems will help social work practitioners develop further competence in using measures. Norms provide information on the typical or average performance of a particular group of clients. They are needed because the raw scores of a measure do not reveal anything about what the client's score means. Norms are developed by administering the measure to a large, representative sample of clients with known characteristics. It is then possible to calculate the mean (average score) and standard deviation (deviation from the mean) for the sample. This allows the practitioner to compare the client with the norm group, and so aids in understanding what other similar individual client scores may mean.

To give further meaning to raw scores, they are statistically converted into derived, or standard, scores and compared with the normalization group (standardization sample). Standard scores are evenly distributed along the normal curve (see figure 3.1) and make it possible to determine the client's standing in relation to the norm group. It is therefore possible to determine whether the client is scoring in the average range. Standard scores make measurements possible across clients and even across measures (Warner, 2008). Some of the derived and standard scoring systems used in normative measurement include cutting points, Z-scores, T-scores, and percentile ranks (Kaplan & Succuzzo, 2009).

Figure 3.1   Standard Scores

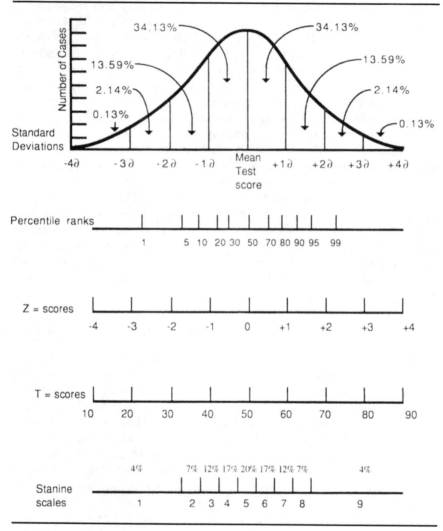

SOURCE: Adapted from Sattler (1988).

Cutting points indicate when a client has moved from the normal to the critical range of performance on a measure. For example, the *Diagnostic and Statistical Manual of Mental Disorders,* fifth edition (DSM-5; American Psychiatric Association [APA], 2013) has provided several crosscutting symptom measures online within the public domain to aid in clinical assessment. If a client scores mild or greater on the depression domain in the broad Level 1 assessment, the clinician is advised to utilize the Level 2 depression measure to further assess the degree of depression and monitor treatment. Most Level 2 measures provide clinical cutting points for disparate levels of severity. The cutting point for mild depression is 55 to 59.9, for moderate depression is 60 to 69.9, and for severe depression is 70 and higher. This indicates that a client with a score of 55 or higher on this measure may be experiencing clinically significant depression that warrants further assessment and treatment.

These cutoff scores are based on percentile ranks (and their related standardized scores) that indicate a client's position relative to the standardization sample. As shown in figure 3.1, the relative standing of a client in a given distribution is presented. A percentile rank is the point in the distribution at or below which a percentage of the normalization group falls in comparison to the client. Z-scores are derived scores that translate into standard scores. A Z-score is a standard score with a mean of 0 and a standard deviation of 1. Frequently, Z-scores are transformed into other standard score systems to eliminate the plus and minus signs. T-scores have a mean (average score) of 50 with a standard deviation of 10. According to the properties of the normal curve, two standard deviations above or below the mean is considered to deviate outside the normal range of functioning. Therefore, those clients scoring 70 or above or 30 or below deviate into the critical range. T-scores are popular standard scores used to interpret many psychological and clinical assessment measures.

T-scores are used to interpret the cutoff severity scores for many of the DSM-5 (APA, 2013) Level 2 measures. These online instruments offer guidance with regard to calculating the scale score, identifying the T-score in the provided table, and interpreting this score. The cutoffs and ranges of T-scores for the DSM-5 Level 2 depression scale, as mentioned above, include 55 to 59.9 for mild depression (.5 to .9 standard deviation above the mean depression score), 60 to 69.9 for moderate depression (1 to 1.9 standard deviations above the mean depression score) and 70 and over (2 or more standard deviations above the mean depression score) for severe depression. Several psychological and clinical measures are scored and interpreted using standard scoring systems based on properties of the normal curve. For example, the popular Wechsler Intelligence Scales (Wechsler Adult Intelligence Scale–Revised and Wechsler Intelligence Scale for Children—Revised) are interpreted with a standard scoring system with a mean of 100 and a standard deviation of 15. The Stanford-Binet Intelligence Test is interpreted similarly with a mean of 100 and a standard deviation of 16. Figure 3.1 further illustrates several standard scoring systems discussed in relationship to the properties of the normal curve.

Norms are essential to standardized measurement and the development of measurement tools and should be considered in relationship to the characteristics of each particular client. Sattler (2001) provides the following three guidelines for evaluating the norms of a measure:

1. Representativeness: Norms are useful only if they share the characteristics of the client. For example, if minorities of color are being assessed using a particular measurement instrument that included no minorities in its normative sample, the available norms are not appropriate for comparison with your client.

2. Size: The larger and more representative the norm group, the better. As a rule, at least one hundred of your clients should be included in a norm group before it is appropriate to use the norms for comparison.

3. Relevance: It is important to determine how relevant a particular norm group is to your client. Because many standardized measures have several different norm samples grouped by client characteristics (e.g., age), it becomes important to choose the norm group that best characterizes your client.

ASSESSMENT OF TREATMENT OUTCOME AND RAPID ASSESSMENT INSTRUMENTS

The fourth step of the EBP process requires that evidence-based practitioners monitor the effectiveness of the implemented practice decision, and this step of the process is consistent with much of what has been emphasized in the practice literature regarding the ongoing nature of assessment throughout the treatment process. Despite the fact that the evidence-based practitioner will select the intervention supported by the best-available evidence with the best fit for the client, it is impossible to be certain that the individual client will benefit from the intervention. There are several reasons why a certain intervention may not work for a client: The practitioner may not deliver the intervention with the same fidelity or level of skill as those in the original research study. The client may differ from those in the research study in significant ways. And even if the client is similar to those in the research study, the client may be more like participants in the experimental group that did not benefit from the intervention. For these reasons, it is essential that evidence-based practitioners engage in an ongoing assessment process of the client's functioning and response to treatment. This type of assessment is usually accomplished using a single-case design, in which the practitioner monitors one or more indicators of change over time, often daily or weekly, to determine whether there is improvement in targeted symptoms. Description of such assessment design is beyond the scope of this chapter; additional reading on feasible ways to implement such designs within the context of EBP is found in Rubin & Bellamy (2012).

Although monitoring treatment outcome does not always necessitate the use of standardized instruments (often the frequency of behaviors, thoughts, and so on, may be more appropriate), there are several rapid assessment instruments that may be beneficial to use in a weekly and/or pretest-posttest manner. Key considerations in selecting a standardized instrument to monitor treatment outcome, in addition to the issues of psychometric adequacy listed earlier, include the following:

- The length and the amount of time required to complete the instrument. The treatment monitoring process should not place an undue burden on the client, and the client should ideally consider it a useful and exciting opportunity to become more engaged in the treatment process.

- The sensitivity of the measure to change. It is essential that the standardized instrument be able to pick up small changes that may be clinically important over the duration of treatment. If there is little change on a measure over time and the sensitivity of the measure is unknown, then it is difficult to know whether the problem of concern is truly not changing or whether the lack of change is an artifact of an insensitive measure. The sensitivity to change is often reported as the average effect size (or magnitude of change) from pretest to posttest that has been achieved in efficacy or effectiveness studies (Burlingame et al., 2005). For this reason, the effect size also provides a baseline with which to benchmark expectations for client gains based on a particular rapid assessment instrument.

COMPUTER-ASSISTED ASSESSMENT TECHNOLOGIES

Research evidence from empirical studies demonstrates the lack of reliability and validity of practitioner-based assessments (Garb, 2000; Grove, Zald, Lebow, Snitz, & Nelson, 2000; Mash & Hunsley, 2005). Grove et al.'s (2000) meta-analysis of 162 studies on computers and prediction confirmed that computers perform well in making clinical judgments and setting tasks, and they usually outperform clinicians who perform such tasks. However, there continues to be a need to further develop well-validated algorithms for making diagnosis and treatment decisions (Percevic, Lambert, & Kordy, 2004; Slade, Lambert, Harmon, Smart, & Bailey, 2008; Wood, Garb, Lilienfeld, & Nezworski, 2002).

The reasons computers tend to perform just as well or better than clinicians are complex. First, practitioners lack the time and resources to check the reliability and validity of assessment information, to analyze the important variables, and to project their possible outcomes. Practitioners have to base their decisions on the information available at a given time, usually during the first or second contact with a client.

Second, lack of standardization in the assessment process leads to inconsistencies in the data gathered and the conclusions drawn. Absence of standardized criteria for making assessment decisions prohibits setting priorities for treatment and development of normative data that may facilitate effectiveness in long-range treatment planning. In addition, a lack of criteria for organizing the existing data and making judgments about the available information makes it difficult for practitioners to accurately discriminate the critical from the less critical variables in making treatment decisions. Practitioners must then rely on the best practice wisdom.

Third, lack of knowledge concerning community resources, availability of those resources, and the criteria for admission into those programs interferes with appropriate treatment decisions and long-term planning.

With the advent of computer technology, a variety of computer-assisted assessment procedures and measurement instruments have been developed. The cost-effectiveness and feasibility of tablets, handheld devices, and personal computers make this technology readily available and useful to practitioners (Ben-Zeev, Davis, Kaiser, Krzsos, & Drake, 2013; Goldstein et al., 2010; Rayner et al., 2014). Several psychological and clinical measures are available in software or on the Internet that may be purchased (or in some cases accessed free of charge; see PROMIS® in table 3.1) from its respective publishers and marketers. Some software examples are the Minnesota Multiphasic Personality Inventory (MMPI), a personality assessment measure that released its third and psychometrically improved version (restructured form), the MMPI-2-RF, in July 2008; the Millon Clinical Multiaxial Inventory (MCMI, MCMI-II, and the more recent MCMI-III; Millon, 1977, 1982, 1994); personality assessment measures; and the Child Behavior Checklist, a behavioral assessment measure for children (Achenbach & Edelbrock, 1983).

These measures are now frequently administered, scored, and interpreted on the computer by Internet or computer software. In some cases, the measures can be mailed in, scored, and received by mail. Computer scoring and interpretation technologies produce client profiles based on the norms of the measure, narrative statements about client characteristics, and alternatives for treatment. (For an example of a computer-generated profile from the MCMI-III, see figure 3.2.) More examples of the interpretive reports and profile information are available and can be obtained from the publisher's Web site.

The MCMI is a clinical personality assessment measure that parallels the DSM. The profile and narrative in the example are from the marital and family practice of one of the authors. The presenting problem of the

Table 3.1   A Comparison of Four Computerized Quality Assurance Systems and Their Measures

Dimensions	OQ®-45[1]	CORE-OM[2]	PROMIS[3]	Previdence Behavioral Risk Management[4]
Source of Information	Patient only	Patient only	Patient only	Clinician and Patient
Length	Variable	Variable	Variable	Variable
Breadth		Behavioral Health	Physical & Behavioral Health	Behavioral Risk
Computerized Assessment System Option	No		Yes, provided online free of charge: http://www.assessmentcenter.net/	
Flexible	Nonflexible	Flexible	Flexible	Flexible
Scoring	Immediate online scoring	Immediate online scoring	Immediate online scoring, scoring program provided: https://www.assessmentcenter.net/ac_scoringservice	
Progress Charts	Yes	Yes	Yes	Yes
Provides Free Access to Database Instruments in Paper Format	No; Fee is Based on Size of Organization	Yes, with purchase of software	Yes, can be downloaded free of charge with or without software use.	
Available on Internet for use on multiple devices	Yes	Yes	Yes	Yes
Reliable Change Index	Yes	Yes	Unknown	Unknown
Provides Alerts	Yes	Yes	No	Yes
Provides Links to Clinical References				Yes
Requires Purchase	Yes	Yes	No	Yes

1. http://www.oqmeasures.com/products/oq-analyst/
2. http://www.coreims.co.uk/About_Core_Software_Overview.html
3. PROMIS® was funded with cooperative agreements from the National Institutes of Health (www.nihpromis.org/) Common Fund Initiative (U54AR057951, U01AR052177, U54AR057943, U54AR057926, U01AR057948, U01AR052170, U01AR057954, U01AR052171, U01AR052181, U01AR057956, U01AR052158, U01AR057929, U01AR057936, U01AR052155, U01AR057971, U01AR057940, U01AR057967, U01AR052186).
4. http://www.previdence.com/aboutUs/

assessed female client used in the example in figure 3.2 was recent problems with illness or fatigue and low self-confidence. The client had also experienced a severe career setback and some interpersonal difficulties

Figure 3.2   Computer-Generated Profile

MILLON CLINICAL MULTIAXIAL INVENTORY - III

CONFIDENTIAL INFORMATION FOR PROFESSIONAL USE ONLY

INVALIDITY (SCALE V) = 0   INCONSISTENCY (SCALE W) = 4
PERSONALITY CODE: 8A 3 ** 2A 2B * 6A 8B 1 + 6B 5 " 7 4 '' // C ** - * //
SYNDROME CODE: A D ** T R * // CC ** - * //
DEMOGRAPHIC CODE: 12566/ON/F/44/W/D/-/--/--/------/--/------/

CATEGORY		SCORE RAW	SCORE BR	PROFILE OF BR SCORES	DIAGNOSTIC SCALES
MODIFYING INDICES	X	163	93		DISCLOSURE
	Y	4	20		DESIRABILITY
	Z	28	90		DEBASEMENT
CLINICAL PERSONALITY PATTERNS	1	13	62		SCHIZOID
	2A	20	83		AVOIDANT
	2B	20	83		DEPRESSIVE
	3	22	93		DEPENDENT
	4	7	12		HISTRIONIC
	5	12	40		NARCISSISTIC
	6A	14	66		ANTISOCIAL
	6B	14	57		SADISTIC
	7	8	16		COMPULSIVE
	8A	24	94		NEGATIVISTIC
	8B	13	65		MASOCHISTIC
SEVERE PERSONALITY PATHOLOGY	S	16	65		SCHIZOTYPAL
	C	23	93		BORDERLINE
	P	15	68		PARANOID
CLINICAL SYNDROMES	A	17	97		ANXIETY
	H	13	66		SOMATOFORM
	N	11	71		BIPOLAR: MANIC
	D	17	88		DYSTHYMIA
	B	8	68		ALCOHOL DEPENDENCE
	T	14	76		DRUG DEPENDENCE
	R	18	76		POST-TRAUMATIC STRESS
SEVERE CLINICAL SYNDROMES	SS	17	70		THOUGHT DISORDER
	CC	21	100		MAJOR DEPRESSION
	PP	7	63		DELUSIONAL DISORDER

Profile of BR scores columns: 0   60   75   85   115

on her job. She sought treatment at the insistence of her husband. As the example illustrates, computer-generated assessments can provide comprehensive information concerning client characteristics and recommendations for treatment. One caveat of these measurement computer-generated profiles, however, is that the reports tend to be canned, and little attention has been given over the past decade to examining the validity and reliability of the computer-generated scoring algorithms and accompanying narrative reports for popular measures like the MMPI-2 and MCMI-II personality assessment measures. Butcher, Perry, and Atlis (2000) reviewed the literature and found only four validity studies on the popular personality measures, and two of the studies showed negative findings. Fortunately, however, there are well developed computer algorithms for predicting violence, suicide, child abuse and neglect, and recidivism among juvenile offenders.

Another example of a measure for which computerized scoring is available is the Structured Clinical Interview for the DSM (SCID-I) (First, Spitzer, Gibbon, & Williams, 2012). The SCID is a semistructured interview that guides DSM assessment and diagnosis. The SCID-I and SCID-II were focused on the DSM-IV (APA, 2000), with the SCID-I used for Axis I Disorders and the SCID-II used to assess Axis II personality disorders. A new computer-assisted, clinician-administered version of the SCID for the DSM-5 (APA, 2013) is in development and should be available for both PC and Internet administration with immediate feedback and scoring in the very near future. The SCID instruments are available for purchase via a computer-assisted program that uses algorithms to structure the questions; the entire instrument is also available for purchase.

The trend in clinical assessment is to use such computer-assisted assessment technologies. These software programs are broader and more inclusive of intake and clinical assessment procedures than older assessments.

Expert Systems and Computer-Assisted Statistical Decision Models

Computer-assisted assessment models and database systems have been suggested as methods to address the foregoing issues and to provide support to practitioners as they make treatment decisions (Baird & Wagner, 2000; Berger, 2006; Butcher, Perry, & Hahn, 2004; Sarrazin, Hall, Richards, & Carswell, 2002). Some studies have demonstrated the superiority of the computer over practitioners in making assessment and treatment decisions. (For a fairly recent review, see Wood et al., 2002.) The sum of these studies indicated that computers usually outperform practitioners by about 10 percent. It has been demonstrated, for example, that the use of computer-based clinical assessment does not compromise the validity of responses among clients receiving substance abuse treatment, even when there are pending legal issues (Sarrazin et al., 2002).

For more than fifty years expert systems and statistical decision models have been discussed as important methods for improving assessment and treatment decisions; the literature has also suggested the advantages of integrating these approaches (Berger, 2006; Butcher et al., 2004; Epstein & Klinkenberg, 2001). Most recent reviews of the use of such technology suggest three main areas of application that are becoming more common: computer-assisted interviewing, computer-assisted technology, and Internet surveys (Epstein & Klinkenberg, 2001). With Internet surveys, an organization's computer administers data collection through a Web site (Pew Research Center, n.d.). These kinds of services are generally available on a pay-by-test basis as opposed to the purchasing of an entire software program. With the expansion of broadband computer networks and increased interest in the availability of psychological assessment instruments online, this may become a more common way to purchase and administer clinical statistical decision models (Berger, 2006; Butcher et al., 2004). However, before such services become available online, Butcher et al. suggest that the following issues need to be further addressed: equivalence between response sets of the Internet-administered tests and tests administered in a standard format; assurance that test norms are appropriate for an Internet application though the collection of Internet-administered samples; and proper test security to prevent use by nonqualified persons or professionals, to protect sensitive information, and to prevent copyright infringement.

One notable trend in computerized assessment systems is the development of adaptive testing (Gibbons et al., 2008). An adaptive test is developed to score each item for an individual as they answer so that subsequent items can best discriminate alternative traits or ability levels and result in a precise diagnosis with fewer questions and less time than a typical standardized instrument. One example of this technology is the computerized version of the Pediatric Symptom Checklist, a parental-report psychosocial problem screen (Gardner, Kelleherk, & Pajer, 2002). When administered in a primary care setting, where efficiency is essential, five or fewer questions were asked for 49 percent of the sample (meaning less screening time), and there were high levels of agreement between this shorter computerized version and the full checklist.

Recent work in the area of quality assurance and in child welfare settings demonstrates that statistical decision models may be combined with standardized measures to greatly improve treatment (Baird & Wagner, 2000; Wood et al., 2002).

Computerized Quality Assurance Measures

Quality assurance measures are computerized and offer ongoing reports to the practitioner about the clinical outcomes of their clients. A special journal issue edited by Lambert (2001) discussed various quality assurance measures and reviewed the strengths and weaknesses of many of the well-known measurement systems (see Barkham et al., 2001; Beutler, 2001; Kordy, Hannover, & Richard, 2001). Since this time, these and other more-recent computerized management systems (Chorpita & Bernstein, 2008; Percevic et al., 2004; Slade et al., 2008) have been developed and used in the United States and Europe to study the effectiveness of psychotherapy and as alternatives to group-oriented, outcome studies on psychotherapy effectiveness (e.g., efficacy and effectiveness studies). Quality assurance systems use individual client data to provide feedback to clinicians (and sometimes clients) on the therapy outcomes. They combine many of the methods previously discussed in this chapter, such as computer algorithms, used with standardized measures and actuarial and statistical decision methods to evaluate the outcomes of individual clients. Sophisticated statistical procedures are used to make decisions about client data, such as probit analysis, survival analysis, and hierarchical linear modeling. These methods help researchers determine the progress and lack of progress of clients in treatment programs, and alert them to the potential risk of client deterioration to prevent harm or drop out (Lambert, Hansen, & Finch, 2001; Slade et al., 2008).

Similar to single-case designs, these procedures focus on individual clients, and clinicians can use them in practice to evaluate the effectiveness of their practices. With more-recent technology, these systems function as dashboards and roadmaps that help clinicians manage their client load, identify further assessment or intervention approaches based on assessment, and prioritize clients that present with higher risks (Chorpita, Bernstein, & Daleiden, 2008). Many of these systems will graph improvement over time within the user interface. For example, figure 3.3 presents the interface of a computerized Behavioral Health Risk and Management System that is being used in the U.S. Army to ensure quality behavioral health treatment and risk management (P. F. Kathleen, personal communication, 2014; U.S. Army Medical Command, Behavioral Health Service Line, 2012). This system, developed by the Previdence Corporation, provides detailed feedback information for practitioners, including graphs of their progress over time. This system, like the other systems listed in table 3.1, assesses clients over time using multiple standardized instruments. These client- or patient-focused measurement systems answer questions that are of interest to practitioners, such as, "Is my client getting better? Is it time to stop treatment? Should I refer this client to someone else?" (Lambert et al., 2001).

Quality assurance systems improve practice by using norms and standardized measures to define clinically significant change and the need for further treatment, and they can feed this information back to clinicians. (For more information on the computerized quality assurance measures and a review of the Outcome Questionnaire, 45.2, see chapter 6).

Figure 3.3   U.S. Army Behavioral Health Risk Management System

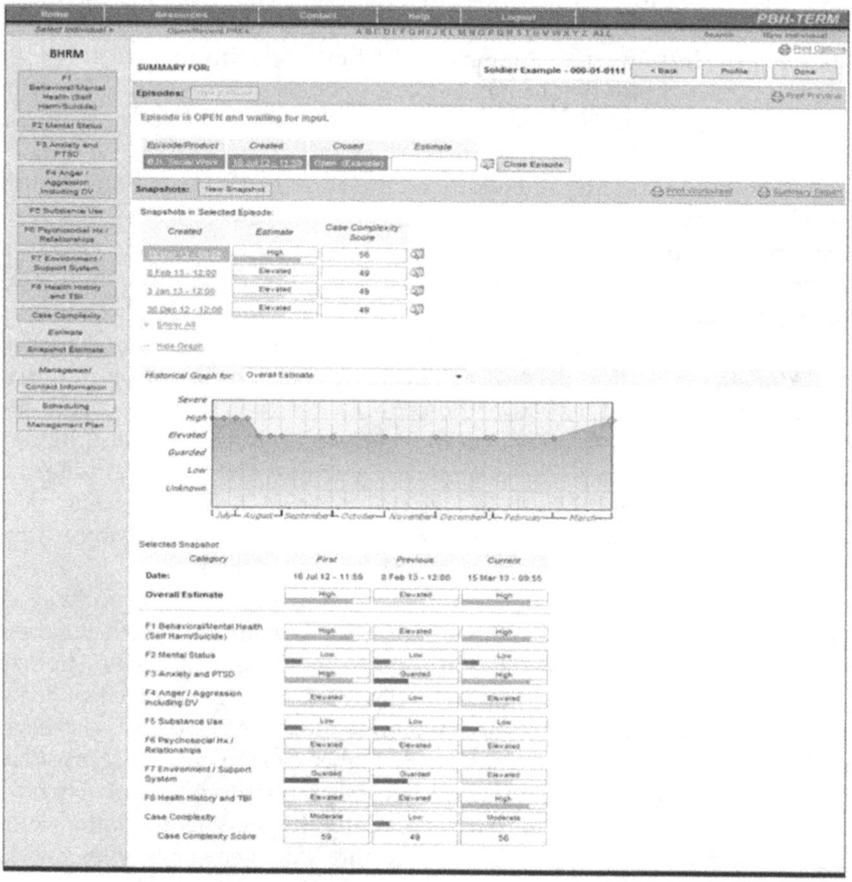

SOURCE: Reprinted with the permission of the U.S. Army Medical Command (system manager) and the Previdence Corporation (system developer).

LIMITATIONS IN STANDARDIZED ASSESSMENT MEASURES

Standardized assessment measures have many strengths: they are quick and efficient to use, they are easy to score and interpret, and they provide sources of data other than those that can be gained in a client interview in that they measure or screen for specific client problems or characteristics. Yet these measures do have some practical weaknesses other than possible limitations in their psychometric properties (e.g., validity, reliability, normalization). Five such limitations follow.

First, standardized assessment measures are subject to demand characteristics or social desirability. Clients may answer the questions on the measure to cast themselves in a favorable or unfavorable light. Clients may seek to please the social worker or give incorrect information on purpose. Some measures include lie scales or faking good scales to try to correct for this limitation. A lie scale is a set of items that tests for false responses on the measure. The Personal Experience Screen Questionnaire, which assesses substance abuse in adolescents, has such a subscale, for example (Winters, 1988).

Second, measures present a narrow band of information; they cannot assess the whole client picture. Some have criticized standardized assessment methods for being unable to assess dynamic interactions or the systems complexities of the real world of clients (Tzuriel, 2001). These critics assert that the measures have limited usefulness because they treat characteristics of clients as if they were static instead of forever changing in response to environmental contingencies. To these practitioners, the psychometric properties of the measures limit their usefulness. Many social workers who take this position object to trying to quantify client behavior. They believe that broader, qualitative methods are more useful for understanding the complexities of client behavior (qualitative assessment methods are covered in chapter 4). The argument that standardized measures cannot capture the complexities and dynamic, fluctuating interactions of client and environment appears to be true; such characteristics are beyond these measures' scope and current level of development.

Third, standardized measures have been criticized for focusing on client problems instead of strengths. In this regard, standardized methods are believed to pathologize clients without pointing to their unique motivation and capacities. Some assessment measures, however, have begun to include scales on coping abilities or problem solving. For example, the MMPI, the popular personality assessment measure, has an ego strengths subscale, and some family measures look at family strengths as well as problems. The Behavioral and Emotional Rating Scale, second edition (BERS-2; Epstein, 2004) is a notable exception. The BERS-2 is a strength-based battery of three instruments that measures functioning in youth across five different areas: interpersonal strength, family involvement, intrapersonal strength, school functioning, and affective strength. A key feature that distinguishes the BERS-2 from many other standardized tools is that it is truly based on a strengths perspective; the wording of the items reflects this perspective.

Fourth, standardized assessment measures have been criticized for their inability to directly link client problems to their interventions; that is, the measures do not prescribe a useful treatment plan, which is the main purpose of assessment (chapter 10 illustrates how to make decisions about treatment plans, based on assessments). Developing a treatment plan involves practitioners using their own cognitive abilities to map out a set of tasks to undertake with the client. Because standardized assessment measures have been combined with computerized assessment technologies, however, these technologies have begun to produce narrative client reports that make recommendations for treatment. Even so, they are still unable to present a complete treatment plan that is relevant to the client's unique experiences and environmental contingencies. The capabilities of standardized measures to help clinicians produce meaningful treatment plans is increasing with the use of the quality assurance measures and patient-focused measurement systems, as discussed earlier.

Fifth, standardized measures are subject to false positives and false negatives like any other standardized assessment procedure. For example, false positives and negatives are often found in tests used in medical practice. It may be necessary to give the test again to verify the results. Errors in the administration of the test, errors in the scoring and interpretation of the test, and measurement error inherent in the psychometric properties of the test can cause a false positive or negative. Researchers have focused on reducing and accounting for measurement error in a standardized assessment measure. In the next section, we discuss in detail measurement error and its implications for interpreting and reporting results on standardized assessment measures.

ETHICAL USE OF STANDARDIZED MEASURES: ATTENDING TO CULTURE AND DIVERSITY

The assessment of and sensitivity to diversity issues in the assessment process is of central importance to EBA and EBP. Diversity issues encompass age, gender, race, ethnicity, culture, disability, sexual orientation, language, socioeconomic status, and any other unique characteristic that may bear on accurate assessment, appropriate choice of intervention, and sensitivity to differences during the treatment process. Of particular importance is attention to ethnic and cultural differences, as recent research has demonstrated that there is often both ethnic and cultural variability in symptom expression and the psychometric appropriateness of commonly used self-report measures (Joneis, Turkheimer, & Oltmanns, 2000). Social workers have a long tradition of working with ethnically and culturally diverse client populations. Consistent with social work values and ethics, social workers should lead the way in ensuring that clinical assessments are not used to mislabel the attributes of ethnic minority clients. Standardized measurement instruments may be biased against certain ethnic and cultural groups. Rubin & Bellamy (2012) provide some guidelines on what to look for in determining whether a measurement instrument is culturally biased (if it was not originally normed with that specific population or culture). In essence, the researcher must make a case for measurement equivalence or a case that the standardized measure measures the same thing in terms of value and meaning with another culture as it did with the original culture or group with which it was normed. This is accomplished by demonstrating the following (Rubin & Bellamy, 2012):

- Linguistic equivalence: This is important when a client speaks a different language from the one with which the original was constructed. It is essential that the questions are asked using the same or very similar wording so that there is no variation in what is being asked. To have confidence that the instruments are linguistically equivalent, the researcher should have worked with two bilingual persons, one of whom translated the instrument from the primary language to the new language and another who translated it back from the new language back to the primary language. If the back-translated version is similar to the original version, there is good evidence of linguistic equivalence.

- Conceptual equivalence: This means that the questions, observed behaviors, or other components of the assessment mean the same thing across cultures. An example of an item that is likely not to have conceptual equivalence for many cultures is the use of the term "blue" from the Generalized Contentment Scale to mean "sad." Conceptually, the statement "I feel blue" is likely to elicit much different responses from those in cultures that do or do not use this colloquialism.

- Psychometric equivalence: This means that the scores are comparable across cultures; it is most important in examining clinical cutoff scores (e.g., what score constitutes certain diagnoses, distress) and in comparing disparate cultures in research. Of course, an instrument cannot have psychometric equivalence if it is not first linguistically and conceptually equivalent.

When all these criteria are met, a practitioner can be more confident that the standardized measure is culturally valid and useful. Moreover, when culturally valid measures are integrated with a thorough cultural formulation of factors related to diagnosis, care, and client preferences (e.g., cultural identity, cultural beliefs regarding presenting problem and help seeking), then the assessment and treatment process is more congruent with the EBA model and culturally sensitive practice (Vergare, Binder, Cook, & Galanter, 2006; for additional information on using standardized measures with American minorities, see chapter 9).

ASSESSING COMORBIDITY

The assessment of comorbidity is a reality of clinical practice. It is quite common for people in real clinical settings to meet the diagnostic criteria for more than one disorder or to have symptoms across disorders (Kazdin, 2005). Recent research has shown that as many as 45 percent of people diagnosed with an anxiety, mood, impulse control, or substance abuse disorder also meet criteria for one or two additional diagnoses (Kessler, Chiu, Demler, & Walters, 2005). The assessment of comorbidity has been recognized as increasingly important, as research has shown that people with comorbid presentations are typically more severely impaired, have chronic mental health histories, and have more physical health problems (Bender, Springer, & Kim, 2006). Also, there is budding evidence that comorbidity may be at least partially linked to core pathological processes whose symptoms cut across disparate disorders (Krueger & Markon, 2006; Widiger & Clark, 2000).

To assess comorbidity, conceptualize the assessment process as having multiple, interdependent stages, with the initial stage addressing more general considerations such as a preliminary evaluation of symptoms and life context (Hunsley & Mash, 2007). To accomplish this assessment, practitioners can use semistructured interviews (some are available for use with both adults and children), multidimensional screening tools, and brief symptom checklists for disorders that are more frequently comorbid with the target disorder, and evaluation of common parameters or domains that cut across the comorbid conditions. According to the DSM-5 (APA, 2013), this comorbidity, which is based on a categorical model of diagnosis, is one of the primary reasons the APA has provided dimensional assessment measures and guidelines to their systematic use (in stages) within the public domain on its Web site (APA, 2015).

CLINICAL UTILITY, COMPETENCY, AND APPROPRIATE USE

Earlier discussion in this chapter made clear that practitioners should choose standardized measures on the basis of their overall quality and purposes. In clinical practice, measures with excellent validity and reliability, sensitivity (when looking to assess over time), and appropriate norms should be selected. Beyond such technical considerations, the practitioner must also consider the clinical utility of the measure. Clinical utility refers to the practical advantages of using a measure to assess clients, to plan interventions, and to obtain accurate feedback (Corcoran & Fischer, 2013). For example, does the measure tap a clinically relevant problem? Is it easy to administer and score? Does it make sense in the particular practice situation? A measure may have excellent technical properties (e.g., validity, reliability) but be too lengthy to administer in a crisis clinic where clients need rapid assessments and immediate assistance—in such a situation, the measure does not have clinical utility.

Clinical utility also has to do with the degree to which using a measure in practice actually "makes a difference with respect to the accuracy, outcome, or efficiency of clinical activities" (Hunsley & Mash, 2007, p. 45). In other words, does using a particular standardized measure or protocol result in better assessment and treatment outcomes for clients? Research has shown that some of the most valid standardized measures may lack clinical utility. For example, a fairly recent study by Lima et al. (2005) examined the clinical utility of the widely used MMPI-2 by randomly assigning patients who had been assessed with the MMPI-2 to a group of therapists who received feedback from the test results and a group of therapists who did not. The results of the study suggest that having the information from this measure did not add to the prediction of positive treatment outcome beyond what other measures in the setting would normally predict (a lack of incremental validity). For that reason, the authors concluded that the measure may not provide clinically useful information. In contrast, the Outcome Questionnaire, 45 (OQ®-45), which measures distress, interpersonal relations, and social functioning, has been shown to have excellent reliability, validity, and sensitivity (Vermeersch et al., 2004). In addition, the contribution of the OQ®-45 to outcome has been assessed in a meta-analysis of three large-scale studies in a similar manner as the MMPI-2 study mentioned previously, and the condition in which practitioners received the ongoing feedback from the OQ®-45 over time ended up with 38 percent fewer clients deteriorating and 67 percent more clients improving, in comparison with the control condition that did not receive such feedback (Lambert et al., 2003). Although this provides good support for the clinical utility of the OQ®-45, the measure remains clinically meaningful only if it taps into a clinically relevant problem for an individual client and is feasible to use.

For this reason, the practitioner should also weigh the clinical benefits of the measure in relationship to its cost. In many instances, measures may prove cost effective and provide rapid and objective assessments of client attributes. This is especially true with the availability of computerized assessment and measurement technology. For example, we discussed earlier that statistical decision models and other computerized database systems are cost effective. The clinical benefits and utility of including standardized measures, however, should be considered in relationship to the needs of the client. Measurement should exist to serve the needs of the client. Does the standardized measure help assess and serve the client better? This should be the primary question all social work practitioners ask before including a measure in their assessment.

Ethical considerations are relevant to the clinical utility of measures. For instance, social workers should use only measures that they are competent to administer. Social workers must be trained in the administration, scoring, and interpretation of the measures they use. This includes training in measurement theory and in evaluation of the quality of various measurement tools, as well as training in scoring and interpreting measures. This chapter has summarized several important issues related to measurement. However, social work practitioners may need additional training in the application of these concepts before they achieve competence in the administration of some measures. Unfortunately, some social workers receive only minimal training in tests and measurement, which precludes their use of many excellent assessment tools. Test publishers are unwilling to sell measurement instruments to unqualified users. Therefore, social workers who want to use such measures in practice may need to seek additional training. This training is indispensable to clinical practitioners who work in settings in which measures are often administered. There are also some measures that can only be administered by other professions, such as psychologists.

A second ethical consideration concerns the responsible and appropriate use of measures. Measures should not be used as single indicators of client characteristics; rather, the use of multiple methods of assessment is recommended (Springer et al., 2002; Vergare et al., 2006). It is appropriate for social work practitioners to use measures along with other sources of assessment information. However, it is not appropriate to use a measurement instrument as a substitute for a clinical interview and other behavioral observations of the client; the practitioner should administer the instrument in conjunction with other clinical assessment techniques. Measures can facilitate good assessments, but they are not an end in themselves. They should be used cautiously, responsibly, and appropriately in service of the client.

A third ethical consideration is confidentiality. Social workers should assure clients of confidentiality of measurement scores in the same way that they hold other client information confidential. When data are being stored via the Internet or computerized system, steps should also be taken to ensure that data are well protected. Social workers should be aware that scores on standardized measures may be used to negatively label clients (e.g., by other clinicians or school personnel). They may also be used politically or legally against clients who are involved with government agencies. In reporting measurement scores, practitioners should always consider other client information. In keeping with social work values, client strengths and resources should be focal to assessment reports.

In selecting standardized measures for use in practice, practitioners should consider the technical considerations of the measure. Equally important is the clinical utility of the measure and ethical considerations regarding its use.

FINDING THE BEST STANDARDIZED MEASURE

In previous chapters we talked about some general ways to locate EBA tools. In addition, a handful of Internet and published resources to support EBA are listed and described briefly here. Although many of the sources are well established, it is not uncommon for Web site addresses to change. If one of these sites has become outdated, try searching by the title of the site instead.

Some Web sites or sources provide access to general information to locate and or search for assessment instruments. For example, the American Psychological Association (n.d.b) FAQ/Finding Information about Psychological Tests Web page provides general guidance on how to locate and stay abreast of most current published and unpublished psychological tests and measures. The Buros Institute of Mental Measurements (www.unl.edu/buros) provides a searchable database of a wide collection of standardized assessment measures. Information is provided on where to obtain the measure, but there is a fee to access the review of each measure's psychometric and clinical utility (Spies, Carlson, & Geisinger, n.d.). University libraries and sometimes public libraries provide free access. The Buros site can be a useful first step to gain a sense of what measurement instruments are available for different assessment topics. The tests or measures in the social sciences pages (such as at the University of Texas Libraries, http://www.lib.utexas.edu/) provides basic information on various measures but does not provide the actual instruments because of U.S. copyright laws. The local library or its interlibrary loan department may be useful in assisting in the location of hardcopies of potentially useful instruments from this site.

The database at the Alcohol and Drug Abuse Institute–University of Washington (n.d.) is designed to help clinicians and researchers find instruments used for screening and assessment of substance use and substance use disorders. Some instruments are in the public domain and can be freely downloaded from the Web; others can be obtained from only the copyright holder. The site provides a searchable engine; a brief description of each scale and its intended use; a general description of its psychometric properties and supporting reference articles, cost, who it is normed on, and length of time required to administer the scale; and who to contact to obtain copies. The American Psychological Association (n.d.a) provides a list of Evidence-based Assessment Resources for the Society of Pediatric Psychology along with the degree of research support each assessment resource has. In addition, the APA has provided measures in the public domain that have been developed to assess and monitor mental health outcomes (APA, 2015). Many of these DSM-5 (APA, 2013) measures were adopted from the PROMIS test bank, which offers hard copies of their measures in health and behavioral health domains, as well as free computer software that utilizes adaptive testing (PROMIS®, n.d.). In addition, the U.S. Department of Veteran Affairs National Center for PTSD (n.d.) provides information on many assessment instruments used to measure trauma exposure and posttraumatic stress disorder, including the updated DSM-5 (APA, 2013) validated measures for PTSD that are available on request. Finally, the U.S. Department of Health and Human Services National Institute on Aging (n.d.) has a Web page devoted to identifying cognitive impairment in older adults.

There are a variety of rapid assessment instruments or brief standardized assessment tools that can be used for assessment or monitoring practice outcomes on the Walmyr Publishing Scales Web site (www.walmyr.com/). This site provides information regarding the psychometric background of the available tests and links for viewing several items within the scales.

With regard to books, Corcoran and Fischer (2013) provide detailed information on more than four hundred rapid assessment instruments in *Measures for Clinical Practice: A Sourcebook*. Likewise, Maltby, Lewis, and Hill (2000) provide various psychological measures in *Commissioned Reviews of 250 Psychological Tests*.

CASE STUDY ALICE: MOVING FROM ASSESSMENT TO INTERVENTION

Alice is a Caucasian female, seventy-five years old, who was recently referred to your outpatient mental health office from a hospital social worker. Alice was recently discharged after spending several weeks in the hospital following a minor stroke. When she was initially admitted, she presented with hallucinations and was very agitated. Over the course of her stay and as she recovered, she no longer experienced the hallucinations or agitation, but disclosed to the social worker that she had been very depressed within the past year after losing her husband. Fortunately, Alice was able to get to the hospital quickly and did not experience major post-stroke symptoms, but she is dealing with some minor memory loss that the hospital social worker believes may be exacerbated by her depression. You plan to coordinate your treatment plan with the hospital's memory clinic, where Alice was also referred for ongoing assessment and treatment for memory loss that utilizes computer-based retraining techniques and supports to manage daily activities.

You have received and reviewed (with the permission of Alice and her primary caregiver, her daughter) the medical files, social worker's psychosocial evaluation, and the psychologist's neurological test results. You note that the psychologist's report indicates that Alice continues to read at above a high-school level, and that she is mobile and continues to be able to drive.

In preparation for your first assessment session with Alice, you plan to utilize the DSM-5 (APA, 2013) Level 1 Crosscutting Symptom Measure for Adults to assist in your gathering of multiple potential domains that may overlap with Alice's depressive symptoms. This measure has been tested in various DSM field trials conducted by the APA (e.g., Narrow et al., 2013), and is available online (APA, 2015). You also note the importance of examining the social support system for older adults, especially following a stroke, so you explore various social support instruments and select the Multidimensional Scale of Perceived Social Support (MSPSS) given its excellent internal validity (.91 with subscales ranging from .90 to .95), and good factorial and concurrent validity given its correlation with depression (Zimet, Dahlem, Zimet, & Farley, 1988). The MSPSS is also of interest given its brevity, use in diverse samples, and ability to measure social support in three areas (subscales): family, friends, and significant other. A copy of this scale can be found in figure 3.4. As

Figure 3.4   The Multidimensional Scale of Perceived Social Support

---

MULTIDIMENSIONAL SCALE OF PERCIEVED SOCIAL SUPPORT ASSESSMENT

Source: The items come from the 12-item Multidimensional Scale of Perceived Social Support. Used with permission

Reference: Zimet, G.D., Powell, S.S., Farley, G.K., Werkman, S. & Berkoff, K.A. (1990). Psychometric characteristics of the Multidimensional Scale of Perceived Social Support. *Journal of Personality Assessment*, 55, 610-17.

Zimet, G.D., Dahlem, N.W., Zimet, S.G. & Farley, G.K. (1988). The Multidimensional Scale of Perceived Social Support. *Journal of Personality Assessment*, 52, 30-41.

Scale Description: A 12-item scale of perceived social support from family and friends. Does not refer to deployment.

Scoring and Algorithm

Note: For each assessment, there is an algorithm leading to one of three acuity ranges. The logic for the user receiving specific feedback is included in the algorithms below.

Scoring, Algorithm and Feedback notes

Each item is scored 1-7 as indicated below. Total is sum of all 12 items, possible range for total is 7-84.

All items are scored:

Very Strongly Disagree = 1
Strongly Disagree = 2
Mildly Disagree = 3
Neutral = 4
Mildly Agree = 5
Strongly Agree = 6
Very Strongly Agree = 7

Algorithm

Total = 69-84   High Acuity
Total = 49-68   Moderate Acuity
Total = 12-48   Low Acuity

Figure 3.4   *Continued*

SOCIAL SUPPORT ASSESSMENT

Instructions: We are interested in how you feel about the following statements. Read each statement carefully. Indicate how you feel about each statement.

Very Strongly Disagree 1	Strongly Disagree 2	Mildly Disagree 3	Neutral 4	Mildly Agree 5	Strongly Agree 6	Very Strongly Agree 7

1.	There is a special person who is around when I am in need.	1 2 3 4 5 6 7
2.	There is a special person with whom I can share my joys and sorrows.	1 2 3 4 5 6 7
3.	My family really tries to help me.	1 2 3 4 5 6 7
4.	I get the emotional help and support I need from my family.	1 2 3 4 5 6 7
5.	I have a special person who is a real source of comfort to me.	1 2 3 4 5 6 7
6.	My friends really try to help me.	1 2 3 4 5 6 7
7.	I can count on my friends when things go wrong.	1 2 3 4 5 6 7
8.	I can talk about my problems with my family.	1 2 3 4 5 6 7
9.	I have friends with whom I can share my joys and sorrows.	1 2 3 4 5 6 7
10.	There is a special person in my life who cares about my feelings.	1 2 3 4 5 6 7
11.	My family is willing to help me make decisions.	1 2 3 4 5 6 7
12.	I can talk about my problems with my friends.	1 2 3 4 5 6 7

*The reproduction of any copyrighted material is prohibited without the express permission of the copyright holder.

illustrated, there are twelve items followed by a seven-point Likert scale. The MSPSS is also easily scored by summing individual items for the total and subscale scores, with a range of 7 to 84. Higher scores indicate higher levels of social support. The first subscale—family—includes items 1, 2, 5, and 10; the second subscale—friends—includes items 1, 2 5, 6, 7, 9, and 12; and the third subscale—significant other—includes items 1, 2, 5, and 10.

When Alice arrives at your office, the receptionist asks her to complete the DSM-5 (APA, 2013) Self-Rated Level 1 Crosscutting Symptoms Measure, and Level 2 Depression Adult Scale, in addition to the MSPSS. You are able to quickly score these instruments prior to meeting with Alice. You observe that Alice rated her depressive symptoms, sleep problems, and memory as moderate or higher on the DSM-5 (APA, 2013) Level 1 measure. You also note that she has scored in the high end of the moderate range on the DSM-5 Level 2 Depression severity measure, as her T-score was 68. You examine the Level 1 instrument to assess whether

Alice has endorsed thoughts of hurting herself, and note that she marked a 0 (or none at all), which suggests low risk of suicide (although you plan to ask follow-up questions regarding potential suicide risk in your face-to-face interview). You also plan to ask follow-up questions regarding sleep from the Level 2 DSM-5 Sleep Disturbance measure to assess severity of recent symptoms, as well as her history of sleep issues and how they may relate to her age, depression symptoms, and recent stroke. Finally, you note that Alice rated most, if not all, of her social support items on the scale as a 3 or lower, indicating neutral or mild disagreement for all items. Realizing the importance of social support for Alice's recovery and general functioning, you plan to conduct a thorough assessment of Alice's social support system within and outside the family.

When you meet with Alice, you begin by introducing yourself and your role. You then let her know that you would like to learn more about her reasons for coming to see you, and ask her to tell you her story. After a more detailed psychosocial assessment, you identify symptoms of a major depressive disorder, with onset of symptoms after the death of her husband a year and a half ago. She also receives a historical (previously identified) diagnosis of mild neurocognitive disorder, due to vascular disease based on neuropsychological testing at the hospital. You wrap up your assessment with Alice and the two of you agree that interpersonal psychotherapy would be a good option for reducing her depressive symptoms given her current challenges with cognition. You also agree to work together to leverage and build Alice's social support system and monitor her depressive symptoms using the Level 2 DSM-5 (APA, 2013) Depression Severity measure on a weekly basis, and refer her for a psychiatric assessment for medication if her symptoms do not improve in the near future. You also plan to monitor her monthly progress on the MSPSS. As Alice leaves, she shares, "I feel better already to know I have your support and that we have a plan."

SUMMARY

This chapter helped social work practitioners become informed consumers in the selection, use, and interpretation of standardized measure evaluation, and interpretation of standardized measures, as well as applications of standardized assessment systems that use computer technologies. This chapter also defined and covered the process of EBA. EBA incorporates theory and research to identify assessment targets, methods, and measures that maximize the effectiveness of the overall assessment process. In addition, EBA focuses on the most effective assessment processes that best fit the client's situation, culture, values, and preferences. Four major factors to consider when engaging in EBA are (a) psychometric adequacy of standardized instruments or assessment protocols, (b) diversity issues and the fit of the procedure with the individual client, (c) issues of comorbidity, and (d) clinical utility of the standardized instruments or assessment protocols. Many valuable resources, several of which are Web-based, are available to support EBA. Finally, case studies showed how to move from assessment to intervention in the selection and use of appropriate standardized measures.

STUDY QUESTIONS

1. What are the key features that distinguish standardized measures from nonstandardized measures?

2. What are the various methods of establishing the reliability and validity of a measure? In what ways are reliability and validity interrelated?

3. Choose a problem area that is of interest to you (e.g., depression, stress) and develop ten items that you think capture your construct of interest. Apply both the rational-intuitive method and the empirical method to examine the content validity of your new items. What advantages and disadvantages did you find for each approach?

4. What are the inherent advantages and challenges associated with practitioners using computer-assisted assessment technologies and standardized assessment measures?

5. Develop a case vignette in which a statistical decision model would potentially aid clinical decision making with a client system. Now develop a case vignette in which a statistical decision model would potentially hinder or complicate clinical decision making. Explore the advantages and disadvantages associated with practitioners using statistical decision models.

6. Your agency administrator has asked you to select a measure to monitor client progress. What criteria would you use to select a measure to aid clinical decision making in practice with clients? Some possible criteria include reliability and validity properties, norms, clinical utility, cost-effectiveness, and ethical considerations. Are any of these criteria more important to you than others? If so, which ones, and why are they more important?

7. Why is incremental validity considered the highest form of validity?

8. Why does every measurement instrument have some measurement error? Come up with at least one example of systematic error and one example of random error that might occur in administering a measurement instrument in clinical practice.

9. Develop a case vignette in which you would use an assessment measure. Locate at least one measure for the vignette and evaluate it for its clinical utility, competency, and appropriateness to the situation.

REFERENCES

Abell, N., Springer, D. W., & Kamata, A. (2009). *Developing and validating rapid assessment instruments.* New York: Oxford University Press.

Achenbach, T. M. (2005). Advancing the assessment of children and adolescents: Commentary on evidence-based assessment of child and adolescent disorders. *Journal of Clinical Child and Adolescent Psychology, 34,* 541–547.

Achenbach, T. M., & Edelbrock, C. S. (1983). *Manual for the child behavior checklist and revised child behavior profile.* Burlington, VT: Thomas M. Achenbach.

Alcohol and Drug Abuse Institute–University of Washington. (n.d.). *Substance use screening and assessment instruments database.* Retrieved from http://lib.adai .washington.edu/instruments/

American Psychiatric Association (APA). (2000). *Diagnostic and statistical manual of mental disorders* (4th ed.; DSM-IV). Washington, DC: Author.

American Psychiatric Association (APA). (2013). *Diagnostic and statistical manual for mental disorders* (5th ed.; DSM-5). Washington, DC: Author.

American Psychiatric Association (APA). (2015). *Online assessment measures (DSM-5).* Retrieved from http://www.psychiatry.org/practice/dsm/dsm5/ online-assessment-measures

American Psychological Association. (n.d.a). *Evidence-based assessment resources for the Society of Pediatric Psychology.* Retrieved from http://www.apadivisions .org/division-54/evidence-based/assessment-resources.aspx

American Psychological Association. (n.d.b). *FAQ: Finding information about psychological tests.* Retrieved from www.apa.org/science/programs/testing/find-tests .aspx

Baird, C., & Wagner, D. (2000). The relative validity of actuarial- and consensus-based assessment systems. *Children and Youth Services Review, 22,* 839–871.

Barkham, M., Margison, F., Leach, C., Lucock, M., Mellor-Clark, J., Evans, C., . . . & McGrath, G. (2001). Computer assisted clinical assessment. *Child and Adolescent Mental Health, 11,* 64–75.

Beidas, R. S., Stewart, R. E., Walsh, L., Lucas, S., Downey, M. M., Jackson, K., . . . & Mandell, D. S. (2015). Free, brief and validated: standardized instruments for low-resource mental health settings. *Cognitive and Behavioral Practice, 22,* 5–19.

Ben-Zeev, D., Davis, K. E., Kaiser, S., Krzsos, I., & Drake, R. E. (2013). Mobile technologies among people with serious mental illness: Opportunities for future services. *Administration and Policy in Mental Health and Mental Health Services Research, 40*(4), 340–343.

Bender, K., Springer, D. W., & Kim, J. S. (2006). Treatment effectiveness with dually diagnosed adolescents: A systematic review. *Brief Treatment and Crisis Intervention, 6,* 177–205.

Berger, M. (2006). Computer assisted clinical assessment. *Child and Adolescent Mental Health, 11,* 64–75. doi: 10.1111/j.1475-3588.2006.00394.x

Beutler, L. (2001). Comparisons among quality assurance systems: From outcome assessment to clinical utility. *Journal of Consulting and Clinical Psychology, 69,* 197–204.

Bloom, M., Fischer, J., & Orme, J. (2008). *Evaluating practice: Guidelines for the accountable professional* (6th ed.). Boston: Allyn and Bacon.

Burlingame, G. M., Dunn, T. W., Chen, S., Lehman, A., Axman, R., Earnshaw, D., & Rees, F. (2005). Selection of outcome assessment instruments for inpatients with severe and persistent mental illness. *Psychiatric Services, 56,* 444–451.

Butcher, J. N., Perry, J. N., & Atlis, M. M. (2000). Validity and utility of computer-based test intervention. *Psychological Assessment, 12,* 6–8.

Butcher, J. N., Perry, J. N., & Hahn, J. (2004). Computers in clinical assessment: Historical developments, present status, and future challenges. *Journal of Clinical Psychology, 80,* 331–345.

Chorpita, B. F., Bernstein, A., & Daleiden, E. L. (2008). Driving with roadmaps and dashboards: Using information resources to structure the decision models in service organizations. *Administrative and Policy in Mental Health and Mental Health Services Research, 35,* 114–123.

Corcoran, K., & Fischer, J. (2013). *Measures for clinical practice: A sourcebook* (5th ed.; 2 Vols.). New York: Oxford University Press.

Cronbach, L. J. (1951). Coefficient alpha and the internal structure of tests. *Psychometrika, 16,* 297–334.

Downie, N. M., & Heath, R. W. (1974). *Basic statistical methods* (4th ed.). New York: Harper and Row.

Epstein, J., & Klinkenberg, W. D. (2001). From Eliza to Internet: A brief history of computerized assessment. *Computers in Human Behavior, 17,* 295–314.

Epstein, M. H. (2004). *Behavioral and Emotional Rating Scale-2: A strength-based approach to assessment* (2nd ed.). Austin, TX: PRO-ED.

First, M. B., Spitzer, R. L., Gibbon, M., & Williams, J. B. (2012). *Structured clinical interview for DSM-IV® Axis I Disorders (SCID-I), Clinician Version, Administration Booklet.* Arlington, VA: American Psychiatric Publication.

Garb, H. N. (2000). Computers will become increasingly important for psychological assessment: Not that there's anything wrong with that. *Psychological Assessment, 12,* 31–39.

Gardner, W., Kelleher, K. J., & Pajer, K. A. (2002). Multidimensional adaptive testing for mental health problems in primary care. *Medical Care, 40,* 812–823.

Garg, A. X., Adhikari, N. K. J., McDonald, H., Rosas-Arellano, M. P., Devereaux, P. J., Beyene, J., . . . & Hyanes, R. B. (2005). Effects of computerized clinical decision support systems on practitioner performance and patient outcomes: A systematic review. *Journal of the American Medical Association, 293,* 1223–1238.

Gibbons, R. D., Weiss, D. J., Kupfer, D. J., Frank, E., Fagiolini, A. Crochocinski, . . . & Immekus, J. C. (2008). Using computerized adaptive testing to reduce the burden of mental health assessment. *Psychiatric Services, 59,* 361–368.

Goldstein, L. A., Connolly Gibbons, M., Thompson, S. M., Scott, K., Heintz, L., Green, P., . . . & Crits-Cristoph, P. (2010). Outcome assessment via handheld computer in community mental health: Consumer satisfaction and reliability. *Journal of Behavioral Health Services & Research, 38,* 414–423.

Grove, W. M., Zald, D. H., Lebow, B. S., Snitz, B. E., & Nelson, C. (2000). Clinical versus mechanical prediction: A meta-analysis. *Psychological Assessment, 12,* 19–30.

Guttman, L. (1945). A basis for analyzing test-retest reliability. *Psychometrika, 10,* 255–282.

Hodges, K. (2000). *The child and adolescent functional assessment scale* (2nd rev.). Ypsilanti: Eastern Michigan University.

Hudson, W. W. (1982). *The clinical measurement package: A field manual.* Homewood, IL: Dorsey Press.

Hudson, W. W. (1999). *Measuring personal and social problems: Methods for scale development.* Unpublished manuscript. Tallahassee, FL.

Hunsley, J., & Mash, E. J. (2003). The incremental validity of psychological testing and assessment: Conceptual, methodological, and statistical issues. *Psychological Assessment, 15,* 446–455.

Hunsley, J., & Mash, E. J. (2005). Introduction to the special section on developing guidelines for the evidence-based assessment (EBA) of adult disorders. *Psychological Assessment, 17,* 251–255.

Hunsley, J., & Mash, E. J. (2007). Evidence-based assessment. *Annual Review of Clinical Psychology, 3,* 29–51.

Joneis, T., Turkheimer, E., & Oltmanns, T. F. (2000). Psychometric analysis of racial differences on the Maudsley Obsessional Compulsive Inventory. *Assessment, 7,* 247–258.

Jordan, C., Franklin, C., & Corcoran, K. (2005). Measuring instruments. In R. M. Grinnell Jr. (Ed.), *Social work research and evaluation: Quantitative and qualitative approaches* (7th ed., pp. 114–131). Itasca, IL: Peacock.

Kaplan, R. M., & Succuzzo, D. P. (2009). *Psychological testing: Principles, applications, and issues.* Belmont, CA: Wadsworth.

Kazdin, A. E. (2005). Evidence-based assessment for children and adolescents: Issues in measurement development and clinical applications. *Journal of Clinical Child and Adult Psychology, 34,* 548–558.

Kessler, R. C., Chiu, W. T., Demler, O., & Walters, E. E. (2005). Prevalence, severity, and comorbidity of 12-month DSM-IV disorders in the National Comorbidity Survey Replication. *Archives of General Psychiatry, 62,* 617–627.

Kordy, H., Hannover, W., & Richard, M. (2001). Computer assisted feedback driven active quality management for psychotherapy provision: The Stuttgart-Heidelberg Model. *Journal of Consulting and Clinical Psychology, 69,* 173–183.

Krueger, R. F., & Markon, K. E. (2006). Reinterpreting comorbidity: A model-based approach to understanding and classifying psychopathology. *Annual Review of Clinical Psychology, 2,* 111–133.

Kuder, G. F., & Richardson, M. W. (1937). The theory of the estimation of test reliability. *Psychometrika, 2,* 151–160.

Kurpius, S. E., & Stafford, M. E. (2006). *Testing and measurement: A user-friendly guide.* Thousand Oaks, CA: Sage.

Lambert, M. J. (2001). Psychotherapy outcome and quality improvement: Introduction to the special section on patient-focused research. *Journal of Consulting and Clinical Psychology, 69,* 147–149.

Lambert, M. J., Hansen, N. B., & Finch, A. E. (2001). Patient-focused research: Using patient outcome data to enhance treatment effects. *Journal of Consulting and Clinical Psychology, 69,* 159–172.

Lambert, M. J., Whipple, J. L., Hawkings, E. J., Vermeersch, D., Neilsen, S. L., & Smart, D. W. (2003). Is it time to track patient outcome on a routine basis? A meta-analysis. *Clinical Psychology: Science and Practice, 10,* 288–301.

Lima, E. N., Stanley, S., Kaboski, B., Reitzel, L. R., Richey, A., Castro, Y., . . . & Joiner, T. (2005). The incremental validity of the MMPI-2: When does therapist access not enhance treatment outcome? *Psychological Assessment, 17,* 462–468.

Maltby, J., Lewis, C. A., & Hill, A. (2000). *Commissioned reviews of 250 psychological tests* (2 Vols.). Wales, UK: Edwin Mellen Press.

Mash, E. J., & Hunsley, J. (2005). Evidence-based assessment of child and adolescent disorders: Issues and challenges. *Journal of Clinical and Adolescent Psychology, 34,* 362–379.

Millon, T. (1977). *Millon Clinical Multiaxial Inventory.* Minneapolis, MN: National Computer Systems.

Millon, T. (1982). *Millon Clinical Multiaxial Inventory.* Minneapolis, MN: National Computer Systems.

Millon, T. (1994). *Millon Index of Personality Styles (MIPS) manual.* San Antonio, TX: Psychological Corporation.

Millon, T., Davis, R., Millon, C., & Grossman, S. (1994). Millon Clinical Multiaxial Inventory-III manual (3rd ed.). Minneapolis, MN: Pearson Assessments.

Narrow, W., Clarke, D., & Kuramoto, S. (2013). DSM-5 field trials in the United States and Canada, Part III: Development and reliability testing of a cross-cutting symptom assessment for DSM-5. *American Journal of Psychiatry, 170*(1), 71–82.

Pew Research Center. (n.d.). *Internet surveys.* http://www.people-press.org/methodology/collecting-survey-data/internet-surveys/

PROMIS®. (n.d.). *Instrument overview.* Retrieved from http://www.nihpromis.org/measures/instrumentoverview?AspxAutoDetectCookieSupport=1

Quay, P. (1987). *The revised behavior problem checklist manual.* Miami, FL: University of Miami.

Rayner, L., Matcham, F., Hutton, J., Stringer, C., Dobson, J., Steer, S., & Hotopf, M. (2014). Embedding integrated mental health assessment and management in general hospital settings: Feasibility, acceptability and the prevalence of common mental disorder. *General Hospital Psychiatry, 36,* 318–324.

Rubin, A., & Babbie, E. (2013). *Research methods for social work* (8th ed.). Belmont, CA: Brooks/Cole.

Rubin, A., & Bellamy, J. (2012). *Practitioner's guide to using research for evidence-based practice.* Hoboken, NJ: John Wiley & Sons.

Sackett, D. L., Straus, S. E., Richardson, W. S., Rosenberg, W. M. C., & Haynes, R. B. (2000). *Evidence-based medicine: How to practice and teach EBM* (2nd ed.). New York: Churchill Livingstone.

Sarrazin, M. S. V., Hall, J. A., Richards, C., & Carswell, C. (2002). A comparison of computer-based versus pencil-and-paper assessment of drug use. *Research on Social Work Practice, 12,* 669–683.

Sattler, J. (1988). *Assessment of children* (3rd ed.). San Diego, CA: Sattler.

Sattler, J. M. (2001). *Assessment of children: Cognitive applications* (4th ed.). San Diego, CA: Author.

Slade, K., Lambert, M. J., Harmon, S. C., Smart, D. W., & Bailey, R. (2008). Improving psychotherapy outcome: The use of immediate electronic feedback and revised clinical support tools. *Clinical Psychology and Psychotherapy, 15,* 287–303.

Spies, R. A., Carlson, J. F., & Geisinger, K. F. (Eds.). (n.d.). *Tests reviewed in the Eighteenth Mental Measurements Yearbook.* Retrieved from http://buros.org/tests-reviewed-eighteenth-mental-measurements-yearbook

Springer, D. W. (1998). Validation of the Adolescent Concerns Evaluation (ACE): Detecting indicators of runaway behavior in adolescents. *Social Work Research, 22,* 241–250.

Springer, D. W., Abell, N., & Hudson, W. W. (2002). Creating and validating rapid assessment instruments for practice and research: Part 1. *Research on Social Work Practice, 6,* 752–768.

Springer, D. W., Abell, N., & Nugent, W. R. (2002). Creating and validating rapid assessment instruments for practice and research: Part 2. *Research on Social Work Practice, 6,* 752–768.

Straus, S. E., Richardson, W. S., Glasziou, P., & Haynes, R. B. (2005). *Evidence-based medicine: How to practice and teach EBM* (3rd ed.). Edinburgh, UK: Elsevier Churchill Livingstone.

Tzuriel, D. (2001). *Dynamic assessment of young children.* New York: Plenum.

University of Miami, Department of Psychology. (n.d.). *Self-report measures available.* Retrieved from www.psy.miami.edu/faculty/ccarver/CCscales.html

University of Texas Libraries. Retrieved from http://libraries.uta.edu/helen/Test&Meas/testmainframe.htm

U.S. Army Medical Command, Behavioral Health Service Line. (2012). *Psychological and Behavioral Health-Tools for Evaluation, Risk and Management (PBH-TERM), Behavioral Health Risk Management (BHRM): User guide,* vers. 2.2. Joint Base San Antonio, Fort Sam Houston, TX: Author.

U.S. Department of Health and Human Services National Institute on Aging. (n.d.). *Instruments to detect cognitive impairment in older adults.* Retrieved from https://www.nia.nih.gov/research/cognitive-instrument

U.S. Department of Veteran Affairs National Center for PTSD. (n.d.). *Assessment overview.* Retrieved from http://www.ptsd.va.gov/professional/assessment/overview/index.asp

Vergare, M. J., Binder, R. L., Cook, I. A., & Galanter, M. (2006). *American Psychiatric Association practice guidelines, psychiatric evaluation of adults* (2nd ed.). Retrieved from http://psychiatryonline.org/pb/assets/raw/sitewide/practice_guide lines/guidelines/psychevaladults.pdf

Vermeersch, D. A., Whipple, J. L., Lambert, M. J., Hawkins, E. J., Burchfield, C. M., & Okiishi, J. C. (2004). Outcome questionnaire: Is it sensitive to changes in counseling center clients? *Journal of Counseling Psychology, 51,* 38–49.

Warner, R. M. (2008). *Applied statistics: From bivariate to multivariate techniques.* Thousand Oaks, CA: Sage.

Widiger, T. A., & Clark, L. A. (2000). Toward DSM-V and the classification of psychopathology. *Psychological Bulletin, 126,* 946–963.

Winters, K. (1988). *Personal Experiences Screen Questionnaire (PESQ) manual.* Los Angeles: Western Psychological Services.

Wood, J. M., Garb, H. N., Lilienfeld, S. O., & Nezworski, T. M. (2002). Clinical assessment. *Annual Review of Psychology, 53,* 519–543.

Zimet, G. D., Dahlem, N. W., Zimet, S. G., & Farley, G. K. (1988). The multidimensional scale of perceived social support. *Journal of Personality Assessment, 52,* 30–41.

CHAPTER 4

Qualitative Assessment Methods

Michelle S. Ballan and Molly Freyer

INTRODUCTION

Qualitative assessment methods are grounded in the need to understand and describe meaningful events in a client's life through words, observations, and graphical depictions rather than numbers. The need for practitioners to emphasize qualitative observations in addition to quantitative measures for client assessments has been a much-debated topic in the field of clinical assessment over the past fifty years (Groth-Marnat, 2000). Furthermore, as with quantitative assessments, the clinician's choice of qualitative methods should be informed by evidence-based assessment (EBA), "the use of research and theory to inform the selection of targets, the methods and measures used in the assessment, and the assessment process itself" (Hunsley & Mash, 2007, p. 29). Evidence-based assessment (EBA) not only involves the use of the best scientific information to inform clinicians' decision making but also requires clinicians to incorporate the clients' preferences and values in applying that evidence (Drisko, 2014). As such, focused qualitative methods are appropriate tools for identifying and addressing client priorities and for ensuring, most often along with conventional quantitative methods, a client-centered EBA.

In this chapter we describe examples of qualitative assessment methods, including interviewing, process recording, case example, observational approaches, self-characterization methods, and portfolio assessments. In addition, we describe how both qualitative and quantitative assessment methods are complementary and can be used together to improve clinical assessments. Finally, we illustrate qualitative assessment methods and how they benefit intervention plans with a case study of an individual's journey from homelessness to housing.

DEFINITIONS AND DESCRIPTIONS

Qualitative assessment methods use words, pictures, diagrams, and narrative instead of numbers and quantitative approaches to understand clients. A clinician may describe the client verbally, use pictures or a diagram to demonstrate the client's life context, or use pictorial language, metaphors, or case-study methods to describe the client and his or her problems (Krysik & Finn, 2010; McLeod, 2011; Parker & Bradley, 2010; Saint Arnault & Shimabukuro, 2012). This rich, in-depth description, sometimes referred to as thick description, is used to provide enriching details about the client's experience to help clinicians gain a full understanding and appreciation for the complexity of a client's problem (Ponterotto, 2006). Instead of relying on quantitative methods such as a measurement instrument to gather information about the client's problems, the social worker using a qualitative approach to assessment becomes the primary data gatherer. For example, instead of labeling the client's marital arguments as severe because of a cutoff score on a quantitative measure or a record of the number of arguments a client has had in a week, the clinician would describe in detail one or more of the arguments using words, narrative, or pictures, and expound on the impact of the arguments on the couple's relationship. This is not to say that numbers cannot be used in a qualitative assessment to describe the client's experience. When numbers are used, however, they are viewed as another method of description, generally as anchors along a continuum that represents the client's experiences.

QUALITATIVE VERSUS QUANTITATIVE ASSESSMENT METHODS: DISTINCT BUT COMPLEMENTARY

In his fifty-year review of psychological assessment, Groth-Marnat (2000) notes the classic work of Hunt (1946), who emphasized that clinical practitioners "should pay more attention to qualitative behavior during the testing situation and rework tests to yield a maximum amount of rich qualitative responses" (Groth-Marnat, 2000, p. 350). So, how does one decide whether to choose a quantitative or a qualitative assessment strategy? We support a synthesis approach and believe that there are many ways to know and empirically report a client's attributes and experiences. Various assessment strategies can provide worthwhile and useful knowledge. Neither qualitative nor quantitative approaches should be privileged, as both have their place in any assessment based on methodological pluralism. It should be noted, however, that regardless of whether the clinician obtains information qualitatively or quantitatively, the clinical judgment in assessment is ultimately a human qualitative judgment that involves subjective appraisal of all the evidence (Friedman & MacDonald, 2006).

The best assessments are a matter of the pragmatics and techniques of the assessment (i.e., what the practitioner does to gather information about the client). The axiom followed throughout this text is this: "If an assessment method is valid and reliable and helps you obtain the type of information needed to help a particular client, then use it." From our perspective, practitioners can use all assessment methods, regardless of their distinct theoretical origins, conjointly to improve the data gathered for an assessment. Multiple methods usually enhance the reliability and validity of clinical information. In particular, qualitative methods add to the detail and thick description of a case assessment and may increase the clinician's understanding of the context and process in which problems occur. Qualitative methods can be used along with the quantitative methods described in chapters 2 and 3; when used together, they may improve our clinical assessments (Franklin, Cody, & Ballan, 2010).

Unique Contributions of Qualitative Assessment

Qualitative assessment methods offer unique contributions to the assessment process. The ability of qualitative assessment methods to uncover personal perspectives is grounded in the flexibility and emphasis on the context and process that clients present in the therapeutic relationship. Qualitative assessments range from behavioral observations to oral and written descriptions of a person's behavior or thoughts, biographical or autobiographical narratives, interviews, experiential exercises, and graphical depictions, all of which are well suited for developing a holistic understanding of the client. The unique contributions that qualitative assessment approaches bring to the assessment process and the helping relationship are discussed in the following sections.

Ability to Uncover and Corroborate Client Viewpoints

A major contribution of qualitative assessment is its ability to uncover social meanings of everyday behavior, the symbolic significance of an individual's behavior. In addition, qualitative assessments are often needed to corroborate and further elucidate the context of quantitative findings. For example, Kolakowsky-Hayner and Caplan (2011) note the utility of qualitative techniques in neuropsychological assessments of clients. The authors describe how clinical observation can assist clinicians in "qualifying the symptom," a process by which the nature and cause of a client's cognitive issues are determined, and supports required to minimize effects on functioning are identified (Kolakowsky-Hayner & Caplan, 2011, p. 2098). Behavioral observations, such as attention to how clients approach tests, formulate strategies, and work toward solutions, enhance quantitative test scores. The authors point out that qualitative findings may prove more meaningful to the client and possibly a caregiver than a quantitative test score; additionally, these observations may have greater bearing on the execution of activities of daily living and ultimately can help inform rehabilitation recommendations.

Adaptability to Assessing Diverse Populations

Standardized instruments have been criticized for their limitations with people of color and other nonmajority populations (Barrera & Jordan, 2011; Dana, 2000). Furthermore, attaining cultural sensitivity for quantitative EBAs necessitates achieving an instrument's measurement equivalence in other cultures (Rubin, 2008). In making assessments across diverse populations, qualitative assessment measures have the advantage of being easily adapted to different populations that vary from the mainstream in ethnic or cultural identity, presence of disabilities, and any life experiences that separate them from the populations on whom tests are usually normed. For example, some Native American tribes do not espouse the concept of depression as a reaction to grief and loss; thus, a standardized depression scale would not be appropriate with this population (Gilbert & Franklin, 2001). The open-ended, process-oriented style of qualitative assessment provides social workers with a window on clients' culturally based thinking and behaviors. Certain Eurocentric values, such as individualism and competition, which are central themes to many dominant theoretical perspectives, directly conflict with values of collectivism and cooperation held by many populations of color. Qualitative assessments allow the social worker to explore cultural scripts and cultural meanings that would not be apparent in standardized assessments. The knowledge gained helps place clients' experiences in a cultural context. This is especially important for identifying clients' strengths, even when their behavioral norms or beliefs do not match the values or norms of the majority culture.

Promotion of the Social Worker's Self-Awareness

The human-to-human interaction of a therapeutic relationship makes individualized assessment possible. The relationship further helps the social worker, as data gatherer, capture unequivocal insights. To understand the subjective human experience, both the social worker's and the client's, the social worker must develop a keen sense of self-awareness. Self-awareness refers to the "therapists' momentary recognition of and attention to their immediate thoughts, emotions, physiological responses and behaviors during a therapy session" (Williams & Fauth, 2005, p. 374). Qualitative assessment requires social workers to be continuously cognizant that their own biases and beliefs may influence their clinical judgment (Malson, 2010). By developing self-awareness, clinicians are able to discern the differences between their interpretations and those of the client. It is essential that clinicians not force their reality or values on a client, because this will lead to misunderstandings of the client's problem and will hamper the assessment process.

Importance of the Client–Social Worker Relationship

Qualitative assessment methods allow for a more holistic, intimate, and cooperative relationship between the client and the practitioner. These methods touch on personal topics that can invoke powerful emotions in both the client and practitioner, allowing the practitioner to interact empathetically in the counseling process (Gilgun, 2013). When conducting quantitative assessment, it may be easy to ignore the reality of the effect of the social worker's presence on the client, even though quantitative approaches suggest that it is important to consider the impact of setting events and the reactions of clients on the results of measures. When using a qualitative approach to assessment, social workers must more readily accept that their presence does affect the client-problem context and that they cannot avoid this. On entering into a relationship with a client, the social worker becomes a part of the problem; only by skillfully comprehending the client's problem definition and unique context can the social worker become part of the solution. To understand the inner workings of the client, the social worker must use assessment methods that unravel human thought and experience and allow the client to become the key informant and primary expert concerning his or her own problems. Qualitative methods therefore call on social workers to have exceptional relationship management skills.

Fit with Many Theoretical and Therapeutic Perspectives and Evidence-Based Standards

Qualitative assessment strategies are flexible to use with many theoretical perspectives (Duffy & Chenail, 2004). The diverse theoretical models that use qualitative methods range from family systems theories to ecological systems models, cognitive-constructivist therapies, and the strengths perspectives. (For a brief review of theoretical models, see chapter 1.) In addition, because qualitative methods emphasize process and preference the experiences of the client, they also fit well with cross-cultural perspectives, feminist theory, and Afrocentric theory. These theories emphasize the contextualized experiences of the client over traditional quantifiable ways of assessing a client. (For a further discussion of how qualitative methods aid the assessment of ethnically diverse clients, see chapter 9.) Therapeutic approaches such as personal construct therapies, cognitive-constructivist therapy, Adlerian therapy, and systemic family therapies (Neimeyer, 2010) also make use of qualitative assessment strategies.

Both qualitative and quantitative assessments play an important role in developing and establishing evidence-based practice (EBP), and qualitative research can inform EBP independent of other research methodologies. Gilgun and Sands (2012) highlight the role of qualitative methods in developmental intervention research, including evaluations of randomized controlled trials. Qualitative research provides critical information regarding how clients respond to aspects of interventions, and how practitioners implement interventions.

Qualitative methods can likewise contribute to the development and evaluation of clinical assessment tools; Gilgun (2004) argues that evaluations of clinical instruments are incomplete if they do not include a qualitative component. Williams (2008), for example, used the qualitative reports of key informants to develop the Self-Awareness and Management Strategies scales for therapists, which have informed numerous interventions. In neuropsychological practice, qualitative aspects of clinical assessment such as the client's affect, mood, "frustration tolerance, ability to attend to the task at hand, manifestations of impulsivity, capacity to switch mental set as needed, nature and pattern of errors, ability to self-monitor, and attempts at self-correction and self-deprecating statements" may be used to enhance the interpretation of numerical scores drawn from clinical testing (Kolakowsky-Hayner & Caplan, 2011, p. 2099).

QUALITATIVE ASSESSMENT METHODS

Interviewing: Ethnographic Interviewing

Interviewing is the most frequently used method for assessing clients, and the face-to-face interview has been the cornerstone of social work practice. Qualitative assessment relies heavily on a form of interviewing known as "ethnographic interviewing" (Berg, 2010). Ethnographic interviewing entails face-to-face speaking, observation, and an abiding respect for context, language, and meaning. This interview format also assumes a position of equality and collaboration between social worker and client, an approach clearly in accordance with the responsibility of practicing clinicians to modify their own behaviors and therapeutic styles to meet the needs of underserved populations (Swartz et al., 2007).

Ethnographic interviewing is highly personal, interpretive, reflective, and elaborative. The interviewer tries to minimize preconceived notions, diagnoses, and hunches about the client and starts out on a journey of understanding. To do so, social workers have to be reflective and in touch with their own feelings, biases, and thoughts about the client. Clients become like teachers telling the social worker about their personal reality. But as every student knows, learning is not totally dependent on the teacher; learners have to be open, flexible, and receptive as well. They also have to be willing to interpret the ideas communicated in the context of the teacher and the concepts being taught. For the social worker conducting ethnographic interviews, interpretations must occur within the client's own framework or worldview, not within that of the social worker.

Ethnographic interviews may be structured, semistructured, or open ended (O'Reilly, 2009); Semistructured or open ended interviews appear to be more suitable to the explorative nature of the ethnographic approach than structured interviews.

A structured interview has a previously formulated set of questions that the social worker asks the client; social workers do not deviate much from their list of questions. Structured interviews are critical to best practices in mental health assessments. For example, Pettit and Joiner (2006) note that, although there is no one extant EBA in the extensive and complex assessment of depression, the structured clinical interview approaches the ideal, particularly when incorporated as an overall assessment strategy.

Semistructured interviews have a previously formulated set of questions, but the social worker may veer from that list as information emerges. Widiger and Samuel (2005) recommend semistructured interviews in a two-stage process of EBA of personality disorders. The first stage involves the administration of a self-report inventory; if the practitioner identifies maladaptive personality traits, a semistructured interview should follow to determine the presence, nature, and severity of any possible personality disorders. The use of established semistructured interviews allows clinicians to give careful attention to the influence of age, gender biases, cultural and ethnic factors, and probable inaccuracies in client self-perception and presentation.

Open-ended interviews have no previously formulated questions; the social worker just begins the interview and sees where it goes. Open-ended ethnographic questions are used both to encourage clients to tell their story and to uncover how clients integrate their beliefs and experiences to create a sense of meaning and coherence (Swartz et al., 2007). In all three types of interviews, a guiding purpose usually directs the interview—for example, to build rapport or to assess whether abuse has occurred.

Within the structure of different ethnographic interviews, the clinician can use various types of questioning techniques to gather information from the client (Berg, 2010; Crabtree & Miller, 1999).

For example, descriptive questions are broadly open ended. Grand-tour descriptive questions attempt to elicit a rich story from the client (e.g., "Describe your experiences at the university after you became disabled," "Tell me about life on the reservation," "Describe your future"). Mini-tour descriptive questions elicit smaller units of experience (e.g., "How did your mother treat you after you began using a wheelchair? Your teachers? Your friends?" "Tell me about your final day of employment at the factory").

Structural questions are inclusive and expand the focus of experience (e.g., "Have you been married before?" "What does she do when she is feeling melancholy?").

Substituting frame questions take a term or phrase the client uses and substitute another question (e.g., social worker: "Tell me what your sister is like"; client: "She comes across like she is better than me and a know-it-all"; social worker: "What else does she come across like?").

Contrast questions are exclusive and expand experience (e.g., "You said that you and Yolanda had some good times together in the past. How has that changed now?" "You mentioned seeing a marital therapist in the past. How is your relationship different now?").

Rating questions ask clients to give differential meaning to their experience (e.g., "What is the best experience you have had since you have been divorced?" "What is the worst thing someone said since you lost your partner?").

Circular questions elicit information about transactions embedded in a system. They focus on the relationships among persons and among the beliefs and views held by individuals (e.g., "How do Mom and Dad solve arguments between them?" "What do you think Brother would say if Dad doesn't pay attention to Mom?").

These types of questions are not used exclusively with ethnographic interviewing; they can be used in other forms of interviewing as well. In chapter 7, for example, we cover how systemic family therapists use circular questions and give examples of such questions in that chapter's appendix.

Clinicians may use ethnographic interviewing to discover the personal meaning clients attribute to their problems, the therapy process, relationship patterns, or any other intrapersonal or interpersonal process. Ethnographic interviewing asks clients to explain in their own words the meanings that they ascribe to processes. Social workers listen intently and probe to understand in more depth what the client is saying. In addition, social workers adopt the language and the meanings of the client when communicating with the client. This aids in their mutual understanding of the world. Ethnographic interviewers know that there are multiple perspectives and that all clients communicate from their own unique social and cultural viewpoints. Ethnographic interviewing is therefore particularly useful for understanding different ethnicities, religions, cultures, and classes. In every interview situation, the ethnographic interviewer becomes like an anthropologist seeking to discover the culture and personal frames of reference of the client. Clients become the key informants and teachers about their social realities.

The *Diagnostic and Statistical Manual of Mental Disorders,* fifth edition (DSM-5) Cultural Formulation Interview (CFI) uses ethnographic interviewing to promote cross-cultural understanding to enhance mental health assessment (American Psychiatric Association [APA], 2013). While the DSM-IV (APA, 2000) provided a basic outline of suggestions for areas of cultural factors to consider in assessment, along with a glossary of "culture-bound syndromes" (p. 897), its lack of guidance in specific lines of questioning hindered its use in practice (Mezzich, Caracci, Fabrega, & Kirmayer, 2009). The CFI addresses this need by providing clinicians with a set of semistructured questions aimed at eliciting the individual client's perception of his or her presenting problem. These questions are informed by the ethnographic traditions of attention to context, language, and meaning, and the assumption of a position of equality and collaboration between social worker and client. The interview begins with an open-ended question. The interviewer is prompted to elicit further information if the client gives only a few details, or mentions only a diagnosis, and is guided to focus on the client's unique way of understanding the problem. (For the full CFI, please refer to the DSM-5 [APA, 2013].)

The interviewer should adopt the language of the client. An additional directive accompanying the opening question notes that interviewers should use the "term, expression, or brief description elicited in question 1 to identify the problem in subsequent questions (e.g., 'your conflict with your son')" (APA, 2013, p. 752). This descriptive question gives clients an opportunity to consider how they would frame their problem for members of their social network, guiding the client to use language one would use with a friend as opposed to a clinician. This line of questioning maintains respect for the client's conceptualization of the problem, and how it is experienced and managed within one's unique social and cultural environment. Mutual understanding of different cultures and religious beliefs forms out of the negotiation and social consensus building that transpire as we openly encounter one another and find ways to communicate. The CFI provides an ethnographically influenced example of how to assess clients, keeping these crucial points in mind.

Narrative Methods

A client may communicate a narrative in oral or written form. The social worker usually captures in written form the essence of the narrative as the client reports but also may communicate the narrative in an oral report, as at a case conference. Written narratives make it possible for social workers to record and reflect on the client's meanings and beliefs, as well as on their own responses to those private thoughts. Written narratives are also used to communicate to others the client's experiences in a manner that provides insight into human behavior and motivations. The following sections cover three narrative methods: process recording, case studies, and self-characterizations.

Process Recording

Process or narrative recording is an intricately detailed and specialized type of written case recording in which social workers document the process of an interview with a client, including his or her actual words and behaviors. In addition, the process recorder identifies his or her feelings or personal reactions to what the client says. The process recording does not necessarily reflect objective events but instead reflects constructions of the social worker and, indirectly, of the client (Gergen, 2003). A supervisor typically reviews the recording and makes other comments about the client–social worker interview (Ortiz Hendricks, Bertrand Finch, & Franks, 2013).

Process recordings help teach social workers interviewing and assessment skills. They also highlight many of the relational or process issues that might emerge in managing a case. Social workers may be able to observe from the process recording something they said wrong or how their attitudes or feelings toward the client caused them to misunderstand the client. Because process recordings are germane to clinical assessment, social workers may be able to observe emerging themes or patterns in the interview that they might have missed if they had used a shorter, less process-oriented recording of the interview.

Despite its usefulness, process recording is time-consuming and impractical for use in everyday practice. It is usually reserved for social work education. It may also be used in agency practice, such as in the context of educational supervision, when a clinician wants guidance with a difficult or unusual case. Conroy (2012) notes that process recordings ought to include the following basic components:

1. Reconstruct the interview.
2. Describe the words [the student/practitioner] spoke and the actions they took.
3. Reflect on the way in which they used themselves in the interview.
4. Assess their practice, and give some examples.
5. Name the specific skill they were using at the time. (Conroy, 2012, p. 88)

The process recording can be relevant to assessing a case, and the information from the recording may be used to formulate an immediate assessment plan. Most process recordings are set up in a column format that provides a place for the different aspects of the recording.

Black and Feld (2006) suggest a learning-oriented thematic approach for the process recording, which affords social work interns an opportunity to analytically reflect or introspect on encounters in their field education setting. They suggest including the following information in a process recording:

1. Statement of Learning Themes and Purpose of the Encounter: This section should be formulated prior to the actual client encounter and includes

    A. Learning theme(s) (student learning objectives targeted by the student and the field instructor for educational attention); and

    B. A succinct indication of the purpose of the encounter: Why is the client/client system being seen? What do you and the client hope to accomplish in this session?

2. Background Information: This section offers a brief indication of the nature of the problem, those present at the session, the setting of the encounter, and any other pertinent information not otherwise known to the field instructor that might orient him or her to the session.

3. Analysis of the Encounter: What happened in the session? Description, reaction, reflection, and analysis. Within the framework of "beginning, middle, and end" of the encounter, the student describes what transpired sequentially in the session, using an "expansion/contraction format. . . . [In contraction, the] practitioner summarizes or bullets the main topics covered in the encounter. . . . [For expansion, in] this core section of the recording, the student details sections of the encounter that relate to the established themes(s) selected for the session. Included is an account of what exactly occurred both verbally and nonverbally, approximating the client/worker dialogue to the extent possible. Interwoven throughout this presentation is an indication of the student's assessment of the emotional climate of the transaction in terms of associated feelings—the client's as well as the students'.

    The practitioner interjects analytical comments regarding the interaction related to what the student was trying to accomplish in a particular exchange including hindsight as well as evaluative comments. Incorporated are segments of the interview that the student can use to demonstrate application or evidence of the theme in operation. For example, this may be an instance of successful implementation of a particular skill or a situation in which the student retrospectively perceives that she or he missed the boat in relation to the targeted skill.

4. Evaluation

    A. Evaluation of learning theme(s) and the extent to which they were addressed

    B. Evaluation of client/client system purpose

5. Future Plans

    A. For self (learning themes for future attention)

    B. For client/client system

6. Supervisory Agenda (questions and issues to discuss with field instructor) (Black & Feld, 2006, pp. 146–147).

The learning-oriented thematic method provides structure but also encourages flexibility. The model further serves to promote student self-awareness and analytical thinking, as well as practice knowledge, values, and skills related to assessment.

Case Studies

Another narrative method of recording and assessment, case studies, assists social workers in assessing different aspects of the client's functioning and related variables that may affect client functioning. A case study is a detailed exploration of a single case study, with the objective of better understanding the characteristics, qualities, and issues presented by the case (Carey, 2012).

Case studies can be completed on individuals, families, groups, or organizations (O'Reilly, 2009; Yin, 2010). They make use of multiple sources of information, including interviews, social histories, life histories, and observations to investigate and communicate relevant clinical data concerning a certain aspect of the case (Yin, 2010). Usually the case study focuses on some descriptively relevant aspect of the case that the practitioner wishes to investigate. The practitioner organizes case information into a narrative summary, to explore or describe the client functioning along certain dimensions. For example, the case study might elucidate the impact of early developmental history on the client's current relationship functioning or discuss the impact of culture on the client's response to treatment.

McLeod (2011) suggests that case studies may address a number of research questions regarding practice effectiveness and outcomes, on both an individual and organization level. These include the following:

1. Outcome questions: "How effective has therapy been in this case? To what extent can changes that have been observed in the client be attributed to therapy?"

2. Theory building questions: "How can the process of therapy in this case be understood in theoretical terms? How can the data in this case be used to test and refine an existing theoretical model?

3. Pragmatic questions: "What strategies and methods did the therapist use in this case that contributed to the eventual outcome? How were therapeutic methods adapted and modified to address the needs of this specific client? What are the principles of good practice that can be derived from this case?

4. Experiential or narrative questions: "What was it like to be the client or therapist in this case? What is the story of what happened, from the client or therapist point of view?

5. Organizational questions: "What is it like to be a counsellor or client in a particular kind of therapy agency? How do organizational factors affect the process and outcomes of therapy? How is the organizational culture and climate of a counseling agency shaped by broader social influences?" (p. 229)

Historically, case studies were the preferred method for clinical investigation in several fields, including social work (Trepper, 1990). The case study method, however, fell into clinical disrepute with the increased focus on empiricism in clinical science. Scientific control of explanatory variables became of great concern, and any treatment outcomes that could not be verified through quantitative measurement methods and statistical models were considered invalid. These attitudes led many to shy away from the case study as a useful method of inquiry (Trepper, 1990). Recent years have witnessed a resurgence of interest in the case study among clinical researchers and practitioners. For example, proponents of single-case-study designs brought a new empiricism to the case study (in chapter 10, we discuss the use of single-case designs).

Throughout the years, the case study has remained a favorite methodology among clinical practitioners. Case studies are presented at conferences in narrative form and on video and are frequently reported in journals and books to illustrate different aspects of clients' functioning and their responses to treatments. To present case studies that are rich in detail and filled with thick description, practitioners must take copious notes of their interviews and observations of the client (Yin, 2010). As they must with all qualitative assessment methods, practitioners creating case studies must make sure they are reporting the empirical processes that emerge from the client's case. In addition, it has been argued that the case study can serve as a prime source of evidence in developing EBA methods (Stickley & Phillips, 2005). Case studies help bridge the gap between research and practice, bringing a "real-life context" to the evidence guiding social workers (Lee, Mishna, & Brennenstuhl, 2010, p. 683).

Following are five guidelines for keeping detailed notes for a case study:

1. Record key pieces of information while interviewing and observing the client. These may be in the form of key words or jottings. Use exact phrases and differentiate clinical impressions from empirical observations when necessary.

2. Limit the time the practitioner comes into contact with the client. For example, limit home visits to one or two hours so that stimulus overload does not occur and you can keep track of the information.

3. Make notes about the sequence of events and context in which they occur.

4. Write up detailed case notes that include a narrative account of the interview, observations, and clinical impressions immediately after or as soon after the client contact as possible.

5. Write your case notes before sharing details of the case or your clinical impressions with anyone, such as a colleague or supervisor.

Copious notes lead to case studies filled with thick description and clinically useful insights. Without detailed case notes, it is not possible to construct a meaningful case study. Once the case notes are written, the social worker must find a method for reflecting on them and interpreting them within the case study. The immersion and crystallization analysis method that is used in qualitative research is useful for examining the case notes to identify clinically relevant patterns and themes (Crabtree & Miller, 1992). Immersion and crystallization analysis comes from the heuristic paradigm in clinical research that emphasizes self-reflection in the research experience. Social workers using the immersion and crystallization analysis method take the following steps in analyzing the case notes. First, as interpreters and reflectors, social workers enter (read) the text (case notes) with the intent of empathetically immersing themselves, until an intuitive insight, interpretation, or crystallization of the text emerges. Second, social workers investigate and interpret the case notes through concerned reflection, intensive inner searching, and the yearning for insight. They rely on clinical intuition to gain insights into the clinical themes and patterns present in the case notes. Third, a cycle of empathic immersion with the case notes and crystallization is repeated until the social worker finds an interpretation. Finally, the results may be reported as a part of the case study. (Appendix 4A presents an example of a case study examining the influence of cultural factors on client engagement in treatment.) This case study was presented to illustrate the response of a Korean college student to an American therapeutic milieu (Seeley, 2004).

Self-Characterizations

Self-characterizations is a self-recording method developed within personal construct theory. The self-characterization assessment technique asks clients to write a description of themselves as if they were a principal character in a play. In writing their description, they are instructed to take the position of an intimate friend or a personal and empathetic confidant. The primary purpose of this description is to assess how clients cognitively construct the world in relation to the roles they believe they must maintain. The unique cognitive structures of clients and the clients' social roles can then be explored and changed in therapy.

Crittenden and Ashkar (2012) provide the following example of a self-characterization, written by a forty-two-year-old male client, "Terry."

> Terry is a real go-getter and has achieved a lot in his life. He has a fairly boring job as an accountant, but he has made a great success of it and made a lot of money. He does not really mind the work, but he can think of a lot of other things he would have wanted to do. He is not all that happy, but believes he does not have any right to complain. He has a great family but he wishes his wife would relax more and be into having fun, especially now that he can afford it. The kids are doing well, but his wife worries about them being spoiled. Terry feels like he is running out of time in some ways and wants to do as much as he can. He would like to be able to talk to his wife about all his interests but she gets irritated and bored. He often feels lonely and depressed. But, hey, he feels he has to keep going to maintain his lifestyle, and anyway he should not be expecting more: he really has it all! (Crittenden & Ashkar, 2012, p. 112).

Using this characterization as a basis for evaluation, the clinician works with the client to identify relevant constructs. These constructs, or personal descriptors, are noted, and the client is asked to verbally elaborate on their meaning. Using the example of Terry, the clinician identified the construct of go-getter and used additional questions to elicit reflection and personal meaning:

> THERAPIST: Can you tell me some more about your image of a go-getter? How would you describe someone like that?
>
> TERRY: Well, you know . . . someone who achieves their goals . . . who knows what he wants and gets it. . . .
>
> THERAPIST: And how would you describe someone who is not like that?
>
> TERRY: Ahh . . . someone who is more easy-going I guess. . . . Someone who doesn't push. . . . I suppose someone who is satisfied with less(Crittenden & Ashkar, 2012, p. 118).

The written description of the self is extremely flexible and may be adapted in various ways to meet the particular assessment or therapeutic needs of the social worker. Therefore, the characterization can, for example, address concepts as diverse as the experience of loss or bereavement (Neimeyer, Keesee, & Fortner, 2000), the various roles individuals play in their lives (i.e., partner, friend, parent), or a characterization of a family (Crittenden & Ashkar, 2012). It has been further noted that the flexibility of this technique minimizes the possibility of the clinician influencing the client in his or her construction of a personal character sketch (Hardison & Neimeyer, 2007).

Graphics Methods

Graphic assessment methods are qualitative assessment tools that make use of pictures, drawings, spatial representations, or images to assess the client. Graphic methods can be useful in contexts in which clients may find it difficult to express themselves verbally, as in working with children or in cross-cultural work with clients whose primary language differs from that of the social worker (Bagnoli, 2009). These graphic methods may likewise help to uncover additional layers of meaning elicited through interviews for experiences that cannot be put into words (Bagnoli, 2009; Sheridan, Chamberlain, & Dupuis, 2011). There are many graphic methods that can be used in social work assessment; full coverage of these methods is beyond the scope of this chapter. We summarize two graphic methods in this chapter to introduce readers to their utility in social work practice.

One graphic method developed by a social worker to assess families is the ecomap (Hartman, 1978). Ecomapping (introduced in chapter 1) provides a pictorial representation of the family and its ecological context from a cross-sectional perspective. An advantage of this approach is that it maps the family and the relationships among family members, as well as the relationship of the family to other social systems, such as schools, social services, and work. (For an example of an ecomap, see figure 4.1.) Ecomaps are excellent tools for creating innovative approaches to assessment. For example, Washington (2009) illustrates how an ecomap can be used to explore the challenges and life contexts of caregivers of children with disabilities. The ecomaps included people, agencies, and/or organizations with whom caregivers interacted. As they designed their ecomaps, the caregivers were asked to think about their perspectives regarding the interactions between family and community as it related to caring for their child with a disability. A questionnaire and interview were utilized to triangulate the information gleaned from the ecomaps, which explored the relationship between the caregiver and the client's community; the supports and stressors inherent to that relationship; and how having a child with a disability affected the caregiver's and family's relationship with others in the community. In addition to providing a visual representation of each caregiver, ecomaps also provided supporting data for themes revealed in caregiver interviews.

A basic genogram of the caregiver's immediate family structure formed the center of the ecomap, surrounded by additional circles representing key elements in the social network. Various lines represent relationships between the individual or family system and the community systems and the flow of resources between the two (Ray & Street, 2005). Thick lines represent stronger or more powerful relationships, dashed lines indicate tenuous relationships, and jagged lines denote conflicted relationships. Descriptive encapsulations and meaningful dates can be written alongside the lines for further context. The resulting visual depiction allows a better understanding of significant stressors, supports, and coping mechanisms available to caregivers (Washington, 2009). (For an example of an ecomap drawn by a female caregiver, see figure 4.1.)

Figure 4.1   Caregiver Ecomap

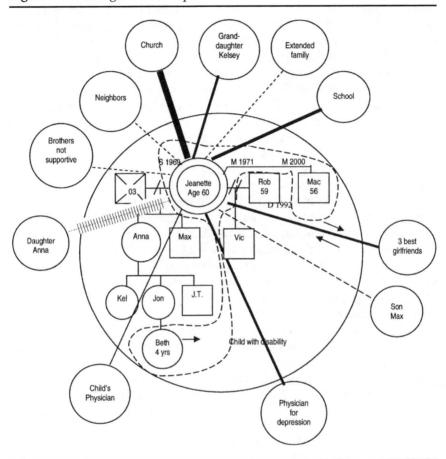

SOURCE: Washington, L. (2009, August 14). A contextual analysis of caregivers of children with disabilities. *Journal of Human Behavior in the Social Environment, 19,* p. 564. Published by Taylor & Francis. Reprinted by permission of the publisher (Taylor & Francis Ltd, http://www.tandfonline.com).

Another type of graphic assessment technique is the lifeline, in which an individual's life history is visually depicted, noting significant events in chronological order and indicating the importance, or meaning, of these events (Gramling & Carr, 2004; Saint Arnault & Shimabukuro, 2012). This method may also be referred to as a timeline (Bagnoli, 2009; Berends, 2011; Patterson, Markey, & Somers, 2012). Lifelines allow social workers to visually organize detailed narrative data (Patterson et al., 2012), and have therapeutic value as a tool for focused reflection and decision-making (Berends, 2011). The concrete, visual depiction of the passage of time and related events occurring within this context helps clients to link past experiences with subsequent actions (Saint Arnault & Shimaburkuro, 2012).

Lifelines have been used in various clinical contexts to allow better understanding of individual life experiences, including the developmental transitions of young women (Gramling & Carr, 2004), the inequity experienced by homeless individuals living with mental illness (Patterson et al., 2012), and the treatment pathways of those with substance abuse issues (Berends, 2011). Saint Arnault and Shimabukuro (2012) used lifelines to examine the interactions between culture, illness, experiences of distress, and help-seeking behaviors among first-generation Japanese women living in the United States. The lifelines were used along with interviews to provide a multifaceted account of each woman's experience. The authors describe the steps used in the process of creating clients' lifelines: "We provided the women a line across a blank sheet of paper, and asked them to situate major events along this line. Next, we asked them to draw another line that indicates the 'ups and downs' or 'highs and lows' of her life along that same lifeline. . . . In describing these times, she discusses how this time in her life felt to her, the symptoms she experienced, the events surrounding them, the meaning she attached to them, and her help seeking" (p. 315). The practitioner used lifelines throughout the interview process to elicit information regarding potential precursors to identified "low" points, as well as related help-seeking behaviors and the impact on relationships with others.

The lifeline, or timeline, method can be tailored to communicate specific experiences, as in the example above, or to describe a more generalized life history. For example, in a case study of identity among young people in England and Italy, Bagnoli (2009) simply asked participants to draw a timeline starting from zero up to their current age, indicating important events and changes that had happened in their lives up to that point. This approach resulted in a biographical depiction of the significant events and personal interests in the lives of each individual, as well as the larger social contexts of family, school, and macrolevel events relevant to their experiences.

Used in combination with interviews in assessment, lifelines facilitate recollection and sequencing of personal events (Berends, 2011). Lifelines can be used to further confirm biopsychosocial information drawn from assessment, or to place a clinical issue within the context of other events (Patterson et al., 2012).

Observational Methods: Participant Observation

Qualitative assessment makes use of two specialized forms of observation: nonstructured and participant observation. Nonstructured observation allows the clinician to observe the client without having a specific preconceived plan to observe particular content. The clinician reflectively records information as it emerges in interactions with the client.

This nonstructured method is in contrast to the structured behavioral observation methods described in chapter 2. Participant observation takes the nonstructured method a step farther by encouraging the practitioner to purposefully observe the client in everyday life and even participate with the client in his or her daily routine, as nonintrusively as possible. This methodology, of course, requires clinicians to get permission from clients to observe them and assumes that the clinician has arranged for a prolonged period of observation.

Participant observation is a humanistic methodology that draws clinicians directly into the lives of clients, allowing for a highly personal view into the dynamics of individuals' lives (Gilgun, 2013). It is considered empowering for both those being observed and for the practitioners, because of the practitioners' ability to study behavior in its natural setting. Participant observation contextualizes culture (Graue & Walsh, 1998) and responds to a variety of abilities (Ward, 1997). It also emphasizes the insider's viewpoint of the participant's everyday life experience.

The participant observation methodology originated in the research of social and cultural anthropologists, and family therapists and other clinicians have adapted it to social work research. It also has clinical utility for social work assessment. Padgett (2008) notes the importance of observation as an adjunct to interviewing, as observation brings in key contextual factors such as nonverbal communication and salient qualities of the environment/setting. For instance, observation may be used to provide illuminating detail in an in-depth case study (Gillham, 2000).

Observation of certain activities and client behaviors may also help in making accurate diagnoses of clients presenting with physical and/or mental health concerns. In the case of autism spectrum disorder, for example, observation of social behaviors in various contexts is crucial to determining an appropriate diagnosis. The DSM-5 diagnostic criteria specify that diagnosis of autism spectrum disorder is contingent on evidence of (a) deficits in social communication and interaction, and (b) restricted repetitive behaviors, interests, and activities (APA, 2013). While rating scales and laboratory-based behavioral observations are commonly used diagnostic tools, naturalistic behavioral observations, in which the individual is observed in his or her normal daily life, provide a highly ecologically valid means of assessment (White, Scarpa, Conner, Maddox, & Bonete, 2014). Please see box 4.1 for the measurement tool provided within the DSM-5 for rating the severity of autism spectrum and social communication disorders (APA, 2013). Observation of the client's behaviors is critical to this measure, both in establishing a baseline of symptoms and noting changes over time.

As an assessment method, participant observation is especially useful when (a) the practitioner knows little about the client, (b) there are important difference between the outsider and insider view, as in the case

Box 4.1
Measurement Tool for Autism

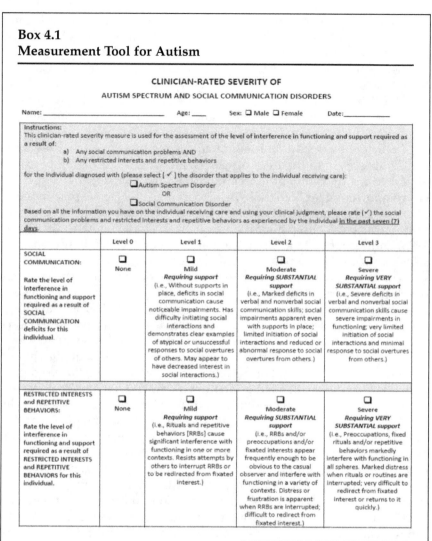

CLINICIAN-RATED SEVERITY OF
AUTISM SPECTRUM AND SOCIAL COMMUNICATION DISORDERS

Name: _____   Age: ____   Sex: ❑ Male ❑ Female   Date: _____

Instructions:
This clinician-rated severity measure is used for the assessment of the level of interference in functioning and support required as a result of:

    a) Any social communication problems AND
    b) Any restricted interests and repetitive behaviors

for the individual diagnosed with (please select [✓] the disorder that applies to the individual receiving care):

    ❑ Autism Spectrum Disorder
    OR
    ❑ Social Communication Disorder

Based on all the information you have on the individual receiving care and using your clinical judgment, please rate (✓) the social communication problems and restricted interests and repetitive behaviors as experienced by the individual in the past seven (7) days.

	Level 0	Level 1	Level 2	Level 3
SOCIAL COMMUNICATION: Rate the level of interference in functioning and support required as a result of SOCIAL COMMUNICATION deficits for this individual.	❑ None	❑ Mild *Requiring support* (i.e., Without supports in place, deficits in social communication cause noticeable impairments. Has difficulty initiating social interactions and demonstrates clear examples of atypical or unsuccessful responses to social overtures of others. May appear to have decreased interest in social interactions.)	❑ Moderate *Requiring SUBSTANTIAL support* (i.e., Marked deficits in verbal and nonverbal social communication skills; social impairments apparent even with supports in place; limited initiation of social interactions and reduced or abnormal response to social overtures from others.)	❑ Severe *Requiring VERY SUBSTANTIAL support* (i.e., Severe deficits in verbal and nonverbal social communication skills cause severe impairments in functioning; very limited initiation of social interactions and minimal response to social overtures from others.)
RESTRICTED INTERESTS and REPETITIVE BEHAVIORS: Rate the level of interference in functioning and support required as a result of RESTRICTED INTERESTS and REPETITIVE BEHAVIORS for this individual.	❑ None	❑ Mild *Requiring support* (i.e., Rituals and repetitive behaviors [RRBs] cause significant interference with functioning in one or more contexts. Resists attempts by others to interrupt RRBs or to be redirected from fixated interest.)	❑ Moderate *Requiring SUBSTANTIAL support* (i.e., RRBs and/or preoccupations and/or fixated interests appear frequently enough to be obvious to the casual observer and interfere with functioning in a variety of contexts. Distress or frustration is apparent when RRBs are interrupted; difficult to redirect from fixated interest.)	❑ Severe *Requiring VERY SUBSTANTIAL support* (i.e., Preoccupations, fixed rituals and/or repetitive behaviors markedly interfere with functioning in all spheres. Marked distress when rituals or routines are interrupted; very difficult to redirect from fixated interest or returns to it quickly.)

Instructions to Clinicians

The Clinician-Rated Severity of Autism Spectrum and Social Communication Disorders is a two-item measure that assesses the level of interference in functioning and support required as a result of difficulties in (1) SOCIAL COMMUNICATION and (2) RESTRICTED INTERESTS and REPETITIVE BEHAVIORS that are present for the individual receiving care. The measure may help with treatment planning and prognostic decision making. The measure is completed by the clinician at the time of the clinical assessment.

Box 4.1 *Continued*

The clinician is asked to rate the level of interference and support required in functioning due to difficulties in each domain as experienced by the individual during the past seven days.

Scoring and Interpretation

Each item on the Clinician-Rated Severity of Autism Spectrum and Social Communication Disorders measure is rated on a 4-point scale (Level 0 = None; Level 1 = Mild/Requiring support; Level 2 = Moderate/Requiring SUBSTANTIAL support; and Level 3=Severe/Requiring VERY SUBSTANTIAL support). The clinician is asked to review all available information for the individual and, based on his or her clinical judgment, select ( ) the level that most accurately describes the severity of the individual's condition. The severity level for each item should be reported separately. A combined score of overall severity should NOT be calculated.

Frequency of Use

To track changes in the individual's symptom severity over time, the measure may be completed at regular intervals as clinically indicated, depending on the stability of the individual's symptoms and treatment status. Consistently high scores on a particular domain may indicate significant and problematic areas for the individual that might warrant further assessment, treatment, and follow-up. Your clinical judgment should guide your decision.

---

of diverse cultures or economic conditions, (c) outsiders usually obscure the phenomenon, as in the case of family life, and (d) the phenomenon is intentionally hidden from public view, as in the case of illegal behaviors (Crabtree & Miller, 1992; Jorgensen, 1989).

The following are suggestions for conducting a participant observation: First, clinicians must gain permission to enter and observe the everyday life of the client. They must decide where to start observing the client and gain supporters from the client's social network who will also agree to the observation. Clinicians must be prepared to reassure clients about concerns regarding their presence in everyday activities. Second, clinicians must establish rapport and develop a trusting and cooperative relationship with those involved in observation. They must fit in with the client's everyday life, be unobtrusive, and play down their evaluative role as an expert. Reflective listening and genuineness are critical skills to be used to gain rapport in participant observation settings. Finally, clinicians should tell the truth about the purpose of their presence but not go into so much detail that they intimidate the client. The initial contact can make or break the observation period. Clinicians should try not to communicate the evaluative nature of their visits. They should, however, be honest if their observations could result in a decision or action that would affect the client's life, as in the case of an adoption home study (Berg, 2010; Crabtree & Miller, 1992; Jorgensen, 1989).

Participant observation uses different types of observations. Descriptive observation is less systematic and represents a shotgun approach in which the clinician observes everything about clients and their situation to get an overall impression of client functioning. Focused observation is based on the specific interests of the assessor. For example, if the client's parenting style is of concern, the social worker might observe the client only in interactions with his or her children, perhaps at playtime, at dinnertime, or at bedtime. Selective observation enables clinicians to concentrate on specific characteristics or attributes. For example, if the social worker is interested in assessing only how the client disciplines his or her children, the social worker might observe specific situations between parent and child in which the parent disciplines the children (Crabtree & Miller, 1992; Jorgensen, 1989).

Clinicians who use participant observation use case notes to keep track of what they observe. A simple format will help the clinician keep case notes to aid in the understanding of client behavior and its context. Notes on observations should be able to answer the following questions:

- Who is present?
- What is happening?
- When does the activity or behavior occur?
- Where is the activity or behavior happening?
- Why is the activity or behavior happening?
- How is the activity or behavior organized? (Crabtree & Miller, 1999)

Recording structured case notes that answer the preceding questions will help clinicians draw on their observations to formulate meaningful client assessments. Keeping track of the sequence of events and the emotions expressed during these events may give clinicians further insights into what motivates the client.

Participant observations have many advantages over other qualitative assessment methods. As time passes in an observation in clients' everyday life, clients are less likely to alter their behavior because of the clinician's presence. Therefore, practitioners may gain a more accurate picture of clients' behavior in an observation than in an interview. The longer the clinician observes clients in their everyday lives, the more likely it is for the clinician to accurately distinguish between real and perceived behavior. Also, participant observation methods help clinicians learn effective ways to communicate with the client and therefore assist in the reconstruction of client beliefs and behaviors (Crabtree & Miller, 1992; Jorgensen, 1989).

Combining Qualitative Methods through Portfolio Assessment

Portfolio or performance-based assessments are multidimensional in nature and blend several types of evaluative approaches. These methods have been particularly popular in educational settings that employ school social workers, and have many different applications (Johnson, Mims-Cox, & Nichols, 2009). Portfolios are defined as a "longitudinal collection of student work that tells a story of the student's efforts, progress, or achievement in a given area" (Swigonski, Ward, Mama, Rodgers, & Belicose, 2006, p. 813). The compilation of artifacts, or the portfolio, is an assortment of various documents: some may be paper-and-pencil tests or classroom observations, while others may be projects, constructions, videotapes, audiotapes, poems, artwork, or stories by the student (Karoly & Franklin, 1996). Portfolios reflect a shift in assessment from a behaviorist framework of learning involving the acquisition of a sequence of component skills through drill and practice to a constructivist lens that regards learning as complex, contextual, and collaborative. Portfolio assessment is culturally sensitive in that it recognizes broad diversity in the pace and style of cognitive and learning development among children from various cultures. This orientation reflects social work's strengths-based focus (Swigonski et al., 2006).

Self-observation and reflection are a part of the portfolio process (Johnson et al., 2009). Reflections are most often written but can also be oral presentations, remarks, or ruminations supplemented by teacher annotations. The process of writing portfolio reflections is a meaning-making process, a way to help learners think critically about assignments they have completed and the relationship of assessments to those performances. It is a way to consciously call to mind effective and ineffective process strategies, to monitor performance objectives in terms of expectations, and to consider steps in the overall learning process that should be adopted, adapted, or eliminated (Fernsten & Fernsten, 2005). Done well, reflection promotes self-regulation and can help students learn to think strategically (Martin-Kniep, 2000). Two assumptions underlie the use of portfolio assessment in schools: (a) Judgments based on portfolios are more reliable and valid because of the comprehensive and inclusive nature of the samples. (b) Portfolios, when used to supplement other methods of measuring learning, will improve the reliability and validity of the evidence (Karoly & Franklin, 1996).

Standards for evaluating performance-based assessments are usually developed after portfolio work has been systematically collected; the portfolio approach is consistent with the qualitative approach to research and evaluation. This method is also in sharp contrast to traditional testing with standardized measures (discussed in chapter 3), which sets specific criteria or develops normative-based samples for comparison before students are evaluated. The rationale for portfolio assessment is that standards should be locally (and realistically) established only after student work has been gathered. Portfolios cannot be reduced to numeric grades; they must be approached qualitatively, through a multidimensional evaluation. The case study assessment at the end of this chapter further clarifies the usefulness of the portfolio or performance-based methods of assessment.

Determining Validity and Reliability of Qualitative Information

Recall from our discussion in chapter 3 that validity and reliability refer, respectively, to the accuracy and consistency of the assessment information. The evaluation of the validity and reliability of qualitative assessment data rests on the credibility, thoroughness, completeness, and consistency of the information; how it is gathered and reported; and the logical inferences and conclusions that the clinician draws from this information about the client. It may not be possible to know from an assessment report whether the clinician is reporting the client's story accurately, but it is possible to view the information in the report, with knowledge of the manner in which it was gathered, and to evaluate the validity and reliability of the clinician's data gathering and the interpretations (Berg, 2010; Franklin et al., 2010). Seven suggestions for evaluating the reliability and validity of qualitative assessment information follow:

1. Does the information tell a complete story, and do the conclusions drawn make sense in relationship to the client's story, as told? For example, are there big gaps in the information? Is the information too sketchy? Does it skip around too much to make a clear connection with the clinician's interpretations?

2. Are there missing details or information that would put the clinician's interpretations in doubt? For example, does the clinician make a diagnosis that the data in the report do not support or fail to disqualify a differential diagnosis that is equally as plausible as the diagnosis given?

3. Are there any contradictions that may disqualify the clinical impressions; if so, does the clinician explain them in the interpretations? For

example, if the clinician interprets that the client had a warm and secure upbringing, but the report gives only minimal information about the client's family history and specifically mentions that the family moved frequently because of personal and economic hardships, perhaps this interpretation should be questioned unless further explanation is provided.

4. Do the metaphors, pictures, or diagrams used make sense, and does the clinician interpret themes and patterns in them? All diagrams and pictures should be provided as part of the assessment report to give others an opportunity to verify the interpretations in the assessment. Although more than one clinical interpretation is possible using these methods, the clinical themes that the clinician interprets and reports should be easy to discern from the data.

5. Did the clinician collaborate with the client in formulating and interpreting the client's problems? Did the clinician check out his or her interpretations with the client? Qualitative assessment relies on the personal stories of clients and their private meanings. Clinicians should assure the readers of the report that they are representing the client's life context appropriately and without undue interpretations or unsupported inferences. Clinicians should use the client's own language throughout and explicitly differentiate their interpretations from the client's report.

6. Were multiple methods used to gather the information? Qualitative assessment relies on triangulation of data-gathering techniques (e.g., client's observation interview, the client's and others' reports). All methods and sources should be compared to determine whether they point to the same conclusion. Did the social worker's observations of the client agree with collateral sources' reports? If there was not agreement, was this inconsistency logically explained?

7. Has the clinician tried to disqualify his or her own interpretations? In qualitative assessment, clinicians should seek to prove themselves wrong by looking for other explanations for a client's behavior. For example, if the clinician believes a client has depression, he or she would look for disconfirming evidence to see whether the judgment holds up to further exploration and probing.

Many of these standards are evident in Gioia's (2009) study of neurocognitive functioning among individuals with schizophrenia. The author used qualitative methods, including ethnographic interviewing and observation, to determine the ecological validity of laboratory-based, quantitative measures of neurocognitive impairments among individuals with schizophrenia. The notion of ecological validity in neuropsychological assessment refers to the relationship, or lack thereof, between laboratory test results and laboratory-based behavioral measures, on the one hand, and behavior and outcomes in real-world settings, on the other.

To address this issue, Gioia (2009) devised an ethnographic approach to determining the ecological validity of neuropsychological testing. The eight-step method (see table 4.1) begins with getting to know the client on an individual level, moving on to prolonged observation of the client in the community, and actively engaging the client in reflecting on these

Table 4.1   Eight Steps in the Ecological Validity Process

Step	Researcher Task
1. Getting to know the participant	Develop rapport, collect quantitative data, schedule community observation.
2. Utilizing prolonged engagement with participants	Spend three consecutive days viewing typical and atypical tasks.
3. Encouraging participant-led activities with opportunity for reflection	Build in time for participant reflection on use of metacognitive processes.
4. Taking field notes	Write notes in a timely manner at the end of each field day.
	Check for gaps in understanding with members of team and return to field to check understanding with participants.
5. Having contact with significant others and community members	Determine depth of interaction with other individuals because they can provide collateral information on functioning.
6. Coding and categorizing observed behaviors and strategies	Use instrumental activities of daily living language to create categories that can be used as a template for additional coders to rate.
7. Employing intercoder agreement as a means to strengthen validity of the data	Use multiple coders for field notes and have them code notes according to types of tasks.
	Generate intercoder reliability scores.
8. Using cocreated results	Check results with the participants for accuracy.
	Share results with scientists working in neuropsychology to increase understanding of ecological validity.

SOURCE: Gioia, D. *Qualitative Health Research* (vol. 19, no. 10), pp. 1495–1503. Copyright © 2009 by SAGE Publications. Reprinted by permission of SAGE Publications, Inc.

activities. Multiple members of the research team reviewed field notes and engaged in coding strategies to ensure the data's reliability, with results continually being checked with clients for accuracy. The real world context of this method should help improve interventions for individuals with neuropsychological disorders affecting cognitive functioning. (See appendix 4B for a detailed description of this approach.)

MOVING FROM ASSESSMENT TO INTERVENTION: PORTFOLIO ASSESSMENT EXAMPLE

Qualitative assessment helps us move from assessment to intervention in that we can view the clinical processes through the thick descriptions that result from the many sources of qualitative data gathered from interactions with clients. In addition, qualitative information provides context and meaning with which to make clinical decisions and intervention plans. The following case study, taken from Sammons (2014), uses rich detail, pictorial language, and descriptive information to detail the assessment-to-intervention continuum of a Mexican American man transitioning from homelessness to a supportive housing program. Qualitative strategies such as culturally sensitive ethnographic assessment, narrative description of the client's life history, and observation of the client's behaviors and physical realities are utilized in this example:

> When I first met Berto, I could not take my eyes off the neat creases in his T-shirt. I'd never seen a carefully ironed T-shirt, and especially not on a man who had been labeled "chronically homeless." From his closely trimmed beard to his sharply ironed khakis and pristine white nonbranded athletic shoes, his meticulous appearance gave no clue that he had just moved to a small single apartment after 21 years of eating, sleeping, and drinking beer on the downtown streets of this southern California metropolis. Well, that wasn't quite true: Sun overexposure had deeply lined and darkened his skin beyond its original Mexican American tone and also added at least 15 appearance years to his 48 chronological ones. His housing services coordinator, Elena, introduced me to my new client since I'd just arrived to fill the clinical social work position at the fledgling Project Home Base multiagency service program in this city's urban core neighborhood. . . . This is the story of how Berto regained his sobriety, his physical and mental health, and his dignity, and how our therapeutic relationship humbled and reinspired me as a social worker.
>
> As a new team member, I had not witnessed Berto's initial entry into this housing first intensive services program. Our outreach worker Patrick had become a familiar presence at the parking lot where Berto slept under a cardboard lean-to attached with bungee cords to a chain-link fence. No one claimed there was any 'befriending' or 'trusting,' just that the daily predawn visits made Patrick's short wiry figure, pale white face, and waist-length dreadlocks a predictable part of the landscape, along with scurrying rats and puddles of urine and vomit in the alley. Like most sidewalk sleepers in this

skid row area, Berto described himself as a 'loner' and 'not a people person,' so what got his attention was not Patrick's socializing attempts but his persistently repeated offer of a sliding-scale rent, no strings attached, room of your own if you just come with me to check it out and sign some papers with the county housing department. . . . He was tired. Tired of being hungry, tired of having to deal with these other unstable guys around him, and especially tired of being dirty. . . . When Patrick caught him on a sober day, Berto agreed to get into the program van and visit the apartment building five blocks away. . . .

As Berto settled into housing, his multiple special needs came into more specific focus. He demonstrated symptoms of severe and recurrent major depression, at times with psychotic features. His lifelong socially phobic behavior patterns suggested avoidance or possibly paranoid personality disorder. But the greatest threat to his housing stability was his alcohol dependence. Berto shared his psychosocial history over a series of interviews that began as just 10-minute check-ins that he maintained primarily because our team was his only social network, and his Mexican American upbringing meant that face-to-face greetings were an important daily ritual for him. I learned of his growing up in the desert town of El Centro, California, dropping out of school in the seventh grade, working for his brother's plumbing business, having a brief marriage, and fathering two daughters. He didn't like to talk about his past, and he really didn't see the point or purpose in meeting with me, but our relationship grew despite his doubts. Instead of focusing on psychiatric symptoms right away, as most mental health clinical social workers are required by their agencies to do, I could turn my attention to whatever mattered most to him in his daily life. . . .

He was initially more comfortable providing health history, so we readily identified and assisted him with concerns such as hypertension, hepatitis C, a history of tuberculosis (treated), and age-related vision impairment. He also had accumulated three police citations, which caused him to sweat with terror whenever he went outdoors, thinking that the police would stop and arrest him. . . .

Berto wanted help with his infractions, so that was my entry into more therapeutic topics. While focusing on his problem, I used generic social work skills in terms of linking him with a legal aid program that advocated on behalf of homeless persons to prevent their incarceration. He also had a desire to eat food that was gentler on his digestions, food that reminded him of his childhood. . . . He had been eating Cup-a-Noodle with pork rinds, candy bars, chips, and grimy coffee from the corner store, but now Berto was thinking more about arroz con pollo, frijoles, warm tortillas, and freshly brewed coffee. With his own kitchen, he could now mobilize his energies to shop for and cook his own meals.

It did not take long for deeper clinical issues to arise. Through formal history gathering and behavioral observations in a variety of settings, the team psychiatrist and I were able to identify significant mood and cognitive dysfunction and to conceptualize them diagnostically. . . . He was well known in this skid row neighborhood as an alcoholic, with the street name of 'Senor.' But less known was the fact that his current binge drinking represented significant progress in a lifelong pattern of polysubstance abuse that began with his father urging him (at age 4) to have sips of beer, and at age 7 sneaking whiskey from his father's hidden bottle. By 11, he was following older male peers down to the convenience store to steal glue and spray paint to inhale. His father's involvement at home had always been minimal and sporadic, but after his mother's death following a brief illness (possibly cancer) when Berto was 14, the family disintegrated. . . . I learned through trial and error that his executive functioning skills were quite impaired, and this exacerbated his social fears and paranoia. For example, his concentration, auditory processing, short-term recall, sequencing, problem-solving skills, and other cognitive functions were very poor, even after his mood improved. The Repeatable Battery for the Assessment of Neuropsychological Status instrument (2013) helped me assess these areas of functioning. This information was critical in coaching him toward enhanced daily coping, as well as for his gradual education about alcoholism.

In keeping with our harm reduction model, I suggested that Berto set a goal of increasing the periods between drinking binges. One very powerful technique we used was a 'sobriety calendar,' which involved a common monthly wall calendar (chosen by him) that was kept in my locked file drawer and brought out at each office session. In reviewing his week, he would put a green sticker on every day that he was sober. We used this visual aid in exploring the detailed nuances of his daily experiences, such as when cravings occurred, what was happening just before, sources of stress, his thought processes, his coping strategies, and so on. . . .

Another successful strategy in Berto's treatment was to incorporate his friend Juan. Although Berto insisted that he did not have friends, that he never had friends, and that he didn't want to make friends, he did frequently describe experiences on the streets with Juan. He would relate that Juan 'had his back' and vice versa. He had urged Juan to come into Project Home Base, and Juan had an apartment in the same building as Berto. He told many warm anecdotes about Juan, and yet, he would not knock on Juan's door in their new building. Juan was actively involved in treatment and had been clean and sober for more than a year, so he was a good role model for Berto. . . . Eventually, and very gradually, they started to initiate contact on their own and even to provide mutual support. . . .

Over an 18-month period, Berto's binges were spaced further apart and shorter in duration. He had recently celebrated his third year of sobriety, his chronic health conditions were in good control, and his overall functioning was probably better than at any other time in his adult life. (Sammons, 2014, pp. 217–224)

REFERENCES

American Psychiatric Association (APA). (2000). *Diagnostic and statistical manual of mental disorders* (4th ed.; DSM-IV). Washington, DC: Author.

American Psychiatric Association (APA). (2013). *Diagnostic and statistical manual of mental disorders* (5th ed.; DSM-5). Washington, DC: Author.

Bagnoli, A. (2009). Beyond the standard interview: The use of graphic elicitation and arts-based methods. *Qualitative Research, 9*, 547–570.

Barrera, I., & Jordan, C. (2011). Potentially harmful practices: Using the DSM with people of color. *Social Work in Mental Health, 9*, 272–286.

Berends, L. (2011). Embracing the visual: Using timelines with in-depth interviews on substance use and treatment. *The Qualitative Report, 16*(1), 1–9.

Berg, B. L. (2010). *Qualitative research methods for the social sciences.* Boston, MA: Allyn and Bacon.

Black, P., & Feld, A. (2006). Process recording revisited: A learning-oriented thematic approach integrating field education and classroom curriculum. *Journal of Teaching in Social Work, 26*(3–4), 137–153.

Carey, M. (2012). *Qualitative research skills for social work: Theory and practice.* Surrey, UK: Ashgate.

Carlsson, E., Paterson, B. L., Scott-Findlay, S., Ehnfors, M., & Ehrenberg, A. (2007). Methodological issues involving people with communication impairments after acquired brain damage. *Qualitative Health Research, 17*, 1361–1371.

Conroy, K. (2012). Student writing in field education. In W. Green & B. L. Simon (Eds.), *The Columbia guide to social work writing* (pp. 85–113). New York: Columbia University Press.

Crabtree, B. F., & Miller, W. L. (Eds.). (1992). *Doing qualitative research.* Newbury Park, CA: Sage.

Crabtree, B. F., & Miller, W. L. (Eds.). (1999). *Doing qualitative research* (2nd ed.). Newbury Park, CA: Sage.

Crittenden, N., & Ashkar, C. (2012). The self-characterization technique: Uses, analysis and elaboration. In P. Caputi, L. L. Viney, B. M. Walker, & N. Crittenden (Eds.), *Personal construct methodology* (pp. 109–128). Oxford, UK: Wiley-Blackwell.

Dana, R. (Ed.). (2000). *Handbook of cross-cultural and multicultural personality assessment.* Mahwah, NJ: Erlbaum.

Drisko, J. (2014). Research evidence and social work practice: The place of evidence-based practice. *Clinical Social Work Journal, 42*, 123–133.

Duffy, M., & Chenail, R. (2004). Qualitative strategies in couple and family assessment. In L. Sperry (Ed.), *Assessment of couples and families: Contemporary and cutting-edge strategies* (pp. 33–63). New York: Brunner-Routledge.

Fernsten, L., & Fernsten, J. (2005). Portfolio assessment and reflection: Enhancing learning through effective practice. *Reflective Practice, 6*(2), 303–309.

Franklin, C., Cody, P. A., & Ballan, M. (2010). Reliability and validity in qualitative research. In B. Thyer (Ed.), *The handbook of social work research methods* (2nd ed., pp. 355–374). Thousand Oaks, CA: Sage.

Friedman, H. L., & MacDonald, D. M. (2006). Humanistic testing and assessment. *Journal of Humanistic Psychology, 46*, 510–529.

Gergen, K. (2003). *An invitation to social construction.* Thousand Oaks, CA: Sage.

Gilbert, D. J., & Franklin, C. (2001). Evaluation skills with Native American individuals and families. In R. Fong & S. Furuto (Eds.), *Culturally competent practice: Skills, interventions and evaluations* (pp. 396–412). Needham Heights, MA: Allyn and Bacon.

Gilgun, J. F. (2004). Qualitative methods and the development of clinical assessment tools. *Qualitative Health Research, 14,* 1008–1019.

Gilgun, J. (2013). Grounded theory, deductive qualitative analysis and social work research and practice. In A. E. Fortune & W. J. Reid (Eds.), *Qualitative research in social work* (pp. 107–135). New York: Columbia University Press.

Gilgun, J. F., & Sands, R. G. (2012). The contribution of qualitative approaches to developmental intervention research. *Qualitative Social Work, 11,* 349–361.

Gillham, B. (2000). *Case study research methods.* London, UK: Continuum.

Gioia, D. (2009). Understanding the ecological validity of neuropsychological testing using an ethnographic approach. *Qualitative Health Research, 19,* 1495–1503.

Gioia, D., & Brekke, J. S. (2009). Neurocognition, ecological validity, and daily living in the community for individuals with schizophrenia: A mixed methods study. *Psychiatry: Interpersonal and biological processes, 72*(1), 93–106.

Gramling, L. F., & Carr, R. L. (2004). Lifelines: A life history methodology. *Nursing Research, 53*(3), 207–210.

Graue, M. E, & Walsh, D. J. (1998). *Studying children in context.* London: Sage.

Groth-Marnat, G. (2000). Visions of clinical assessment: Then, now, and a brief history of the future. *Journal of Clinical Psychology, 56,* 349–365.

Hardison, H. G., & Neimeyer, R. A. (2007). Numbers and narratives: Quantitative and qualitative convergence across constructivist assessments, *Journal of Constructivist Psychology, 20,* 285–308.

Hartman, A. (1978). Diagrammatic assessment of family relationships. *Social Casework, 59,* 465–476.

Hunsley, J., & Mash, E. J. (2007). Evidence-based assessment. *Annual Review of Clinical Psychology, 3,* 29–51.

Hunt, W. A. (1946). The future of diagnostic testing in clinical psychology. *Journal of Clinical Psychology, 2,* 311–317.

Johnson, R. S., Mims-Cox, J. S., & Nichols, A. R. (2009). *Developing portfolios in education: Reflection, inquiry and assessment.* Thousand Oaks, CA: Sage.

Jorgensen, D. L. (1989). *Participant observation: A methodology for human studies.* Newbury Park, CA: Sage.

Karoly, J. C., & Franklin, C. (1996). Using portfolios to assess students' academic strengths: A case study. *Social Work in Education, 18,* 179–185.

Kidd, S. A., & Kral, M. J. (2005). Practicing participatory action research. *Journal of Counseling Psychology, 52*(2), 187–195.

Kolakowsky-Hayner, S. A., & Caplan, B. (2011). Qualitative neuropsychological assessment. In J. S. Kreutzer, J. DeLuca, & B. Caplan (Eds.), *Encyclopedia of clinical neuropsychology* (pp. 2098–2099). New York: Springer.

Krysik, J. L., & Finn, J. (2010). *Research for effective social work practice* (2nd ed.). London: Routledge.

Lawton, M., & Brody, E. (1969). Assessment of older people: Self-maintaining and instrumental activities of daily living. *Gerontologist, 9*(3), 179–186.

Lee, E., Mishna, F., & Brennenstuhl, S. (2010). How to critically evaluate case studies in social work. *Research on Social Work Practice, 20*(6), 682–689.

Lysaker, P. H., Carcione, A., Dimaggio, G., Johannesen, J. K., Nicolo, G., Procacci, M., & Semerari, A. (2005). Metacognition amidst narratives of self and illness in schizophrenia: Associations with neurocognition, symptoms, insight and quality of life. *Acta Psychiatrica Scandinavica, 112*(1), 64–71.

Malson, H. (2010). Qualitative methods from psychology. In I. Bourgeault, R. Dingwall, & R. DeVries (Eds.), *The SAGE handbook of qualitative methods in health research* (pp. 193–212). London: Sage.

Martin-Kniep, G. O. (2000). *Becoming a better teacher: Eight innovations that work.* Alexandria, VA: Association for Supervision and Curriculum Development.

McLeod, J. (Ed.). (2011). *Qualitative research in counselling and psychology* (2nd ed). London: Sage.

Mezzich, J. E., Caracci, G., Fabrega, H., & Kirmayer, L. J. (2009). Cultural formulation guidelines. *Transcultural Psychiatry, 46*(3), 383–405.

Neimeyer, R. A. (2010). *Constructivist psychotherapy: Distinctive features.* New York: Taylor and Francis.

Neimeyer, R. A., Keesee, N. J., & Fortner, B. V. (2000). Loss and meaning reconstruction: Propositions and procedures. In R. Malkinson, S. Rubin, & E. Witzum (Eds.), *Traumatic and non-traumatic loss and bereavement* (pp. 197–230). Madison, CT: Psychosocial Press.

O'Reilly, K. (2009). *Key concepts in ethnography.* Los Angeles: Sage.

Ortiz Hendricks, C., Bertrand Finch, J., & Franks, C. L. (2013). *Learning to teach, teaching to learn: A guide for social work field education.* Alexandria, VA: CSWE Press.

Padgett, D. K. (Ed.). (2008). *Qualitative methods in social work research.* Thousand Oaks, CA: Sage.

Parker, J., & Bradley, G. (Eds.). (2010). *Social work practice: Assessment, planning, intervention, and review* (3rd ed.). Exeter, UK: Learning Matters.

Patterson, M. L., Markey, M. A., & Somers, J. M. (2012). Multiple paths to just ends: Using narrative interviews and timelines to explore health equity and homelessness. *International Journal of Qualitative Methods, 11*(2), 132–151.

Pettit, J. W., & Joiner, T. E. (2006). *Chronic depression: Interpersonal sources, therapeutic solutions.* Washington, DC: American Psychological Association.

Ponterotto, J. G. (2006). Brief note on the origins, evolution, and meaning of the qualitative research concept "thick description." *Qualitative Report, 11*(3), 538–549.

Ray, R. A., & Street, A. F. (2005). Ecomapping: An innovative research tool for nurses. *Journal of Advanced Nursing, 50*(5), 545–552.

Rubin, A. (2008). *Practitioner's guide to using research for evidence-based practice.* Hoboken, NJ: John Wiley & Sons.

Saint Arnault, D., & Shimabukuro, S. (2012). The clinical ethnographic interview: A user-friendly guide to the cultural formulation of distress and help seeking. *Transcultural Psychiatry, 49,* 302–322.

Sammons, C. (2014). Case study 6-3: Project Home Base: How Berto came indoors after 20 years of sidewalk sleeping. In C. W. LeCroy (Ed.), *Case studies in social work practice* (3rd ed., pp. 217–224). Hoboken, NJ: John Wiley & Sons.

Seeley, K. (2004). Short-term intercultural psychotherapy: Ethnographic inquiry. *Social Work, 49,* 121–130.

Sheridan, J., Chamberlain, K., & Dupuis, A. (2011). Timelining: Visualizing experience. *Qualitative Research, 11*(5), 552–569.

Stickley, T., & Phillips, C. (2005). Single case study and evidence-based practice. *Journal of Psychiatric and Mental Health Nursing, 12,* 728–732.

Swartz, H. A., Zuckoff, A., Grote, N. K., Spielvogle, H. N., Bledsoe, S., Shear, K. M., & Frank, E. (2007). Engaging depressed patients in psychotherapy: Integrating techniques from motivational interviewing and ethnographic interviewing to improve treatment participation. *Professional Psychology: Research and Practice, 38,* 430–439.

Swigonski, M., Ward, K., Mama, R. S., Rodgers, J., & Belicose, R. (2006). An agenda for the future: Student portfolios in social work education. *Social Work Education, 25*(8), 812–823.

Trepper, T. S. (1990). In celebration of the case study. *Journal of Family Psychotherapy, 1,* 5–13.

Ward, L. (1997). *Seen and heard: Involving disabled children and young people in research and development projects.* York, UK: York Publishing Services for the Joseph Rowntree Foundation.

Washington, L. (2009). A contextual analysis of caregivers of children with disabilities. *Journal of Human Behavior in the Social Environment, 19,* 554–571.

White, S. W., Scarpa, A., Conner, C. M., Maddox, B. B., & Bonete, S. (2015). Evaluating change in social skills in high-functioning adults with autism spectrum disorder using a laboratory-based observational measure. *Focus on Autism and Other Developmental Disabilities, 30,* 3–12. doi: 10.1177/1088357614539836

Widiger, T. A., & Samuel, D. B. (2005). Evidence based assessment of personality disorders. *Psychological Assessment, 17,* 278–287.

Williams, E. N. (2008). A psychotherapy researcher's perspective on therapist self-awareness and self-focused attention after a decade of research. *Psychotherapy Research, 18,* 139–146.

Williams, E. N., & Fauth, J. (2005). A psychotherapy process study of therapist in session self-awareness. *Psychotherapy Research, 15,* 374–381.

Willis, G. B. (2005). *Cognitive interviewing: A tool for improving questionnaire design.* Thousand Oaks, CA: Sage.

Wolcott, H. F. (1995). *The art of fieldwork.* Lanham, MD: AltaMira Press.

Yin, R. K. (2010). *Case study research: Design and methods.* Newbury Park, CA: Sage.

PART III

Clinical Assessment with Populations

Special populations have unique issues that can and should be addressed during assessment. Part III identifies these issues for children, adults, and families. Chapter 5, "Children and Adolescents," acknowledges childhood experts' disagreement on the appropriate method of diagnosing children's problems, with the growing neuroscience evidence to clarify this issue, and discusses different diagnostic methods. It also reviews multicultural issues of child assessment. Chapter 6, "Adults," summarizes types of questions and assessment methods that practitioners can use to gain information from adults at different ages and stages of life. Chapter 7, "Family Systems," reviews and summarizes selected assessment and developmental frameworks for understanding the normative characteristics of families, as well as methods that can be used as family information-gathering techniques. Chapter 8, "Families Who Are Multi-stressed," reviews families experiencing stressors, including families of gay and lesbian persons and families experiencing child maltreatment. Chapter 9, "Multicultural Assessment," covers the limitations of assessment methods and provides an overview of ethnic-sensitive assessment strategies for four groups: (a) American Indians and Alaska Natives, (b) African Americans and blacks, (c) Hispanics and Latinos, and (d) Asian and Pacific Islander Americans.

CHAPTER 5

Children and Adolescents

Catheleen Jordan and Alexa Smith-Osborne

INTRODUCTION

The special issues of child and adolescent populations are the focus of this chapter, which reviews assessment and measurement techniques and presents a case study. The important environmental interactions for this group occur in the school and neighborhood (including the biosphere), at home, and with peers.

COMPLETE CHILDHOOD ASSESSMENT

Before conducting a formal assessment with a child, it is important to understand the factors that have caused and that are contributing to the child's problem. A thorough assessment requires an understanding of the biopsychosocial and spiritual perspectives, including the child's age, his or her development in comparison to age-peers, health status, culture, race, gender, socioeconomic status, family background, personality, and intellectual capacities. In assessing a child or adolescent, it is "critical to consider the child holistically (i.e., thought, affect, behavior, culture, race/ethnicity, spirituality)" (Yalof & Abraham, 2007, p. 19).

Clinical assessment is different from diagnosis or testing, however. Diagnosis relies on nosological systems like the *Diagnostic and Statistical Manual of Mental Disorders*, fifth edition (DSM-5; American Psychiatric Association [APA], 2013) to provide a medical/psychiatric label of the client's symptoms and problems. Testing uses an instrument or procedure to measure the magnitude of a problem area using an assessment instrument. Assessment is a problem-solving process in which the assessor uses tests as a tool in combination with his or her knowledge, skill, and experience, and in the context of historical information, referral information, and behavioral observations to arrive at a "cohesive and comprehensive understanding of the person being evaluated" (Handler & Meyer, 1998, pp. 4–5). An assessment that considers all aspects of a child's life provides information that aids clinicians in developing an appropriate intervention and treatment plan (Yalof & Abraham, 2007).

Childhood experts disagree on the appropriate method of diagnosing children's problems. The following sections discuss different diagnostic methods and the multicultural issues of child assessment.

Diagnosis

There are three perspectives on child diagnosis: (a) categorical-dimensional, (b) empirical, and (c) behavioral (Bornstein & Kazdin, 1985; Harper-Dorton & Herbert, 1999).

Categorical-Dimensional Diagnosis. The most widely used categorical system for diagnosing persons with mental disorders, regardless of age, has been the DSM-5 (APA, 2013). The goal of a categorical system is to establish whether a diagnosis is present or absent. Categorical diagnosis describes client symptoms and features such as age at onset, predisposing factors, and prevalence. It also provides diagnostic criteria that are based on the most recent scientific evidence. In general, corrections are made as new data become available. The categories in the DSM system (APA, 2013) have been atheoretical, derived from evidence for practice, reviewed by panels of multidisciplinary experts, and subjected to experimental trials in the field.

However, the DSM-5 departs for the first time from the categorical approach and shifts to a dimensional approach emphasizing measurement of frequency and severity; this new approach should be useful in treatment decisions. Criticisms of the DSM's prior categorical approach include lack of detailed assessment criteria for children who experience multiple problems. However, the DSM-5 appears to have resolved the latter limitation by updating severity specifier criteria based on specific behavioral indicators and by requiring recording of diagnoses and other issues for clinical attention in order of the urgency presenting at the time of the diagnostic session. The addition of these dimensional scales (e.g., new severity specifier system) to the categorical diagnostic approach represents a significant advance in classification systems useful to child clinicians.

In the DSM-5 many of the changes from the previous edition were made on the basis of syntheses of new brain imaging and genetic, neuro-chemical, and treatment outcome research, consistent with a dimensional approach. For example, the DSM-5 does not include the category of Infant, Child, and Adolescent Disorders due to continued conflicting evidence on the duration of dysfunction or age of onset for some disorders, and solid new evidence establishing the similar presentation at the brain level of the early onset and typical onset types of each disorder. The DSM-5 adds a new disorder, Disruptive Mood Dysregulation Disorder, to address the dimensionality of severe, nonepisodic irritability presentation, which could be accounted for in the prior categorical the DSM approach only by bipolar disorder; this was implicated to an increase in early onset bipolar diagnoses. It also eliminates the "Not Otherwise Specified" option, to reduce diagnosis of spurious comorbidities under the prior categorical approach. The dimensional approach is more consistent with neuroscience and genomic evidence about mental disorders in being more sensitive to gender and age variance, and underlying genetic and neural variations.

The DSM-5 also endorses use of validated instruments in the diagnostic process, thus incorporating the empirical diagnostic approach, and emphasizes careful observation and measurement of specific behaviors in assessing condition severity, thus incorporating the behavioral approach. Many standardized screening and diagnostic instruments, as well as the Diagnostic Interview Schedule for Children (Columbia University DISC Development Group, 2006)—a widely used structured clinical interview guide—are currently undergoing revision to be consistent with the changes in the DSM-5.

Empirical Diagnosis. In addition to identifying groupings of symptoms or syndromes that have been empirically derived, empirical diagnosis uses multivariate classification (use of several different measures) to diagnosis a problem. Reviews of these multivariate studies show similarities.

Advantages of empirically derived diagnosis include evaluating the child across all areas (factors) included in the empirically derived test. Because testing provides an empirically derived score, children's problems can also be prioritized, an advantage over the earlier editions of the DSM. Finally, because tests provide interpretive data that enable comparison of the child's score with a normative group, empirically derived tests help establish how children compare with their peers.

Limitations of empirically derived testing include variation in a given analysis resulting from such factors as rater reliability, appropriateness of the clinical sample, and item content. Furthermore, data collected are often from parent or teacher reports rather than from observations of behavior. Such reports are not always verified by comparison with direct observation of the problem behavior.

Finally, parents may suffer from their own marital or individual problems that influence the ratings.

Behavioral Diagnosis. One characteristic of behavioral diagnosis is emphasis on a functional analysis of behavior rather than on a categorical-dimensional system such as the DSM. Functional analysis seeks to identify or operationalize children's specific problematic behaviors and the controlling conditions that continue or promote those behaviors. The behaviors, in turn, are targeted for modification. A behavior observation that measures the frequency of specific behaviors in a given time is a prerequisite to a functional analysis. The behavior observation provides data to conduct a functional analysis of a child with problems in the classroom. For example, a behavior observation may reveal that a child initiates conversations with other children and leaves his seat without permission approximately three times per half hour of observation period. A functional analysis may reveal that these incidents occur only in reading class, where the teacher has a somewhat authoritarian disciplinarian style that seems to elicit disruptive behavior from the child.

A second characteristic of behavioral diagnosis is the classification of behavior into broad categories, such as excesses and deficits. In the foregoing example, the child is excessively out of his seat.

A third characteristic relies on direct measurement of the specific problem behavior. The teacher might measure or count the number of incidents of disruptive behavior (e.g., number of times child left seat).

One advantage of behavioral diagnosis is that it is highly individualized. It provides an in-depth analysis of a specific child's problematic behavior, the controlling conditions, and the modifications necessary for change. Behavioral diagnosis provides information on specific problems targeted for change, which facilitates an easy transition from assessment to treatment.

Limitations of behavioral diagnosis relate to the lack of a classification system, which hampers accumulation of knowledge. Also, because behavioral diagnosis is oriented toward assessing the problem in the present rather than looking into the past, relevant historical factors (e.g., onset, depth of dysfunction) may be overlooked. The behavioral literature does not reflect what types of clients have which types of problems.

In contrast to classifying children's problems according to diagnostic or other criteria, psychological theories explain how children acquire behavior, problematic or otherwise. The next section reviews prominent child developmental theories.

In summary, the strongest child assessment includes all three types of diagnosis—categorical-dimensional, empirical, and behavioral. Using all three methods together, the social worker can get a complete picture of the child's problems and strengths. Theories of child development guide the social worker's selection of assessment tools.

Psychological Issues

Psychological issues are considered in a complete childhood assessment. Those psychological issues discussed next include neuroscience, psychological, cognitive, affective, and learning theories.

Neuroscience Theories. Recent advances in neuroscience are beginning to elucidate brain biochemical, morphologic, and genetic indicators relevant to preventive and treatment outcome specificity and sensitivity for the mental disorders across the life span, already yielding promising new avenues for treatment. Genomic studies have also identified specific alleles that appear to operate protectively to shield some environmental risk-exposed and/or genetically predisposed children from onset of a range of mental disorders, while their relatives (even twins) without the allele succumb (Kim-Cohen et al., 2006; Smith-Osborne, Wilder, & Reep, 2013). As genetic testing technology advances, with concomitant decreases in cost and increases in accuracy of endophenotypic correlates with protective alleles, these genomic research results will assist child clinicians in targeting early environmental and intervention modifications to those most at risk. In the meantime, detailed assessment of the family history of mental disorders, symptoms, and related behaviors, especially among first-degree relatives, continues to be supported as an important part of the clinical assessment and diagnostic evaluation of children and adolescents. Continuum theories suggest that the family history should include consideration of subclinical threshold symptom clusters.

Continuum theories of mental disorder etiology are suggested by growing genetic evidence on gene sharing and common structure and function across major depressive disorder, bipolar disorder, schizophrenia, autism spectrum disorder, and attention deficit/hyperactivity disorder (ADHD) (Cross-Disorder Group of the Psychiatric Genomics Consortium, 2013). Gene sharing and common features have also been found across obsessive-compulsive disorder, Tourette's syndrome, other tic disorders, and trichotillomania (both hair- and skin-picking varieties; Bienvenu et al., 2009), and across generalized anxiety disorder, panic disorder, and agoraphobia. A linkage has been found between genetic heritability and all the anxiety disorders in children and adolescents, ranging from 36 to 65 percent, with panic disorder showing the highest genetic component (Sadock, Sadock, & Ruiz, 2015). Animal and situational phobias also show gene sharing, with social phobia–sharing genes with those as well as with the generalized anxiety disorder cluster (Hettema, Neale, & Kendler, 2001). Biochemical and molecular studies using brain imaging have also found shared neural circuit and connectivity deficit similarities among these same clusters of disorders. More-precise, individualized device and medication treatments, as well as refinements to behavioral treatments such as reconsolidation in fear extinction (Inda, Muravieva, & Alberini, 2011), are under study to build on these findings.

Neuroscience advances have also clarified that parental behaviors (e.g., substance abuse, mental illness) formerly hypothesized as causal environmental factors for conditions such as autism spectrum disorder and ADHD are in fact spurious, as they are actually correlates for third variable causation—namely, shared genetic predisposition. The parental behaviors are results or correlates of their untreated disorder or associated endophenotypes in the parents, and are consistent with longitudinal comorbidity studies that have shown, for example, that ADHD untreated in childhood is associated with higher rates of substance abuse in adolescence and adulthood than in both treated and healthy peers. Similar correlates may be involved in a proportion of parental/family environmental factors contributing, along with genetic factors and other neurobiological factors (e.g., decreased gray matter), to the etiology of conduct disorder (Sadock et al., 2015). Such combined factors appear to have different effects on girls and on boys in the development of conduct disorder (Sadock et al., 2015); this may explain the typically later age of onset for girls than for boys.

Environmental risks that have been validated by neuroscience studies on brain development suggest targets for autism spectrum disorder/ADHD preventive work by social workers, especially during the prenatal and neonatal periods. These include maternal nutrition; maternal stress/trauma; traffic-related air pollution; organophosphate pesticides; lead residues in soil, water, children's costume jewelry, and imported candies; and chemicals (i.e., phthalates) contained in perfume, cosmetics, and shampoo (Rosenberg & Pascual, 2015). Prevention of ADHD has longer-term implications for downstream conditions linked in a developmentally sequential trajectory from untreated and undertreated ADHD: oppositional defiant disorder and conduct disorder (Burke, Loeber, & Birmaher, 2004). These models also suggest that public health measures to improve overall ecological, physical, and social welfare can contribute to preventing these childhood-onset mental disorders or reducing severity, especially when these measures are targeted to the prenatal and neonatal life stages.

Major depression evidence consistently concludes the neurobiology underpinnings are the same across the lifespan, although clinical presentation may differ in the early onset forms (Sadock et al., 2015). Depressive disorders with child or adolescent onset have been found to have a genetic heritability component of 40 to 50 percent, with environmental stressors such as parental loss contributing a larger component in earlier childhood among those with genetic vulnerability (Luecken & Roubinov, 2012). Identified genetic vulnerability factors to depression include the lack of one to two long alleles in one serotonin transporter polymorphism (Caspi et al., 2003). Childhood onset depressive disorders are often preceded by a lengthy prodromal period characterized by anxiety, social withdrawal, and cognitive deterioration, and there is significant comorbidity of the mood and anxiety disorders across the life span (Sadock et al., 2015). Brain circuit models of depression have been derived from brain imaging studies across the life span. They suggest that appropriate and properly executed combinations of psychotherapy and medication are effective because they produce decreased cerebral blood flow targeted to two areas of the prefrontal cortex concomitant with reciprocal modulation of glucose metabolism in two other areas in the limbic and cortical brain regions. As discrete biomarkers of the mental disorders along the continuum and their individual variations are identified, their use can accelerate work to increase therapeutic effectiveness and to harness neural plasticity more fully as the operative mechanism of behavioral, device, and medication treatment. More efficacy trials are needed on the known psychotherapy modalities to investigate the range of operative fidelity, as effectiveness trials do not address this question of what level of treatment precision is necessary to produce effective outcomes (Rosenberg & Pascual, 2015).

Psychological Theories.   Barth (1986) suggests that children's problems may be time limited, because children often outgrow their problems. Stage theories of development, such as the theories of Piaget (1947/2001) and Erikson (1993), suggest that children go through fixed developmental stages. Given more credence in recent years, however, are theories that show the developmental process to be more flexible; that is, children must have the maturational readiness and learning opportunities in the environment before they can move ahead. Therefore, children develop at different rates. This also implies that all children can learn and change. The major child developmental theories can be categorized as cognitive, affective, or learning (Bloom, 1984).

Cognitive Theories.   The cognitive theories of Kohlberg (1981) and Piaget (1947/2001) describe development from the perspective of how one's mental processes perceive and affect one's experience in the world. The development of mental processes or structures is the focus of the theory. Information is believed to be assimilated into existing mental structures, which are represented as schemata; integration of new experiences occurs by accommodation. Piaget described four discrete stages to explain this development.

The first stage, the sensorimotor period, describes cognitive development from birth to two years of age. During this period, an infant's contact with the world is through the senses—that is, by sucking, tasting, touching, hearing, and seeing. Piaget (1947/2001) describes the essential tasks that infants have during this period: differentiation of self from others, or object permanence; recognition that external people or objects can be experienced through more than one sense; and beginning formation of cognitive schemata through interaction with others or objects.

The second stage, the preoperational period, occurs from ages two to seven and is composed of two phases, egocentric and intuitive. Egocentricism describes the child who is more attentive to current experiences and environment but who, through language development, begins to develop symbolic processing. This symbolic processing is continued in the intuitive phase.

The third stage, the period of concrete operations, lasts from ages seven to eleven. The development of logical thinking, classification, seriation, and conservation characterizes this stage, as does what Piaget (1947/2001) calls decentering, or moving away from the previous egocentric view of the world.

The fourth stage is the period of formal operations and lasts from ages eleven to fifteen. In this, the highest form of cognitive development that Piaget (1947/2001) described, children develop the ability to logically reason, both inductively and deductively.

Piaget (1947/2001) described children's moral development as occurring in two stages: heteronomy and autonomy. Children's adherence to the fixed rules of others, particularly the parents, characterizes the first stage. Children gradually move into the second phase, which is characterized by rules that can be negotiated and changed by mutual consent.

Kohlberg (1981) furthered the discussion of children's moral development by describing three levels of moral development: (a) premoral, (b) conventional, and (c) postconventional. Each level has two stages that describe the choices individuals have at each stage.

The premoral phase coincides with the preoperational stage of cognitive development. The two stages are punishment and obedience, in which the child obeys the rules to avoid being punished; and instrumental behavior, in which the child obeys to be rewarded.

The conventional phase is reached after the period of concrete operations begins. The two stages are conformity, in which the child seeks approval and tries to avoid disapproval from others; and law and order, in which the child obeys because of a respect for law and order.

The postconventional level is reached after the formal operations stage. The two stages are social contracts, in which the child makes rational decisions but the law is the final word; and the perception of universal ethical principles, in which the child bases moral decisions on his or her conscience.

The strongest research support for the cognitive model appears to be for the substages in the sensorimotor stage and for the concrete operational stage. Findings from studies on the other stages are less clear cut. Both Piaget (1947/2001) and Kohlberg (1981) have been criticized for the difficulty of replicating their research findings and by critics who believe that their view minimizes the role of the environment.

Affective Theories. Numerous theorists and practitioners concerned with personality development from the affective perspective have extended the work of Sigmund Freud. The affective perspective of child development is concerned primarily with the role of feelings in human behavior rather than the rate of thought, as with the cognitive theories described previously. Freud's work is described in five dimensions: (a) dynamic, (b) genetic or developmental, (c) topographical or depth, (d) structural, and (e) economic.

The dynamic dimension describes instinctual psychological energy, innate structures that direct behavior (e.g., the libido, an unconscious force that is expressed sexually). Freud also described the pleasure principle, a child's tendency to seek pleasure and avoid painful experiences or tensions.

The genetic or developmental dimension describes stages or periods that Freud believed to be a part of every individual's history. First, the oral period is represented by the infant's mouth and the taking in of food, and symbolically the taking in of other nourishment such as emotional warmth. The developing child then faces the challenge of toilet training, which leads to the second stage, which Freud called the "anal stage." The child's ability to exert control over his or her bodily functions, and perhaps to be in conflict with parental demands, may contribute to problems that continue in the individual's adult life. The third stage is referred to as the phallic period and involves the child's developing awareness of his or her genitalia. The next stage, the latency period, is a time when sexual issues are suppressed when the child enters school and becomes refocused on other issues. However, in the genital period, which begins in puberty, sexual issues again become important to the developing child. Children are believed to need to achieve mastery in each of these stages before they can successfully move on to the others. If children do not achieve mastery, they can become fixated at any one point and will display signs of this lack of resolution.

In the topographical or depth dimension, Freud described three personality components believed to account for behavior: (a) the unconscious, (b) the conscious, and (c) the preconscious. The unconscious component is outside of the person's awareness and believed to be mostly composed of the id. The conscious component is a smaller area of awareness, focused on something in the present. The preconscious is outside current awareness but accessible. The material in the unconscious is believed to be accessible only through mechanisms such as a slip of the tongue or somatically as in the case of phobias.

The structural dimension describes the personality, as divided into id, ego, and superego. The id is believed to be unconscious and represents the primitive portion of the personality, which operates on the basis of the pleasure principle. The ego develops next and is the rational portion of the personality. It seeks to express id impulses in a more rational fashion. Finally, the superego is composed of the ego ideal—that is, the information about good and bad that the child learns from the parents, the conscience, and the information about good and bad that the child learns from the parent's actions.

The economic dimension describes how children use their inherent energy. Psychic investment toward a specific object is called "cathexis." External conditions may prohibit expending energy toward an object, which is called "anticathexis." In the latter case, the child forms internal mechanisms to block or delay the energy.

Erikson (1993) described eight psychosocial developmental issues: trust, autonomy, initiative, industry, identity, intimacy, generativity, and integrity. These issues correspond to eight stages of the life span, from infancy and early childhood to old age. As did Freud, Erikson postulated that the child had to resolve the tasks of one stage before moving on to the tasks of the next stage.

Affective theories have been criticized for their lack of empirical evidence and for the difficulty involved in operationalizing the concepts. However, recent attempts to study psychoanalytic theory have provided some support for some of the concepts.

Learning Theories.   So far, we have reviewed thinking and feeling theories of child development. Learning theories focus on acting, which is behavior itself. Three learning models are discussed here: (a) respondent or classical conditioning, (b) operant conditioning, and (c) social learning theory. These models share the common idea that behavior is learned.

Pavlov's (1927/1960) respondent, or classical, conditioning model illustrates the learning process as follows: Pavlov found that food (a natural or unconditional stimulus) elicited a salivation response. He paired the natural stimulus with another stimulus, a bell. This second stimulus, after repeated pairings with the natural stimulus, also elicited the salivation response without the presentation of the food. The second stimulus is now called the "conditioned stimulus" and has the power to condition other stimuli. This conditioning process occurs with objects, persons, and verbal behavior as well; for example, a baby is comforted by his or her baby blanket, which was conditioned by pairings with mother and feedings.

Skinner's (1972) operant conditioning model proposes that behavior is learned as a consequence of the rewards or punishments that follow the behavior. If the behavior is positively reinforced, it is more likely to occur again; if an aversive experience follows the behavior, it is less likely to occur again. If the parent or teacher gives attention only when a child acts disruptively at home or in class, the child will continue to be disruptive.

Schedules or contingencies of reinforcement determine how quickly behavior is learned and how well established it will be. Continuous reinforcement encourages behavior to be emitted more quickly, whereas intermittent reinforcement establishes behavior at a slower rate. Behavior reinforced intermittently maintains longer after cessation of reinforcement than does behavior reinforced continuously. For example, if a child is rewarded with candy every time she carries her dishes to the sink, she will learn this behavior quickly but stop the behavior if the reward is stopped. A child rewarded only some of the time will take longer to learn the behavior; however, once the child learns the behavior, he or she will maintain it for a longer time, because the child thinks a reward could be forthcoming.

Bandura's (1977) social learning theory elaborates on learning by respondent or operant mechanisms, which contributes the idea of vicarious learning; that is, learning may occur by observation of a model and by observation of the consequences of the model's behavior. Bandura's studies on the vicarious development of aggressive social behavior have contributed to the debate on causes of aggressive behavior in children and others. Bandura showed that children viewing adults modeling aggressive behavior were more likely to exhibit the same aggressive behavior than children who did not view these adult models.

Learning theorists have contributed more empirical research to support their theoretical views than have cognitive or affective schools of thought. Bloom (1984) recommends, however, that "until such time as enough of the evidence is in to maintain or to discontinue use of one or another theory, the student is probably most wise to study their major representatives and try to become facile in all of them" (p. 312). The following sections review social theories, familial theories, and environmental theories.

Social Issues

Child problems are a symptom not of individual pathology but of a malfunctioning ecosystem, according to some (Barth, 1986; Harper-Dorton & Herbert 1999; Janzen, Harris, & Jordan, & Franklin, 2005). These researchers assert that positive changes are longer lived when children's problems are assessed and treated in the broader context of the family and the environment. Next, we review issues related to familial and environmental theories that affect child problems.

Familial Theories.   Children's problems are related to the number of stressful events the family experiences. Also, as children grow, their normal developmental changes may lead to maladjustment. Isolated families and those living in rural settings often have limited resources to help their children adjust to developmental changes (Barth, 1986). Family isolation with limited access to resources and supportive extended family members can be a stress factor for both parents and children (Openshaw & Halvorson, 2005).

Physical or mental issues, or parent or family morale problems, may affect children (Jordan & Hoefer, 2002). Domestic violence, either a single incident or long-term violence, affects a child's emotional state and development. The more intense and long lasting the exposure, the more severely the child is affected. Direct exposure to violence, such as when the child is hit, or indirect exposure, such as when the child merely hears parents fighting, both have devastating effects on children (Openshaw & Halvorson, 2005). Likewise, child abuse and neglect influence the child's development. Early trauma or emotional neglect interferes with the brain's development of explicit memory and the capacity for empathy and modulation of impulses. Continued trauma may also affect cognitive and social development. Persistent and severe abuse may result in pervasive developmental delays (Davies, 2004; Nelson & Carver, 1998; Perry, 1997).

Trauma that results from abuse, neglect (e.g., removal from the home or placement in foster care), and exposure to violence may interfere with a child's cognitive development. According to Perry (2002), trauma can create a lifetime loss of potential. Accordingly, assessment of cognitive abilities must consider exposure to trauma.

Family changes or transitions cause stress (Jordan & Cobb, 2001). The traditional family that consists of a father who goes out to work and a mother who stays home with the two kids is virtually nonexistent. New family styles, such as dual working couples, single-parent families, and remarried or blended families all have associated stressors. Other family transitions, such as the birth or adoption of a sibling or children leaving for college, can also cause stress on the family system. Any family change may be expected to cause at least temporary discomfort for the parents and children, and any loss of money or status can be extremely devastating.

Although more and more mothers work outside the home and share the role of provider, women still do the majority of the housework, with resultant fatigue, morale problems, and resentment. A mother's working outside the home may benefit the family by helping her feel better about herself and by enhancing the family income. Problems may arise, however, when family members move from work or school to home life. Other parental job factors that may affect children's adjustment include parental job loss or transfer. Parent psychopathology, divorce, or spouse abuse can also affect children.

Environmental Theories.   Parents' friendships and other external relationships define their perception of their children's adjustment (or lack of it) (Barth, 1986). Parents learn what is "normal" and how their children stack up to other children by comparing them with others in their neighborhood. Parents' social supports, friends, family, and neighbors all informally support parenting efforts. Some communities have more formal support systems, such as parenting classes and alcoholic support groups for parents.

The primary settings in which children are expected to perform are the home and the school (Barth, 1986). Studies show that children's personalities and environments determine their behavior. Some studies find that children behave differently at home than at school, but others find that children's behavior is consistent across settings. Children need social, cognitive, and self-management competencies to be successful at home and at school.

Social competencies include the ability to accept influence, exert influence, learn from models, accept reprimands, negotiate with others, protect oneself from others, groom oneself, engage the company of others and avoid isolation, and resolve conflicts with strategies such as problem solving.

Cognitive competencies include cognitive skills for solving interpersonal problems: identifying the problem, generating alternative solutions, seeing the other party's viewpoint, seeing the consequences of the alternative solutions, evaluating the consequences, and choosing the best solution.

Self-management competencies include commitment, goal setting, arousal management, self-monitoring, evaluation, and self-administration of consequences (self-reinforcement).

Individual factors, such as social competencies, cognitive abilities, and self-management skills, contribute to a child's ability to thrive in difficult situations. Likewise, the child's family and environment may aid the child's normal development. Family factors that encourage the child's normal development include secure attachment with a positive and warm parental relationship, parental support during stress, parental marital stability, structure, and high parental expectations. Environmental factors that aid a child's normal development include middle-class and above socioeconomic status, available health-care and social services, consistent parental employment, adequate housing, family religious participation, good schools, and supportive adults outside the family (Davies, 2004).

The child's level of motivation—the interaction between individuals and their environments—is an important part of the environmental picture. A lack of motivation indicates that social or material incentives should be considered for the child. For example, parents can reward the child for completing homework assignments with a point system. The child can then exchange points for toys, privileges, and so forth.

Finally, the child's culture is an important part of assessing the child's environment. It is important to know how the members of the child's culture and ethnic background define child problems, child discipline, and so forth, as discussed in the following section on children of color.

Issues of Children of Color

Children and families of color require special consideration and should be assessed as framed by Erikson's (1993) developmental stages with ecological systems, and with a cross-cultural perspective (Gibbs & Huang, 2003; Janzen et al., 2005). Canino and Spurlock (2000) discuss a multiaxial approach to assessment and intervention with children of color. This approach should be spearheaded by a culturally competent practitioner who is willing to consider ethnicity and immigration status in assessment and who is willing to advocate for change in larger systems, such as school and community, as part of the intervention process.

Psychosocial Adjustment.   Individual psychosocial adjustment includes several special considerations. Low-income minority children may suffer from the effects of malnutrition, which leads to lack of energy and stunted growth; therefore, a physical exam may be indicated. Children's affect may be a product of cultural variation; for example, not making eye contact may indicate respect for adults rather than lack of respect. Particular ethnic groups may differently define self-esteem, interpersonal competence, achievement, and attitudes toward autonomy; therefore, it is important to check one's assumptions and determine the norms for ethnic groups. Ethnicity and culture affect all aspects of a child's life. Migration and acculturation experiences vary among minorities and can be stressful events, especially if a youth emigrates from a war-torn country. Psychosocial adjustment should be carefully assessed in this context (Guarnaccia & Lopez, 1998). Achievement might be defined in ways other than the traditional majority-culture definition of educational achievement (Nurmi, 1993); if so, assessment should focus on the child's success in other areas, such as sports or music. Beliefs about development and behavior vary widely cross-culturally. Even the emergence of language is regarded uniquely according to ethnicity. Some cultures value characteristics such as dependence and passivity, whereas others prize independence and assertiveness (Johnson-Powell, Yamamoto, & Arroyo, 1997). Ethnic groups have different methods of teaching children how to manage aggression and control impulses. Some may use guilt, and others may use shame. Finally, the child's coping and defense mechanisms that protect the child from anxiety may be either externalizing (e.g., acting out, yelling) or internalizing (e.g., withdrawing from social situations).

Relationships with Family.   A second area for assessment is family relationships. Ethnicity and social class influence family size, structure, traditions, and so forth, all of which influence the child's role in the family. Some important characteristics that may prescribe norms or expectations for children include age, sex, birth order, physical characteristics, and personality traits. Families also differ in terms of parental authority, disciplinary practices, communication styles, and language fluency, all of which should be topics in the assessment. Recognizing the family beliefs, the level of acculturation and the degree of involvement in neighborhood and community can provide important information in assessment, as can religion. In some cases, religion plays an important role in health issues as well as in the family value system. Acknowledging not only the parents but also extended family, and significant adults such as healers and religious leaders, can improve the prospects for successful intervention (Barona & de Barona, 2000; Canino & Spurlock, 2000).

School Adjustment and Achievement.   School adjustment and achievement should be assessed from four perspectives: (a) psychological adjustment, (b) behavioral adjustment, (c) academic achievement, and (d) relationships with peers. Children from low-income minority families sometimes have difficulty making the transition to school environment from homes that are different from the societal norm. Families may lack education and view the educational system negatively, they may be unfamiliar with school requirements, or they may have language and other difficulties. Therefore, a review of records, sensitive interviews with parents and children, and interviews with teachers can establish rapport and enlist needed support for intervention. Furthermore, expectations and cultural norms can emerge to direct the clinician in interpreting the assessment in the appropriate ethnic context. When assessing or testing a minority child, the practitioner may want to suspend some procedures. For example, use of time-limited standardized tests may work unnecessarily against the child (Gopaul-McNicol & Armour-Thomas, 2001).

Adolescents may fear school or fear the rejection they may suffer from being different. Minority children account for a proportion of students with behavior problems that result from their propensity to solve problems or to cope with the environment by acting out. Behavior problems, however, may be symptoms of other, more worrisome problems, such as poor health from inadequate nutrition or health care. In addition, the social pressures of being a minority, of feeling disempowered, of chronic poverty, and anxiety predispose these children and adolescents to depression (Roberts & Chen, 1995; Siegel, Aneshensel, Taub, Cantwell, & Driscoll, 1998). Minority students do not generally do as well in school as white students and have more problems with dropping out and with expulsion and suspension. Some of the problems may lie with inappropriate testing procedures; IQ and achievement tests might not be culturally sensitive. Also, children may have motivational deficits or lack of parental support. The child's study skills should also be assessed.

Peer Relationships.   Peer relationships are an indicator of the minority child's well-being. Peer interactions, or lack thereof, and degree of involvement may indicate the child's perception of self in relation to the larger society. Peer-group assessment should be done at both the school and the community level, as the child may have different experiences in the two settings. Peer interactions, and particularly opposite-sex relationships, may be an issue for biracial youths.

Adaptation to the Community.   The child's overall community relationships should be assessed, as these may indicate the child's adjustment. Specific areas to look for include the child's group and community involvement, as well as special interests or abilities that could help the child develop a sense of competence. Gibbs and Huang (2003) stress that these assessment guidelines should serve as general guides to assessing children in their unique culture. They point out that there is variation within ethnic groups and that one should consider the uniqueness of each child.

One must always, also, be aware of the conditions by which the child arrived in the mainstream culture. Immigrant children have unique issues, such as, for example, issues resulting from the trauma of hurriedly leaving a country torn by war or political upheaval, whereas children of color who were born into minority status may be fully acculturated. In all cases, children may experience a sense of belonging to both or neither culture (the minority and the majority culture). In assessing this factor, clinicians should consider, too, how willing the majority culture has been to confer equal status on these children and their families (Canino & Spurlock, 2000).

In summary, a complete childhood assessment should address four broad areas: (a) diagnosis, (b) psychological issues, (c) social issues, and (d) issues of children of color. The following section reviews methodologies available to aid the assessment process.

ASSESSMENT METHODS

This section reviews some of the many assessment tools currently available to assist in the assessment of children. These tools can be categorized as global techniques and rapid assessment scales. To be valid, an assessment must consider the individual's unique experience and research specific to the individual's problem. Global techniques, such as ecomaps or genograms (qualitative), help the social worker get a big picture of how the child is functioning and in which areas problems exist. For instance, a genogram may reveal a family history of depression, which helps explain the child's behavioral symptoms. This can guide the social worker to then use a self-report (quantitative) instrument to explore and measure the child's depression. Furthermore, measurement of depression may use a depression instrument that focuses on cognitive, affective, or behavioral symptomatology according to the manner in which the child expresses his or her depression.

Evidence-Based Assessment

Relevant research consists of a combination of cross-sectional and longitudinal surveys, experimental research, and case studies. Relevant and sound research findings provide base-rate estimates (incidence and prevalence) of specific problems in the community, estimate the rates of co-occurring problems, and identify key risk and resiliency factors (both developmental and current) that are expected to contribute to the client's problems or predict recovery. Research also provides estimates for the relative strength of risk and resiliency factors, explains the multidimensional nature of the individual's problems, supports or invalidates theories, and provides an empirical and theoretical basis for testing (O'Hare, 2005). Practitioners must review the professional literature for studies that measure the effectiveness of various assessment tools to select the one that is most appropriate for each client. Many assessment tools may be found on Web sites, some of which list articles that provide evidence of the effectiveness of that assessment tool.

Global Techniques

Global techniques for assessing children help obtain a global picture of children's functioning and the problems they encounter. The three qualitative techniques mentioned here are (a) interviews, (b) play, and (c) sculpting or other family techniques.

Interviews.   Interviews are the most effective qualitative assessments. "To conduct an informed qualitative assessment, practitioners must choose a human behavior model that is relevant to the client's presenting problems and based on research specific to the relevant problem area" (O'Hare, 2005, p. 15; see also Wakefield, 1996). Interviews are the most commonly used technique for assessing children, parents, and teachers (Hughes & Baker, 1991; McConaughy, 1996). Sattler (1988) reviewed the use of interviews for gleaning information from children and their parents. Goals for the interview include establishing rapport, understanding the presenting problem, and obtaining information from a broad range of perspectives. In addition to the guidelines presented in chapter 1 for the integrative skills protocol, important areas to include in the assessment interview of children are interests, school, peers, family, fears or worries, self-image, mood or feelings, somatic concerns, thought disorders, aspirations, expectations, and fantasies. Additional topics for adolescents include heterosexual or homosexual relationships, sexual activity, and drug or alcohol usage.

Structured and semistructured interviews can elicit this wide range of information. Some structured interviews require lengthy time to administer and, in some cases, extensive training for the clinician; laypersons can conduct and score others. Examples of structured interviews that do not require specialized training include the Diagnostic Interview Schedule for Children (Columbia University DISC Development Group, 2006) and the Diagnostic Interview for Children and Adolescents–Revised (Reich & Welner, 1990). These instruments yield information that is easily codified for data analysis and for diagnosing mental disorders in children and adolescents. However, these instruments may not be as flexible as semistructured interviews, which provide not only standardized questions but also some adaptability for the age and personality of the child. The Diagnostic Interview Schedule for Children is being revised for the DSM-5 dimensional approach, which will allow more adaptability for these factors.

The Semistructured Clinical Interview for Children and Adolescents (McConaughy & Achenbach, 2001) was specifically designed for use with children aged six to eighteen years. This instrument allows the interviewer to adjust the order of questions to the natural order of the discussion with the child; it also provides information about a variety of facets in the child's life, including peer group and school, not just mental health status. The Semistructured Clinical Interview for Children and Adolescents shows moderate to good test-retest reliability (0.54 to 0.89) for all of its subscales and generally good concurrent validity (McConaughy, 1996). Social workers should be mindful that the reliability of all interviews rests solidly with the interviewer—that is, in how careful the interviewer is in following testing protocol, how prepared the interviewer is to work with the child, and how conscientiously the interviewer scores the data. In general, the reliability of interviews across time and sometimes across subjects (child and parent) can be questionable, particularly structured interviews with children younger than twelve.

Interviewing parents generates essential information in the assessment of and intervention with children and adolescents. Barkley (2005) recognized parent interviews not only as a source for diagnosis but also as the primary way to gauge the level of family distress and to understand more about the child's problems with relationships. In addition, interviewing the parents gives them the chance to express their concerns, their frustrations, and their systems for coping with the child's problems. This process establishes rapport with the parent that is fundamental to successful intervention or treatment later on (Jenson & Potter, 1990).

The practitioner should ask parents about the referral problem; the ways they have attempted to deal with the problem; the child's medical, developmental, educational, and social history; family history; prior treatment for the problem; results of past treatment; and expectations about the evaluation. As with child interviews, parents can provide more comprehensive information through semistructured interviews that may include standardized rating scales such as the Child Behavior Checklist (Achenbach, 1991) or the Basic Assessment System for Children (Reynolds & Kamphaus, 2003). A primary goal of interviews with parents is to define the child's problems in observable, discreet behaviors that facilitate targeted intervention and measurable progress.

Teachers should also be interviewed when appropriate. It is appropriate to involve teachers when the child's problem is exhibited in the school setting. They should be asked about their view of the referral problem, the antecedents and consequences of the problem, any attempts that have been made to solve the problem, how others (teachers and students) react to the problem, school academic performance, their view of the family, and their expectations and suggestions for school-based interventions (McConaughy, 1996). Standardized teacher rating scales include the Basic Assessment System for Children (Reynolds & Kamphaus, 2003) and the Behavior Evaluation Scale-2 (McCarney & Leigh, 1990). More-specific problems, such as attention and hyperactivity or social skills difficulty, are addressed by scales like the Conners's Teacher Rating Scale (Conners, 2008) and the School Social Behavior Scales (Merrell, 1993, 2007). Of course, personal interviews with teachers are useful, as well, and can uncover any negative feelings the teacher has toward the child or any underlying reasons for referral.

The family may also be interviewed as a whole. Information about the following subjects can be obtained from the social worker's observation of the family or through direct questioning: each member's view of the child's problem(s); family interactional patterns; family communication patterns; family social and cultural norms and values; and child's behavior individually, as compared with child's behavior in the family group. The Darlington Family Assessment System (Wilkinson, 2000) presents a thorough method for describing and assessing families by providing information from the child's point of view, the parents' point of view, and the total family point of view. This framework offers a semi-structured interview and rating scale with explicit directions about how to implement the system in clinical work with children and families. A fundamental advantage to this model is its adaptability to a variety of families and theoretical approaches.

Sattler (1988) gives guidelines for interpreting the assessment data and sharing it with the child and parents. Before practitioners meet with the child and parents, they should synthesize the data gathered from the interview and evaluate their own feelings about it, look for common patterns or themes, try to account for any discrepancies they may find, look for indicators of the child's strengths and weaknesses, and look for resources for change or for coping. Then practitioners should meet with the child to provide reassurance, verify their hypothesis about the problem(s), and present findings. The practitioner can meet with the parents to describe the child's problems and the plan for treatment and to address any parental issues or problems that may affect the child. Practioners should be sensitive to the parents' feelings while also protecting the child's right to confidentiality.

Play.   With younger children, the social worker can gather information during games or other play activities more efficiently than in a formal interview session. Asking children to engage in unstructured play, such as drawing pictures of themselves or their family and then telling about what they have drawn or making models of themselves out of clay, may help the social worker establish rapport and learn valuable information. Structured therapy games are also available (e.g., the *Thinking, Feeling, and Doing Game,* 1973) and may serve the same purpose.

Sattler (1988) offers guidelines for interpreting children's unstructured play. These include how the child enters the room, initiates play activities, expends energy while playing, moves while manipulating the play materials, paces him- or herself during play, moves his or her body in play, verbalizes while playing, integrates play activities, exhibits creativity, uses products, and reflects attitudes about adults during play. Other important considerations in assessing children's play are the age appropriateness of the child's play, as well as the tone of play (e.g., hostile, impatient). Cross-culturally, children's play mirrors social role and family structure and may display symptoms of family problems such as uninvolved or neglectful parenting (Berk, 2007).

Sculpting or Other Family Techniques.   Older children may be assessed in the context of the family system by using techniques such as sculpting (Frieson, 1993) or ecomapping (Sheafor, Horejsi, & Horejsi, 1988). These qualitative techniques also can help establish rapport with an older child who may be reluctant, at first, to sit down and participate in a formal interview. Sculpting requires the child or other family member to address family members as if they were made of clay and mold them accordingly. The social worker might request that the child mold the family to depict a typical family scenario, such as when they have supper together. The child then places members in relation to one another and molds their faces to convey moods. The child would also place him- or herself in the picture. Then the family would be asked to talk about how it felt to be in the scene and whether they agreed with the depiction. Other members might then remold the family as they see it.

Ecomapping depicts the family in the larger community or societal system. It is done with paper and pencil and requires family members to identify external, environmental issues that affect each member (see figure 1.2). This form of assessment not only sets up collaboration between the clinician and the family but also encourages interaction among family members that may facilitate needed change. In addition, ecomapping allows parents to view their families more objectively, which may obviate defensiveness and resistance (Miley, O'Melia, & DuBois, 2006).

Frieson (1993) describes other family techniques that might be helpful to children and their families. The family may be asked to construct a family floor plan. Each member draws his or her house floor plan and then answers questions about each room: What is the mood of the room? What are the smells, sounds, colors? Is there a special room? Are there issues of closeness or privacy in the house? How does the house fit in with the neighborhood? Frieson also discusses the use of metaphors (e.g., animals, objects) to describe oneself or other family members.

Self-Report Techniques and Scales

Self-report techniques give children the opportunity to give information about themselves and their problems after rapport has been established using the qualitative methods described in the preceding section. The measures described here are (a) standardized instruments, (b) self-anchored and other rating scales, and (c) self-observation. Because evaluating children is typically a multiaxial process, many standardized instruments have companion scales for parents and teachers. Obtaining multiple views of the child's problem helps provide a more complete picture of the situation.

Standardized Instruments.   The Depression Self-Rating Scale, identified by Corcoran and Fischer (2000; see figure 5.1), was designed by P. Birleson to measure the extent and severity of depression in children ages seven to thirteen. The scale asks questions about children's mood and thoughts, as well as physiologic or somatic problems. The test has fair reliability (alpha = 0.86 and 0.73, test-retest = 0.80) and good validity (correlation = 0.81) with the Children's Depression Inventory. The Children's Depression Inventory (Kovacs, 1992) was created to determine depressive symptoms in children ages seven to seventeen. Based on the Beck Depression Inventory, the Inventory requires that children identify statements that characterize themselves over the course of the previous two weeks on a scale of 0 to 2. Although the test-retest reliability of the Children's Depression Inventory is moderate (0.38–0.87), it has shown good internal consistency (Cronbach's alpha of 0.80), and it was normed on a sample of more than 1,200 boys and girls from various ethnic and socioeconomic backgrounds.

The Hare Self-Esteem Scale, another commonly used scale, measures children's self-esteem in three settings: (a) at home, (b) at school, and (c) with peers. Each of the three subscales comprises ten items; a total score is computed, and higher scores indicate higher self-esteem. Reliability for the general scale is 0.74; validity was 0.83 with both the Coopersmith Self-Esteem Inventory and the Rosenberg Self-Esteem Scale (Corcoran & Fischer, 2000). The population sampled to norm the measures was fifth- and eighth-grade students, including 41 Blacks and 207 Whites, 115 boys and 137 girls (Corcoran & Fischer, 2000).

Figure 5.1   Depression Self-Rating Scale

Please answer as honestly as you can by indicating at left the number that best refers to how you have felt over the past week. There are no right answers; it is important to say how you have felt.

> 1 = Most of the time
> 2 = Sometimes
> 3 = Never

____   1. I look forward to things as much as I used to.
____   2. I sleep very well.
____   3. I feel like crying.
____   4. I like to go out to play.
____   5. I feel like running away.
____   6. I get tummy aches.
____   7. I have lots of energy.
____   8. I enjoy my food.
____   9. I can stick up for myself.
____   10. I think life isn't worth living.
____   11. I am good at things I do.
____   12. I enjoy the things I do as much as I used to.
____   13. I like talking with my family.
____   14. I have horrible dreams.
____   15. I feel very lonely.
____   16. I am easily cheered up.
____   17. I feel so sad I can hardly stand it.
____   18. I feel very bored.

SOURCE: Used with permission of Peter Birleson, Royal Children's Hospital, Fleminton Road, Parkville, Victoria 3052, Australia.

The Multidimensional Self-Concept Scale (Bracken, 1992) was designed for use with children age nine to nineteen. Comprising 150 items, this four-point Likert scale contains six subscales: social, competence, affect, academic, family, and physical. This scale shows test-retest reliability coefficients ranging from 0.85 to 0.97 in the subscales, with higher coefficients for the total scale ranging from 0.97 to 0.99. In addition, concurrent validity of 0.69 to 0.83 has been established with the Coopersmith Self-Esteem Inventory.

The Assessment of Interpersonal Relations (Bracken & Kelley, 1993) was constructed to evaluate the interpersonal relationships between children and their peers, parents, and teachers. Children are asked to rate their level of agreement with the same thirty-five statements as they pertain to all three groups. Normed on 2,501 U.S. children and adolescents aged nine to nineteen, this assessment displays high test-retest reliability (0.93–0.96) and good discriminant validity across the subscales. This multidimensional instrument yields comprehensive information about the quality of relationships from the child's perspective.

The Impulsivity Scale (figure 5.2) was designed by Hirschfield, Sutton-Smith, and Rosenberg and measures the child's tendency toward restlessness, rule breaking, and indulgence in horseplay. Reliability was good (test-retest = 0.85), and criterion-referenced validity was established by significant correlations with teacher ratings of children. The test was normed on 127 fifth and sixth graders.

Other children's scales include the Children's Action Tendency Scale, by Deluty; the Children's Cognitive Assessment Questionnaire, by Asher; the Common Belief Inventory for Students, by Hooper and Layne; and the Compulsive Eating Scale, by Kagan and Squires (see Corcoran & Fischer, 2000). In their review of clinical measures for social workers, Corcoran and Fischer included a number of family relationship scales appropriate for children to complete. The best example is the Hudson Family Scale Package, which measures the child's relationship with mother, father, and siblings, as well as the child's overall family satisfaction.

Self-Anchored and Other Rating Scales. Children can rate the intensity of problems such as depression or anxiety on self-anchored scales (figure 5.3). Children may be asked, for example, to develop anchors for a one- to seven-point scale describing their depression from the lowest to the highest they could possibly imagine. Anchors are the specific behavioral indicators of depression for that child.

Another type of self-rating scale used with children measures their anxiety on a one-hundred-point scale (Jordan, Franklin, & Corcoran, 2010). The scale can be drawn to look like a thermometer, with a red center that moves up and down. When children push the red part all the

Figure 5.2   Impulsivity Scale

Decide whether each statement is true as applied to you or false as applied to you. If a statement is True or Mostly True as applied to you, circle T. If a statement is False or Mostly False as applied to you, circle F.

T F   1. I like to keep moving around.
(I don't like to keep moving around.)

T F   2. I make friends quickly.
(I don't make friends quickly.)

T F   3. I like to wrestle and to horse around.
(I don't like to wrestle and to horse around.)

T F   4. I like to shoot with bows and arrows.
(I don't like to shoot with bows and arrows.)

T F   5. I must admit I'm a pretty good talker.
(I must admit that I'm not a good talker.)

T F   6. Whenever there's a fire engine going someplace, I like to follow it.
(If there's a fire engine going someplace, I don't usually like to follow it.)

T F   7. My home life is not always happy.
(My home life is always happy.)

T F   8. When things get quiet, I like to stir up a little fuss.
(I usually don't like to stir up a little fuss when things get quiet.)

T F   9. I am restless.
(I am not restless.)

T F 10. I don't think I'm as happy as other people.
(I think I'm happy as other people.)

T F 11. I get into tricks at Halloween.
(I don't get into tricks at Halloween.)

T F 12. I like being "it" when we play games of that sort.
(I don't like being "it" when we play games of that sort.)

T F 13. It's fun to push people off the edge into the pool.
(It's not fun to push people off the edge into the pool.)

T F 14. I play hooky sometimes.
(I never play hooky.)

T F 15. I like to go with lots of other kids, not just one.
(I usually like to go with one kid, rather than lots of them.)

T F 16. I like throwing stones at targets.
(I don't like throwing stones at targets.)

T F 17. It's hard to stick to the rules if you're losing the game.
(It's not hard to stick to the rules even if you are losing the game.)

T F 18. I like to dare kids to do things.
(I don't like to dare kids to do things.)

T F 19. I'm not known as a hard and steady worker.
(I'm known as a hard and steady worker.)

SOURCE: Used with permission of Paul Hirschfield, Hirschfield and Associates, 529 Pharr Road, Atlanta, GA 30305.

Figure 5.3   Children's Self-Anchored Anxiety at Bedtime Scale

1 .... 2 .... 3 .... 4 .... 5 .... 6 7
Least Anxiety   Mid-Level Anxiety   Most Anxiety

Relaxed, sleeps peacefully through the night.	Falls asleep, wakes 1–2 times during the night, reports bad dreams in the morning.	Trouble falling asleep, sleeps fitfully, nightmares or wakes up screaming.

way up (scale reads one hundred points), they are told this indicates that they are the most anxious they could ever imagine. When they lower the reading to zero, they are told that they are not anxious at all. Children are then instructed to move the red center to indicate their current amount of anxiety.

Self-Observation.   Children may be asked to observe their own behavior. One format is to make a simple problem checklist that asks children to check off the specific problems for which they would like help. This type of problem checklist can be made to reflect agency services. An example of such a checklist developed for completion by children receiving social work services in a school setting appears in figure 5.4. Children may also be asked to collect data on their own or other's behavior using simple data collection methods. For example, children can staple a three-by-five card to the inside of their school folder and keep a tally of the number of times they talk in class or the number of times they get out of their chair. Children may be asked to record information about family members or peer interactions using similar methods.

Ratings by Others

Parents and teachers are frequently asked to provide information about children's problems. Sometimes other professionals are asked to help in the assessment. One popular instrument is the Achenbach Child Behavior Checklist (Achenbach & Edelbrock, 1983). This is perhaps the most frequently used scale of its type. It has been shown to provide less-accurate results for children who are mildly retarded, but it has demonstrated clear accuracy for children of color when used in translation, identifying not only the impairment but also its severity (Bird, Gould, Rubio-Stipec, Staghezza, & Canino, 1991; Embregts, 2000). The Child Behavior Checklist has been used to analyze premorbid behavioral differences among young adults diagnosed with schizophrenia and to analyze behavior functioning

Figure 5.4   Problem Checklist

Name _____   Age _____   Grade _____
Who referred you to the social worker? _____

The following list are problems about which other kids at school have talked to the social worker. Please check all of the following that are problems for you.

____ New student adjustment
____ Failing grades
____ Lack of motivation in class
____ Disruptive classroom behavior
____ Truancy
____ Problems with a teacher
____ Excessive tardiness
____ Drug policy violation
____ Organization skills
____ Problems with peers
____ Conflicts with siblings-parents
____ Low self-concept
____ Poor social skills
____ Concern about friend
____ Depression
____ Withdrawn and isolated
____ Aggressive behavior
____ Failure to serve detention
____ Overweight or other physical problems
____ Physical abuse by parents
____ Other (please specify) _____

---

for children in foster care (Armsden, Pecora, Payne, & Szatkiewicz, 2000; Rossi, Pollice, Daneluzzo, Marinangeli, & Stratta, 2000).

Functional behavioral assessments are conducted in schools to determine the antecedents and consequences of specific behaviors. A behavior observation monitors an individual's actions by visual or electronic means while recording quantitative and/or qualitative information about those actions (Cohen & Swerdlik, 2005). "A functional assessment of behavior asks what the behavior is, when it occurs, what the activating events are, and what happens as a result of the behavior both positive and negative" (Openshaw, 2008, p. 39; see also Boys Town, 1989).

Derived from the Child Behavior Checklist, the Child Behavior Checklist–Depression scale (Clarke, Lewinsohn, Hops, & Seeley, 1992) was designed to identify symptoms of depression as noted by both adolescents and parents. Each checklist has fifteen items. Although it possesses adequate criterion-related validity with diagnoses of depression from psychiatrists and acceptable concurrent validity with other measures of depression, the Child Behavior Checklist–Depression has demonstrated only moderate ranges of reliability (test-retest = 0.20–0.57; interrater = 0.35–0.59). It remains useful, however, as a general index of depression and for its adaptability across sources.

The Inventory of Children's Individual Differences (Halverson et al., 2003) provides researchers with an age- and culture-neutral instrument designed specifically to assess the five-factor model of personality in children and adolescents ages two to fifteen using parental, nonparental, or self-reports (Deal, Halvorson, Martin, Victor, & Baker, 2007).

Another frequently used instrument is the Hilson Adolescent Profile (Inwald, Brobst, & Morrisey, 1988). Appendix 5A presents a copy of the computer-generated report provided when the test is sent in for computer scoring. In addition to these specially designed instruments, parents, teachers, or other significant people in the child's environment may fill out the same self-report measures mentioned in the previous section. For example, if the child is asked to complete the Hare Self-Esteem Scale, the parent is also asked to fill out the measure for the child. This way, the social worker has two different perspectives on the child's self-esteem.

Parents and teachers, as well as social workers, may do direct observation and recording of children's behavior. Four types of recording are recommended. Narrative recording is a qualitative recording of an event. Special attention is given to the behavior and to the setting in which the behavior occurs. For example, a child may be observed while interacting in the classroom. The social worker might look for specific behaviors to occur, such as getting out of one's seat. Other, external conditions that might affect the child would also be observed and noted, such as actions of the teacher, actions of other students, and distracting aspects of the classroom setting itself. Interval recording is continuous, direct observation of the child during specified time periods divided into equal intervals. For example, the social worker may look to see whether a child got out of his seat during a given interval. Frequency recording notes each occurrence of the behavior. For example, each occurrence of the child getting out of his seat would be counted. Duration recording is concerned with the length of each occurrence of the behavior, for example, how long the child was out of his seat.

Child protective services caseworkers may record information about children in a form such as the Children's Restrictiveness of Living Environments Instrument (figure 5.5). This instrument provides an indicator of factors related to out-of-home placement (Thomlison & Krysik, 1992). Magura and Moses (1985) have developed a set of scales to measure outcomes for child welfare services.

Figure 5.5   Children's Restrictiveness of Living Environments Instrument

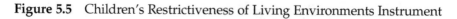

Children's Restrictiveness of Living Environments

Instructions for calculating the restrictiveness of children's living environments:
A. Complete the child and rating information.
B. On the right side of the items in column B, number the child's placements in
   sequential order and record the corresponding number of days in each placement,
   e.g., (1,30) indicates first placement, 30 days.
C. Record the corresponding Restrictiveness Score for each placement into the
   Restrictiveness Formula in column C, i.e., Rp1, represents the restrictiveness score
   of the child's first placement. Calculate the totals.
D. Record the corresponding per diem cost and the number of days in each placement
   in column D. Calculate the totals.

A. Child Name: _____   Rater Name: _____

   Child Birthdate: _____/_____/_____   Date Completed: _____/_____/_____
                    (year) (month) (day)   (year) (month) (day)

   Child Identification: _____

B. Restrictiveness Scores	C. Restrictiveness Equation
1.51 Self-maintained residence 2.10 Private boarding home 2.18 Home of child's friend 2.33 Home of family friend 2.40 Home of relative 2.45 Home of biological parent 2.60 Homeless 2.66 Adoptive home 2.75 Supervised independent living 3.09 Independent living prep. group home 3.13 Regular foster care home 3.38 Family emergency shelter	R_{p1}____ − R_{p2}____ = ____ R_{p2}____ − R_{p3}____ = ____ R_{p3}____ − R_{p4}____ = ____ R_{p4}____ − R_{p5}____ = ____ Total ____

B. (continued)	D. Cost Equation
3.48 Receiving foster care 3.57 Treatment foster family care home 3.58 Special needs foster home 3.61 Long-term group home 3.85 Youth emergence shelter 3.86 Receiving group home 4.00 Medical hospital 4.14 Private residential school 4.18 Wilderness camp 4.45 Ranch-based treatment center 4.60 Open youth correction facility 4.62 Adult drug/alcohol rehab. center 4.63 Cottage based treatment center 4.85 Psychiatric group home 4.97 Youth drug/alcohol rehab. center 5.13 Armed services base 5.40 Young offender group home 5.50 Psychiatric ward in a hospital 6.10 Psychiatric institution 6.40 Closed youth correction facility 6.56 Adult correction facility 6.58 Secure treatment facility	T_{p1}____ × C_{p1}____ = ____ T_{p2}____ × C_{p2}____ = ____ T_{p3}____ × C_{p3}____ = ____ T_{p4}____ × C_{p4}____ = ____ T_{p5}____ × C_{p5}____ = ____ Total # Days Total Cost in Placement ___ of Placement ___

SOURCE: Used by permission of Barbara Thomlison (1992), Faculty of Social Work, The University of Calgary.

Standardized Tests. Quantitative data derived from some of the tests used with children are designed to measure intelligence, achievement, or special problems or abilities. Social workers do not usually administer these tests but refer children to other trained personnel when appropriate. Social workers may administer screening inventories such as the Attention Deficit Hyperactivity Disorder Rating Scale (DuPaul, 1992) or the Conners' Continuous Performance Test II (CPT IIV.5), but comprehensive evaluations for ADHD or other complicated disorders require specialized training and skill. When referring a child for testing, you as the social worker should follow these guidelines: have a specific reason for referring a client; explain to the psychologist what questions you want answered; provide information you have collected to the psychologist; prepare the client for what to expect at the psychologist's office; do not have unrealistic expectations of what the testing will provide, because testing is only one tool for assessing the client; and ask the psychologist to explain any limitations of the specific tests that your client has been given (Sheafor et al., 1988). To further promote the process, social workers can learn more about testing instruments, their interpretation, and implications. Social workers can also help other professionals understand the parameters of social service and child welfare systems (Kayser & Lyon, 2000).

As a response to federal initiatives to improve education, such as No Child Left Behind Act of 2001 and the 2004 Individuals with Disabilities Education Improvement Act (IDEIA) revisions, many states and school districts are adopting a cross-battery assessment system. The cross-battery approach provides a conceptual model for measurement and interpretation of cognitive abilities. The cross-battery approach gives educators the means to "make systematic, valid, and up-to-date interpretations of intelligence batteries, and to augment them with other tests (e.g., academic ability tests) in a way that is consistent with the empirically supported Cattell-Horn-Carroll (CHC) theory of cognitive abilities" (Flanagan, Ortiz, & Alfonso, 2007, p. 1). The psychometrically and theoretically defensible cross-battery approach principles and procedures represent an improved method of measuring cognitive abilities (Carroll & Kaufman 1998; Kaufman, 2000; Flanagan et al., 2007). In a cross-battery assessment, "many scale and composite measures on intelligence are mixed containing excess reliable variance with a construct irrelevant to the one intended for measurement and interpretation. The cross-battery approach ensures that assessments include composites or clusters that are relatively pure representations of CHC broad and narrow abilities, allowing for valid measurement and interpretation of multiple unidimensional constructs" (Flanagan et al., 2007, p. 3).

The use of new testing procedures in the schools ensures that children and adolescents are labeled accurately and, when needed, correctly placed in programs that provide the types of assistance students need to thrive in school.

CASE STUDY ANTHONY: MOVING FROM ASSESSMENT TO INTERVENTION

The following case study illustrates the various systemic factors and personal difficulties that families face today. We use this case study to illustrate the correct assessment tools for the child and a treatment plan.

Client Identifying Information

Name: Anthony Estrada
Date of Birth: 11/09/2007
Ethnicity: Hispanic
Address: 1112 N. Clement Street, Mayfield, Texas
Phone: 555.123.4567 (home), 555.890.1112 (cell)

Family Members Living in the Home

Anthony Estrada	Client	8 y.o.	2nd grade
John Estrada	Brother	11 y.o.	5th grade
Robert Estrada	Brother	10 y.o.	3rd grade
Lydia Estrada	Sister	6 y.o.	1st grade
Hector Estrada	Father	35 y.o.	Construction
Alina Estrada	Mother	30 y.o.	Classroom assistant

Family Income.   The family income is $3,500 and $4,000 per month, depending on the mother's employment. She works part time at the elementary school during the school year.

Presenting Problem.   Anthony has been suspended from school for hitting a teacher while on the playground. He did not want to go inside at the end of recess and struck her in his frustration. His teacher complains that he's had a bad attitude all year, and the principal is suggesting placement for him in an alternative school.

Previous Counseling.   None.

Source of Data.   In-office assessment visit with Anthony and his parents. Additional information from the pediatrician, the teachers, and the school counselor.

Nature of Presenting Problem.   In the past two years, Anthony has changed from an energetic, loving child to a moody, irritable child. Although Anthony has always been "busy and active," his mother reports that he has become more competitive with his older brothers and that he is easily frustrated if he cannot beat them at sports or other games. She reports that if Anthony loses a board game, he will sulk and say that he is "stupid" or that his brothers cheated. Often, he himself will cheat in an attempt to win. About a month ago, as the boys were playing soccer in their backyard, Anthony became so upset that he began to scream at his brothers and say that he wished he were dead. Shocked by this outburst, the mother tried to comfort Anthony, but she said that he resisted her effort and finally calmed down only at the urgings of his oldest brother. Since that incident, the family has tried to avoid making Anthony too angry.

Despite their efforts to mollify him, however, the mother reports that Anthony has become "sassy" and that, increasingly, she must discipline him for hitting his siblings and for not obeying her. She attempts to spank him, but she says that when she does that, he only tries to hit her back. More often, now, she sends him to his room. Although he obeys his father, who uses corporal punishment, Anthony seems to ignore his mother's requests that he pick up his clothes and toys and that he complete his homework. She says that it is difficult to get him up in the mornings and that he dawdles rather than dressing himself and gathering his supplies for school as his brothers do. She finds that she must spend as much time helping Anthony get ready in the mornings as she does his younger sister. Sometimes, they are all late for school because of Anthony's dilatory actions or because of one of his angry outbursts, when he feels that everyone is pushing him and causing him to be late.

With incomplete homework and, sometimes, incomplete work in school, Anthony's grades have suffered this year. The teacher says that Anthony is inattentive and that he bothers other children, often distracting them from their work and provoking them into confrontations with him. She believes that Anthony is smart enough to learn the material but that he does not seem to want to. She reports that his work is careless and that he often leaves worksheets incomplete. In her exasperation, she enlisted help from the school counselor, who assisted her in setting up a classroom behavior management plan of rewards and consequences for directing Anthony's behavior. Although Anthony responds to this system, the teacher says that the time she must spend managing Anthony's behavior takes away from class time that would normally be devoted to all of the children. She believes that Anthony should be transferred to a class for emotionally disturbed children, where his behavior can be monitored more closely in a smaller class of students.

The teacher reports that Anthony is able to play with peers most of the time, but she notes that his angry behavior alienates some children. In all competitive instances, he becomes frustrated and aggressive if he is unable to win or to perform as well as he wants to. The day of the playground incident, Anthony was playing in a group of children who were divided into teams for kickball. Anthony's team was behind, and when the teacher said that recess was over, Anthony was upset because he wanted to continue playing until his team could catch up. When the teacher refused to extend recess, he hit her in the back with his fist. She immediately took him to the principal, who called Anthony's mother and suspended Anthony from school for three days. During the suspension, the principal and the teacher arranged to meet with Anthony and his parents to discuss appropriate ways to help him control his behavior and be more successful in school. The school social worker was asked to attend this meeting.

Anthony has several strengths. His parents are devoted to their family and are genuinely concerned for their son. They are willing to participate in recommended plans for intervention both at school and at home, but they strongly advocate for their son's continued placement in a regular classroom. Anthony's personal strengths include his ability to maintain focus on certain types of projects in school, his apparent ability to master second-grade work, and a stated understanding of why he has been suspended. He says that he is sorry for hitting his teacher.

The school prioritizes the problems (with 1 being the most severe) in the following order: (a) aggressive behavior, (b) distracting other students, (c) inability to focus on schoolwork. The parents prioritize the problems similarly: (a) angry behavior, (b) argumentativeness, (c) poor grades.

Client Interpersonal Issues

Cognitive Functioning.   Anthony's school achievement tests indicate that he is capable of mastering second grade. He consistently scores in the fiftieth percentile, but his teacher thinks that he is capable of more. Neither his pediatrician nor his parents report any type of cognitive developmental delay. In fact, when he was young his mother thought that he was exceptionally bright because he could figure out how to get out of his crib and how to take apart most toys. Anthony has mastered all developmental tasks at age-appropriate times. The teacher reports that if she works with Anthony individually he can learn anything, but he becomes easily distracted when she works with students as a group or when he must work alone.

Emotional Functioning.   During the assessment visit, Anthony seemed like a quiet child. He sat between his parents, closer to his mother, during most of the interview, showing appropriate anxiety about being in a meeting with adults. He warmed up quickly, however, to the interviewer and answered questions easily, although he did show some discomfort while discussing the playground incident. Only after about thirty minutes did he begin to fidget by swinging his legs against the chair, finally standing up and walking around the room as the adults continued to talk.

Behavioral Functioning.   Anthony exhibited no unusual behaviors during the assessment session. His impatience and need to move after thirty minutes were within normal limits for his age. In fact, he asked his father if he could stand up before he began to walk around. He sighed occasionally to display his boredom, but he did not interrupt the conversation by talking. His parents reported that Anthony has never enjoyed paperwork such as drawing and coloring; he prefers to climb, run, and jump. His parents recounted several events of inappropriate angry behavior over the past six months, but Anthony did not exhibit such behavior in this session. In fact, his behavior in this session indicated some strength in self-control and coping. His weakness in this area seems to be with coping in the classroom environment.

Physiologic Functioning.   Anthony's medical records reveal essentially normal development. Anthony is in the fiftieth percentile for both height and weight, his immunizations are up to date, and he currently takes no medication. His illness history is not remarkable, although he did require minor surgery for repeated ear infections when he was three years old. Since that time, he has shown no delay in speech or hearing. He has had only minor colds and infections that have responded to conservative medical intervention. Although teachers complain about Anthony's handwriting, he does not demonstrate any unusual deficit in fine-motor skills. His drawings are not detailed, but they are not immature for his age. Anthony can dribble a basketball and throw a baseball within the appropriate range for his age. Neither the pediatrician nor the PE teacher reports any physical limitations, although the PE teacher says that he seems clumsy at times and that he needs to "run off steam" during PE class.

Developmental Considerations.   Anthony has met developmental milestones within normal time ranges. Anthony's birth history reveals that he was delivered spontaneously and without complications at forty-one weeks gestation with an Apgar rating of nine, as reflected by the parents and the medical record. He weighed seven pounds, ten ounces.

Client Interpersonal Issues: Family

Anthony resides with his parents, his two older brothers, and his younger sister in a modest home in Mayfield. Anthony's parents are first-generation Mexican Americans. Both sets of grandparents migrated to Texas from northern Mexico. Anthony's mother grew up in a small border town, where she says that she liked school but often missed class to babysit for her younger siblings while her mother worked. She dropped out of high school in eleventh grade because she was somewhat behind in her studies, and she had found a good job as a seamstress. She later acquired her GED by studying at night in an adult education class before her first child was born. Having the GED allows Mrs. Estrada to work as a classroom assistant for the elementary school Anthony attends. Anthony's father grew up in the same small border town, where he worked in fields from the time he was a boy. He reports that school was boring for him and that he preferred the physical activity of the fields but that he stayed in school until high school. He dropped out before his junior year. He says that teachers sometimes called him inattentive and disruptive because he found it hard to pay attention to things that did not matter to him. He currently works as a foreman for a local construction company. He says that he has always preferred being outdoors and working with his hands.

Mrs. Estrada has learned behavioral disciplining techniques, such as time-out, in her job, and she thinks these techniques work with her children when she is not too stressed to employ them. Mr. Estrada thinks these techniques are fine, but he prefers corporal punishment because he thinks that it works best and that children should have a "healthy fear" of their parents. Mr. Estrada leaves much of the discipline to his wife because she is with the children more than he is, but when he is home he intervenes if he finds that the children are not responding appropriately to him or to their mother. He says that he has had to spank Anthony more than the other children lately, and he admits that the spankings seem to escalate Anthony's anger.

The other Estrada children, John, Robert, and Lydia, are healthy and developing normally. A fifth grader, John makes good grades and is well liked by his peers. He is in the highest performance groups for reading and math. Schoolwork appears to come easily for him, but his passion is baseball, where he is demonstrating talent as a pitcher. He is a confident and bright boy. Anthony seems closer to him than he is to Robert, who is only eighteen months older than he is. Robert, a third grader, is described as the "squeaky wheel" of the family. Like John, Robert performs well in school, but his parents and teachers describe him as competitive and whiny, although he has never displayed the anger problems that Anthony has. Robert excels in art. His drawings show dimensional depth and detail that are unusual for his age. Lydia is in first grade, where she seems to be on level. She is described as quiet and is the "baby" of the family. The parents insist that the boys protect her and not tease or aggravate her.

Mrs. Estrada is with the children most of the time because her job allows her to leave for school and return with her children. In good weather, Mr. Estrada works many evenings and weekends. When he is home, he is often too tired to play with the children, but sometimes he throws a ball with the boys. Mrs. Estrada reports that all of the children want to spend more time with their father. Because the family depends heavily on Mr. Estrada's income, however, she acknowledges that he must work hard to maintain his job.

Client Interpersonal Issues: School

The school counselor reports that she observed Anthony's behavior in the classroom on several occasions, at the request of his teacher. The counselor found that Anthony was often off-task, playing with his pencil or talking to classmates, and that he seemed unable to follow oral directions for the entire class. At times, the more he was corrected by the teacher, the more disruptive Anthony became.

The school counselor reports that Anthony responded well to the token economy system she set up for improving his focus in the classroom. She says that he was willing to work for the tokens and stayed on task better when he knew that his teacher would reward him. This focus, in turn, reduced his disruptive behavior with his peers and seemed to improve his schoolwork. Reviewing his test scores, she reported that she could see some disparity between Anthony's ability and performance scores, a disparity that continues in the classroom. She expresses some concern that if his school problems continue, he will fall behind in his schoolwork and lose interest completely. She recognizes that he must gain some control of his temper and his attention span if he is to succeed in the classroom.

Client Interpersonal Issues: Peers

Anthony and his parents report that he has some friends, but that sometimes people do not like to play with him because he gets so angry. The counselor reports that students in second grade try to stay out of trouble, and they fear that Anthony will get them in trouble with the teacher. Anthony is signed up for soccer this year, but the soccer season has not yet started. His parents hope that sports will give him an outlet for his energy and that he will make friends.

Context and Social Support Networks

The family has been somewhat isolated since their move from a town on the border two years ago, where they left behind both sets of grandparents and a large extended family of aunts, uncles, and cousins. Mrs. Estrada stays busy with her work, her home, and her children. She does enjoy her colleagues at work, but she is busy the rest of the time meeting the needs of four active children. With his long work hours, Mr. Estrada is not often available to help with family and housekeeping tasks. He is, himself, exhausted with his labors. The children are each expected to do chores, but Mrs. Estrada admits that sometimes she does the work herself to ensure that it is done well and in a timely manner. The family does attend a Catholic church nearby, but they have not become active in the church community, though all of their children have participated in first communion and will likely continue all of their religious education through confirmation.

Mr. and Mrs. Estrada are happy with their family and their circumstances. They believe that they have provided well for their children. Although they miss the support of extended family, they believe that the move has been beneficial financially and that they and their children will have more opportunity in Mayfield than in their home town.

Measurement

Individual Functioning: Assess for Depression.   Evidence-based support for assessment with Anthony should include the use of a multidimensional functional assessment. Because children often mask depression with anger, multiple observations should be conducted under different situations, and data should be obtained from multiple informants (O'Hare, 2005). The assessment should cover three modes of expression: (a) Anthony's cognitive appraisal of the events in his life; (b) physiological symptoms, such as any somatic complaints; and (c) behaviors associated with depression (O'Hare, 2005). Tools to be used should include the Children's Depression Inventory (Kovacs, 1992), the Depression Self-Rating Scale (Birleson, Hudson, Buchanan, & Wolff, 1987), and the Children's Depression Rating Scale (Poznanzski, Cook, & Carroll, 1979).

Assess for Anger and Noncompliance.   Evidence-based support for assessment includes a functional analysis of Anthony's angry outbursts and noncompliance. This analysis would delineate the patterns and sequencing of the antecedents and consequences of his negative behaviors (O'Hare, 2005). His teacher should conduct behavior observations throughout the school day to see when the behavior occurs, and what consequences follow it. Likewise, Mrs. Estrada should design a daily behavioral checklist and record the number of Anthony's noncompliances, compliances, and angry outbursts. Instruments that could assist in the analysis include the Revised Behavior Problem Checklist (Quay, 1983), the Eyberg Child Behavior Inventory (Eyberg & Robinson, 1983), and the New York Teacher Rating Scale (Miller et al. 1995; O'Hare, 2005).

Family Functioning.   The social worker should administer the Hudson Index of Family Relations (Inwald et al., 1988) and the Family Adaptability and Cohesion Evaluation Scales, currently in its fourth revision (FACES IV), which measures cohesiveness and flexibility in family functioning (Franklin, Streeter, & Springer, 2001; O'Hare, 2005; Olsen, Russell, & Sprenkle, 1989).

Box 5.1 provides a treatment plan that was developed for Anthony.

BOX 5.1
Treatment Plan: Anthony Estrada

Problem: Child behavior problems; parental lack of skills

Definitions: Distractibility, inattentiveness, angry outbursts, and occasional aggression for child. Have skills deficit in parenting and use corporal punishment instead of positive discipline, such as rewards.

Goals: 1. To improve attentiveness at home and at school
2. To eliminate angry outbursts and aggression
3. To improve overall parent-child relationship

Objectives:	Interventions:
1. Parents will learn how to help Anthony stay on task, as measured by behavioral checklist.	1. Teach parents use of a reward system for when a child stays on task. Teach parents to redirect inappropriate behaviors. Refer child for ADHD test.
2. Anthony will learn to control his anger, as measured by behavioral checklist.	2. Teach Anthony anger management skills, such as time-out, mindful breathing, and focusing.
3. Family relationships will improve, as measured by the Index of Family Relationships	3. Teach family to have family meetings and outings.

Diagnosis: Consider 314.01 Attention-Deficit/Hyperactivity Disorder, Combined Type

---

SUMMARY

This chapter described assessment of children and adolescents. The special issues important in assessing this population are diagnosis, psychological theories, social theories, and ethnicity: Childhood diagnosis is done from three different perspectives: categorical-dimensional, empirical, and behavioral. Psychological theories explain child development from cognitive, affective, and learning perspectives. Development is assumed to occur at different rates for different children, depending on maturational readiness and environmental opportunities. Social theories explain children's behavior in the broader context of family and society. Issues that influence assessment of children of color include psychosocial adjustment, relationship with family, school adjustment and achievement, peers, and community.

Measures available for assessment of children and adolescents should be empirically supported with evidence-based outcome research. Measures should include global techniques such as interviews, use of play, and sculpting and other family techniques. Self-report measurement techniques include standardized instruments, self-anchored and other rating scales, self-observation, and ratings by others. Finally, the chapter presented the case of Anthony, an eight-year-old boy with problems including distractability, inattentiveness, angry outbursts, and social aggression.

STUDY QUESTIONS

1. Use psychological, social, and color guidelines from the chapter to assess a child you know. What are the strengths and weaknesses of each approach?

2. Using the same case study as in question 1, design a measurement system that includes both qualitative (play or sculpting) and quantitative (standardized measures, self-anchored scales) techniques.

3. Review the Web sites of assessment tools listed at the end of this chapter. Which assessment tools are evidence-based and which are not? What is the most effective way to ensure that an assessment tool is effective?

WEB SITES

Evidence-Based Assessment Materials

American Psychiatric Association, http://www.psychiatry.org/practice/managing-a-practice/practice-management-guides

Campbell Collaboration, http://www.campbellcollaboration.org/resources/research/new_information_retrieval_guide.php

Cochrane, http://www.cochrane.org/news/updated-list-cochrane-priority-reviews-now-available

Various Assessments of Children

Child Abuse and Neglect, https://www.childwelfare.gov/topics/preventing/

Anatomically Detailed Dolls

Institute for Psychological Therapies, http://www.ipt-forensics.com/library/special_problems5.htm

Learning

Pearson Assessment (for the Beery Visual Motor Integration, ages 2 to 18, includes helpful information about the test and developmental learning materials), http://www.pearsonclinical.com/therapy/products/100000663/the-beery-buktenica-developmental-test-of-visual-motor-integration-6th-edition-beery-vmi.html

Social-Emotional

Children's Depression Inventory, ages 7 to 17, http://www.mhs.com/product.aspx?gr=edu&id=overview&prod=cdi2

Reynolds Adolescent Depression Scale (ages 11 to 20, includes critical items), http://www4.parinc.com/Products/Product.aspx?ProductID=RADS-2

Feifer Assessment of Reading, http://www4.parinc.com/products/Product.aspx?ProductID=FAR

Emotional-Behavioral Screening

Behavior Assessment System for Children (different forms cover ages 2.5 to 18), http://www.pearsonclinical.com/education/products/100001402/behavior-assessment-system-for-children-third-edition-basc-3.html

Pearson Instructional Resources, http://www.pearsonschool.com/

Achenback System of Empirically Based Assessment, Child Behavior Checklist (ages 1.5 to 18), http://www.aseba.org/

Personality-Projective Tests

Children's Apperception Test (covers ages 3 to 10), Adaptive Behavior Assessment System http://www.pearsonclinical.com/psychology/products/100001262/adaptive-behavior-assessment-system-third-edition-abas-3.html

Intellectual Assessments

Wechsler Preschool and Primary Scale of Intelligence (3rd ed.; covers ages 2 to 3), Harcourt Assessment, http://www.pearsonclinical.com/psychology/products/100000422/wechsler-preschool-and-primary-scale-of-intelligence—third-edition-wppsi-iii.html

Achievement Tests

Woodcock Johnson III (measures academic achievement, ages 2 to 90+), http://www.cps.nova.edu/~cpphelp/WJIII-ACH.html

REFERENCES

Achenbach, T. M. (1991). *Manual for the youth self report and 1991 profile.* Burlington: University of Vermont, Department of Psychiatry.

Achenbach, T. M., & Edelbrock, L. (1983). *Manual for the child behavior checklist and revised child behavior profile.* Burlington, VT: Queen City Printers.

American Psychiatric Association (APA). (2013). *Diagnostic and statistical manual of mental disorders* (5th ed.; DSM-5). Washington, DC: Author.

Armsden, G., Pecora, P. J., Payne, V. H., & Szatkiewicz, J. P. (2000). Children placed in long-term foster care: An intake profile using the child behavior checklist/4-18. *Journal of Emotional and Behavioral Disorders, 8,* 49–64.

Bandura, A. (1977). *Social learning theory.* Englewood Cliffs, NJ: Prentice Hall.

Barkley, R. (2005). *Attention deficit hyperactivity disorder: A handbook for diagnosis and treatment* (2nd ed.). New York: Guilford Press.

Barona, A., & de Barona, M. S. (2000). Assessing multicultural preschool children. In B. Bracken (Ed.), *The psychoeducational assessment of preschool children* (pp. 282–297). Boston: Allyn and Bacon.

Barth, R. (1986). *Social and cognitive treatment of children and adolescents.* San Francisco: Jossey-Bass.

Berk, L. E. (2007). *Infants, children and adolescents* (6th ed.). Boston: Allyn and Bacon.

Bienvenu, O. J., Wang, Y., Shugart, Y. Y., Welch, J. M., Grados, M. A., Fyer, A. J., ... & Nestadt, G. (2009). Sapap3 and pathological grooming in humans: Results from the OCD collaborative genetics study. *American Journal of Medical Genetics Part B: Neuropsychiatric Genetics, 150*(5), 710–720.

Bird, H. R., Gould, M. S., Rubio-Stipec, M., Staghezza, B., & Canino, G. (1991). Screening for childhood psychopathology in the community using the child behavior checklist. *Journal of the American Academy of Child and Adolescent Psychiatry, 30,* 116–123.

Birleson, P., Hudson, I., Buchanan, D. G., & Wolff, S. (1987). Clinical evaluation of a self-rating scales for depressive disorder in childhood (Depression Self-Rating Scale). *Journal of Child Psychology and Psychiatry, 28,* 43–60.

Bloom, M. (1984). *Configurations of human behavior.* New York: Macmillan.

Bornstein, P., & Kazdin, A. (1985). *Handbook of clinical behavior therapy with children.* Homewood, IL: Dorsey Press.

Boys Town. (1989). *Working with aggressive youth.* Boys Town, NE: Author.

Bracken, B. A. (1992). *Multidimensional self-concept scale: Examiner's manual.* Austin, TX: PRO-ED.

Bracken, B. A., & Kelley, P. (1993). *Assessment of interpersonal relations.* Austin, TX: PRO-ED.

Burke, J. D., Loeber, R., & Birmaher, B. (2004). Oppositional defiant disorder and conduct disorder: A review of the past 10 years, part II. *Focus, 2,* 558–576.

Canino, I. A., & Spurlock, J. (2000). *Culturally diverse children and adolescents: Assessment, diagnosis, and treatment* (2nd ed.). New York: Guilford Press.

Carroll, J. B., & Kaufman, A. (1998). Foreword. In K. S. McGrew & D. P. Flanagans, *The intelligence test desk reference (ITDR): GF-Gc cross-battery assessment* (pp. xi–xii). Boston: Allyn and Bacon.

Caspi, A., Sugden, K., Moffitt, T. E., Taylor, A., Craig, I. W., Harrington, H., . . . & Pouton, R. (2003). Influence of life stress on depression: Moderation by a polymorphism in the 5-HTT gene. *Science, 301*, 386–389. doi: 10.1126/science.1083968

Clarke, G. N., Lewinsohn, P. M., Hops, H., & Seeley, J. R. (1992). A self- and parent-report measure of adolescent depression: The Child Behavior Checklist Depression Scale. *Behavioral Assessment, 14*, 443–463.

Cohen, R. J., & Swerdlik, M. E. (2005). *Psychological testing and assessment: An introduction to tests and measurement* (6th ed.). Boston: McGraw-Hill.

Columbia University DISC Development Group. (2006). *Diagnostic interview schedule for children.* New York: Author.

Conners, K. C. (2008). *Conners' rating scales manual* (3rd ed.). North Tonawanda, NY: Multihealth Systems.

Corcoran, K., & Fischer, J. (2000). *Measures for clinical practice.* New York: Free Press.

Cross-Disorder Group of the Psychiatric Genomics Consortium. (2013). Identification of risk loci with shared effects on five major psychiatric disorders: A genome-wide analysis. *Lancet, 381*, 1371–1379.

Davies, D. (2004). *Child development: A practitioner's guide* (2nd ed.). New York: Guilford Press.

Deal, J. E., Halverson, C. F. Jr., Martin, R. P., Victor, J., & Baker, S. (2007). The inventory of children's individual differences: Development of validation of a short version. *Journal of Personality Assessment, 89*, 162–166.

DuPaul, G. J. (1992). How to assess attention deficit hyperactivity disorder within school settings. *School Psychology Quarterly, 7*, 60–74.

Embregts, P. (2000). Reliability of the child behavior checklist for the assessment of behavioral problems of children and youth with mild mental retardation. *Research in Developmental Disabilities, 21*, 31–41.

Erikson, E. (1993). *Childhood and society.* London: Norton.

Eyberg, S. M., & Robinson, E. A. (1983). Conduct problem behavior: Standardization of a behavioral rating scale with adolescents. *Journal of Clinical Child Psychology, 12*, 347–357.

Flanagan, D., Ortiz, S. O., & Alfonso, V. C. (2007). *Essentials of cross-battery assessment* (2nd ed.). Hoboken, NJ: John Wiley & Sons.

Franklin, C., Streeter, C., & Springer, D. (2001). Validity of the FACES IV family assessment measure. *Research on Social Work Practice, 11*, 576–596.

Frieson, J. (1993). *Structural-strategic marriage and family therapy.* New York: Gardner.

Gibbs, J., & Huang, L. (2003). *Children of color.* San Francisco: Jossey-Bass.

Gopaul-McNicol, S., & Armour-Thomas, E. (2001). *Assessment and culture: Psychological test with minority populations.* San Diego, CA: Academic Press.

Guarnaccia, P. J., & Lopez, S. (1998). The mental health and adjustment of immigrant and refugee children. *Child and Adolescent Psychiatric Clinics of North America, 7,* 537–553.

Halverson, C. F., Havil, V., Deal, J. E., Baker, S., Victor, J., & Pavlopoulos, V. (2003). Personality structure as derived from parental ratings of free descriptions of children: The Inventory of Child Individual Differences. *Journal of Personality, 71,* 995–1026.

Handler, L., & Meyer, G. J. (1998). The importance of teaching and learning personality assessment. In L. Handler & M. J. Hilsenroth (Eds.), *Teaching and learning personality assessment* (pp. 3–30). Mahwah, NJ: Erlbaum.

Harper-Dorton, K., & Herbert, M. (1999). *Working with children and their families* (2nd ed.). Chicago: Lyceum Books.

Hettema, J. M., Neale, M. C., & Kendler, K. S. (2001). A review and meta-analysis of the genetic epidemiology of anxiety disorders. *American Journal of Psychiatry, 158,* 1568–1578.

Hughes, J., & Baker, D. B. (1991). *The clinical child interview.* New York: Guilford Press.

Inda, M. C., Muravieva, E. V., & Alberini, C. M. (2011). Memory retrieval and the passage of time: From reconsolidation and strengthening to extinction. *Journal of Neuroscience, 31,* 1635–1643.

Individuals with Disabilities Education Improvement Act of 2004 (IDEIA), Pub. L. 108-446, 118 Stat. 2647 (2004).

Inwald, R. E., Brobst, K. E., & Morrisey, R. F. (1988). *Hilson adolescent profile.* Kew Gardens, NY: Hilson Research.

Janzen, C., Harris, O., Jordan, C., & Franklin, C. (2005). *Family treatment: Evidence-based practicer with populations at risk* (4th ed.). Belmont, CA: Brooks/Cole.

Jenson, B. F., & Potter, M. L. (1990). Best practices in communicating with parents. In A. Thomas & J. Grimes (Eds.), *Best practices in school psychology II* (pp. 183–193). Washington, DC: National Association of School Psychologists.

Johnson-Powell, G., Yamamoto, J., & Arroyo, W. (1997). *Transcultural child development.* New York: John Wiley & Sons.

Jordan, C., & Cobb, N. (2001). Competency-based treatment for persons with marital discord. In K. Corcoran (Ed.), *Structuring change* (2nd ed.; chap. 10). Chicago: Lyceum Books.

Jordan, C., Franklin, C., & Corcoran, K. (2010). Development of measuring instruments. In R. Grinnell (Ed.), *Social work research and evaluation* (pp. 196–215). New York: Oxford University Press.

Jordan, C., & Hoefer, R. (2002). Work versus life: Family friendly benefits in non-profit organizations. *National Social Science Journal, 17,* 16–25.

Kaufman, A. S. (2000). Foreword. In D. P. Flanagan, I. S. McGrew, & S. O. Ortiz (Eds.), *The Wechsler intelligences scales and GF-Gc theory: A contemporary approach to interpretation* (pp. xiii–xv). Boston: Allyn and Bacon.

Kayser, J. A., & Lyon, M. A. (2000). Teaching social workers to use psychological assessment data. *Child Welfare, 79,* 197–222.

Kim-Cohen, J., Caspi, A., Taylor, A., Williams, B., Newcombe, R., Craig, I. W., & Moffitt, T. E. (2006). MAOA, maltreatment, and gene–environment interaction predicting children's mental health: New evidence and a meta-analysis. *Molecular Psychiatry, 11*, 903–913. doi: 10.1080/15402000701557383

Kohlberg, L. (1981). *Essays on moral development:* Vol. 1. *The philosophy of moral development.* San Francisco: Harper and Row.

Kovacs, M. (1992). *Children's depression inventory.* Los Angeles: Multi-Health Systems.

Luecken, L. J., & Roubinov, D. S. (2012). Pathways to lifespan health following childhood. *Social and Personality Psychology Compass, 6*, 243–257. doi: 10.1111/j.1751-9004.2011.00422.x

Magura, S., & Moses, B. (1985). *Outcome measures for child welfare services.* Washington, DC: Child Welfare League of America.

McCarney, S. B., & Leigh, J. E. (1990). *Manual for the behavior evaluation scale 2.* Columbia, MO: Educational Services.

McConaughy, S. H. (1996). The interview process. In M. Breen & C. Fiedler (Eds.), *Behavioral approach to assessment of youth with emotional/behavioral disorders: A handbook for school-based practitioners* (pp. 181–223). Austin, TX: PRO-ED.

McConaughy, S. H., & Achenbach, T. M. (2001). *Manual for the semistructured clinical interview with children and adolescents.* New York: Guilford Press.

Merrell, K. W. (1993). Using behavior rating scales to assess social skills and antisocial behavior in school settings: Development of the School Social Behavior Scales. *School Psychology Review, 22*, 115–133.

Merrell, K. W. (2007). *Behavioral, social, and emotional assessment of children and adolescents* (3rd ed.). Hillsdale, NJ: Erlbaum.

Miley, K. K., O'Melia, M., & DuBois, B. (2006). *Generalist social work practice: An empowering approach.* Boston: Allyn and Bacon.

Miller, L. S., Klein, R. G., Piacentini, J., Abikoff, H., Shah, M. R., Samoilov, A., & Guardino, M. (1995). The New York Teacher Rating Scale for disruptive and anti-social behavior. *Journal of the American Academy of Child and Adolescent Psychiatry, 34*, 359–370.

Nelson, C. A., & Carver, L. J. (1998). The effects of stress and trauma on brain and memory: A view from developmental cognitive neuroscience. *Development and Psychopathology, 10*, 793–809.

No Child Left Behind Act of 2001, Pub. L. 107-110 (2002).

Nurmi, J. E. (1993). Adolescent development in an age graded context: The role of personal beliefs, goals, and strategies in the tackling of developmental tasks and standards. *International Journal of Behavioral Development, 16*, 169–189.

O'Hare, T. (2005). *Evidence-based practices for social workers: An interdisciplinary approach.* Chicago: Lyceum Books.

Olsen, D. H., Russell, C., & Sprenkle, D. (1989). *FACES III manual.* St. Paul: University of Minnesota Press.

Openshaw, L. (2008). *Social work in schools: Principles and practice.* New York: Guilford Press.

Openshaw, L., & Halvorson, H. (2005). The co-occurrence of intimate partner violence and child abuse. In L. H. Ginsberg (Ed.), *Social work in rural communities* (4th ed., pp. 207–221). Alexandria, VA: Council on Social Work Education.

Pavlov, I. P. (1960). *Conditional reflexes.* New York: Dover. (Original published in 1927).

Perry, B. D. (1997). Incubated in terror: Neurodevelopment factors in the cycle of violence. In J. D. Osofsky (Ed.), *Children in a violent society* (pp. 124–149). New York: Guilford Press.

Perry, B. D. (2002). Helping traumatized children: A brief overview for caretakers. In *Parent and caregiver education series of the Child Trauma Academy.* Retrieved from http://www.childtrauma.org

Piaget, J. (1951). *The psychology of intelligence.* London: Routledge and Kegan Paul. [*La psychologie de l'intelligence* (1947)].

Piaget, J. (2001). *Psychology of intelligence.* Florence, KY: Routledge. (Original published 1947).

Poznanzski, E. O., Cook, S. C., & Carroll, B. J. (1979). A depression rating scale for children. *Pediatric, 64,* 442–450.

Quay, H. C. (1983). A dimensional approach to behavior disorder: The Revised Behavior Problem Checklist. *School Psychology Review, 12,* 244–249.

Reich, W., & Welner, Z. (1990). *Diagnostic interview for children and adolescents– Revised.* St. Louis, MO: Washington University, Division of Child Psychiatry.

Reynolds, C. R., & Kamphaus, R. W. (Eds). (2003). *The handbook of psychological and educational assessment of children:* Vol. 1. *Aptitude and achievement.* New York: Guilford Press.

Roberts, R. E., & Chen, Y. W. (1995). Depressive symptoms and suicidal ideation among Mexican-origin and Anglo adolescents. *Journal of the American Academy of Child and Adolescent Psychiatry, 34,* 81–90.

Rosenberg, R. N., & Pascual, J. M. (Eds.). (2015). *Rosenberg's molecular and genetic basis of neurological and psychiatric disease* (5th ed.). New York: Elsevier.

Rossi, A., Pollice, R., Daneluzzo, E., Marinangeli, M. G., & Stratta, P. (2000). Behavioral neurodevelopment abnormalities and schizophrenic disorder: A retrospective evaluation with child behavior checklist (CBCL). *Schizophrenia Research, 44,* 121–128.

Sadock, B. J., Sadock, V. A., & Ruiz, P. (2015). *Kaplan & Sadock's synopsis of psychiatry* (11th ed.). Philadelphia: Wolters Kluwer.

Sattler, J. (1988). *Assessment of children* (3rd ed.). San Diego, CA: Author.

Sheafor, B., Horejsi, C., & Horejsi, G. (1988). *Techniques and guidelines for social work practice.* Newton, MA: Allyn and Bacon.

Siegel, J. M., Aneshensel, C. S., Taub, B., Cantwell, D. P., & Driscoll, A. K. (1998). Adolescent depressed mood in a multi-ethnic sample. *Journal of Youth and Adolescence, 27,* 413–427.

Skinner, B. F. (1972). *Beyond freedom and dignity.* New York: Bantam Vintage.

Smith-Osborne, A., Wilder, A., & Reep, E. (2013). A review of reviews examining neurological processes relevant to impact of parental PTSD on military children: Implications for supporting resilience. *Journal of Aggression, Maltreatment, & Trauma, 22*, 461–481. doi: 10.1080/10926771.2013.785454

Thinking, feeling, and doing game, The. (1973). Developed by John Gardner. Card game. Cresskill, NJ: Creative Therapeutics.

Thomlison, B., & Krysik, J. (1992). The development of an instrument to measure the restrictiveness of children's living environments. *Research on Social Work Practice, 2*, 207–219.

Wakefield, J. C. (1996). Does social work need the eco-systems perspective? *Social Service Review, 70*, 1–32.

Wilkinson, I. (2000). The Darlington Assessment System: Clinical guidelines for practitioners. *Journal of Family Therapy, 22*, 211–224.

Yalof, J., & Abraham, P. (2007). Personality assessment in schools. In S. R. Smith & L. Handler (Eds.), *The clinical assessment of children and adolescents: A practitioner's handbook* (pp. 19–35). Mahwah, NJ: Erlbaum.

CHAPTER 6

Adults

Elizabeth C. Pomeroy and Kathleen Hill Anderson

INTRODUCTION

Social workers assess clients across the life cycle from the cradle to the grave and frequently work with adult clients at different ages and stages of life. This chapter discusses the use of a different perspective to assess adult clients, incorporating examples across the life cycle and highlighting different problem areas that adults may experience. The chapter also offers further suggestions for the types of assessment methods that practitioners can use when assessing adults. We summarize several methods for assessing adult clients that are consistent with the types of assessment and measurement techniques described in chapters 2, 3, and 4, including interview questions, diagnostic systems like the *Diagnostic and Statistical Manual of Mental Disorders,* fifth edition (DSM-5; American Psychiatric Association [APA], 2013), mental status interviews, standardized measures, quality assurance systems, and other rating scales. Finally, a case study offers an opportunity for readers to practice moving from assessment to intervention planning.

ASSESSMENT METHODS

Interview Questions

While social workers are examining aspects of the adult client's functioning, they also must keep in mind the complex interplay among the various personal issues being presented. For example, clients' culture and ethnicity have pervasive implications throughout all aspects of the client's life experience and can affect the client's ability to obtain adequate mental health care (Broman, 2012; Carpenter-Song et al., 2010; Snowden, 2003). Moreover, multicultural sensitivity and competence during the clinical interview and diagnostic process is paramount to alliance building and to the engagement and retention of racial/ethnic minorities in treatment (Alcántara & Gone, 2014). Although some factors distinguish assessment of adults from assessment of children and adolescents, it is important to note that, in cases of serious mental illness, boundaries may be blurred depending on the client's level of functioning. In general, when assessing adults it is important to recognize that there is normally an extensive history of life experiences that affect the client's presentation, that coping mechanisms are more solidified and complex and often less mutable, and that there are additional areas for inquiry based on adult functioning and interactions. The goal of an assessment with an adult client is to gain a comprehensive profile of the client's present functioning in all areas of life. Box 6.1 provides a list of questions that a social worker can use depending on the particular needs of an adult client. These questions are designed to guide social workers in developing their own questions to ask the client; that is, social workers do not simply ask the client these questions—rather, they carefully choose wording that is sensitive, culturally appropriate, and at the client's developmental and intellectual level.

Box 6.1
Interviewing Questions

Appearance
How is the client dressed (e.g., neatly, professionally, disheveled, colorfully, coordinated)?
What is the client's level of personal hygiene?
What is the client's physical appearance (e.g., overweight, underweight, marked physical anomalies)?

Biomedical/Organic
What is the client's medical history?
What is the family's medical history?
Are there any physical disabilities or limitations?
Are there any cognitive disabilities or limitations (e.g. aphasia, ataxia, echolalia)?
Does the client take any prescribed drugs?
What are the client's eating patterns?
What are the client's sleeping patterns?
Has the client experienced any exposure to chemical or environmental toxins that may produce behavioral abnormalities?
How does the client describe his or her recent general state of health?
Has the client discovered solutions for any concerns?
What is the impact of the above concerns regarding family, friends, school/work, or community?

Box 6.1 *Continued*

Developmental Issues or Life Transitions
Is the client experiencing any developmental issues or life transitions
(e.g. adolescent individuation, marriage, birth or adoption of a child,
divorce, death of a family member, aging, retirement)?
How is the client affected by his or her current life cycle tasks and
demands?
Does the client have support systems available to help in these transitions?
Has the client discovered solutions to any concerns?
What is the impact of any concerns on family, friends, school/work, or
community?

Problem Solving/Coping Skills
What type of coping styles does the client demonstrate (e.g., problem
solving, relational, avoidance, emotion-focused, task-focused)?
What type of coping skills does the client use?
Does the client believe that his or her coping mechanisms are effective in
dealing with problems?
Does it appear that the client's coping mechanisms are problematic?
Has the client discovered solutions to any concerns?
What is the impact of any concerns on family, friends, school/work, or
community?

Stressors
What are the primary stressors in the client's current life situation?
How long have these stressors been affecting the client?
Are the stressors internal or situational?
Is there a pattern of stress in the client's life (e.g., chronic, occupational,
or relational problems)?
Are there any environmental or cultural stressors (e.g., neighborhood
violence, acculturation issues, minority status)?
Has the client discovered solutions to any concerns?
What is the impact of any concerns on family, friends, school/work, or
community?

Relationship and Social Capacities
Who are the client's significant others?
With whom does he or she reside?
What are the client's communication skills?
In what activities outside the home does the client participate?
How does the client perceive his or her level of social support?
Are there noteworthy relationship patterns?
Does the client appear to have the ability to form lasting relationships?
Does the client have the capacity for empathy toward others?

Box 6.1 *Continued*

Does the client experience significant stress, fear, or anxiety concerning
  interpersonal contacts?
Is the client currently experiencing any relationship difficulties?
Has the client discovered solutions to any concerns?
What is the impact of any concerns on family, friends, school/work, or
  community?

Behavioral Functioning
Does the client display any unusual behavioral characteristics (e.g., tics,
  tremors, violence, hyperactive movements, responses to unobserved
  stimuli)?
Does the client appear to behave appropriately in the interview?
How comfortable is your interaction with the client?
Does the client report problems in psychosocial functioning because of
  behavioral issues?
Has the client discovered solutions to any concerns?
What is the impact of any concerns on family, friends, school/work, or
  community?

Sexual Functioning
Does the client report any sexual difficulties?
If so, are the problems emotional, physical, or cultural in origin?
What is the duration of these problems?
Have any problems affected other areas of functioning?
Has the client discovered solutions to any concerns?
What is the impact of any concerns on family, friends, school/work, or
  community?

Cognitive Functioning
(Use the Mini-Mental State Exam [MMSE] that follows to determine the
possibility of cognitive impairment.)

What are the results of the mental status exam?
What is the client's intellectual capacity and level of education?
Is there a history of cognitive/neurological problems in the client system?
Does the client display or report any delusional thinking (e.g., paranoid
  ideations, grandiosity, delusions of reference)?
Does the client use bizarre expressions?
Is the client able to use language to express him- or herself clearly?
Does the client appear to have good judgment or "common sense"
  (i.e., does the client have a realistic plan for his or her life, does the
  client recognize risks and consequences of decisions, and is the client
  able to choose appropriate solutions to problems)?

Box 6.1 *Continued*

Has the client discovered solutions to any concerns?

What is the impact of any concerns on family, friends, school/work, or community?

Emotional Functioning

What is the client's general affective presentation (e.g., flat, manic, sad, content, anxious)?

Is the client's mood or affect stable or labile? Is any lability situation-related?

Is the client's mood or affect appropriate to his or her current circumstances?

Is the client's mood or affect creating problems in his or her psychosocial functioning? If so, what is the duration of these problems?

Has the client discovered solutions to any concerns?

What is the impact of any concerns on family, friends, school/work, or community?

Self-Concept

Does the client view him- or herself as a valuable, worthwhile individual?

Does the client see him- or herself as competent?

Does the client have a reality-based perception of self?

Does the client report any problems with self-concept or self-esteem?

Has the client discovered solutions to any concerns?

What is the impact of any concerns on family, friends, school/work, or community?

Motivation

Does the client report a desire to change?

How strong is the client's motivation to make changes?

What are the client's external and internal motivators for change?

Does the client have goals for him- or herself?

Can the client imagine ways of changing and can the client visualize improvement?

Has the client discovered solutions to any concerns?

What is the impact of any concerns on family, friends, school/work, or community?

Culture and Ethnic Identification

Does the client identify with particular cultural and/or ethnic group(s)? Does the client gain strength from any such identification(s)?

Does the client experience conflict related to his or her ethnic/cultural identity?

Does the client feel oppressed by membership in this group or population?

What cultural barriers are experienced by the client, if any?

Box 6.1 *Continued*

Has the client discovered solutions to any concerns?
What is the impact of any concerns on family, friends, school/work, or
community?

Role Functioning
What roles does the client currently fulfill?
How were these roles acquired (i.e., voluntarily or involuntarily)?
Is the client having difficulty with any of these roles or balancing these
roles?
Has the client discovered solutions to any concerns?
What is the impact of any concerns on family, friends, school/work, or
community?

Spirituality and Religion
Does the client adhere to a particular spiritual belief system or religion?
Does the client view his or her spiritual or religious orientation, if any, as a
strength?
Does the client view his or her spiritual or religious orientation, if any, as a
problem?
What is the client's sense of life purpose?
Do the client's beliefs hinder his or her psychosocial functioning in any way?
Has the client discovered solutions to any concerns?
What is the impact of any concerns on family, friends, school/work, or
community?

Other Strengths
Does the client identify any other strengths or talents?

Diagnostic Systems

Psychiatric classifications and assessment tools assess various mental
health problems and are useful for determining whether a client has one
or more major mental disorders. It is important for social work practitioners to have a thorough grounding in nosological assessment systems,
such as the DSM-5 (APA, 2013) and to learn how to give a client a mental
status exam to assess the client's current functioning and make an accurate diagnosis of a mental disorder, when appropriate to do so.

The DSM-5 (APA, 2013) provides criteria that help practitioners
decide whether a client has one or more mental disorders, as well as various psychosocial issues. Even in a brief interview, for example, it is
important to find out about the presenting problems of clients and to

assess clients for serious mental illnesses, such as schizophrenia spectrum and other psychotic disorders, depressive disorders, anxiety disorders, and substance-related disorders. The practitioner must be aware of serious impairments, such as the anxious distress specifier associated with bipolar and major depressive disorders and suicidal behavior, which place the client and others at significant risk of harm. Extreme moods, hallucinations, delusions, and other signs of thought disorders are major concerns, and the DSM criteria can help us sort through the myriad of symptoms and presentations of different problem areas.

There are several other advantages to being trained in using the DSM. For example, the DSM diagnostic criteria are widely accepted in practice settings, descriptive in nature, and not tied to any particular theoretical framework. The manual takes a dimensional, developmental, and lifespan approach to mental and emotional disorders found in children, adolescents, and adults. Diagnoses are made according to clinical judgment, referencing the clinical disorder with separate notation of medical problems, psychosocial stressors (e.g., V and Z codes), and disability issues in order to be consistent with the *International Classification of Diseases* codes (APA, 2013). Although some mental disorders such as Alzheimer's disease and sleep disorders require medical evaluation by a neuropsychologist and other doctors, most others can be assessed by master's-level social workers who have a license to practice clinical social work.

Specific Criticisms of the DSM for Social Work Practice.   The DSM is first and foremost a psychiatric textbook for diagnosing clients, and its credibility and use are somewhat controversial among professionals (Bentall, 2014; Carney, 2014). As discussed in chapter 1, for example, practitioners trained in the strengths perspective do not prefer the use of diagnostic labels because they may marginalize the client. Other practitioners, such as those trained in solution-focused brief therapy and behavioral perspectives, prefer more-empirical and more-functional ways to describe the problems of clients over diagnostic labels. Practitioners also believe that the diagnostic labels used in the DSM pathologize clients instead of empowering them to overcome their psychosocial problems. Diagnostic labels, in fact, may be used by some clients to disempower, excuse dysfunctional behavior, and remove the personal incentives and self-determination necessary to change. Many therapists, including family therapists and others practicing from the systems perspectives, brief therapists, cognitive constructivist therapists, and behaviorist practitioners, express some skepticism about the usefulness of the DSM nosological system. They do not see diagnostic labels as helpful because they do not describe the specific behaviors of the client that are a problem for the client and others. Neither do they specify change goals that are necessary for the client to solve his or her presenting problems.

Beyond the critiques offered by social work practitioners and therapists working from differing models, the DSM has also been criticized for its lack of research into the validity and reliability of its diagnostic categories. It is necessary for a measurement instrument or an assessment tool to demonstrate validity and reliability before it is useful to practitioners (Kendell & Jablensky, 2003). The social work researchers Kutchins and Kirk (1997) have offered some of the most compelling criticisms of the research for the manual, showing that the categories lack reliability. The ongoing question of clinical utility has affected both the *International Classification of Diseases* and the DSM (Reed, 2010; Stein et al., 2010). Other practice researchers have pointed to the political and social constructivist nature of the diagnoses in the DSM. These researchers demonstrate that the diagnoses are maintained or deleted from the manual based on social political processes such as associations of pharmaceutical industries to the DSM instead of empirical research (Cosgrove & Krimsky, 2012; Robbins, 2014). Some social constructivists and advocates for the oppressed groups of mental health patients go so far as to say that the DSM is neither valid nor helpful to clients, but that it serves instead to maintain the power of an elite group of psychiatrists and therapists. The social work profession in general does not prefer the categorical, noncontextual view of human behavior of the DSM.

According to Hare (2004) and the International Federation of Social Workers, fundamental to social work practice worldwide is the person-in-environment concept. Unfortunately, however, the person-in-environment assessment approach does not yet have validity and reliability studies, which limits its usefulness to clinical practice. Moreover, evidence-based practice will continue to inform social workers with the goal being to deliver the highest quality, ethically sound, and clinically useful interventions for clients (Pace, 2008).

Improving the DSM for Social Workers.   Over the years, the developers of the DSM have worked to address criticisms of it; the current DSM (DSM-5; APA, 2013) offers more of a person-in-environment approach to assessment for making a diagnosis. DSM-5 accomplishes this through clustering related disorders, including dimensional versus strictly categorical diagnostic classifications, as well as the continued focus on cultural concepts in the diagnostic process (e.g., cultural formulation interview). Future editions of the DSM are likely to continue to address criticisms. It is not likely, however, that any revision will totally satisfy practitioners who have theoretical or epistemological concerns about the helpfulness of psychiatric diagnosis.

Importance of Using the DSM. The DSM is the most frequently used diagnostic system in mental health assessment. Despite the limitations of the DSM-5 (APA, 2013), the most current version of the manual, it is important for social workers to learn to use the DSM. According to a congressional research service publication, clinical social workers are estimated to make up the largest percentage of mental health providers nationally (Heisler & Bagalman, 2014). One national survey conducted by the Substance Abuse and Mental Health Services Administration (SAMHSA) board found that clinical social workers outnumber psychiatrists and psychologists by five to one and two to one, respectively, in the provision of mental health and substance abuse treatment (SAMHSA, 2013). Majorities of practicing social workers are employed in mental health or school mental health services followed by health-care and substance abuse services (Bureau of Labor Statistics, 2014). The manual is constantly used in health and mental health services and in work with clients and insurance reimbursement, and other mental health professionals consider it the state of the art in mental health assessment. Because social workers often collaborate with other health-care professionals, they need to be familiar with the content of the DSM to communicate effectively about their clients with other professionals. The DSM delineates the symptoms, diagnostic features, development and course, gender/cultural and risk factors, including suicide risk, differential diagnoses, comorbidity, and prevalence rates that must be examined thoroughly in a complete psychosocial assessment. For this reason, this chapter also uses DSM diagnostic categories and their measurements when discussing assessment methods for adult clients.

ASSESSING MAJOR MENTAL ILLNESSES IN ADULTS

Social workers assess adult clients with major mental illnesses, such as schizophrenia spectrum and bipolar illnesses, and other neurocognitive disorders such as delirium. It is important that practitioners be astute in diagnosing these symptoms in clients to ensure that clients get the proper help and treatment and familiarize themselves with standardized neuropsychological assessment tools. The mental status exam has long been used to help examine current mental functioning and to assess serious mental disorders. Depression, anxiety disorders, trauma- and stressor-related disorders, substance-related disorders, and personality disorders are covered later in this chapter.

Mini-Mental State Exam

The MMSE, published by Folstein, Folstein, and McHugh (1975), is a frequently used assessment tool designed to evaluate the mental state of clients in both clinical and research settings (Crum, Anthony, Bassett, & Folstein, 1993; Molloy & Standish, 1997). It assesses cognitive impairments like delirium, and other neurocognitive disorders. The MMSE consists of brief and basic items that allow for a time-efficient and effective evaluation of various cognitive domains, including orientation, encoding, attention, recall, language, reading, writing, and drawing (Folstein et al., 1975). The eleven-item scale has a possible total of thirty points and requires less than ten minutes to administer. The MMSE has been widely used to detect cognitive difficulties in special populations, such as the elderly, clients with head injury, and individuals with severe mental illness (Lezak, 1995).

When using the MMSE, a cutoff score of 23 or 24 is generally accepted in order to separate patients with cognitive impairment from those who are cognitively intact (Anthony, LeResche, Niaz, von Korff, & Folstein, 1982; DePaulo, Folstein, & Gordon, 1980). Research indicates that a cutoff score of 23 for clients with mental health issues is acceptable (Folstein et al., 1975). However, some studies have suggested a lower sensitivity level for those clients with less education, clients of certain ethnicities, or older clients (Fillenbaum, Heyman, Willians, Prosnitz, & Burchett, 1990; Launer, Dinkgreve, Jonker, Hooijer, & Lindeboom, 1993; Murden, McRae, Kaner, & Bucknam, 1991). The MMSE is published in the *Journal of Psychiatric Research,* thus was formerly in the public domain; a small fee is now required to use it.

Use of Mini–Mental State Examination in Concert with Other Information

The Structured Clinical Interview for the DSM-IV Axis I Disorders (SCID-I; APA, 2000; First, Spitzer, Gibbon, & Williams, 2002) is the most common clinical interview used with adults with mental disorders. It is a comprehensive assessment that is based on the DSM-IV decision tree and is currently being updated to comply with the DSM-5 (APA, 2013) with an expected release in Spring 2015. The SCID-I requires a fair degree of clinical judgment and includes several open-ended questions that help account for self-report. The SCID-I is an extensive tool that can be used to diagnose many disorders.

RAPID ASSESSMENT OF COMMON PROBLEMS IN ADULT CLIENTS

Two of the most prominent types of problems that adult clients experience are depression and anxiety. Other frequent problems include trauma- and stressor-related disorders as well as substance-related disorders. To develop accurate assessments of these disorders, a social worker can use a set of rapid assessment instruments specific to the particular diagnoses. The following sections introduce some of the prominent rapid assessment tools recommended for assessment purposes. Recall from chapter 3 that these standardized measures are meant to offer quick, valid, reliable assessments of a client's characteristics. As screening tools, rapid assessment measures can provide one part of the information necessary to make a diagnosis. If the client scores are clinically significant on one of these rapid assessment measures, the practitioner can follow up with more thorough diagnostic interviews and procedures to determine whether the person qualifies for the diagnosis. The measures are also helpful in outcomes monitoring. (For more ideas about measuring outcomes, see chapter 10.)

Major Depressive Disorder

In practice, a social worker is likely to encounter clients with a variety of depressive disorders; their diagnostic features along with a large number of applicable specifiers are detailed in the DSM-5 (APA, 2013). Accordingly, a major depressive disorder is characterized by the presence of a depressed mood and/or anhedonia over a two-week period that causes clinically significant impairment, as well as four or more of the following seven symptoms nearly every day:

- Significant weight loss or gain
- Insomnia or hypersomnia
- Psychomotor agitation or retardation
- Fatigue
- Feelings of worthlessness or inappropriate guilt
- Diminished ability to concentrate or think
- Recurrent thoughts of death or suicide

Persistent depressive disorder is characterized by many of the same symptoms as major depressive disorder, and research has shown that both disorders can be equally disabling. Diagnostic criteria include a continuous depressed mood and the occurrence of a minimum of two out of six symptoms (e.g., poor appetite, insomnia or hypersomnia, low energy, low self-esteem, poor concentration, and feelings of hopelessness). Furthermore, the symptoms must be present most of the time over a two-year period and cause clinically significant impairment (APA, 2013).

Depression may be an accompanying symptom with other disorders (e.g., adjustment disorder with depressed mood). Although the use of clinical tools for the assessment of depression may be necessary, self-report instruments are also valuable. With regard to suicide risk, assessment must be consistent and ongoing. The following sections cover some examples of validated instruments to appropriately screen for major depression, persistent depressive disorder, as well as other specified and unspecified depressive disorders. Screening tools should be used to supplement but never replace clinical judgment or the clinical interview.

Beck Depression Inventory.   The mostly widely known and extensively used assessment instrument for ascertaining depressive symptomatology in adults is the Beck Depression Inventory II (Beck, Steer, & Brown, 1996). First developed in 1961 by Aaron Beck (1961), the Beck Depression Inventory consists of twenty-one items rated on a four-point scale (0 to 3) to assess the intensity of depression in adult clients. The current version, the Beck Depression Inventory II, was revised from earlier versions to be congruent with the text revision DSM-IV-TR (APA, 2000). The self-administered instrument takes between five and ten minutes to complete and should be filled out in the presence of a doctoral-level clinician trained in the use of the instrument. It has excellent reliability with a test-retest coefficient of 0.90. Hundreds of research studies have been conducted using the Beck Depression Inventory over the past fifty-five years, which attests to its concurrent and criterion validity. A score of 0 to 13 indicates normal levels of depressive symptoms, 14 to 19 indicates mild to moderate levels of depression, 20 to 28 indicates moderate to severe levels of depression, and 29 to 63 indicates extremely severe levels of depression. The social worker needs to be able to comprehend these scores provided by the doctoral-level administrator to facilitate treatment strategies for the client.

The Patient Health Questionnaire–9 Depression Scale.   The Patient Health Questionnaire–9 depression scale (Spitzer, Kroenke, & Williams, 1999) is a self-administered version of the Primary Care Evaluation of Mental Disorders (Spitzer et al., 1994) for screening depression severity (Kroenke & Spitzer, 2002; Kroenke, Spitzer, & Williams, 2001). The questionnaire has nine items that are scored on a Likert scale from 0 (not at all) to 3 (nearly every day), with totals ranging from 0 to 27. The Patient Health Questionnaire–9 can be used as a diagnostic tool (i.e., depression is indicated when five items are scored greater or equal to 2), but it is used most often to screen for depression (i.e., cutoff scores of 5, 10, and 15 indicating mild, moderate, and severe levels of depression). Kroenke et al. reported internal consistency ranging from .86 to .89 and identified a cutoff score of 10 or greater had a sensitivity of 88 percent and a specificity of 88 percent for major depression. Later research by Chagas et al. (2013) identified a threshold score of 9 or higher having a sensitivity of 100 percent and specificity of 83.1 percent.

Center for Epidemiological Studies Depression Scale–Revised.
Another commonly used instrument to assess depression is the Center for
Epidemiologic Studies Depression Scale (Radloff, 1977), revised in 2004
(Eaton, Muntaner, Smith, Tien, & Ybarra, 2004). This self-report, twenty-
item scale has been found to be highly reliable with populations of vary-
ing ages, ethnicities, and cultures in addition to underserved populations
such as economically disadvantaged and elderly (Eaton et al., 2004; Van
Dam & Earleywine, 2011). Both the Patient Health Questionnaire–9 (see
www.phqscreeners.com) and the Center for Epidemiologic Studies
Depression Scale–Revised (see www.cesd-r.com) are in the public domain.

Anxiety Disorders

In addition to depression, clients often encounter problems with anxiety.
There is growing evidence of a strong relationship between depression
and anxiety disorders. The genetic causes of depression and generalized
anxiety disorder have striking similarities (Sullivan, Neale, & Kendler,
2000). Clients often qualify for both diagnoses; the coexistence of both
disorders constitutes a greater mental health burden than previously
acknowledged (Moffitt et al., 2007). Furthermore, the DSM-5 recognizes
the comorbidity of anxiety disorders with each other and defines anxiety
disorders as those "that share features of excessive fear and anxiety and
related behavioral disturbances" (APA, 2013, p. 189). Here again, clinical
judgment is key to determining what may be interpreted as excessive.
Other symptoms might include restlessness, concentration difficulties,
sleep problems, tension, and irritability. According to the DSM-5, the
variety of anxiety disorders includes separation anxiety, specific phobias,
social anxiety, panic disorder, agoraphobia, generalized anxiety disorder,
and anxiety disorders of varied etiologies (e.g., substance or medication
induced, or due to another medical condition). Anxiety can be assessed
using multiple methods, including standardized measurement tools.
Detailed diagnostic criteria for assessing anxiety disorders can be found
in the DSM-5 (APA, 2013).

State Trait Anxiety Inventory.   The State Trait Anxiety Inventory is a
standardized two-part, self-report instrument. The state and trait sections
each contain twenty items, which the respondent rates from "not at all" to
"very much so" on a scale of 1 to 4. The scale has been validated and
shown to have alpha reliability coefficients ranging from 0.86 to 0.95
(Spielberger, Gorsuch, Lushene, Vagg, & Jacobs, 1983). Several of the items
are reverse scored. Examples of items include "I feel tense," "I feel upset,"
and "I feel secure." Additionally, a brief instrument that can help screen
for anxiety symptoms is the Generalized Anxiety Disorder seven-item
scale (Spitzer, Kroenke, Williams, & Löwe, 2006); this tool can be found in

the public domain on the screening tools Web site (www.integration .samhsa.gov). Furthermore, the DSM-5 contains a brief, crosscutting symptom measure (Level 1) and a more specific (Level 2) questionnaire to help assess symptoms of anxiety (e.g., the PROMIS® Emotional Distress–Anxiety short form), which can be found under "online assessment measures" on the APA DSM-5 Web site (PROMIS®, 2011).

Panic Attack Symptoms Questionnaire. The Panic Attack Symptoms Questionnaire (Clum, Broyles, Borden, & Watkins, 1990) is a thirty-three-item instrument measuring the severity of symptoms the client experiences during a panic attack. Items are rated from 0 to 5, where 0 = "Did not experience this" and 5 = "Experienced it protractedly (1 day to 2 days or longer)." The instrument has good reliability, with an alpha of 0.88. The scale can be used to differentiate between individuals who do and do not have panic attacks (Corcoran & Fisher, 2013).

Trauma- and Stressor-Related Disorders

Trauma- and stressor-related disorders are classified in terms of psychological symptoms and behaviors that emerge in response to an external event or stressor, which is a critical diagnostic condition (APA, 2013). These disorders often share overlapping symptoms on the diagnostic spectrum with the surrounding chapters (e.g., anxiety, obsessive compulsive, and dissociative disorders). Some appropriate assessment measures include the following:

The Posttraumatic Stress Disorder Checklist for the DSM-5. The Posttraumatic Stress Disorder Checklist for the DSM-5 (PCL-5; Weathers et al., 2013) is a twenty-item, self-report instrument that adheres to the DSM-5 (APA, 2013) diagnostic criteria for posttraumatic stress disorder (PTSD). This assessment tool takes under ten minutes to complete and is available in three formats (i.e., without Criterion A component, with Criterion A component, with expanded Criterion A component). The PCL-5 can be used for screening purposes, provisional diagnosis or to measure change over time. Item responses are measured on a five-point scale from 0 = "not at all" to 4 = "extremely." Scoring instructions vary depending on purpose (e.g., total symptom severity score or provisional diagnosis). Preliminary validation of the psychometric properties of the PCL-5 appears to be adequate. However, cutoff scores for monitoring progress are still being established. Further information is available at www.ptsd.va.gov/ professional/assessment/adult-sr/ptsd-checklist.asp. Additionally, the Acute Stress Disorder scale (Bryant, Moulds, & Guthrie, 2000) is a nineteen-item, self-report instrument that measures symptoms of acute stress disorder with good psychometrics (total scale internal consistency alpha = .96

and test-retest reliability = .94), and convergent, construct and predictive validity (Corcoran & Fisher, 2013).

Trauma Symptom Checklist 33 and 40.   The Trauma Symptom Checklist 33 (TSC-33; Briere & Ruentz, 1989) and Trauma Symptom Checklist 40 (TSC-40; Elliot & Briere, 1992) are self-report instruments, with thirty-three and forty items respectively, that have been used in clinical research as a measure of childhood or adult traumatic effect. Both instruments have been shown to have reliable psychometrics and internal consistency for total scales and subscales as well as predictive and discriminant validity (Briere & Ruentz, 1989; Dutton, 1995). The respondent rates a list of thirty-three or forty items (from 0 = never to 3 = very often). Examples of the items include "insomnia," "feeling isolated from others," and "trouble getting along with others."

Personality Disorders

Clients with personality disorders often have difficulty functioning in work and social settings. Personality disorders in the DSM-5 are divided into three clusters based on symptom presentation, including cluster A (e.g., paranoid, schizoid, and schizotypal), cluster B (e.g., antisocial, borderline, histrionic, and narcissistic), and cluster C (e.g., avoidant, dependent, and obsessive compulsive). An alternative model for personality disorders can be found in Section III of the DSM-5 (APA, 2013). These disorders tend to require extensive therapeutic intervention, and clients may be at risk for harming themselves and others, as is the case with clients who have antisocial and borderline diagnoses. A social worker can augment clinical judgment with the use of standardized measurement instruments and appropriate developmental history.

Structured Clinical Interview for the DSM-IV Axis II Personality Disorders.   One method a social worker can use to ensure an appropriate diagnosis is to rely on standardized, structured interviews for assessing psychopathology. Interviews such as the Structured Clinical Interview for the DSM-IV Axis II Personality Disorders (SCID-II; APA, 2000; First, Gibbon, Spitzer, Williams, & Benjamin, 1997) can improve the reliability and validity of diagnosis among clinicians. The SCID-II is the recognized benchmark for the diagnosis of personality disorders. This semistructured instrument can make a diagnosis by either the presence/absence of symptoms or by counting (summing scores) the number of criteria needed to meet diagnosis. The SCID-V will be released in Spring 2015. Although the diagnostic criteria for the personality disorders in the DSM-5 (APA, 2013) are unchanged, revisions in the 2013 edition have improved clinical utility. Many argue that the assessment of personality disorders is strengthened when clinicians are trained in the use of semi-structured instruments (Duggan & Gibbon, 2008). A social worker can also use other standardized measures to assess a client's personality or refer the client to an experienced psychologist for a more formal personality assessment.

Minnesota Multiphasic Personality Inventory. The standardized measures covered in chapter 3 are among the best self-report assessment tools for measuring personality functioning. Other personality assessment measures, such as the Minnesota Multiphasic Personality Inventory (MMPI) and the MMPI-2, are based on the original work of Hathaway and McKinley (1943). The MMPI-2 was updated with the help of James Butcher and others (Butcher, 2004; Butcher, Graham, Williams, & Ben-Porath, 2007; Butcher, Williams, & Fowler, 2000). A restructured form with new scales (MMPI-2-RF; Ben-Porath & Tellegen, 2008/2011; Tellegen & Ben-Porath, 2008/2011; Tellegen et al., 2003) contains 338 items (dichotomously scored) and takes from thirty to fifty minutes to complete. (For a list of the fifty-one scales of the MMPI-2-RF, see appendix 6A.) The original MMPI-2 is a widely used comprehensive instrument with years of supportive research behind it, and the MMPI-2-RF appears to be a promising tool for diagnosing personality disorders as conceived in Section III of the DSM-5 (APA, 2013; Ben-Porath, 2012; Finn, Arbisi, Erbes, Polusny, & Thuras, 2014). Clinicians must be trained in the administration and scoring of this scale.

Self-Report Standardized Assessment of Personality Abbreviated Scale. Another useful self-administered instrument for screening purposes is the Self-Report Standardized Assessment of Personality Abbreviated Scale (Germans, Van Heck, Moran, & Hodiamont, 2008) that is based on the original Standardized Assessment of Personality Abbreviated Scale (Hesse & Moran, 2010; Moran et al., 2003). This eight-item dichotomously rated measure for personality disorders screens for the presence of a general personality disorder versus diagnosing which disorder may be present. Summing items produces a total score ranging from 0 to 8, with higher scores indicating greater likelihood for the presence of a personality disorder. The cutoff score of 4 correctly identifies the presence of a DSM-IV personality disorder in 80 percent of participants (sensitivity of .83, specificity of .80) and a test-retest coefficient of .89 (Germans et al., 2008).

Millon Clinical Multiaxial Inventory and Coolidge Axis II Inventory. Psychologists, clinical social workers, and other clinicians can also use other standardized personality assessment measures, such as the

Millon Clinical Multiaxial Inventory (Millon, 1997; Millon & Davis, 1997) and the Coolidge Axis II Inventory (Coolidge, 2005; Coolidge & Merwin, 1992). The Millon consists of 175 true/false items designed primarily to detect a variety of personality disorders as well as additional subscales for detecting some of the more common co-occurring mental disorders. In its third edition, this instrument reflects the diagnostic constructs for the ten personality disorders found in the DSM-5 (APA, 2013), as well as forty-two Grossman Facet Scales. Similar to other NCS Pearson products, the Millon instrument has been well researched and validated in its various versions. Details and psychometrics can be found in the authors' test manual (Millon, Millon, Davis, & Grossman, 2006). The Coolidge consists of 250 questions designed to measure personality disorders based on current diagnostic criteria. Each item is self-rated on a four-point scale, ranging from "strongly false" to "strongly true." A shorter, seventy-item version (Coolidge, 2001) is also available with psychometrics similar to its parent (Coolidge, Segal, Cahill, & Simenson, 2010). Additionally, the DSM-5 (APA, 2013) contains new disorder specific assessment measures (e.g., Personality Inventory for the DSM-5–Brief Form) for both adults and children; these can be found under online assessment measures (PDFfiller, n.d.).

Substance-Related Disorders

Substance-related disorders and the severity of substance use are important issues to consider when assessing adult clients. The DSM-5 (APA, 2013) offers a detailed way to diagnose ten classes of substances, including alcohol, cannabis, opioids, hallucinogens, inhalants, sedatives, hypnotics, stimulants, tobacco, and caffeine. Adults can be diagnosed with substance intoxication, withdrawal, or one or more substance-use disorders based on their ingestion of different substances and patterns of use. While this chapter cannot cover every substance-related disorder that may be assessed in clinical practice, it provides an overview of important assessment issues to consider when working with adult clients. It is important, for example, to assess for substance use in every client because substance use is often comorbid with other mental illnesses and is a common presenting problem even though clients may not volunteer to discuss such use openly. Substance use may be a major contributor to other mental disorders including depression, anxiety, and stress-related symptoms and personality disorders. This means that social workers assessing clients that present with these types of problems must also consider if these disorders are caused by or exacerbated by a substance-related disorder. In fact, the DSM-5 even provides diagnostic criteria for various mental illnesses that may be caused because of substance use so that practitioners can report when a client is having symptoms that are associated with a substance-related mental disorder.

Alcoholism is a frequent diagnosis that is encountered in adult clients of all ages, including older adult populations. For many years alcoholism has been recognized as a medical disease and has been included in the *International Classification of Diseases* (World Health Organization, 2010) as a persistent progressive, and potentially fatal disease. Binge drinking and alcohol misuse is the nation's third-leading cause of preventable death, and alcoholism may also contribute to other medical complications such as diabetes, heart disease, and liver failure (Stahre, Roeber, Kanny, Brewer, & Zhang, 2014). This suggests that it is important for practitioners to assess the health risks of binge drinking and alcohol-related disorders. The importance of assessment is highlighted by the fact that a SAMHSA study (2006) reported that about 54 million (23 percent) of Americans binge drink (i.e., five or more alcoholic drinks on the same occasion on at least one day in the past thirty days), which puts many adults at risk for alcohol-use disorders. This section explores substance-related disorders and provides important issues to consider and assessment methods for accurately diagnosing substance-related disorders.

First, as noted, the symptoms of substance use may be comorbid with other mental disorders or may even cause symptoms of a mental disorder. Many clients may also qualify for a dual diagnosis where they have both a mental illness and a substance-related disorder. For example, clients that may be diagnosed with a substance-related disorder may have mood swings between periods of elation and apparent depression (e.g., restlessness, irritability, discontent); however, only some clients may actually have a dual diagnosis of bipolar disorder and substance-related disorder, while other clients' mood swings are attributable to substance use alone. This makes the diagnosis of substance use complicated, requiring accurate knowledge of the client's history, detailed observation, and information from collateral sources in order to develop a thorough understanding of the problems the client may be experiencing.

How to Determine Severity of Substance Use

The DSM-5 (APA, 2013) describes four primary categories of clinical syndrome: substance use, substance withdrawal, and substance- or medication-induced mental disorders.

Substance-use disorder refers to a maladaptive pattern of using substances that has resulted in clinically significant impairment or distress. Depending on whether withdrawal-related symptoms have been empirically supported for a specific disorder, this category of disorder contains ten to eleven criteria for diagnostic purposes. To establish a diagnosis, two or more symptoms shall concur at any time during the same one-year period. Tolerance, one of the criteria for substance, is defined as a need for increased amount of the substance to achieve the desired effect, or a diminished effect with continued use of the same amount of the substance

(APA, 2013). Usually, to ascertain the degree of an individual's tolerance for any specific substance, lab results may be necessary. According to DSM-5 (APA, 2013), severity for substance use disorder depends on how many symptoms are identified over this one-year period.

Withdrawal from a substance is a second clinical syndrome of substance-related and addictive disorders. Withdrawal is also a physiological response to the discontinuation or dramatic reduction of a substance. While this disorder can be applied to all ten classes of substance, some substances such as phencyclidine, hallucinogens, and inhalants lack withdrawal symptoms that are empirically validated. According to DSM-5 (APA, 2013), avoiding withdrawal by ingestion of a similar substance is also considered a symptom.

Finally, there are three primary criteria necessary for establishing a diagnosis of substance- or medication-induced mental disorders: (1) the symptoms must meet the criteria for a mental disorder, (2) symptoms must occur within one month of substance or medication usage, and (3) the resulting mental disorder must be caused by the usage of specific substance and/or medication. It is important to note that individuals may respond to various medications differently; as a result, this disorder can occur after the consumption of some over-the-counter or prescribed medication according to a physician's advice (APA, 2013). However, for individuals with a high sensitivity to regular medications, symptoms are usually temporary and generally diminish within a short period.

The remaining possible symptoms are more psychologically oriented. Loss of control is manifested by an individual taking the substance in larger amounts or over a more extended period than was intended. Symptoms of persistent desire or failure to cut down or control substance use are referred to as "cravings." Other symptoms of this category's disorder include (1) spending a great deal of time in activities necessary for substance access or recovery, (2) important activities (e.g., social, recreational, psychological) affected by using or recovering from substance use, and (3) continuing the substance use despite the individual's being aware of physical and/or psychosocial problems that are likely triggered by substance use (APA, 2013).

To indicate severity of substance-related disorders (mild, moderate, or severe), the number of symptoms should be recorded. Two or three symptoms indicates a mild severity, and four or five symptoms indicates a moderate severity. For individuals manifesting six or more symptoms, a severe substance-use disorder diagnosis should be offered.

Gambling disorder is currently the only non-substance-related addictive disorder in the DSM-5 (APA, 2013), with other similar addictive disorders (e.g., Internet addiction) anticipated to be forthcoming. A diagnosis of gambling disorder comprises a persistent and recurrent pattern of behavior in which gambling is unable to stop despite negative consequences. In general, individuals with gambling disorder exhibit addictive-like behaviors. The client usually engages in lying to conceal the amount of gambling, participates in illegal activities to fund the gambling, and fails to end the behaviors even after his/her awareness of the impairments in relationships, occupational opportunities, and social connections.

Assessment Instruments for Substance-Related Disorders.   There are a variety of assessment instruments that social workers can use to determine the presence, nature, and treatment directions with regard to clients with potential substance abuse problems. For an extensive list of assessment tools, clinicians can visit the National Institute on Alcohol Abuse and Alcoholism online (www.niaaa.nih.gov). The updated 2005 edition of *Helping Patients Who Drink Too Much: A Clinician's Guide* (National Institute on Alcohol Abuse and Alcoholism, 2005) can assist with collecting sensitive information by providing tools for assessment and intervention, patient education materials, and other useful clinical support. The guide is available free online and includes printable materials for use in the clinical setting (National Institute on Alcohol Abuse and Alcoholism, 2005).

There is a wealth of validated screening and assessment tools to determine the severity and extent of substance use, as well as the impact of substance abuse on an individual's functioning. The following sections present three of the most commonly used and widely accepted assessment tools used to guide the clinical interview: CAGE-AID, the Alcohol Use Disorders Identification Test-C, and the Michigan Alcohol Screening Test.

CAGE-AID.   The CAGE-AID (Brown & Rounds, 1995) screening tool (CAGE stands for cut, annoyed, guilty, eye opener; AID stands for adapted to include drugs) was developed by John Ewing, founding director of the Bowles Center for Alcohol Studies, at the University of North Carolina at Chapel Hill (Mayfield, McLeod, & Hall, 1994). The CAGE-AID test is an internationally used assessment instrument for identifying clients with alcohol and other substance use disorders. It is particularly useful as an initial screening tool, and the test has been translated into several languages. The practitioner asks the patient four questions:

1. Have you ever felt you ought to cut down your drinking (or drug use)?
2. Have people annoyed you by criticizing your drinking (or drug use)?
3. Have you ever felt bad or guilty about your drinking (or drug use)?
4. Have you had a drink (or used drugs) first thing in the morning (eye opener) to steady your nerves or get rid of a hangover?

Affirmative answers to two or more questions is a positive screen and should prompt further history. This screening tool is in the public domain.

Scoring and psychometric information can be found at SAMHSA–Health Resources and Services Administration (SAMHSA-HRSA; n.d.).

The Alcohol Use Disorders Identification Test-C. The Alcohol Use Disorders Identification Test (AUDIT-C; Bush, Kivlahan, McDonell, Fihn, & Bradley, 1998) was developed from a six-country World Health Organization collaborative project as a screening instrument for hazardous and harmful alcohol consumption. The AUDIT-C (Bush et al., 1998) is a short version of the AUDIT (2001); AUDIT-C consists of three items that covers the domains of alcohol consumption, drinking behavior, and alcohol-related problems. Responses to each question are scored from 0 to 12, with a maximum possible score of 36. An AUDIT-C score of 4 or more indicates hazardous or harmful alcohol use for men and a score of 3 or more for women indicates a potential alcohol-use disorder. The AUDIT-C provides a simple method for early detection of harmful alcohol use (Frank, DeBenedetti, Volk, Williams, Kivlahan, & Bradley, 2008). The AUDIT-C is available in both English and Spanish. It takes only about five minutes to complete, has been tested internationally, and has high levels of validity and reliability. (For a downloadable version complete with scoring instructions, see SAMHSA-HRSA, n.d., Drug and Alcohol Screening Tools).

The Michigan Alcohol Screening Test. The Michigan Alcohol Screening Test ([MAST] Selzer, 1971; see appendix 6B) is a written, twenty-five-item screening test that may be given to a patient initially or in follow-up to another screening test, such as CAGE-AID. Its brevity makes it useful as an outpatient-screening tool. Cutoff scores correlate well with more-extensive diagnostic tests for alcohol disorders. The MAST has been modified for drug abuse (i.e., Drug and Alcohol Screening Test). The instrument is in the public domain and clinicians can download it for use (MAST, n.d.).

Other Resources

SBIRT (Screening, Brief Intervention, Referral, and Treatment) is a comprehensive approach to providing early intervention and treatment services to individuals who have substance-use problems. Screening occurs during routine medical care (e.g., doctor or dental visit) via a brief questionnaire developed by the National Institute on Drug Abuse and the National Institute on Alcohol Abuse and Alcoholism. Additional information can be found at SAMHSA-HRSA (n.d.a). In addition, Section III of the DSM-5 (APA, 2013) includes emerging measures that can be used to assist clinical decision-making, including the National Institute on Drug Abuse–modified ASSIST for assessment of substance use in adults (National Institute on Drug Abuse, 2014; APA, 2015).

In summary, substance abuse disorders are complex problems with a variety of etiologies and outcomes. Social work practitioners can use the previously noted assessment tools to assess substance abuse disorders. If you, as a social worker, have a large clientele of substance users or abusers, special training would be valuable and important.

SPECIAL ISSUES IN WORKING WITH OLDER ADULTS

With increasing advances in medical technology during the past two decades, there has been a corresponding increase in the number of older persons in the population. Data from the 2010 Census showed that the population of individuals aged sixty-five and older in the United States is rapidly growing and equals 13 percent of the total U.S. population, which is the highest level for any Census (Werner & U.S. Census Bureau, 2011). Older adults experience many of the same emotional problems that younger adults experience. For example, older adults can be diagnosed in any of the adult categories for mental disorders found in the DSM. In contrast, depression and neurocognitive disorders are two psychobiological and emotional problems that are prevalent in the older adult population. In addition, medical or physical problems may be confounding factors for older adults and may mask emotional symptoms such as depression that older adults experience. In the older adult population, it is also important to be able to differentiate between an emotional or medical problem and normal aging. Therefore, assessment instruments that specifically focus on the problems confronting older adults have been developed to address the psychological and medical issues that are prevalent in this population.

One of the most common emotional disorders experienced by older adults is depression. As do other adults, older persons display symptoms of sadness, hopelessness, fatigue, loss or increase of appetite, difficulty sleeping, and other symptoms outlined in the DSM. However, in addition to those symptoms, older adults may also experience memory loss and cognitive impairment when depressed. Practitioners are cautioned that depressive symptoms can often be confused with more serious neurocognitive disorders (Korczyn & Halperin, 2009).

Other symptoms that may be present in depressed, younger adults, such as a decline in sexual interest and other somatic complaints, may be normal signs of aging in older adults and not an indication of depression. Because of these differences in psychological symptomatology among older adults, specific scales, such as the Geriatric Depression Scale (GDS), have been designed to measure depression in the elderly.

The GDS is a well-known instrument designed to assess depressive symptoms in older adults (Brink et al., 1982). It is available in a thirty-item version and a highly correlated fifteen-item shorter version. The GDS has high internal consistency and has been validated in many studies (Burns,

Lawlor, & Craig, 2002; Marc, Raue, & Bruce, 2008). Because depression in older adults is often first assessed in a physician's office, it is helpful to have a questionnaire that requires only a short time to complete. The GDS is often used as an initial screening tool to diagnose depressive symptoms in the elderly. If an elderly person scores above the cutoff point on this scale, it is likely that a significant depressive symptomatology exists, and the practitioner should pursue a fuller assessment. Social workers who have elderly clients can use this instrument during an initial interview or at any time the client appears to be displaying depressive symptoms. Box 6.2 presents the short form of the scale and instructions for scoring. The scale is in the public domain, can be used by practitioners without permission from the authors, and is available in the short or long version with scoring instructions (Stanford University, n.d.).

Box 6.2
Geriatric Depression Scale

Mood Scale (Short Form)

1. Are you basically satisfied with your life?	YES/**NO**
2. Have you dropped many of your activities and interests?	**YES**/NO
3. Do you feel that your life is empty?	**YES**/NO
4. Do you often get bored?	**YES**/NO
5. Are you in good spirits most of the time?	YES/**NO**
6. Are you afraid that something bad is going to happen to you?	**YES**/NO
7. Do you feel happy most of the time?	YES/**NO**
8. Do you often feel helpless?	**YES**/NO
9. Do you prefer to stay at home, rather than going out and doing new things?	**YES**/NO
10. Do you feel you have more problems with memory than most?	**YES**/NO
11. Do you think it is wonderful to be alive now?	YES/**NO**
12. Do you feel pretty worthless the way you are now?	**YES**/NO
13. Do you feel full of energy?	YES/**NO**
14. Do you feel that your situation is hopeless?	**YES**/NO
15. Do you think that most people are better off than you are?	**YES**/NO

Answers in **bold** indicate depression. Score 1 point for each bolded answer.
A score > 5 points is suggestive of depression.
A score ≥ 10 points is almost always indicative of depression.
A score > 5 points should warrant a follow-up comprehensive assessment.

SOURCE: Sheikh, J. I., & Yesavage, J. A. (1986). Geriatric Depression Scale (GDS). Recent evidence and development of a shorter version. In T. L. Brink (Ed.), *Clinical Gerontology: A Guide to Assessment and Intervention* (pp. 165–173). New York: The Haworth Press, Inc.

Functional Status of Older Adults

Another important factor to consider in assessing older adults is their functional status. Functional status refers to the person's ability to take care of him- or herself, to perform physical activities, and to participate in activities of daily living. Older adults who have difficulties in their functional status may require additional community resources such as home health services, home-delivered meals, visiting nursing services, or housekeeping assistance. Elderly persons can range from mildly to severely impaired in their ability to perform functional activities. Current recommendations from the U.S. Preventive Services Task Force suggest that early recognition of cognitive impairment, in addition to helping make diagnostic and treatment decisions, enables clinicians to anticipate problems the patients may have in understanding and adhering to recommended therapy (Lin, O'Connor, Rossom, Perdue, & Eckstrom, 2013). This information may also be useful to the patient's caregiver and family members in helping anticipate and plan for future problems that may develop as a result of cognitive impairment progression. Clinicians should assess cognitive function whenever they suspect cognitive impairment or deterioration, through direct observation, patient report, or concerns that family members, friends, or caretakers raise. One evidence-based tool that clinicians and gerontologists have widely used is the World Health Organization Disability Assessment Schedule 2.0 (WHODAS 2.0). This tool is in the public domain and can be found along with scoring instructions in Section III of the DSM-5 (APA, 2013, pp. 745–748) or online (APA, 2015). We describe the WHODAS 2.0 and its usage in more detail in the following section.

WHODAS 2.0: Administration and Scoring.   The WHODAS 2.0 is a thirty-six-item, self-administered measure that assesses functional impairment and disability dimensions over the past thirty days across six functioning domains: (a) cognition/communication, (b) mobility, (c) self-care, (d) getting along with others, (e) activities of daily living (i.e., work, school/education, and household), and (f) involvement in society. The WHODAS 2.0 has good psychometrics, high test-retest reliability and correlation to other known related instruments of functioning. The WHODAS 2.0 has been used with diverse populations and is a recognized assessment measure of health and disability. It is also available in a twelve-item version (World Health Organization, 2010, 2012).

Quality Assurance and Brief Assessment Screening and Outcome Measures for Adults

Rapid assessment tools like those covered in the sections on depression and anxiety provide a general screening for specific problem areas.

More-comprehensive assessment measures like the MMPI-2-RF (appendix 6A) covered in the section on personality disorders provide a comprehensive screen of major mental health diagnosis and psychological characteristics but are time consuming and expensive to use in practice. In today's fast-paced, managed-care, practice settings it is not always desirable or cost-effective to perform a comprehensive assessment or to give a client a long measure like the MMPI-2 or the Millon measure described earlier. In fact, surveys of psychologists indicate that the whole field of psychological assessment is being challenged to change and is evolving because of managed care. Increasingly, psychologists are using fewer standardized measures for traditional psychological assessment batteries. Standardized brief screening and outcomes measurement instruments, as well as quality assurance systems that provide specific feedback on individual clients for treatment planning and outcomes monitoring, are replacing traditional psychological assessment batteries (Baker, McFall, & Shoham, 2009). Chapter 3 introduced computerized quality assessment systems and their measures. Such measurement systems are able to assess client functioning quickly (as are rapid assessment instruments) but include several problem areas instead of one specific area like depression. They also give specific feedback on high-risk areas, such as suicide and violence, and provide both graphic and narrative reports that practitioners can use in treatment planning and outcome monitoring.

When used in quality assurance systems, brief screening instruments can assess several problem areas and measures, either by acting as a screen of several different areas or by making it possible for clinicians to combine rapid assessment questions as needed from different test-item banks or measurement tools. Some systems even allow the clinician to add client data from more-traditional instruments such as the MMPI or Millon. The latter choices give clinicians more flexibility in assessment and can be individualized for client need. (For a review of several quality assurance systems and their measures, see table 3.1.) Quality assurance measurement systems generally provide the following:

- A screen of several problem areas that is completed in a short time and that is directly linked with treatment planning
- Clinically significant scores based on normative data
- A risk assessment profile
- A projection for client outcome
- An ongoing monitor of treatment effectiveness through the completion of repeated measures
- A signal for the practitioner if treatment is not progressing

- A clinical change score and reliability of change index for showing client improvement
- Graphic displays and/or narratives that the practitioner can use

These types of measurement tools meet all the criteria and common themes that chapter 1 identified as important for social work assessment. Problem identification, task planning, and treatment monitoring, for example, are inherent in these quality assurance measurement systems. These types of measurement systems are also easy to use in single-case designs and practice evaluation, as discussed in chapter 10. One shortfall of many of the quality assurance measurement systems, however, is that they often rely exclusively on client self-reports. Recall from earlier chapters that it is usually important to include more than one source of data in building valid and reliable assessments of clients. Some quality assurance systems correct for this possible information bias by including the practitioner's and other persons' perspectives as well.

One of the most popular measures is the Outcome Questionnaire (OQ®-45.2). The OQ®-45.2 is a computerized, self-report measure belonging to a family of outcomes measures. The measure is available online and is instantly scored (OQ® Measures, n.d.). The OQ®-45.2 has a clinical support technology known as a "signal-detecting device," which can alert clinicians to treatment progress or failure.

The OQ®-45.2 is a brief, forty-five-item, self-report outcome and tracking instrument designed for repeated measurement of client progress through the course of therapy and following termination. It can be completed in five minutes and is inexpensive to use, which makes it cost effective and suitable for agency-based practice. It offers measures of social functioning and appears to have excellent potential for social work practice.

The OQ®-45.2 measures functioning in three domains—subjective distress or symptom dysfunction (items loaded for depression and anxiety); interpersonal functioning; and social role, which enables the practitioner to assess functional level and change over time. The OQ®-45.2 contains risk assessment items for suicide potential, substance abuse, and potential violence at work. This questionnaire is available in Windows-based and Web-based versions, and it graphically reports treatment progress in real time. It has decision support features and numerous standard reports. Each item on the measure is rated on a five-point Likert scale from 0 (never) to 4 (almost always). The overall score is recommended for tracking progress in treatment because the number of items on the individual scales is small.

The OQ®-45.2 provides a signal-detecting system that alerts clinicians to the status of the client's treatment and the need to adjust the treatment plan. Feedback dots appear on the report. White feedback indicates that the client is functioning in the normal range and may be ready for termination. Green feedback suggests that the change the client is making is in the normal range and everything is all right; no change in treatment plan is needed. Yellow feedback indicates that the change the client is making is less than expected and that some adjustment in treatment plan is needed. Red feedback tells the practitioner that the client is not making progress and may terminate prematurely with no benefit from therapy.

The validity and reliability of the OQ®-45.2 are acceptable, and it is one of the better measures in the quality assurance area. It has a large national normative base and good internal consistency reliability (r = 0.93). The test-retest reliability after three weeks (r = 0.84) is acceptable. The measure has also demonstrated construct validity in factor-analytic studies showing a three-factor solution. Studies into concurrent validity have been done with acceptable results, and it has been shown to be sensitive to clinical change. A reliable change index has also been calculated: a score of fourteen is regarded as having made reliable change during treatment (Boswell, White, Sims, Harrist, & Romans, 2013; Lambert, Hansen, & Finch, 2001).

The OQ®-45.2 is among the first quality assurance measures to demonstrate in quantitative research, thereby providing outcome information to practitioners that can make a difference in the treatment outcomes of clients (Lambert et al., 2001; Lambert, Gregersen, & Burlingame, 2004).

Recent experimental design studies indicate that, when combined with other clinical support tools such as empirically derived problem-solving tools, an alliance measure, and a measure of social support, the OQ®-45.2 and its signal-detecting device is effective at improving treatment outcomes (Harmon et al. 2007; Slade, Lambert, Harmon, Smart, & Bailey, 2008; Lambert, 2013).

To further improve their evidence-based practices, social work clinicians and administrators should consider the benefits of using quality assurance systems that produce client-focused feedback in real time with empirically derived feedback systems like the OQ®-45.2 and its associated clinical support tools.

MOVING FROM ASSESSMENT TO INTERVENTION

Several other chapters in this book provide examples of assessment reports and intervention plans. This chapter gives each reader a chance to practice developing an intervention plan. In the case study that follows, we encourage readers to practice deciding what diagnosis, assessment tools, and treatment goals are appropriate. Read the following case study and use it as a learning tool to reflect on and answer the following questions and tasks. (You may also wish to consult chapters 5, 7, and 8 for examples of completed assessments to help you answer.):

- Develop a DSM-5 diagnosis based on the information presented in the case.
- What is this client's current mental status?
- Which measures covered in this chapter are most suitable for this client?
- Develop an intervention plan by identifying symptoms that may require referral to other professionals (e.g., physician, psychologist, psychiatrist, career counselor) and by identifying the availability of client resources (e.g., social support systems, transportation, housing, finances, recreational outlets).
- What are the most pressing issues for this client? What needs to be done first to help? Second? Third?
- What types of treatment goals might you be able to form with this client? How might the client suggest his or her main goals?
- Which measurement tools will you use in outcomes monitoring?

CASE STUDY CHRISTOPHER: MOVING FROM ASSESSMENT TO INTERVENTION

Christopher T. Hager, a sixty-two-year-old Caucasian man, appeared for the first interview wearing a wrinkled cardigan, blue jeans, and plaid shirt. He was unshaven and appeared to have just woken up. His hair was uncombed, and he had dark circles under his eyes. Chris was slightly underweight and had a subtle tremor in his hands.

When asked about his medical history, he replied that he had recently gone to the doctor complaining of headaches. Chris reported that the doctor found no physiological reason for the pain he was experiencing. He also remarked, "My headaches really made it hard to eat, so I've lost some more weight. I think I really need to gain a few pounds." Chris stated that there had been no prominent family history of illness, although he noted one of his uncles had committed suicide. He reported having tried Advil, Tylenol, and aspirin for the headaches but that he has taken no other prescribed medication on a regular basis to alleviate the chronic pain. He also stated that he sometimes has a nightcap to help him fall asleep, which has become more difficult lately.

The client's family physician had referred him to this behavioral health center for a psychological assessment. Chris readily agreed to make an appointment at the center because his twenty-four-year-old daughter, a graduate student in social work, supported the physician's recommendation.

Chris was employed for thirty years at a well-known, high-tech computer corporation as an electronics engineer. He recently took early retirement because of the company's employee layoffs and their offer of a compelling severance package. Chris stated that he missed the routine of getting up and going to work every morning, although he did not miss the pressure of trying to "keep up with young, new college grads."

Chris noticed that, after being out of work for approximately one month, he felt more lethargic and was having difficulty pursuing activities that he normally enjoyed. He mentioned that he often was bored and sometimes "didn't know what to do" with himself. Another difficulty he encountered was that he no longer saw friends from work—for lunch or for weekend activities. When asked about solutions to this problem, he said, "I don't really have the energy to make plans with the guys." He reported that his daughter, Catherine, has been urging him to get out of the house and socialize. However, Chris stated that he "just can't get going on anything these days."

Throughout the course of this assessment, Chris seemed to be using avoidance coping strategies to deal with his current problems. Rather than asserting himself on his own behalf, Chris tended to passively wait for others to initiate activities and solutions. When asked whether he believed his coping mechanisms are effective, he answered, "No, but I don't know what else to do."

In addition to his headaches and the loss of his job, Chris stated that he was divorced from his wife, Connie, approximately five years ago and that he is still disturbed by the divorce. When the social worker probed further, Chris revealed that his wife had left him after twenty-eight years of marriage. He stated angrily, "She was fed up with the whole thing." He also believed that Catherine had been caught in the middle, which prompted her to go to school in another state. Following the divorce, Chris moved from his comfortable, four-bedroom home in the suburbs to a small apartment downtown. Despite the manageable size of his present residence, he reportedly still has difficulty adjusting to taking care of the apartment and with other activities of daily living (e.g., laundry, cleaning, self-care).

Chris has weekly phone contact with Catherine. She is his only child. He no longer is in contact with his former wife, except on rare occasions. His primary companion is his bloodhound named Blue. Chris is quite committed to his dog, and spoke at length about Blue's pedigree and how he takes Blue for long walks late at night. He constantly made references to Blue throughout the conversation (e.g., "Blue and I had macaroni and cheese for dinner," "Blue and I like to walk to the grocery store and get coffee in the mornings").

Chris noted that "in his day," he was an eloquent speaker, a member of a large social network (primarily through playing golf), and a good communicator. However, he lamented that he no longer felt like part of a community, as he was when he was working. He stated that he lost many of his golfing partners because they had been work colleagues and they would make plans to golf at the end of the day. He also said that he was a member of several engineering organizations but that he had lost interest in those functions since he left his job. He also indicated that he used to play a lot of bridge when he was married but that, since the divorce, he had no one to partner with. He said he was embarrassed to go to bridge tournaments by himself. Chris stated that he felt he had been robbed not only of his professional title but also of his role as a husband. He stated that he had been married for so long that he did not know how to function as a single person. He did, however, mention one person, Mack, who played golf with him occasionally and who also went out to dinner with him at times.

Throughout the interview, Chris appeared sad when discussing his divorce and job loss. He seemed engaged in the conversation and showed no signs of psychotic behavior. He did appear to have a slight trembling in both hands but made no mention of this problem during the session.

When asked about romantic interests, Chris laughed and responded, "Are you kidding? I haven't even looked at a woman since my wife left me." On inquiry, Chris noted that, although his first few years married to his wife were "romantic and fun," approximately five years before his wife left the couple began sleeping in separate rooms. He noted in a defensive tone, "I snore pretty loudly." Chris was vague in response to questions about his sex life, but he did add, "I'm not what I used to be, if you know what I mean."

The social worker administered the MMSE to Chris before the interview. Chris scored in the normal range on the scale. He showed no signs of cognitive impairment, loss of memory, or thought disorder. He reported no history of cognitive problems. His thinking appeared to be clear, focused, and well organized, and he had no difficulty engaging in conversation with the social worker. Although he seemed to have some difficulty finding solutions to his present life problems, he appeared to have good judgment and decision-making capacities.

Chris consistently had flat affect during the assessment. Even his sporadic laughter at his own jokes was forced. He has a tendency toward sarcasm and a pessimistic attitude, as evidenced by his statement, "Even though I want things to be different, I am what I am. Guess you can't expect me to change after all these years." When asked whether he has times when he feels good, he replied, "There are times when I feel a bit better or worse, but I haven't really ever felt like myself since my wife left." He added that retirement is a challenge to a "workaholic like me." When asked about the impact of his mood on others, he expressed the belief that his daughter avoids spending time with him because she feels frustrated about his situation.

Although it was apparent that Chris viewed himself as a valuable worker and father, his self-esteem seems to have diminished since he left his job. His relatively recent divorce also seems to have deflated his sense of self-worth. Although he did not offer a great deal of information about his marriage or causes of the divorce, it was evident that the divorce was a traumatic event in his life. He appeared to be feeling somewhat hopeless about developing new relationships with others. His low self-esteem also seems to be preventing him from seeking out friends and other social supports with whom he could be involved.

Although Chris's low self-esteem and sadness appear to be preventing him from finding solutions to his present difficulties, he verbally expressed a strong desire to make changes in his life. For example, he stated, "I just don't want to continue living this way," and "Something's got to change in my life." Catherine seems to be a strong support and motivator for Chris to resolve his feelings of loss. He obviously respects her opinions and acknowledged that she "knows a whole lot more about this type of thing [feelings] than I do." When the social worker asked about any goals he might have for the future, Chris stated that it is all he can do to get through a day and that he does not think beyond that very much. However, he stated that he used to always set goals and was a fairly driven person when employed. When the social worker asked whether he could imagine ways that things could improve, Chris replied that he thought he might be drinking more than usual and that he needed to cut down on his alcohol consumption. "I think it may be clouding my vision right now." Chris exhibits some ambivalence about the work involved in making some of these changes. "One day I tell myself I'm going to stop drinking and start finding some healthy outlets for myself, and the next day I can't get out of bed. Two days last week, I never got out of my pajamas and Blue and I just spent the day watching videos and eating popcorn."

When asked about his culture and ethnicity, Chris reported that he is "Irish-Catholic." He jokes, "No wonder I'm the way I am, right?" When asked to elaborate, he noted that he comes from a long line of "stoic, hard-working, hard-drinking" men. He stated that his grandparents came to the United States when his parents were children. He did not know any more details about the family history. When asked about strengths and solutions that have come from his ethnic culture, he noted that he attributes his sense of humor, determination, and "realistic expectations" to his Irish heritage.

As referred to earlier, Chris considers himself Catholic. He reported that he used to go to church, at least on holidays, but that he has not gone since his divorce. He believes that God punishes people for sins. Through further inquiry, it became clear that Chris feels that because of his divorce, drinking, and his perception of a lack of contribution to society, there is "no way I can squeeze my way through the 'pearly gates.'" When asked about his life purpose, Chris responded, "At this point, just getting through the day." When pressed, he noted gaining strength from his belief that "I'm really Blue's 'higher power,' I suppose. He needs me." Chris is apparently experiencing some role transition and confusion.

He has lost his former roles of professional and husband. He has been having a great amount of difficulty transitioning to other roles in his life. He seems to enjoy the role of caretaker for his dog, but he appears to need other roles to gain a sense of self-fulfillment. It does not appear that Chris is ready to accept the role of retired person and may need to find another part-time position or to volunteer in the nonprofit sector to gain a sense of self-worth.

When asked whether he had anything to add to the assessment, he noted that he used to be an avid woodworker. He told the social worker that he made much of the furniture in his home. He expressed some pride in his work but noted that it has been so long since he has done such work that he does not even know where his tools are.

SUMMARY

This chapter described how to assess adult clients at different points in the life cycle and with diverse problem areas, as well as several methods of assessing adults using interview questions, the DSM diagnosis, standardized assessment measures, and other rating scales. A case study provides an opportunity for the reader to practice moving from assessment to intervention with an actual client situation. Assessment of adults from a strengths-based systems perspective is a crucial component in the social worker's repertoire of skills. Learning how to make accurate diagnoses and how to use different methods that aid assessment with adults can improve social workers' assessment skills.

STUDY QUESTIONS

1. How is the DSM used in practice?
2. What are three criticisms of the DSM?
3. What are three measures for depression and anxiety? Describe them.
4. What are two specific considerations in assessing older adult clients?
5. What are nine characteristics of quality assessment measurements used in managed care?

WEB SITES

Campbell Collaboration, www.campbellcollaboration.org
Cochrane Collaboration, www.cochranecollaboration.org
Psych Web, www.psychweb.com
DSM-5 Prelude Project, www.dsm5.org

REFERENCES

Alcántara, C., & Gone, J. P. (2014). Multicultural issues in the clinical interview and diagnostic process. In F. T. L. Leong (Ed.), *APA handbook of multicultural psychology: Vol. 2. Applications and training* (pp. 153–164). Washington, DC: American Psychological Association. Retrieved from http://gonetowar.com/wp-content/uploads/2014/01/Multicultural-Dx.pdf

American Psychiatric Association (APA). (2000). *Diagnostic and statistical manual of mental disorders* (4th ed.; DSM-IV). Washington, DC: Author.

American Psychiatric Association (APA). (2013). *Diagnostic and statistical manual of mental disorders* (5th ed.; DSM-5). Washington, DC: Author.

American Psychiatric Association (APA). (2015). *Online assessment measures (DSM-5).* Retrieved from http://www.psychiatry.org/practice/dsm/dsm5/online-assessment-measures

Anthony, J. C., LeResche, L., Niaz, U., von Korff, M. R., & Folstein, M. F. (1982). Limits of the mini-mental state as a screening test for dementia and delirium among hospital patients. *Psychological Medicine, 12,* 397–408.

Baker, T. B., McFall, R. M., & Shoham, V. (2009). Current status and future prospects of clinical psychology: Toward a scientifically principled approach to mental and behavioral health care. *Psychological Science in the Public Interest: A Journal of the American Psychological Society, 9*(2), 67–103.

Beck, A. T., Steer, R. A., & Brown, G. K. (1996). *Manual for the Beck Depression Inventory* (2nd ed.). San Antonio, TX: Psychological Corporation.

Beck, A.,Ward, C. H., Mendelson, M., Mock, J., & Erbaugh, J. (1961) An inventory for measuring depression. *Archives of General Psychiatry,4,* 561–571.

Ben-Porath, Y. S. (2012). *Interpreting the MMPI-2-RF.* Minneapolis: University of Minnesota Press.

Ben-Porath, Y. S., & Tellegen, A. (2011). *MMPI-2-RF (Minnesota Multiphasic Personality Inventory-2 Restructured Form): Manual for administration, scoring, and interpretation.* Minneapolis: University of Minnesota Press. (Originally published 2008).

Bentall, R. P. (2014). The search for elusive structure: A promiscuous realist case for researching specific psychotic experiences such as hallucinations. *Schizophrenia Bulletin, 40*(4), S198–S201.

Boswell, D. L., White, J. K., Sims, W. D., Harrist, R. S., & Romans, J. S. (2013). Reliability and validity of the Outcome Questionnaire-45.2. *Psychological Reports, 112*(3), 689–693.

Briere, J., & Ruentz, M. (1989). The TSC (TSC-33): Early data on a new scale. *Journal of Interpersonal Violence, 4,* 151–163.

Brink, T. L., Yesavage, J. A., Lum, O., Heersema, P., Adley, M. B., & Rose, T. L. (1982). Screening tests for geriatric depression. *Clinical Gerontologist, 1,* 37–44.

Brion, J. M., Dawson Rose, C., Nicholas, P. K., Sloane, R., Voss, J. G., Corless, I. B., . . . & Rosa, M. (2011). Unhealthy substance-use behaviors as symptom-related self-care in persons with HIV/AIDS. *Nursing & Health Sciences, 13*(1), 16–26.

Broman, C. L. (2012). Race differences in the receipt of mental health services among young adults. *Psychological Services, 9*(1), 38–48.

Brown, R. L., & Rounds, L. A. (1995). Conjoint screening questionnaires for alcohol and other drug abuse: criterion validity in primary care practice. *Wisconsin Medical Journal, 94*(3), 135–140.

Bryant, R. A., Moulds, M. L., & Guthrie, R. M. (2000). Acute Stress Disorder Scale: A self-report measure of acute stress disorder. *Psychological Assessment, 12*(1), 61–68.

Bureau of Labor Statistics. (2014). U.S. Department of Labor, Occupational Outlook Handbook, 2014–15 edition, Social Workers. Retrieved from http://www.bls.gov/ooh/community-and-social-service/social-workers.htm

Burns, A., Lawlor, B., & Craig, S. (2002). Rating scales in old age psychiatry. *British Journal of Psychiatry, 180,* 161–167.

Bush, K., Kivlahan, D. R., McDonell, M. B., Fihn, S. D., & Bradley, K. A. (1998). The AUDIT Alcohol Consumption Questions (AUDIT-C): An effective brief screening test for problem drinking. Ambulatory Care Quality Improvement Project (ACQUIP). *Archives of Internal Medicine, 158*(16), 1789–1795.

Butcher, J. N. (2004). *A beginner's guide to the MMPI-2* (2nd ed.). Washington, DC: American Psychological Association.

Butcher, J. N., Graham, J. R., Williams, C. L., & Ben-Porath, Y. S. (2007). *Development and use of the MMPI-2 content scales* (3rd ed.). Minneapolis: University of Minnesota Press.

Butcher, J. N., Williams, C. L., & Fowler, R. D. (2000). *Essentials of MMPI-2 and MMPI-A interpretation* (2nd ed.). Minneapolis: University of Minnesota Press.

Carney, J. (2014). Where are the social workers? One social worker's road to active opposition to the new DSM. *Ethical Human Psychology & Psychiatry, 16*(1), 63–79.

Carpenter-Song, E., Chu, E., Drake, R. E., Ritsema, M., Smith, B., & Alverson, H. (2010). Ethno-cultural variations in the experience and meaning of mental illness and treatment: Implications for access and utilization. *Transcultural Psychiatry, 47*(2), 224–251.

Chagas, M. H., Tumas, V., Rodrigues, G. R., Machado-de-Sousa, J. P., Filho, A. S., Hallak, J. E., & Crippa, J. A. (2013). Validation and internal consistency of Patient Health Questionnaire-9 for major depression in Parkinson's disease. *Age Ageing, 2*(5), 645–649.

Clum, G. A., Broyles, S., Borden, J., & Watkins, P. L. (1990). Validity and reliability of panic attack symptoms and cognition questionnaire. *Journal of Psychopathology and Behavioral Assessment, 12,* 233–245.

Coolidge, F. L. (2001). Short-form of the Coolidge Axis II Inventory (SCATI): Manual. Colorado Springs, CO: Author.

Coolidge, F. L. (2005). *The Coolidge Axis II Inventory Manual–Revised.* Colorado Springs, CO: Author.

Coolidge, F. L., & Merwin, M. M. (1992). Reliability and validity of the Coolidge Axis Two Inventory: A new inventory for the assessment of personality disorders. *Journal of Personality Assessment, 59,* 223–238.

Coolidge, F. L., Segal, D. L., Cahill, B. S., & Simenson, J. T. (2010). Psychometric properties of a brief inventory for the screening of personality disorders: The SCATI. *Psychology & Psychotherapy: Theory, Research & Practice, 83*(4), 395–405.

Corcoran, K., & Fisher, J. (2013). *Measures for clinical practice and research: A sourcebook: Vol. 2. Adults* (5th ed.). New York: Oxford Press.

Cosgrove, L., & Krimsky, S. (2012). A Comparison of DSM-IV and DSM-5 Panel Members' Financial Associations with Industry: A Pernicious Problem Persists. *Plos Medicine, 9*(3), 1–4.

Crum, R. M., Anthony, J. C., Bassett, S. S., & Folstein, M. F. (1993). Population-based norms for the mini-mental state examination by age and education level. *Journal of the American Medical Association, 18*, 2386–2391.

DePaulo, J. R., Folstein, M. F., & Gordon, B. (1980). Psychiatric screening on a neurological ward. *Psychological Medicine, 10*, 125–132.

Duggan, C., & Gibbon, S. (2008). Practical assessment of personality disorder. *Psychiatry, 7*(3), 99–101.

Dutton, D. G. (1995). Trauma symptoms and PTSD-like profiles in perpetrators of intimate violence. *Journal of Traumatic Stress, 8*, 299–316.

Eaton, W. W., Muntaner, C., Smith, C., Tien, A., & Ybarra, M. (2004). Center for Epidemiologic Studies Depression Scale: Review and revision (CESD and CESD-R). In: M. E. Maruish, (Ed.), *The Use of Psychological Testing for Treatment Planning and Outcomes Assessment* (3rd ed., pp. 363–377). Mahwah, NJ: Lawrence Erlbaum.

Elliot, D. M., & Briere, J. (1992). Sexual abuse trauma among professional women: Validating the Trauma Symptom Checklist-40 (TSC-40). *Child Abuse & Neglect, 16*, 391–398.

Fillenbaum, G., Heyman, A., Willians, K., Prosnitz, B., & Burchett, B. (1990). Sensitivity and specificity of standardized screens of cognitive impairment and dementia among elderly black and white community residents. *Journal of Clinical Epidemiology, 43*, 651–660.

Finn, J. A., Arbisi, P. A., Erbes, C. R., Polusny, M. A., & Thuras, P. (2014). The MMPI–2 Restructured Form Personality Psychopathology Five Scales: Bridging DSM–5 Section 2 Personality Disorders and DSM–5 Section 3 Personality Trait Dimensions. *Journal of Personality Assessment, 96*(2), 173–184.

First, M. B., Spitzer, R. L., Gibbon M., & Williams, J. B. (2002). *Structured Clinical Interview for DSM-IV-TR Axis I Disorders,* Research Version, Patient Edition. (SCID-I/P). New York: Biometrics Research, New York State Psychiatric Institute.

First, M. B., Spitzer, R. L., Gibbon, M., Williams, J. B., & Benjamin, L. S. (1997). *Structured clinical interview for DSM-IV Axis II Personality Disorders* (SCID-II). Washington, DC: American Psychiatric Press.

Folstein, M. F., Folstein, S. E., & McHugh, P. R. (1975). Mini-mental state: A practical method for grading the cognitive state of patients for the clinician. *Journal of Psychiatric Research, 12*, 189–198.

Frank, D., DeBenedetti, A. F., Volk, R. J., Williams, E. C., Kivlahan, D. R., & Bradley, K. A. (2008). Effectiveness of the AUDIT-C as a Screening Test for Alcohol Misuse in Three Race/Ethnic Groups. *JGIM: Journal of General Internal Medicine, 23*(6), 781–787.

Germans, S., Van Heck, G. L., Moran. P., & Hodiamont, P. P. G. (2008). The self-report Standardized Assessment of Personality-Abbreviated Scale; Preliminary results of a brief screening test for personality disorders. *Personality and Mental Health, 2,* 70–76.

Hare, I. (2004). Defining social work for the 21st century. The International Federation of Social Workers' revised definition of social work. *International Social Work, 47,* 407–424.

Harmon, S. C., Lambert, M., Smart, D. M., Hawkins, E., Nielson, S., Slade, K., & Lutz, W. (2007). Enhancing outcome of potential treatment failures: Therapist-client feedback and clinical support tools. *Psychotherapy Research, 17,* 379–392.

Hathaway, S. R., & McKinley, J. C. (1943). *Minnesota Multiphasic Personality Inventory.* Minneapolis: University of Minnesota Press.

Heisler, E. J., & Bagalman, E. (2014, January). *The mental health workforce: A primer.* (CRS report No. R43255). Retrieved from http://www.fas.org/sgp/crs/misc/R43255.pdf

Hesse, M., & Moran, P. (2010). Screening for personality disorder with the Standardised Assessment of Personality Abbreviated Scale (SAPAS): Further evidence of concurrent validity. *BioMed Central Psychiatry,* 101–106. Retrieved from http://www.biomedcentral.com/1471-244X/10/10

Kendell, R., & Jablensky, A. (2003). Distinguishing between the validity and utility of psychiatric diagnoses. *American Journal of Psychiatry, 160*(1), 4–12.

Korczyn, A. D., & Halperin, I. (2009). Depression and dementia. *Journal of Neurological Sciences, 283*(1), 139–142.

Kroenke K., & Spitzer R. L. (2002). The PHQ-9: A new depression diagnostic and severity measure. *Psychiatric Annals, 32,* 509–521.

Kroenke K., Spitzer, R. L., & Williams, J. B. W. (2001). The PHQ-9: Validity of a brief depression severity measure. *Journal of General Internal Medicine 16*(9), 606–613.

Kutchins, H., & Kirk, S. A. (1997). *Making us crazy—DSM: The psychiatric bible and the creation of mental disorders.* New York: Free Press.

Lambert, M. J. (2013). Outcome in psychotherapy: The past and important advances. *Psychotherapy, 50*(1), 42–51.

Lambert, M. J., Gregersen, A. T., & Burlingame, G. M. (2004). The Outcome Questionnaire-45. In M. E. Mariush (Ed.), *The use of psychological testing for treatment planning and outcomes assessment* (3rd ed., pp. 191–234). Mahwah, NJ: Erlbaum.

Lambert, M. J., Hansen, N. B., & Finch, A. E. (2001). Patient-focused research: Using patient outcome data to enhance treatment effects. *Journal of Consulting and Clinical Psychology, 69,* 147–149.

Launer, L. J., Dinkgreve, M. A., Jonker, C., Hooijer, C., & Lindeboom, J. (1993). Are age and education independent correlates of the Mini-Mental State Exam performance of community-dwelling elderly? *Journal of Gerontology, 48*, 271–277.

Lezak, M. D. (1995). *Neuropsychological assessment* (3rd ed.). New York: Oxford University Press.

Lin, J. S., O'Connor, E., Rossom, R. C., Perdue, L. A., & Eckstrom, E. (2013). Screening for cognitive impairment in older adults: A systematic review for the U.S. Preventive Task Force. *Annals of Internal Medicine, 159*, 601–612.

Marc, L. G., Raue, P. J., & Bruce, M. L. (2008). Screening performance of the Geriatric Depression Scale (GDS-15) in a diverse elderly home care population. *American Journal of Geriatric Psychiatry: Official Journal of the American Association for Geriatric Psychiatry, 16*(11), 914–921.

Mayfield, D., McLeod, G., & Hall, P. (1994). The CAGE questionnaire: Validation of a new measure. *American Journal of Psychiatry, 131*, 1121–1123.

Michigan Alcohol Screening Test (MAST). (n.d.). *Michigan Alcohol Screening Test.* Retrieved from http://adai.washington.edu/instruments/pdf/Michigan_Alcoholism_Screening_Test_156.pdf

Millon, T. (1997). *The Millon inventories: Clinical and personality assessment.* New York: Guilford Press.

Millon, T., & Davis, R. D. (1997). The MCMI-III: Present and future directions. *Journal of Counseling & Development, 68*, 69–85.

Millon, T., Millon, C., Davis, R. D., & Grossman, S. D. (2006). *Millon Clinical Multiaxial Inventory III (MCMI-III) manual* (3rd ed.). Minneapolis, MN: Pearson Assessments.

Moffitt, T. E., Harrington, H., Caspi, A., Kim-Cohen, J., Goldberg, D., Gregory, A. M., & Poulton, R. (2007). Depression and generalized anxiety disorder: Cumulative and sequential comorbidity in a birth cohort followed prospectively to age 32 years. *Archives of General Psychiatry, 64*(6), 651–660.

Molloy, D. W., & Standish, T. I. (1997). A guide to the standardized Mini-Mental State Examination. *International Psychogeriatrics, 9*, 87–94.

Moran, P., Leese, M., Lee, T., Walter, P., Thornicroft, G., & Mann, A. (2003). Standardised Assessment of Personality-Abbreviated Scale (SAPAS): Preliminary validation of a brief screen for personality disorder. *British Journal of Psychiatry, 183*, 228–232.

Murden, R. A., McRae, T. D., Kaner, S., & Bucknam, M. E. (1991). Mini-Mental State Exam scores with education in blacks and whites. *Journal of the American Geriatrics Society, 43*, 138–145.

National Institue on Alcohol Abuse and Alcoholism. (2005). *Helping patients who drink too much: A clinician's guide.* Washington, DC: Author. Retrieved from http://pubs.niaaa.nih.gov/publications/Practitioner/CliniciansGuide2005/clinicians_guide.htm

National Institute on Drug Abuse. (2014). *American Psychiatric Association Adapted NIDA Modified ASSIST Tools.* Retrieved from http://www.drugabuse.gov/ nidamed-medical-health-professionals/tool-resources-your-practice/screening-assessment-drug-testing-resources/american-psychiatric-association-adapted-nida

OQ® Measures. (n.d.). *OQ®-45.2.* Retrieved from http://www.oqmeasures.com/ measures/adult-measures/oq-45/

Pace, P. (2008). Evidence-based practice moves ahead. *NASW News, 53*(1). Retrieved from http://www.socialworkers.org/pubs/news/2008/01/evidenceBased.asp

PDFfiller. (n.d.). *Fillable Personality Inventory for DSM-5: Brief form (PID-5-BF) Adult.* Retrieved from http://www.pdffiller.com/35573588-ThePersonality InventoryForDSM5BriefFormAdultpdf-The-Personality-Inventory-for-DSM-5Brief-Form-PID-5-BFAdult-Various-Fillable-Forms

PROMIS®. (2011). *PROMIS instruments available for use.* Retrieved from http://www.nihpromis.org/Documents/Item_Bank_Tables_Feb_2011.pdf? AspxAutoDetectCookieSupport=1

Radloff, L. S. (1977). The CES-D scale: A new self-report depression scale for research in the general population. *Applied Psychological Measurement, 1*, 385–401.

Reed, G. M. (2010). Toward ICD-11: Improving the clinical utility of WHO's *International classification of mental disorders. Professional Psychology: Research and Practice, 41*(6), 457–464.

Robbins, S. P. (2014). From the editor: The DSM-5 and its role in social work assessment and research. *Journal of Social Work Education, 50*(2), 201–205.

Selzer, M. L. (1971). The Michigan Alcoholism Screening Test: The quest for a new diagnostic instrument. *American Journal of Psychiatry, 127*, 89–94.

Sheikh, J. I., & Yesavage, J. A. (1986). Geriatric Depression Scale (GDS). Recent evidence and development of a shorter version. In T. L. Brink (Ed.), *Clinical gerontology: A guide to assessment and intervention* (pp. 165–173). New York: Haworth Press.

Slade, K., Lambert, M. J., Harmon, S. C., Smart, D. W., & Bailey, R. (2008). Electronic feedback and revised clinical support tools. *Clinical Psychology and Psychotherapy, 15*, 287–303.

Snowden, L. R. (2003). Bias in mental health assessment and intervention: Theory and evidence. *American Journal of Public Health, 93*, 239–243.

Spielberger, C. D., Gorsuch, R. L., Lushene, R., Vagg, P. R., & Jacobs, G. A. (1983). *Manual for the state-trait anxiety inventory.* Palo Alto, CA: Consulting Psychologists Press.

Spitzer, R. L., Kroenke, K., & Williams, J. W. (1999). Validation and utility of a self-report version of PRIME-MD: The PHQ primary care study. Primary care evaluation of mental disorders. Patient Health Questionnaire. *Journal of the American Medical Association, 10*(282), 1737–1744.

Spitzer, R. L., Kroenke, K., Williams, J. B. W., & Löwe, B. (2006). A brief measure for assessing generalized anxiety disorder. *Archives of Internal Medicine, 166,* 1092–1097.

Spitzer, R. L., Williams, J. B., Kroenke, K., Linzer, M., deGruy, F. V., Hahn, S. R., Brody, D., & Johnson, J. G. (1994). Utility of a new procedure for diagnosing mental disorders in primary care: The PRIME-MD 1000 study. *Journal of the American Medical Association, 14*(272), 1749–1756.

Stahre, M., Roeber, J., Kanny, D., Brewer, R. D., & Zhang, X. (2014). Contribution of excessive alcohol consumption to deaths and years of potential life lost in the United States. *Preventing Chronic Disease, 11,* 1–12. Retrieved from http://www.cdc.gov/pcd/issues/2014/pdf/13_0293.pdf

Stanford University. (n.d.). *Geriatric Depression Scale.* Retrieved from http://www.stanford.edu/~yesavage/GDS.html

Stein, D. J., Phillips, K. A., Bolton, D., Fulford, K. M., Sadler, J. Z., & Kendler, K. S. (2010). What is a mental/psychiatric disorder? From DSM-IV to DSM-V. *Psychological Medicine, 40*(11), 1759–1765.

Substance Abuse and Mental Health Services Administration (SAMHSA). (2006). *Results from the 2005 National Survey of Drug Use and Health: National findings* (NSDUH Series H-30, No. (SMA) 06-4194m). Rockville, MD: Author.

Substance Abuse and Mental Health Services Administration (SAMHSA). (2013). *Behavioral health, United States, 2012.* HHS Publication No. (SMA) 13-4797. Rockville, MD: Author. Retrieved from http://www.samhsa.gov/data/sites/default/files/2012-BHUS.pdf

Substance Abuse and Mental Health Services Administration–Health Resources and Services Administration Center for Integrated Health Solutions (SAMHSA-HRSA). (n.d.a). *SBIRT: Screening, brief intervention, and referral to treatment.* Retrieved from http://www.integration.samhsa.gov/clinical-practice/SBIRT

Substance Abuse and Mental Health Services Administration–Health Resources and Services Administration Center for Integrated Health Solutions (SAMHSA-HRSA). (n.d.b). *Screening tools.* Retrieved from http://www.integration.samhsa.gov/clinical-practice/screening-tools

Sullivan, P. F., Neale, M. C., & Kendler, K. S. (2000). Genetic epidemiology of major depression: Review and meta-analysis. *American Journal of Psychiatry, 157*(10), 1552–1562.

Tellegen, A., & Ben-Porath, Y. S. (2011). *MMPI-2-RF (Minnesota Multiphasic Personality Inventory-2 Restructured Form): Technical manual.* Minneapolis: University of Minnesota Press. (Original published 2008).

Tellegen, A., Ben-Porath, Y. S., McNulty, J. L., Arbisi, P. A., Graham, J. R., & Kaemmer, B. (2003). *MMPI-2 Restructured Clinical (RC) Scales: Development, validation, and interpretation.* Minneapolis, MN: University of Minnesota Press.

Van Dam, N. T., & Earleywine, M. (2011). Validation of the Center for Epidemiologic Studies Depression Scale—Revised (CESD-R): Pragmatic depression assessment in the general population. *Psychiatry Research, 186*(1), 128–132.

Weathers, F. W., Litz, B. T., Keane, T. M., Palmieri, P. A., Marx, B. P., & Schnurr, P. P. (2013). *The PTSD Checklist for DSM-5 (PCL-5)*. Scale available from the National Center for PTSD at www.ptsd.va.gov

Werner, C. A., & U.S. Census Bureau. (2011). *The older population: 2010*. [Washington, DC]: U.S. Dept. of Commerce, Economics and Statistics Administration, U.S. Census Bureau.

World Health Organization. (2010). *International classification of diseases* (10th rev.; ICD-10). Retrieved from http://www.who.int/classifications/icd/en/

World Health Organization. (2012). *Measuring health and disability: manual for WHO Disability Assessment Schedule (WHODAS 2.0)*. Geneva: Author.

CHAPTER 7

Family Systems

Cynthia Franklin, Laura Hopson, Yuqi Guo, and
Anao Zhang

INTRODUCTION

This chapter provides several methods for conducting a family assessment and summarizes key concepts and issues to consider in the evaluation of family systems. We review and summarize selected assessment for understanding families, as well as techniques for gathering information on families. Specifically, we briefly review standardized measures, interviewing techniques, family-task observations, graphic, problem-oriented, and specific methods for assessing family strengths. Finally, this chapter provides family assessment reports illustrating the integration of multiple sources to create a family intervention plan from that information and how to move from assessment to intervention.

KEY ISSUES FOR FAMILY SYSTEMS ASSESSMENT

Thinking about families from a systems perspective focuses our attention on the way the family functions as an entity rather than on the individual behavior or attributes of one of its members. Systems theorists have often said, "The whole is greater than the sum of its parts." Wholeness or whole-systems functioning means that the family system is not just the sum of its parts viewed separately; the family members' interactions produce a unique type of behavior pattern all its own (Goldenberg, Goldenberg, & Pelavin, 2013; Sperry, 2011).

Several family systems models have emerged in clinical practice: structural, strategic, behavioral-functional, psychodynamic-transgenerational, experiential, and communication. Other strengths-based models have also been developed, such as solution-focused brief therapy, narrative, feminist, and multicultural. A comprehensive discussion of these models is beyond the scope of this chapter (for a review, see Gurman & Kniskern, 2014) but some discussion on how families are understood using family systems perspectives is relevant to learning how to assess family functioning.

Family Structure

Family structure relates to the way family members organize themselves into interactional patterns (Minuchin & Fishman, 1982; Segrin & Flora, 2014). It also includes the family constellation, which describes the nature of the family (e.g., single parent, intact family) and number of family members. For example, a recently divorced father is depressed over his divorce and fears that it will damage his two teenage sons and complicate his already strained relationship with them. The father attempts to form a blended family in which the father and his two children cohabitate with the father's new partner. The following structural interactional pattern emerges: The father does not enforce the rules because he is used to a mother figure assuming the discipline of the children. When his partner attempts to step in and enforce the rules, the children resist the discipline because she is not "their mother." The partner and the children get into a screaming match, and the father becomes involved and tries to negotiate. The children refuse to obey the father because he is siding with the partner against them. This angers the father, who threatens the children with a severe punishment (e.g., taking their transportation away) but then changes his mind after further argument, in exchange for the boys' half-hearted compliance. By that time, however, everybody is mad at everybody else, including the father and his partner.

If this type of structural interactional pattern occurs over time, it becomes well-rehearsed and well known. This behavior pattern involves every member of the family and composes part of the structural, interactional sequences of the family system. In this example, it is impossible to identify a simple cause-and-effect relationship for the dysfunctional pattern of this family. Causes and effects feed into one another to produce complex and interactive behavioral chains (e.g., partner looks to father to intervene with children, partner intervenes, father reacts to screaming, children resist, father chastises children, children comply, father backs down, partner looks to father to intervene). For questions that you can use to assess family structure, see the section on interviewing in this chapter and review the information on circular questions in appendix 7A.

Relationship and Communication Patterns

Social workers must gain an understanding of the health of dyads and triads in the family. Dyadic relationships such as couples function most harmoniously when those involved function in a complementary pattern rather than a symmetrical one based on competition and conflict. Complementary patterns denote shared roles and reciprocal interaction and a harmony between roles and responsibilities (Watzlawick, Bavelas, &

Jackson, 2011). For example, in a couple's relationship, one may be assertive and more of a leader, while the other is passive and more of a follower. When they disagree, the submissive partner may defer to the more assertive one. Such reciprocal interaction is characterized as "complementarity," a term from systems theory that suggests that opposites may function well together. Another couple may both be assertive and, during disagreements, find themselves in an argument over who is right. The second couple's relationship is symmetrical, and although it is more equal, it is also more at risk for escalations, quarrels, and competition.

Triadic relationships in families are especially important to observe. In family systems, the triad (triangle) is believed to be the basic building block of relationships (Bowen, 1978). Triangulation occurs when any two members of a family experience too much stress between them. These two members may pull a third member into their relationship, thus regulating the stress between them. Another way to think about a triad is in terms of its ability to defocus conflict. This process is known as "detouring"; for example, parents might focus on a child's behavior instead of on their own issues (Minuchin, Nichols, & Lee, 2006). Family relational processes often consist of a series of interlocking triangles that may extend across generations and that lend stability to the system but also cause family dysfunction (Bowen, 1978). Social workers assessing such processes must evaluate the nature of these triangles to understand the network of relationships in the family system.

Communication is important to the competent functioning of family systems. For communication to be effective between family members, it must be open, direct, clear, and congruent at different levels, such as the tone and content of one's message. There are three basic levels of communication: verbal communication, nonverbal communication, and metacommunication. Verbal communication refers to the words and content of the message, nonverbal communication refers to the body posture and subtle innuendoes sent with a message, and metacommunication (communication about communication) refers to the context of the communication, such as voice tone, tenor, and timing (Janzen, Harris, Jordan, & Franklin, 2005).

In most families that present with problems to be solved, members have difficulty communicating with one another. It is common to observe members of such families sending messages through a third party (e.g., the daughter tells the father why the mother is mad at him). Dysfunctional families also withhold information or send confusing and double-binding messages to one another. Here is an example of a double-binding message: A mother says to her daughter that she can confide in the mother about her relationship with her boyfriend (content level) and that the mother will be accepting and not upset (voice rising sharply and arms crossed at nonverbal level) if she confides that she has chosen to have sex with the boyfriend.

Rules and Myths

Families are rule-governed systems, and rules define the relationship agreements among family members (Janzen et al., 2005). Some rules are explicit and clearly stated (e.g., this family goes to church every Sunday). Other rules are implicit or covert and may not be as clearly stated. For example, it may be an implicit rule that a family does not talk about sex in front of members of the opposite sex or that the family does not discuss Grandpa's drinking problem at all. Rules dictate much of the family members' behavior toward one another.

Family myths, like rules, contribute considerably to a family's behavior. Myths, here, are family members' shared beliefs and expectations concerning one another (Janzen et al., 2005). A family may develop a type of shared mythical reality concerning the behavior of one of its members. For example, the highly successful, artistic son of a conventional, enmeshed family may receive the label "queer" or "deviant." The family may view him as inadequate, even though he wins a scholarship to study art at a prestigious university and later establishes a successful art gallery. Such an inadequate view of an obviously creative and successful young man is a family myth that serves an important function in that family.

Problem Solving, Negotiation, and Decision Making

Functional family systems have good problem-solving skills and are able to brainstorm solutions and come to agreement about how to proceed to solve a problem. Families that can effectively solve problems may have special times to meet to discuss problems and come up with solutions (e.g., a weekly family gripe session). They may also have a way to monitor the progress of proposed solutions, such as a daily report card or a meeting to discuss outcomes (Dinkmeyer, McKay, & Dinkmeyer, 1997).

Like problem solving, negotiation is important to the functioning of family systems. Couples in particular must learn to negotiate roles and power between them and model those behaviors to their children. The adage goes "the two shall be one," but the ultimate task may be to negotiate which one. Families work out different ways to negotiate for the things that each member wants. For example, some couples work out relationship agreements in which one member exchanges something for something else. In this bargaining type of relationship, one may be willing to do the laundry if the other washes the cars, or each may care for the children alone one night in exchange for a free night out. These are sometimes referred to as quid pro quo relationships (Stuart, 2004). Other families take a more giving attitude in which members go out of their way to please one another. Members of such families behave similarly toward one another. Some families have difficulty negotiating their relationships; the result may be endless and relentless power struggles and conflict.

Decision making, like negotiation, is central to the functioning of a family system. Who makes the decisions and how they do so are critical determinants of how the family operates. Equally important is who appoints the decision maker. Observing the pattern of decision making is important to understanding a family. In some families, for instance, one person (e.g., the father) makes major decisions. Other families make decisions in an egalitarian, democratic fashion. In most families, the patterns of decision-making shift from situation to situation or role to role. For example, one partner may be responsible for making major decisions about the home and the other for making decisions about the finances. Some families delegate decision-making to the members most proficient in those tasks, whereas others rigidly follow the terms established in their family of origin. Some families have difficulty deciding who will make the decisions and how they will be made. Such families may argue over decisions or shift responsibility for making the decisions from one person to another in a chaotic manner. As part of a family assessment, social workers need to become acquainted with the problem-solving and negotiation skills, as well as the decision-making processes of the family.

Individual Dynamics and Biological Systems

Thus far, this review of major concepts for understanding families has focused on families as a social system. In keeping with the holistic view of systems theory, social workers also need to assess psychological and biological competencies and vulnerabilities of families (Hepworth, Rooney, Rooney, Strom-Gottfried, 2013; Levine, 2012). There is increasing evidence that major mental disorders like schizophrenia and major depression have neurobiological determinants. In addition, there is other evidence suggesting genetic links and biological vulnerabilities for problems such as attention deficit/hyperactivity disorder, depression, alcoholism, and antisocial behavior and other problems. It is impossible for social workers to effectively treat such disorders in families until there have been interventions that address mental illnesses and behavioral health issues that may require psychotropic medications and other medical interventions.

Teamwork and collaboration with medical professionals need to be a routine part of a family assessment for high-risk families. For example, a family brings a hyperactive and disruptive child with severe behavior problems to a social worker for treatment. In this case, there is a repeated family history of alcoholism and mood disorders; in particular, several relatives have been diagnosed with bipolar disorder. Disruptive behavior in this context may be a combination of biopsychosocial factors and the child him- or herself may be at risk for developing one or more mental disorders. In such a case the social worker would need to consider the correct diagnosis as a part of the assessment. Depending on the diagnosis and as a part of a good social work assessment, the social worker may also need to refer and consult with medical professionals to help the client obtain the proper combination of medical and family interventions for the child and family. (For examples of questions for assessing the individual and biological aspects of children and adults, see chapters 5 and 6.)

Family Strengths

It is important to assess strengths in families and to encompass both individual and environmental factors. The individual factors are often referred to as resilience, whereas the environmental factors are referred to as protective. Some examples of resilience include social skills and competencies, as well as the ability to set goals and to have a future orientation. Protective factors include characteristics of the environment, such as having a caring family or other adults, safe schools, and parental monitoring. A strengths perspective assumes that clients who come for help are more than their problems and circumstances dictate. All clients have competencies, knowledge, hidden resources, and resilience that they can use to reverse the misfortunes of their life struggles. Therapists practicing from a strengths perspective are convinced that clients have aspirations, motivation, untapped goals, and spiritual fortitude that they can muster against the impossible odds of their disabilities and social environment. Clients have self-determination and are able to resist and shape their environments and can use hidden resources in their environments (Franklin, 2002).

Many popular and effective approaches to couple and family therapy (including solution-focused brief therapy, narrative, and multisystemic models) use client strengths in therapy (Franklin, Jordan, & Hopson, 2015). Psychotherapy research indicates that positive belief and expectation for client change is a prerequisite for effective therapy, regardless of the model used. Practicing from a strengths perspective incorporates a value system that encompasses beliefs in the dignity and worth of individuals, their self-determination, and the transformative power of humans and human relationships. Regardless of the model the practitioner uses, practicing with clients from a strengths perspective means viewing them through a humanistic lens that assumes that all clients can grow and change (Franklin, 2002).

Ethnicity, Culture, and Gender

The behaviors, expectations, and prescribed roles that emerge from clients' social class, ethnicity, culture, and gender roles are sometimes outside their awareness; at other times, clients' awareness of these viewpoints may restrict or oppress them so that they believe they have limited options. For example, after facing incidents of discrimination in trying to find housing in middle-class neighborhoods, African American clients may feel that their options have been limited because of race and then transfer these feelings to other areas of their life or even have similar experiences that validate these social realities.

As another example, a woman may experience depression because she feels trapped in an unhappy marriage with a domineering husband. She may be unaware, however, that the gender roles of each partner are partly responsible for this dilemma. Both she and her husband have internalized culturally prescribed roles for how men and women are to behave in relationship to each other. She wants more intimacy, and he has difficulty sharing feelings, for example.

As a part of the assessment process, the practitioner assesses a person's culture, ethnicity, and social class and develops an understanding of strengths and resources, as well as an understanding of the effects of social oppression. To understand a client's culture and ethnic experiences, it is important to use interpersonal skills and cross-cultural competence to form a helping relationship with a client (Whaley & Davis, 2007). Some strategies that can facilitate the relationship-building and assessment process include the following:

- Remain open and nonjudgmental to alternative life styles. Clearly communicate to clients that you know there are many different ways of living and doing things. Cite examples and initiate conversation into an area so that the client will feel comfortable talking to you about his or her family and life situation.

- Disclose patterns and ways of doing things in your family and culture, and ask the client to describe how things are handled in his or her family and culture. A comparison conversation may facilitate information exchange and mutual understanding.

- Ask, "How do you do that in your family or culture?" Or, "What does this mean in your culture?"

- Be self-aware and explore possible cultural biases with a supervisor.

- Ask for and accept feedback from the client about your level of cultural knowledge and sensitivity. Tell clients what you are thinking, and ask them to comment on whether your thoughts and beliefs are accurate from their viewpoint.

Thus far in this chapter, we have summarized some major concepts important for understanding how families function as a system and family assessment considerations. Next, we review assessment approaches that have research evidence and standardized measurement instruments that help us assess family functioning.

Olson Circumplex Family Model

The Olson Circumplex Family Model derives from systems theory. It provides a classification schema for understanding couple and family functioning, which provides a typology of family functioning along three important dimensions: cohesion (emotional bonding), adaptability or flexibility (degree of change in family rites and structure), and communication (facilitative dimension). The communication dimension is important for establishing appropriate levels of the other two dimensions.

Through research on more than one thousand families over the past decade, Olson, Russell, and Sprenkle (2014) developed several empirically derived family inventories that measure these three dimensions of family life. Family assessment instruments, including the Family Satisfaction Scale and the Family Communication Scale, have been developed for the model.

The most famous and up-to-date of the self-report measures is the Family Adaptability and Cohesion Scales, currently in its fourth revision (FACES IV), which measures the two central dimensions of the Circumplex Model of Marital and Family System: Family Cohesion and Family Flexibility (Olson, 2008, 2011). The FACES IV was developed to be (a) self-report scales that tap the full dimensions of cohesion and flexibility as defined in Circumplex Model; (b) self-report scales that are reliable, valid, and clinically relevant; and (c) a family assessment tool that is useful for research and clinical work with families (Olson, 2008). The FACES IV scale contains forty-two items, including six scales, to assess the dimensions of family cohesion and family flexibility. These six scales include two balanced and four unbalanced scales; all have good levels of reliability and validity (e.g., Baiocco, Cacioppo, Laghi, & Tafà, 2013; Marsac & Alderfer, 2011). The FACES IV package is a sixty-two-item, normative-based, paper-and-pencil, self-report inventory that operationalizes the Circumplex Model. Besides the FACES IV measures the first two dimensions of the Circumplex Model of marital and family systems, additional scales of Family Communication Scale (ten items), and Family Satisfaction Scale (ten items) are used to measure family communication and family satisfaction.

The original Circumplex Model posits a curvilinear understanding of family functioning that emphasizes the need for balance in family relationships. Families that fall along extreme dimensions of functioning in cohesion, adaptability and flexibility, or communication are believed to be at risk of dysfunction. Those that fall into balanced or midrange dimensions are believed to be better adjusted. The FACES IV measure categorizes families into twenty-five types with five levels of cohesion and flexibility. The main advantage of the dimension score is that it makes it possible to plot the location of the individual/family on the Circumplex with a formula (see figure 7.1).

Figure 7.1   Family Adaptability and Cohesion Scales (FACES-IV)

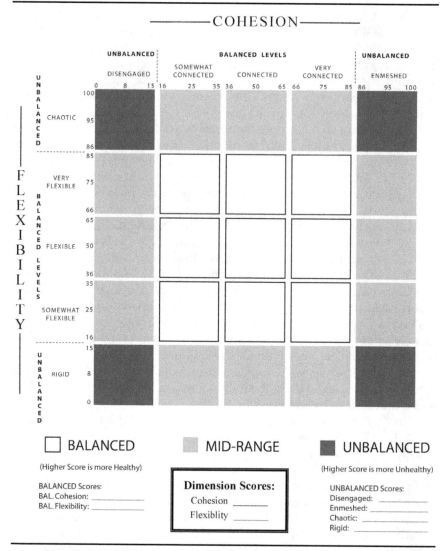

SOURCE: Olson, D. (2011). FACES IV and the Circumplex Model: Validation study. *Journal of Marital and Family Therapy*. Copyright © 2011 American Association for Marriage and Family Therapy. Reproduced with permission by John Wiley and Sons.

FACES IV continues to be a leader in its ongoing empirical work to establish a useful measure for family practice (Olson, Gorall, & Tiesel, 2007). Recent work on the clinical assessment shows that high levels of concurrent, construct, and discriminant validity and reliability were found in the six scales (Olson, 2011). There is a relationship between extreme scores on the dimensions of the model and family dysfunction, which shows the clinical usefulness of the Circumplex Model (Craddock, 2001). Researchers currently use FACES to assess family cohesion in studies investigating a range of topics, including the effects of trauma (Lohan & Murphy, 2007; Uruk, Sayger, & Cogdal, 2007), eating disorders (Franko, Thompson, Bauserman, Affenito, & Striegel-Moore, 2008), and ethnic differences (Baer & Schmitz, 2007). More than 1,200 studies using FACES measures and several studies using the Clinical Rating Scale support the major hypotheses of the Circumplex Model (Olson, 2011).

Beavers Systems Model

The Beavers Systems Model, originally called the "Beavers Timberlawn Family Evaluation Scales," developed over twenty-five years from clinical observations of both dysfunctional and healthy, competent families in treatment and research settings. From this work, three assessment instruments have been developed: the Beavers Interactional Scales, the Family Competence and Style Scales, and the Self-Report Family Inventory. The first two scales are observational clinical rating scales. The third is a self-report instrument completed by family members (Beavers & Hampson, 2003). Multiple studies by the Beavers research team have documented the reliability and validity of the measures (Hampson & Beavers, 2011).

The Beavers Systems Model (Hampson & Beavers, 2011) integrates family systems theory and developmental theory; it is widely used in clinical practice. It seeks to understand the health and competence of families in relationship to their ability to produce healthy and competent children. This model classifies families on the axes of family competence and family style. The competence axis classifies families into types that fall along a continuum according to their level of functioning: optimal, adequate, midrange, borderline, disturbed, and severely disturbed. The style axis classifies families according to their quality of interaction: centripetal and centrifugal. Centripetal families turn inward and seek pleasure and gratification from within the family. Centrifugal families turn outward and seek fulfillment in relationships outside the family. Both family competence and style converge to produce levels of family functioning, which are believed to have implications for the types of difficulties children may have, as defined by psychiatric categories. Figure 7.2 is a visual representation of the Beavers Systems Model. Figure 7.3 shows the areas of family life used to obtain an assessment of the family competence and style dimensions on the Beavers Systems Model as described by Beavers (2003). When the two dimensions of the Beavers Systems Model, family competence and family style, are combined, nine distinct family groups diagrammatically emerge on the basis of clinical observation and empirical research. Three of the groups are considered functional, whereas six are problematic and require clinical intervention (Hampson & Beavers, 2011).

Figure 7.2   Beavers Systems Model

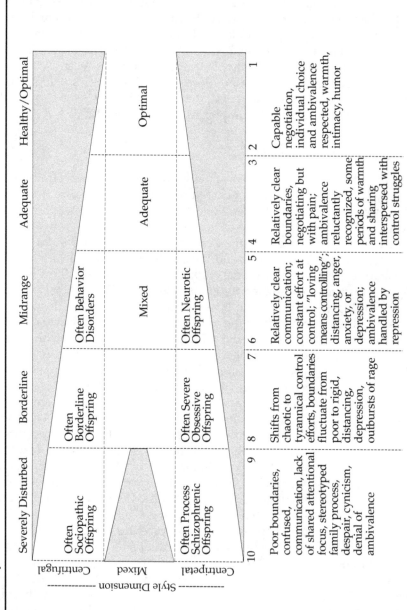

Figure 7.3   Assessing Family Competence and Style Dimensions, Beavers Systems Model

---

I. Structure of the family
  A. Overt power: chaotic vs. egalitarian
  B. Parental coalition: parent-child coalitions vs. strong parental coalition
  C. Closeness: indistinct boundaries vs. close, distinct boundaries
II. Mythology: congruent vs. incongruent reality perception of the family
III. Goal-directed negotiation: efficient vs. inefficient problem solving
IV. Autonomy
  A. Clarity of expression: directness of expression of thoughts and feelings, from less clear to clear
  B. Responsibility: voicing responsibility for personal actions, from taking responsibility to taking no responsibility
  C. Permeability: open vs. unreceptive to statements of others
V. Family affect
  A. Range of feelings: broad range vs. limited range of feelings
  B. Mood and tone: open and optimistic vs. cynical and pessimistic
  C. Unresolvable conflict: chronic underlying conflict vs. ability to resolve conflict
  D. Empathy: empathic vs. inconsiderate of individual feelings
VI. Global health pathology scale: optimal/adaptive (1) vs. severely dysfunctional (10)
VII. Family style
  A. Dependency needs: discouraged/ignored vs. encouraged
  B. Adult conflict: quite open vs. indirect, covert, hidden
  C. Proximity: all members give and expect lots of room between members vs. all members stay physically close with much touching
  D. Social presentation: try hard to appear well behaved and to make a good impression vs. seem unconcerned with appearances and social approval
  E. Expression of closeness: consistently emphasize that they are close vs. deny that they are close
  F. Assertive/aggressive qualities: discourage aggressive or disruptive behavior and expressions vs. solicit or encourage assertive, even aggressive behavior and expressions
  G. Expression of feelings: express positive feelings more often vs. express negative feelings more often
  H. Global centripetal/centrifugal style: total inward oriented vs. total outward oriented

---

In the Beavers Systems Model, family competence and family style are combined and nine distinct family groups diagrammatically emerge on the basis of clinical observation and empirical research. Three of the groups are considered functional, whereas six are problematic and require clinical intervention (Beavers & Hampson, 2000).

Development of the model, as with all assessment models, is ongoing. The recent introduction of a self-report version of the family assessment instrument has added to the clinical utility of the model. The Self-Report Family Inventory measures two dimensions of family functioning (Hampson & Beavers, 2011).

McMaster Family Model

The McMaster Family Model (Epstein, Baldwin, & Bishop, 2013) is another widely used family assessment model that evolved from clinical practice. The model was developed over fifteen years with families in the Brown University and Butler Hospital Family Research Program. This model assesses whole-systems functioning of the family and evaluates family structure, organization, and transactional patterns that distinguish healthy from unhealthy families. Two assessment instruments have emerged from this work: the McMaster Clinical Rating Scale, and a self-report family measure, the McMaster Family Assessment Device (FAD), version 3.

These scales assess seven dimensions of family functioning: (a) problem solving, (b) communication, (c) roles, (d) affective responsiveness, (e) affective involvement, (f) behavior control, and (g) overall family functioning:

Family Problem Solving.   Family problem solving refers to how families solve both instrumental (e.g., financial) and affective (e.g., social support and nurturance) problems. Families are considered most effective when they follow seven steps in their problem-solving efforts:

1. Problem identification
2. Communication of the problem to the appropriate family members
3. Development of a plan and subsequent alternatives (brainstorming)
4. Commitment to a plan
5. Action on that plan
6. Accountability and monitoring of the action
7. Outcome evaluation

Families are considered least effective in their problem solving if they cannot accomplish the first step.

Communication.   Families with the most-effective communication use a clear, direct style. Those with the least-effective communication have a masked, indirect style. For example, a husband might say, "It really bothers me when you don't call before you come home if you are going to be late," rather than refusing to speak to his wife all evening because she was late.

Roles.   Roles refer to how the family assigns instrumental, affective, and mixed-dimension (e.g., system maintenance, teaching independent living skills) role functions and how it handles accountability for those functions. Families are considered to have effective role assignments when all the necessary family functions have been clearly allocated to appropriate family members and when some form of monitoring and accountability takes place. Least-effective role functioning occurs when the necessary family functions are not addressed or when accountability for those functions is not maintained.

Affective Responsiveness.   Affective responsiveness refers to how families respond to crises and the degree to which emotional responses are aimed at the well-being of family members. Families are considered to have appropriate affective responses when they can demonstrate a full range of emotional responses that are consistent in degree and congruent with context. Families are least effective when the type and severity of emotional responsiveness is incongruent with context.

Affective Involvement.   Affective involvement refers to a range of emotional involvement, from absence of involvement to symbiotic involvement. Families are considered most effective when they express empathic involvement and least effective when they express an absence of involvement.

Behavior Control.   Behavior control refers to a range of styles from rigid to chaotic. Control of behavior is assessed in three areas: dangerous or threatening situations, meeting and expressing of family members' needs and drives (e.g., eating, sleeping, sex), and monitoring of interpersonal socializing both inside and outside the family. Flexible behavior control is assessed as most effective and chaotic behavior control is assessed as least effective.

Overall Family Functioning.   Although there has been some debate over the past few years about whether the FAD scoring procedures should be reorganized to reflect higher-order factors from self-report measures (Ridenour, Daley, & Reich, 2000), Miller, Ryan, Keitner, Bishop, and Epstein (2000) argue that the overall ecological validity of the scale, with the backing of numerous studies, suggests an absence in the utility of higher-order factors. Clinical assessments using FAD have attested to the validity of measuring family functioning from self-report (Georgiades, Boyle, Jenkins, Sanford, & Lipman, 2008). In addition, Miller et al. suggest that the most important issue regarding any scale is its clinical utility and validity, which the FAD has demonstrated repeatedly.

Moos Family Environment Scale

The Moos Family Environment Scale (FES) (Moos & Moos, 2013) evolved from research on social climates—that is, from research on the unique personality or attributes of social environments. The FES is a self-report measure that assesses whole-family functioning and is compatible with social and systems ecological theory. It has been widely used in both clinical research and in practice and has been demonstrated to be an effective outcome measure. The FES evaluates families' perceptions of their social or interpersonal climate along three dimensions: (a) relationship, (b) personal growth, and (c) systems maintenance dimensions. Each dimension comprises subscales that evaluate diverse areas of family functioning.

Relationship Dimensions.   The first three dimensions measured by FES assess how involved people are in their family and how openly they express both positive and negative feelings in a bipolar dimension of cohesion versus conflict, and then in a unipolar dimension of organization versus control.

The cohesion subscale measures the degree of commitment, help, and support family members provide for one another (e.g., the way they support one another, the amount of energy they put into what they do at home, how much feeling of togetherness there is in the family).

The expressiveness subscale taps the extent to which family members are encouraged to act openly and to express their feelings directly (e.g., how openly family members talk around home, how freely they discuss their personal problems, how often they just pick up and go if they feel like doing something on the spur of the moment).

The conflict subscale measures the amount of openly expressed anger, aggression, and conflict among family members (e.g., frequency of fights, whether family members sometimes get so angry that they throw things, how often they criticize each other).

Personal Growth Dimensions.   The personal growth, or goal orientation, subscales make up another set of FES dimensions. This set focuses on the family's goals by tapping the major ways in which a family encourages or inhibits personal growth.

The independence subscale measures the extent to which family members are assertive and self-sufficient and make their own decisions (e.g., the extent to which family members are encouraged to be independent, how much they think things out for themselves, how freely they come and go in the family).

The achievement orientation subscale taps the extent to which activities, such as school and work, are cast into an achievement-oriented or competitive framework (e.g., how important they feel it is to do their best and to get ahead, how competitive they are).

The intellectual-cultural orientation subscale assesses the degree of interest in political, social, intellectual, and cultural activities (e.g., how often family members talk about political or social problems, how often they go to the library, how much they like music, art, and literature).

The active-recreational orientation subscale taps the extent of participation in social and recreational activities (e.g., how often friends come over for dinner or to visit, how often family members go out, how often family members go to movies, sports events, camping).

The moral-religious subscale measures the degree of emphasis on ethical and religious issues and values (e.g., how frequently family members attend church, synagogue, or Sunday school, how strict their ideas are about right and wrong, how much they believe that some things must be taken on faith).

Systems Maintenance Dimensions.   The last set of dimensions the FES measures assesses the family's emphasis on clear organization, structure, rules, and procedures in running family life.

The organization subscale measures the importance of clear organization and structure in planning family activities and responsibilities (e.g., how carefully activities are planned, how neat and orderly family members are, how clearly each person's duties are defined).

The control subscale assesses the extent to which set rules and procedures are used to run family life (e.g., how much one family member makes the decisions, how set the ways of doing things are at home, how much emphasis is on following rules in the family).

Because the FES is easy to administer, it has become one of the most popular environmental measures in clinical and family research, even though not all subscales of FES are reliable (Moos & Moos, 2013). Chipuer and Villegas (2001) and others have found a potential problem with using the three-factor structure of the FES across different groups of respondents. In particular, their study of wives' and husbands' responses to the perceptions of their family environment did not support the Moos and Moos three-factor model. Rather, they found evidence supporting a two-factor solution—cohesion versus conflict and organization versus control. They recommend using the two-factor, second-order solution to compare perceptions of spouses and to provide the best fit across data for wives and husbands (Boake & Salmon, 1983; Chipuer & Villegas, 2001).

Family Assessment Measure

The Family Assessment Measure (FAM; Skinner, Steinhauer, & Santa-Barbara, 2009) is based on the process model of family functioning, which describes how to conduct family assessments based on seven dimensions: (a) affective involvement, (b) control, (c) task accomplishment, (d) role performance, (e) communication, (f) affective expression, and (g) values and norms. Each dimension is measured at three levels: whole-family systems, dyadic relationships, and individual functioning.

Affective Involvement.   Assesses how much interest and concern family members show. There are five types: uninvolved, devoid of feeling, narcissistic, empathic, and enmeshed.

Control.   Assesses how family members influence each other's behavior, techniques, and strategies. These include rigidity, flexibility, and chaotic.

Task Accomplishment.   Assesses three types of family tasks, which are defined in a cultural context: basic tasks, developmental tasks, and crisis tasks.

Role Performance.   Tied to task accomplishment and assesses three distinct operations: each family member's assigned role, the agreement of each family member to accept his or her role, and actual enactment of those roles and behaviors.

Communication.   Assesses how affective role performance and tasks are accomplished. Three forms of communication are assessed: affective, instrumental, and neutral.

Affective Expression.   Assesses the content, intensity, and timing of affective expression. This is considered the most important form of communication for the family system in how it expresses itself.

Values and Norms.   Assesses basic family processes in terms of values and norms. The focus is on whether family rules are explicit or implicit, how free family members are to determine and express their own attitudes, and whether the family values and norms are consistent with those in the society at large.

After twenty years of work of development the FAM has four self-report components, including the general scale, which has fifty items and nine subscales; the dyadic relationship scales, with forty-two items and seven subscales; the self-rating scale, with forty-two items and seven subscales; and the brief FAM with fourteen items. FAM is demonstrated as a reliable tool to measure family function in different cultures settings; therefore clinicians can use FAM to measure cross-culture families (Laghezza, Delvecchio, Pazzagli, & Mazzeschi, 2014). The measure has demonstrated good reliability and discriminant validity (Skinner et al., 2009). For clinical guidelines for using the FAM, see box 7.1.

Box 7.1
Clinical Guidelines for Using the Family Assessment Measure

1. This is a good instrument for obtaining an overall index of family functioning, especially in time-limited situations.
2. This instrument helps to pinpoint gaps in the assessment.
3. This instrument helps identify areas of confusion where family members' perceptions of a situation are quite different from each other.
4. This instrument provides an independent and objective validation of the clinical assessment.
5. This instrument identifies a starting point for circular questioning.
6. This instrument allows the nonverbal members of the family a forum for expressing themselves.
7. This instrument provides good visual representation of the strengths and weaknesses of the family.
8. This instrument helps both the therapist and family members define treatment goals.
9. This instrument shows a quantitative measure of change in response to treatment.

SOURCE: Skinner, H. A., Steinhauer, P. D., & Santa-Barbara, J. (2009). The Family Assessment Measure. *Canadian Journal of Community Mental Health, 2*(2), 91–103.

Problem-Oriented Standardized Measures

Many other measures for assessing family problems exist beside those covered in the previous section. Comprehensive reviews of available measures for family assessment are provided by Sherman, Fredman, Sherman, & Fredman (2013), Thomlison (2015), and Toulitas, Perlmutter, and Straus (2000). Corcoran and Fischer (2013) provide a review of several rapid assessment instruments that can be used to assess marital and family systems, and the Society of Pediatric Psychology of American Psychological Association (n.d.) offers a list of measures on family functioning. Recall from the discussion on standardized measures in chapter 3 that several different types of standardized measures exist, ranging from global, multidimensional measures to specific, unidimensional problem inventories. Standardized measures are most effective when administered as part of a comprehensive clinical assessment and evaluation. Using standardized clinical measures in any other way to screen or diagnose a client or client system is ineffective clinical practice. One family measure that is useful assessing families, the Mediator's Assessment of Safety Issues and Concerns (MASIC), is in the public domain and is provided in appendix 7B.

DSM-5 AND FAMILY ASSESSMENT METHODS

The fifth, and most recent, revision of the *Diagnostic and Statistical Manual of Mental Disorders,* fifth edition (DSM-5; American Psychiatric Association [APA], 2013) includes a section on relational problems that may affect the course, prognosis, or treatment of disorders included in the manual. The DSM-5 designates a series of problems related to family upbringing, including "Parent-child relational problems" (Z62.820), a diagnosis applied when the parent-child relationship affects the diagnosis or treatment of a mental disorder. It may be applied when families are struggling in the areas of parental control or supervision or when parents are exerting excessive pressure on a child. Other diagnoses include "Sibling relational problem" (Z63.5), which applies when a child's relationship with a sibling is disruptive to treatment; "Upbringing away from parents" (Z63.8), when treatment is compromised by a child who has been raised away from parents; and "Child affected by parental relationship distress" (Z62.898), when parents' marital discord presents barriers to treatment. Figure 7.4 provides an example of standardized measure for assessing battering in families: the Abusive Behavior Inventory.

Other diagnostic codes are used in cases when there are relationship problems in the primary support that get in the way of treatment of mental disorders. These include "Disruption of family by separation or divorce" (Z63.5); "High expressed emotion level within the family" (Z63.8), which is applied when family members are directing high levels of hostility and criticism toward the identified patient; and "Uncomplicated bereavement" (Z63.4), when the identified patient is reacting to the death of a loved one.

Another category of DSM-5 (APA, 2013) diagnostic codes that applies to family assessment involves assessing for child maltreatment, since current or past abuse and neglect influences the diagnosis and treatment of a number of mental disorders. The diagnostic codes end with an A if the patient is currently receiving treatment for child maltreatment, and they end in a D to indicate that the patient has received prior treatment. Diagnoses include "Child physical abuse, confirmed" (T74.12XA; T74.12XD), "Child physical abuse, suspected" (T76.12XA, T76.12XD), "Child sexual abuse, confirmed" (T74.22XA, T74.22XD), "Child sexual abuse, suspected" (T76.22XA, T76.22XD), "Child neglect, confirmed" (T74.02XA, T74.02XD), "Child neglect, suspected" (T76.02XA, T76.02XD), "Child psychological abuse, confirmed" (T74.32XA, T74.32XD), "Child psychological abuse, suspected" (T76.32XA, T76.32XD).

OTHER FAMILY ASSESSMENT METHODS

Even though standardized family assessment measures and DSM-5 (APA, 2013) diagnoses may be useful for family assessment, practitioners

Figure 7.4   Abusive Behavior Inventory Partner Form

Here is a list of behaviors that many women report have been used by their partners or former partners. We would like you to estimate how often these behaviors occurred during the six months prior to your beginning this program. Your answers are strictly confidential.

CIRCLE a number of each of the items listed below to show your closest estimate of how often it happened in your relationship with your partner or former partner during the six months before he started the program.

1 = Never
2 = Rarely
3 = Occasionally
4 = Frequently
5 = Very frequently

1. Called you names and/or criticized you. `1 2 3 4 5`
2. Tried to keep you from doing something you wanted to do (example: going out with friends, going to meetings). `1 2 3 4 5`
3. Gave you angry stares or looks. `1 2 3 4 5`
4. Prevented you from having money for your own use. `1 2 3 4 5`
5. Ended a discussion with you and made the decision himself. `1 2 3 4 5`
6. Threatened to hit or throw something at you. `1 2 3 4 5`
7. Pushed, grabbed, or shoved you. `1 2 3 4 5`
8. Put down your family or friends. `1 2 3 4 5`
9. Accused you of paying too much attention to someone or something else. `1 2 3 4 5`
10. Put you on an allowance. `1 2 3 4 5`
11. Used your children to threaten you (example: told you that you would lose custody, said he would leave town with the children). `1 2 3 4 5`
12. Became very upset with you because dinner, housework, or laundry was not ready when he wanted it or done the way he thought it should be done. `1 2 3 4 5`
13. Said things to scare you (example: told you something "bad" would happen, threatened to commit suicide). `1 2 3 4 5`
14. Slapped, hit, or punched you. `1 2 3 4 5`
15. Made you do something humiliating or degrading (example: begging for forgiveness, having to ask his permission to use the car or do something). `1 2 3 4 5`
16. Checked up on you (example: listened to your phone calls, checked the mileage on your car, called you repeatedly at work). `1 2 3 4 5`
17. Drove recklessly when you were in the car. `1 2 3 4 5`
18. Pressured you to have sex in a way that you didn't like or want.
19. Refused to do housework or child care. `1 2 3 4 5`
20. Threatened you with a knife, gun, or other weapon. `1 2 3 4 5`
21. Spanked you. `1 2 3 4 5`
22. Told you that you were a bad parent. `1 2 3 4 5`
23. Stopped you or tried to stop you from going to work or school. `1 2 3 4 5`
24. Threw, hit, kicked, or smashed something. `1 2 3 4 5`
25. Kicked you. `1 2 3 4 5`
26. Physically forced you to have sex. `1 2 3 4 5`
27. Threw you around. `1 2 3 4 5`
28. Physically attacked the sexual parts of your body. `1 2 3 4 5`
29. Choked or strangled you. `1 2 3 4 5`
30. Used a knife, gun, or other weapon against you. `1 2 3 4 5`

SOURCE: Shepard, M. F., & Campbell, J. A. *Journal of Interpersonal Violence* (vol. 7, no. 3), pp. 291–305. Copyright © 1992 by SAGE Publications. Reprinted by permission of SAGE Publications, Inc.

should not exclusively rely on such approaches—there are many other methods for assessing family functioning (DeMaria, Weeks, & Hof, 2013; Holland, 2010). This section covers some of the other methods: those that are consistent with the types of assessment methods summarized in chapter 2 on quantitative assessment and in chapter 4 on qualitative assessment. Specifically, this section covers (a) interviewing techniques, (b) family-task observations, (c) graphic measures, and (d) assessing family strengths and resilience. The assessment methods presented here are not comprehensive but provide practitioners with several useful techniques for collecting assessment information on families.

Interviewing Techniques

Social workers frequently rely on talking with family members as their primary way of gathering assessment information. Interviewing is one of the most important practice skills for a social worker to acquire (Bogo, 2006; Kadushin & Kadushin, 2013). Throughout this chapter we provide several examples of questions to guide social workers through the interview and to aid in gathering pertinent information concerning family process and behavior. Practitioners can interview family members together or apart, depending on the type of information the social worker is seeking. For example, in exploring problems such as family roles or rules, the social worker may include everyone because such issues affect the entire family; however, the social worker would interview only the parents when exploring problems in the couple's sexual relationship.

Regardless of how many family members the practitioner interviews at one time, he or she should remember that the members being interviewed are part of a larger family system. In essence, when interviewing families social workers always have two clients: the family as a system and the individual members of that system (Schulman, 2011). This makes interviewing families complex and calls on the social worker to engage all family members, to observe their interactions, and to assess the family at different levels. For example, the social worker may need to assess the behavior of an individual family member, such as eight-year-old Chad, who has disruptive behavior. Chad started rocking back and forth on a chair in the social worker's office, distracting his parents from the meeting. The social worker not only recognized the disruptive behavior but also assessed a parental subsystem interaction—the parenting-skills deficits of the parents, who are unable to set appropriate limits on the boy's behavior. In addition, the social worker noted a systems-level interaction—Chad's behavior of jumping on the chair started immediately after the parents made critical remarks about his poor school performance and compared it with the superior performance of his twelve-year-old brother, Chip.

The social worker then observed the following interactional sequence: The father yells at the boy to stop his behavior of jumping on the chair (parent-child subsystem interaction). The older brother, Chip, joins in the interaction by calling Chad stupid for acting the way he does (sibling subsystem interaction and parent-child coalition). The social worker observes this interaction so that she can see the interactional functioning. The mother intervenes and tells Chip not to call his brother stupid (parental subsystem interaction). The mother also told the father not to raise his voice at Chad (parent-child coalition). The father told the mother to stop interfering in his discipline and stated that she is too easy on Chad (parental subsystem interaction). At the same time, Chad jumped out of the chair, sat in another chair near the mother, and began to pick a fight with his older brother. They exchanged a few putdowns (sibling subsystem interaction). Chip asked the parents to stop Chad from picking on him (parent-child subsystem interaction). The parents then united and told Chad to stop picking on Chip, and the mother stated that they both owe each other an apology (parental subsystem interaction). Chip said angrily, "You always stick up for Chad" and pouted, refusing to apologize (parent-child subsystem interaction). Chad went and sat away from the family in the chair in which he was rocking back and forth before he moved to taunt his brother (individual member interaction).

Both parents turned to the social worker and denied that they give preferential treatment to one child over the other. Chip shook his head no. The father looked at the social worker and said that it is difficult to have peace in the family when Chad throws such fits. The mother agreed that there is much tension in the family but added that it is not all Chad's fault. The father added that Chad wears his feelings on his sleeve and does not cooperate. Chad started rocking in the chair again (systems/contextual level).

In such a scenario, the social worker uses the face-to-face interview to observe the multiple interactions of the family. Interviewing in this context requires expert observation skills and the ability to engage the family verbally. It might be helpful, at this point, to refer back to the assessment protocol in chapter 1 and review some of the important information on family functioning that can be gathered during a comprehensive assessment.

As has been emphasized throughout this chapter, it is important to assess the family as a system and to understand how all the members' separate behaviors fit together into the complex interactions known as "systemic functioning." One interviewing technique that helps assess the complexities of how families work as systems is circular questioning. Circular questions provide a structure for eliciting information from various family members about the transactions and operations embedded in the family system. The structure of circular questions is nonthreatening to the family because the questions generally ask family members to comment on the family process from the viewpoint of a different family member. Thus, a father might be asked to comment on how he believes a son is responding to the behavior of the mother or a sister might be asked how she believes her brother might be feeling in response to his mother.

Circular questions can be divided into categories of information-eliciting probes. O'Brien and Bruggen (1985) offer five categories for organizing different types of circular questions:

1. Relationship to others: These questions may refer to the relationship between two people in a family (e.g., "How do your mom and dad solve disagreements between them?").

2. Relationship to events in family life: These questions refer to how people organize meanings around events or time (e.g., "When Mom comes home late from work, what does Dad do?").

3. Ranking behavior in the family: Actual or hypothetical situations can be used (e.g., "Who is most strict, your mother or your father?" "Pretend for a moment that I am a magic fairy with the powers to send you on a vacation to an adventurous island. Who in your family would you take with you?").

4. Relationships to time: Both events in time and specific points in time may be used (e.g., "How was your husband different before you moved to this city?" "How were things different between you a year ago?").

5. Eliciting information from the perspective of the silent member: This may include members not present at family sessions or those who will not or cannot talk (e.g., "If your father were here in the session, what do you think he might say about your family?" "If your brother were to answer my question, what do you think he might say?").

Fleuridas, Nelson, and Rosenthal (1986) offer a more-detailed categorization for understanding different types of circular questions, as presented in appendix 7A.

Family-Task Observations

Observations of family members undertaking structured tasks provide an important way for social workers to observe and assess family functioning. Such tasks as playing a game, planning a vacation, solving a problem, and making a decision have been used. As an example of making a decision, the social worker may ask families to decide on their main issue in therapy while the social worker observes them from the corner of the room or through a one-way mirror. Observing families in such a task allows the social worker to view many aspects of family functioning, such as roles, power, communication, and decision-making processes.

Enactment is a structured family task in which the family replays a previous situation in the family. For example, the practitioner might ask a couple who complains that they argue about how to spend their free time on weekends to reconstruct or reenact an argument while the practitioner observes. The practitioner might instruct a wife who complains that she cannot talk to her husband to tell her husband those feelings in the session and to talk to him about them. Enactments help social workers understand both the strengths and the weaknesses of family process and provide meaningful information on which the social workers may base their interventions.

Family sculpting is an experiential task in which the social worker asks an individual family member to place other family members in stationary positions that represent what the family is like from that individual's perception. The individual places him- or herself among the family members. Significant therapeutic information is believed to emerge from the sculpting. For example, a woman sculpting her family placed herself on the floor with her husband's foot on top of her. From a family sculpture, social workers can assess such family dynamics as power, cohesion, affective responses, coalitions, and triangles. The experiential aspects of the sculpture also serve as a powerful tool that may help family members gain insight into the interactions in their own family.

Graphic Measures

Family therapists have developed several pictorial and graphic methods for assessing family functioning. One of the most popular graphic methods is the genogram, which was popularized through the Bowenian approach to family therapy (Bowen, 1976). The genogram provides an assessment of the family from an intergenerational context and provides a map of the family from a longitudinal perspective across three generations. Symbols are used to depict the types of family members and different aspects of family functioning. For example, a square symbolizes males and a circle symbolizes females. A horizontal line symbolizes a marriage and a vertical line symbolizes offspring. The genogram also provides a method for gathering psychosocial information from the family. Such information as family members' cultural and ethnic backgrounds, socioeconomic status, religions, dates of marriage, dates of birth or adoption, birth order, dates of divorce, deaths, amounts of contact with and social support from family members, and other significant events (e.g., serious illnesses, abortions, personal tragedies) can be recorded on the genogram. Some social workers also record personal information about family members, such as descriptions of personality characteristics and personal and emotional problems. The genogram can provide a wealth of assessment information, and it is not unusual for transgenerational patterns of a certain type of family difficulty to emerge.

Assessing Family Strengths and Resilience

From a strengths perspective a definition of strengths is always associated with resilience. Family strengths and resilience have a strong connection when we look at a definition of strength as "the capacity to cope with difficulties, to maintain functioning in the face of stress, to bounce back in the face of significant trauma, to use external challenges as a stimulus for growth, and to use social supports as a source of resilience" (McQuaide & Ehrenreich, 1997, p. 203). Family researchers and practitioners have also developed specific methods for assessing family strengths and resilience. There are several measures that have been developed to assess family strengths and that have been modified for those purposes by practitioners. Box 7.2 offers a list of strengths-based measures that are designed for evaluating families, children, and adolescents.

Rawana and Brownlee (2009) built the Strength, Assessment, and Treatment Model to enhance family strengths and resilience. This model emphasizes four foundational components: (a) engagement, (b) exploration, (c) expansion, and (d) evolution (Rawana & Brownlee, 2009). The second step of this model, exploration, means assessing family strengths. Rawana pointed out that practitioners can use a structured questionnaire to enhance the interview process. Examples are the Behavioral and Emotional Rating Scale (Buckley & Epstein, 2004), the Clinical Assessment Package for Risks (Gilgun, 2001), and the Strengths and Difficulties Questionnaire (McQuaide & Ehrenreich, 1997).

Graybeal (2001) discusses ways that social workers can include strengths in traditional psychosocial assessments by using the ROPES interviewing approach. The acronym ROPES reminds the practitioner to consider all the following approaches:

- Resources: Personal, family, social environment, organizational, community.

- Options: Present focus, emphasis on choice. What can be accessed now? What is available and has not been tried or used yet?

- Possibilities: Future focus, imagination, creativity, vision of the future, play. What have you thought of trying but have not tried yet?

- Exceptions: When is the problem not happening? When is the problem different? When is part of the hypothetical future solution occurring? How have you survived, endured, thrived?

- Solutions: Focus on constructing solutions, not solving problems. What is working now? What are your successes? What are you doing that you would like to change?

The ROPES interviewing approach encourages practitioners to think about strengths in areas they are already assessing. For example, they assess exceptions to the problem when collecting information about presenting problems or list resources when describing the family and social

Box 7.2
Strengths-Based Measures for Families and Children

Strengths-based Family Instruments

Name of Instrument	Reliable	Valid	Appropriateness in Clinical Settings	Appropriateness in Research Settings
Family Assessment Device (FAD)	Yes	Yes	Appropriate	Appropriate
Family Functioning Style Scale (FFSS)	Yes	Yes	Unknown	Appropriate
Parent Perception Inventory	Yes	Yes	Unknown	Appropriate
Developmental Assets Profile (DAP)	Yes	Yes	Unknown	Appropriate
Parent-Adolescent Communication Scale	Yes	Unknown	Appropriate	Inconclusive
Family Assessment Measure (FAM-III)	Yes	Unknown	Appropriate	Inconclusive
Family Resource Scale (FRS)	Unknown	Yes	Unknown	Inconclusive
Family Support Scale (FSS)	Yes	Unknown	Unknown	Inconclusive
Family Empowerment Scale (FES)	Yes	Unknown	Unknown	Inconclusive

Strengths-Based Children and Adolescents Instruments

Name of Instrument	Reliable	Valid	Appropriateness in Clinical Settings	Appropriateness in Research Settings
Behavioral and Emotional Rating Scale (BERS)	Yes	Yes	Unknown	Appropriate
Developmental Assets Profile (DAP)	Yes	Yes	Unknown	Appropriate
Social Skills Rating System (SSRS)	Yes	Moderate	Unknown	Inconclusive
Behavioral Assessment System for Children (BASC)	Yes	Moderate	Unknown	Inconclusive
Multidimensional Student Life Satisfaction Survey	Yes	Moderate	Unknown	Appropriate
School Social Behavior Scale-2 (SSBS-2)	Yes	Moderate	Unknown	Appropriate
California Healthy Kids Survey–Resilience Youth Development Module (RYDM)	Yes	Moderate	Unknown	Appropriate

SOURCE: Franklin, C., Trepper, T. S., Gingerich, W. J., & Mccollum, E. E. (2012). *Solution-Focused Brief Therapy: A handbook of evidence-based practice.* New York: Oxford University Press.

environment of the client. The ROPES approach can also be used in the following areas in a traditional assessment of clients:

- Presenting problems: Add exceptions, solutions, and options to your assessment.
- Background information: Add resources and options to your social assessment.

- Goal setting: Add exceptions and coconstruct options and possibilities to your set of goals for the client change.
- Intervention plan: Add possibilities and solutions to the set of recommendations for your assessment report.

We have discussed several different methods for assessing families. All of them are useful in helping social workers learn about family functioning. It is not practical, however, for social workers to use all these methods in an assessment situation with a family, because different families may respond to some techniques better than others. For example, Ho (2003) indicates that Hispanic families may respond favorably to the genogram technique because of their multigenerational family orientation. Individual social workers may also find a certain set of techniques more effective in helping them assess family processes. Social workers must choose among the assessment options and use knowledge of their clientele and practice wisdom to help them decide which methods to use in a family assessment. Social workers are encouraged to develop their own personal assessment outline that may guide them in practice. Chapter 3 provides guidelines for using multiple methods for assessing clients.

MOVING FROM ASSESSMENT TO INTERVENTION

What follows covers a family assessment completed by a social worker practicing in a juvenile justice setting. The report illustrates how to use the multiple sources of information gathered during an assessment to develop an assessment report on a client, including how to integrate standardized family assessments into the assessment report. In addition, the assessment report illustrates how to use assessment information to develop an intervention plan. It is important to note that, even though this is an actual assessment report on a client, the identifying information has been changed to protect the confidentiality of the clients.

Peggy Weeks, MSSW, LCSW, is a social worker employed in a youth shelter for juvenile offenders. She frequently conducts family assessments to make recommendations to the court concerning youths who are brought to the shelter. Weeks employs several of the assessment methods discussed previously in her data-gathering process, usually relying on interviews with family members, family-task observations, and standardized measures. The major purpose of an assessment is to make decisions about treatment. Weeks used multiple methods in her assessment: interviews, task observations, and a standardized measure guided her decision about what she would recommend to the court concerning the youth she was working with, Madie Williams.

For example, from her family assessment information she was able to conclude that Madie's family had many strengths. They were loving and supportive, and capable of providing the structure and guidance that Madie needed. In contrast, the family had experienced many stressors and had some significant cross-generational conflicts that needed resolution. These stressors, however, did not appear to interfere with Mr. and Mrs. Williams's functioning as parents. Therefore, the social worker concluded that they were competent parents and able to provide a good home for Madie.

The social worker's assessment uncovered many emotional and psychological issues contributing to Madie's behavior problems. She was able to use this information to make a clinical judgment concerning what types of issues she should address in a treatment plan. Thus, in the recommendation section of the assessment report, Weeks outlined Madie's emotional issues (i.e., loss, depression, anger) and suggested that these issues be addressed in therapy. She also interpreted those emotional issues in relationship to Madie's adolescent developmental issues. She further looked at the severity of her behavior problem (e.g., running away) and inferred that Madie would need a fairly intensive treatment program that provided additional supports and structures besides those her family could provide. The social worker, therefore, recommended the day treatment program as an intervention for Madie.

The therapist used the information uncovered in the assessment and written in the report to develop the recommendations section of the assessment report. The recommendations section is the first step toward developing a treatment plan for a client. Treatment plans generally flow out of and are the next step to be completed after the assessment (see chapter 10). The process by which Weeks used the assessment information to create her recommendations for Madie is complex: she drew on her knowledge of child development, psychopathologies, and family practice theories, as well as her clinical experiences with adjudicated youths. That is, Weeks used her clinical expertise to infer from the assessment information and make decisions about needed treatments. All practitioners must rely on their clinical judgment when they move from assessment to intervention; this is not a completely objective or linear process but rather is a process that can follow the steps of evidence-based practice described in previous chapters of this book.

Here are some guidelines for using the assessment information to construct treatment recommendations. Begin by reviewing information on the presenting problems. Focus on resolution of the presenting problems (in Madie's case, running away). Next, focus on resolving associated problems (in Madie's case, depression and identity disturbance). Ask yourself what interventions are needed to resolve these problems. Focus on the other dimensions (e.g., developmental context of the client's life, history, family situation) and decide what is affecting the presenting problems and how that needs to be considered in the treatment process. Consider all the assessment information in terms of resolving the problems, and then construct a set of recommendations.

ASSESSMENT REPORT: THE WILLIAMS FAMILY

The Williamses are an African American family of four: Will (father), Lisa (mother), Tiffany (daughter), and George (son). They reside at 1200 Wagon Street, Hays, Texas.

The following assessment information is based on two interviews with the parents on February 7 and 9, one interview with the whole family on February 11, and two separate interviews with the daughter, Tiffany, while she was in detention on February 6 and 7 at the youth shelter of Travis County. Behavioral observations of the family carrying out a task and scores from the administration of the FES, a standardized measure, were also used to determine the family's overall level of functioning. All interviews took place in the shelter except for one of the parental interviews, which took place in the family home.

Presenting Problem

Tiffany Williams, a fourteen-year-old female detained at the shelter for stealing two packs of cigarettes while awaiting a detention hearing, was assigned to the social worker, Peggy Weeks. On February 6, Judge Lyndon L. Roberts ordered Weeks to assess the family and be prepared to recommend placement in the best interest of Tiffany Williams, a juvenile.

Individual Characteristics

Tiffany Williams is a fourteen-year-old African American female, and is the older child in a family of two children. She is in the eighth grade at Johnson High School. Mrs. Williams reports that Tiffany has never failed a grade or had any significant academic problems. She has consistently been on the honor roll at school. There are no reports of significant behavior problems until age twelve, when Tiffany became openly defiant of authority and began to lie persistently and be truant from school. Mr. and Mrs. Williams also stated that Tiffany's "feelings are easily hurt, and that in the past she has allowed herself to be easily taken advantage of by friends just so she wouldn't lose them." Mrs. Williams believes that Tiffany became depressed about age thirteen and began stealing at about age fourteen. Tiffany reportedly has run away from home overnight on two occasions since age thirteen. At age fourteen she left home with a boyfriend for five days. Police picked her up, she returned home, and she promised not to leave again. From reports of both parents, the onset of Tiffany's behavior problems at age twelve occurred when she found out from the Jeffersons, Mrs. Williams's parents, that Lisa Williams was not Tiffany's biological mother. This incident was reported to have happened during a family argument where some "pretty mean things were said."

Madeline Jones is Tiffany's biological mother. Her whereabouts are unknown, and she has not been heard from since she left Tiffany at the age of eighteen months with her father, Mr. Williams. Less than a year after Tiffany found out about the identity of her biological mother, she allegedly started a fire in her grandmother's house that destroyed the house and injured her grandmother and her brother.

Lisa Williams is a thirty-six-year-old African American female. She is articulate and intelligent. She is stepmother to Tiffany and biological mother of George, Tiffany's brother. Mrs. Williams has cared for Tiffany since she was eighteen months old, and she states that she "loved her like her own." Williams works as an assistant at the Austin library and is the primary financial support for the family. She reports that she is currently estranged from her family, the Jeffersons, in Dallas because of the fire at her parent's house, their negative comments, and their attitude toward Tiffany and Will. She states that those family relationships are very stressful, but she truly believes her mother and father have misjudged the situation and that the fire was started by accident because Tiffany was trying to hide her smoking from them. Mrs. Williams graduated from high school and attended college, where she met her husband.

Will Williams is a thirty-five-year-old African American male. He is articulate. He is the biological father of both Tiffany and George. Williams graduated from high school and attended college. He played football through college and for eight years as a professional for the Los Angeles Unicorns. Williams has worked only part-time outside the home in the past five years. He provides child care and attends to the needs of the family at home. He began his current job as a part-time night stocker at a grocery store six months ago.

George Williams is an eleven-year-old African American male. He is in the fifth grade at Travis Elementary School, is consistently on the honor roll, and has won several trophies for his athletic abilities in baseball. He has a speech impediment, a stutter, which his parents report he has always had. He receives speech therapy at his school. He also reports feeling very close to his sister and being worried that she "may be in very big trouble."

Family Background and History

Mr. and Mrs. Williams met in Dallas, Texas, nineteen years ago while attending Dallas County Community College. They have been married for thirteen years. Mr. Williams was previously involved in a relationship with Megan Jones, with whom he fathered one child, Tiffany, in 1977. When Tiffany was eighteen months old, Megan Jones disappeared, leaving Tiffany in the care of the child's father, who married Lisa Jefferson shortly thereafter. The family moved to Los Angeles in 1979, after Mr.

Williams was recruited out of college to play football for the Los Angeles Unicorns, a professional team. Their son was born one year later, in 1980. Mrs. Williams worked as an assistant in a library while Mr. Williams played football for eight years. As a result of numerous knee injuries, Mr. Williams was dropped from the team in December 1988, and the family moved to Dallas, Texas, where they lived with Mr. and Mrs. John Jefferson, Mrs. Williams's parents. Mr. Williams held odd jobs, mostly as a security guard, and Mrs. Williams worked at a Dallas library.

Nine months after moving in with the Jeffersons, a fire completely destroyed the house. Mrs. Jefferson and George were injured in the fire but recovered in a few weeks. Tiffany was arrested, placed on probation for arson, and sent to Buckner Children's Home for two weeks. Tiffany appears to have been arrested because the fire was started in or near her room, and the Jeffersons believed that she had set the fire with a lighter later found on her person. Tiffany and her parents maintain that she did not start the fire on purpose but that it did result from her smoking in her room. Relations between the Williamses and the Jeffersons deteriorated, and one year after moving to Dallas the family decided to move to Hays. Mr. Williams moved first and found a job at a grocery store. He later took a similar job at a large grocery chain. Lisa, Tiffany, and George followed three months later, after Lisa was able to get a job at the Hays library.

Social Support and Current Living Arrangements

The Williamses live in a single-family home that they own. The home is spacious, with three bedrooms and two baths, and the social worker noted that it is tidy and well kept. Both Tiffany and George have their own rooms, and the home is enriched with music, art, and literature that Mrs. Williams provides. The family home is located in a middle-class neighborhood with parks and recreational facilities. The neighborhood is well integrated ethnically, and the family reports that the neighbors are friendly with one another. Mr. and Mrs. Williams socialize with one couple in the neighborhood and know several others. Both Tiffany and George state that they have friends that live on their street.

The family is very involved in the local Protestant church, and the parents state that religion is important to the family life. Mr. Williams says the minister had been a comfort to them during this "trial with Tiffany," and that several people in the church had offered emotional support to them.

Both Mr. and Mrs. Williams are involved in several civic and recreational groups. They belong to and attend meetings at the neighborhood association. Mr. Williams belongs to a fraternity and frequently plays sports with a few of the men from that group. Mrs. Williams loves African art and serves on the committee of the local art museum. Both children have been active in sports; George is especially involved in baseball and Tiffany in track. Family members report that they have been satisfied with the quality of their social relationships and that they like their neighborhood.

Both Mr. and Mrs. Williams have expressed regret, however, that they were not close to their extended family members and hope that something could be done about the problem between Mrs. Williams and her parents in the future.

The family at this time has adequate financial resources and expresses no concern for their financial well-being. Mr. Williams, however, expresses a concern that he should make plans to develop a new career now that he has left football.

Results of the Family Environment Scale

The FES, a standardized measure, was used to assess the family's social climate as it compares with a normative group. The social worker administered the measure to each family member during the family interview on February 11. The results from the FES appear to be valid and consistent with the social worker's observations of the family (tables 7.1 and 7.2, figure 7.5).

According to the FES scores, this is a relationship-oriented family that encourages personal growth. The family also scored above average in achievement and support orientation. The family incongruence score indicates that they are a highly congruent family; they answered fifty-two questions out of ninety the same. Given the results, the below-average score for Tiffany on the independence subscale can be explained as normal for an adolescent trying to master developmental goals of separation and individuation.

Table 7.1   Family Environment Scale Raw Scores on Subscales

	Mother	Father	Daughter	Son
Relationship Dimensions Cohesion (C)	9	8	8	9
Expressiveness (Ex)	3	5	6	5
Conflict (Con)	1	4	2	1
Independence (Ind)	5	8	4	7
Achievement Orientation (AO)	7	9	7	6
Intellectual-Cultural Orientation (ICO)	7	9	9	7
Achievement-Recreational (ARO)	8	7	7	8
Moral-Religious Emphasis (MRE)	7	6	5	6
Organization (Org)	8	5	7	7
Control (Ctl)	5	8	7	7
Family Incongruence Score: 13.66				

Table 7.2   Family Environment Scale Raw Scores on Subscales

	Mrs. Williams	Mr. Williams	Madie	Player
C	90	80	80	90
Ex	30	50	60	50
Con	10	40	20	10
Ind	50	80	40	70
AO	70	90	70	60
ICO	70	90	90	70
ARO	80	70	70	80
MRE	70	60	50	60
Org	80	50	70	70
Ctl	50	80	70	70

Figure 7.5   Family Environment Scale Scores Graphed

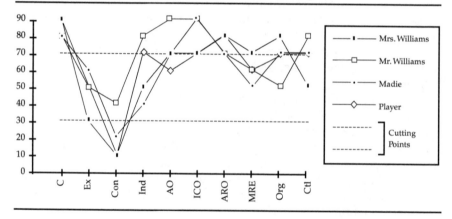

All family members' scores indicate a high degree of cohesiveness. They appear to be very committed to and supportive of one another. Their feelings of togetherness as a family are above average. Mr. Williams described his family as his "heartbeat." When he said this, the family members all embraced one another.

Mr. Williams and both children report an average feeling of openness; they can express their feelings openly and discuss their personal problems. Mrs. Williams, however, scored considerably below average on the expressiveness subscale, which is consistent with her observed quieter demeanor; she was the least outspoken and did not offer any information without being asked a direct question. Mrs. Williams and both children scored below average on the conflicts subscale, which indicates a lack of aggression or fighting in the family. All members agreed that "if there's a disagreement in our family, we try hard to smooth things over and keep the peace," that they "do not fight a lot in our family," that "family members do not get so angry that they throw things," and that "family members do not hit each other." This family appears to show a preference for conflict avoidance and agreement. The social worker also observed these patterns during the family interview; family members were quick to come to the aid and defense of one another.

Except for the independence subscale, this family measured above average in encouraging personal growth. The family measured well above average on the achievement orientation subscale. Their dedication to school and sports clearly illustrates this pattern. They all report that it is important to be the best at whatever they do, and "work before play is the rule in our family." Given these results, the below-average score for Tiffany on the independence subscale may be related to her own personal turmoil over her identity and recent psychosocial stressors. It may also reflect Tiffany's own sense of powerlessness over the situation and her level of depression.

The family scores were average for the intellectual and cultural orientation subscale, which is consistent with the social worker's observations of their experience. The Williamses are very culturally aware and proud of their African heritage. They report that they have been discriminated against because of their race but continue to encourage their children to be proud of and to preserve their African heritage. Their political and social interests, however, do not go much beyond their immediate life. The average subscale measure is consistent with the social worker's own observations and conversations with them. The Williamses are involved in their children's athletic activities at an above-average level, according to the measure score. Mr. Williams reports that he is Tiffany's trainer for track.

The Williamses range from average to well above average on the moral-religious emphasis subscale. The family attends church on a regular basis and reports that they say prayers, believe that sin will be punished, and that there is a heaven and a hell.

This family is highly organized and structured. Their activities and responsibilities are planned and clear. The social worker's observation while in their home on one occasion is consistent with these outcomes. Their home is neat and orderly, as are their persons. When Mr. Williams observed his daughter being escorted from detention to the courtroom, his first comment to her was, "Baby, look at your hair! Why didn't you comb it?"

The measures on the control subscale also fell into the well-above-average range. Mr. Williams, who is clearly the head of the house, scored above average on this subscale. The score appears to reflect both his cultural and his religious beliefs concerning the gender roles of men in a family. All family members agreed that Mr. Williams makes most of the final decisions. They agreed that there are set ways of doing things at home and that there is a strong emphasis on following rules in the family.

Recommendation to the Court

The social worker recommends that Tiffany be returned to her family. They are able to and have in the past provided needed support and structure for her. Tiffany's decline can be traced directly to several major events in her life: at the age of ten, she and her family moved from Los Angeles to Dallas, a major disruption that required a great deal of adjustment. At that time, Tiffany also discovered that Lisa Williams was not her biological mother, which caused a major shift in her self-image and in their relationship. She subsequently developed several behavior problems. Next, her grandparents' house burned down, injuring her grandmother and her brother. Tiffany was arrested, charged with arson, placed on probation, and briefly removed from her home when she was sent to the Buckner Children's Home. These events confirmed Tiffany's distorted beliefs that the Jeffersons were correct: "She wasn't good enough to be Lisa's daughter." To complicate matters, Tiffany entered adolescence at this time. It is believed that Tiffany may suffer from depression associated with these stressors. Tiffany will benefit from individual and family counseling that helps the family better address her behavior problems. She needs a safe place to explore and talk about her feelings of loss at suddenly becoming a stepchild, anger toward her parents for keeping her ignorant of her biological mother, anger about the events that occurred in Dallas, and shame over her behavior in the past two years. It is believed that the family also needs help in adjusting to their stresses, their extended family conflicts, and the issues regarding Tiffany's runaway, stealing, and identity problems. To facilitate Tiffany's adjustment in the home, the social worker also recommended that she attend an alternative school or day treatment program so that she can receive the extra support and the structure needed to resolve her difficulties. She can do this best with the loving support of her family.

SUMMARY

This chapter has reviewed several methods for conducting a family assessment and has summarized key concepts and issues to consider in evaluating family systems. We discussed selected assessment approaches for understanding families, as well as techniques for gathering information on families. Specific assessment methods covered include standardized measures, interviewing techniques, family-task observations, family goal recording, and specific methods for assessing family strengths.

Finally, this chapter demonstrated how to move from assessment to intervention by providing a family assessment report that illustrated how to integrate multiple sources of information into a family assessment and how to create an intervention plan from this information.

STUDY QUESTIONS

1. What are five key characteristics of family systems?
2. How do whole-systems measurement instruments help family practitioners?
3. Develop a family genogram on yourself or a friend.

WEB SITES

American Association of Marriage and Family Therapy, www.aamft.org
Minuchin Center for the Family, www.minuchincenter.org/
Solution-Focused Brief Therapy Association, www.sfbta.org

REFERENCES

American Psychiatric Association (APA). (2013). *Diagnostic and statistical manual of mental disorders* (5th ed.; DSM-5). Washington, DC: Author.

Baer, J. C., & Schmitz, M. F. (2007). Ethnic differences in trajectories of family cohesion for Mexican American and non-Hispanic white adolescents. *Journal of Youth and Adolescence, 36,* 583–592.

Baiocco, R., Cacioppo, M., Laghi, F., & Tafà, M. (2013). Factorial and construct validity of FACES IV among Italian adolescents. *Journal of Child and Family Studies, 22*(7), 962–970.

Beavers, W. R., & Hampson, R. B. (2000). The Beavers Systems Model of family functioning. *Journal of Family Therapy, 22,* 128–133.

Beavers, W. R., & Hampson, R. B. (2003). Measuring family competence: The Beavers systems model. In F. Walsh, *Normal family processes: Growing diversity and complexity* (3rd ed., pp. 549–580). New York: Guilford Press.

Boake, C., & Salmon, P. G. (1983). Demographic correlates and factor structure of the Family Environment Scale. *Journal of Clinical Psychology, 39,* 95–100.

Bogo, M. (2006). *Social work practice: Concepts, processes, and interviewing.* New York: Columbia University Press.

Bowen, M. (1976). Theory in the practice of psychotherapy. In P. J. Guerin (Ed.), *Family therapy: Theory and practice* (pp. 24–90). New York: Gardner.

Bowen, M. (1978). *Family therapy in clinical practice.* New York: Aronson.

Buckley, J. A., & Epstein, M. H. (2004). The Behavioral and Emotional Rating Scale-2 (BERS-2): Providing a comprehensive approach to strength-based assessment. *The California School Psychologist, 9*(1), 21–27.

Chipuer, H. M., & Villegas, T. (2001). Comparing the second-order factor structure of the Family Environment Scale across husbands' and wives' perceptions of their family environment. *Family Process, 40,* 187–199.

Corcoran, K., & Fischer, J. (Eds.). (2013). *Measures for clinical practice and research:* Vol. 1. *Couples, families, and children.* New York: Oxford University Press.

Craddock, A. E. (2001). Relationship between family structure and family functioning: A test of Tiesel and Olson's Circumplex Model. *Journal of Family Studies, 7,* 29–39.

DeMaria, R., Weeks, G., & Hof, L. (2013). *Focused genograms: Intergenerational assessment of individuals, couples, and families.* London: Routledge.

Dinkmeyer, D., McKay, G. D., & Dinkmeyer, D. (1997). *Systematic training for effective parenting: The parents' handbook.* New York: STEP.

Epstein, N., Baldwin, L., & Bishop, D. (2013). McMaster Family Assessment Device. In R. Sherman, N. Sherman, & N. Fredman, *Handbook of measurements for marriage and family therapy* (pp. 171–180). New York: Routledge.

Fleuridas, C., Nelson, T. S., & Rosenthal, D. M. (1986). The evolution of circular questions: Training family therapists. *Journal of Marital and Family Therapy, 12,* 113–127.

Franklin, C. (2002, March/April). Becoming a strengths fact finder. *Family Therapy Magazine, 1*(2), 30–33.

Franklin, C., Jordan, C., & Hopson, L. (2015). Effective couple and family treatment. In K. Corcoran (Ed.), *Social workers desk reference* (3rd ed., pp. 438–447). New York: Oxford University Press.

Franko, D. L., Thompson, D., Bauserman, R., Affenito, S. G., Striegel-Moore, R. (2008). What's love got to do with it? Family cohesion and healthy eating behaviors in adolescent girls. *International Journal of Eating Disorders, 41,* 360–367.

Georgiades, K., Boyle, M. H., Jenkins, J. M., Sanford, M., & Lipman, E. (2008). A multilevel analysis of whole family functioning using the McMaster Family Assessment Device. *Journal of Family Psychology, 22*(3), 344–354.

Gilgun, J. F. (2001). CASPARS: New tools for assessing client risks and strengths. *Families in Society: The Journal of Contemporary Human Services, 82,* 450–459.

Goldenberg, I., Goldenberg, H., & Pelavin, E. G. (2013). Family therapy. In D. Welding & R. J. Corsini (Eds.), *Current psychotherapies* (10th ed., pp. 373–407). Belmont, CA: Brooks/Cole.

Graybeal, C. (2001). Strengths-based social work assessment: Transforming the dominant paradigm. *Families in Society: The Journal of Contemporary Human Services, 82,* 233–242.

Gurman, A. S., & Kniskern, D. P. (Eds.). (2014). *Handbook of family therapy. Routledge.*

Hampson, R. B., & Beavers, W. R. (2011). Observational assessment. In L. Sperry (Ed.), *Family assessment: Contemporary and cutting-edge strategies* (2nd ed., pp. 83–114). New York: Routledge.

Hepworth, D. H., Rooney, R., Rooney, G. D., & Strom-Gottfried, K. (2013). *Direct social work practice: Theory and skills* (9th ed.). Belmost, CA: Brooks/Cole.

Ho, M. (2003). *Family therapy with ethnic minorities.* Newbury Park, CA: Sage.

Holland, S. (2010). *Child and family assessment in social work practice.* Thousand Oaks, CA: Sage.

Janzen, C., Harris, O., Jordan, C., & Franklin, C. (2005). *Family treatment: Evidence-based practice with populations at-risk* (4th ed.). Belmont, CA: Brooks/Cole.

Kadushin, A., & Kadushin, G. (2013). *The social work interview.* New York: Columbia University Press.

Laghezza, L., Delvecchio, E., Pazzagli, C., & Mazzeschi, C. (2014). The Family Assessment Measure III (FAM III) in an Italian sample. *BPA-Applied Psychology Bulletin (Bollettino Di Psicologia Applicata), 269,* 17–28.

Levine, J. (2012). *Working with people* (9th ed.). New York: Pearson.

Lohan, J. A., & Murphy, S. A. (2007). Bereaved mothers' marital status and family functioning after a child's sudden violent death: A preliminary study. *Journal of Loss and Trauma, 12,* 333–347.

Marsac, M. L., & Alderfer, M. A. (2011). Psychometric properties of the FACES-IV in a pediatric oncology population. *Journal of Pediatric Psychology, 36*(5), 528–538.

McQuaide, S., & Ehrenreich, J. H. (1997). Assessing client strengths. *Families in Society: The Journal of Contemporary Human Services, 78,* 201–212.

Miller, I. W., Ryan, C. E., Keitner, G. I., Bishop, D. S., & Epstein, N. B. (2000). Why fix what isn't broken? A rejoinder to Ridenour, Daley. *Family Process, 39,* 381–385.

Minuchin, S., & Fishman, H. C. (1982). *Family therapy techniques.* Cambridge, MA: Harvard University Press.

Minuchin, S., Nichols, M. P., & Lee, W. Y. (2006). *Assessing families and couples: From symptom to system.* Boston: Pearson/Allyn and Bacon.

Moos, R. H., & Moos, B. S. (2013). Family Environment Scale. In R. Sherman, N. Fredman, & N. Fredman, *Handbook of measurements for marriage and family therapy* (pp. 82–86). New York: Routledge.

O'Brien, C., & Bruggen, P. (1985). Our personal and professional lives: Learning positive connotation and circular questioning. *Family Process, 24,* 311–322.

Olson, D. H. (2008). *FACES IV manual.* Minneapolis, MN: Life Innovations.

Olson, D. H. (2011). Faces IV and the circumplex model: Validation study. *Journal of Marital & Family Therapy, 3*(1), 64–80.

Olson, D. H., Gorall, D. M., & Tiesel, J. W. (2007). *FACES IV manual.* Minneapolis, MN: Life Innovations.

Olson, D. H., Russell, C. S., & Sprenkle, D. H. (2014). *Circumplex model: Systemic assessment and treatment of families.* New York: Routledge.

Rawana, E., & Brownlee, K. (2009). Making the possible probable: A strength-based assessment and intervention framework for clinical work with parents, children and adolescents. *Families in Society: The Journal of Contemporary Social Services, 90*(3), 255–260.

Ridenour, T. A., Daley, J. G., & Reich, W. (2000). Further evidence that the Family Assessment Device should be reorganized: Response to Miller and colleagues. *Family Process, 39,* 375–381.

Schulman, L. (2011). *Brooks/Cole empowerment series: The skills of helping individuals, families, groups, and communities.* Belmont, CA: Cengage Learning.

Segrin, C., & Flora, J. (2014). *Family communication* (2nd ed.). New York: Routledge Communication Series.

Shepard, M., & Campbell, J. A. (1992). The abusive behavior inventory: A measure of psychological and physical abuse. *Journal of Interpersonal Violence, 7,* 291–305.

Sherman, R., Fredman, N., Sherman, R., & Fredman, N. (2013). *Handbook of measurements for marriage and family therapy.* New York: Routledge.

Skinner, H. A., Steinhauer, P. D., & Santa-Barbara, J. (2009). The Family Assessment Measure. *Canadian Journal of Community Mental Health, 2*(2), 91–103.

Society of Pediatric Psychology of American Psychological Association. (n.d.). Assessment resource sheet: Family measures. Retrieved from http://www.apa divisions.org/division-54/evidence-based/family-assessment.aspx

Sperry, L. (Ed.). (2011). *Family assessment: Contemporary and cutting-edge strategies* (2nd ed.). New York: Routledge.

Stuart, R. B. (2004). *Helping couples change: A social learning approach to marital therapy.* New York: Guilford Press.

Thomlison, B. (2015). *Family assessment handbook: An introductory practice guide to family assessment.* Boston, MA: Cengage Learning.

Toulitas, J., Perlmutter, B. F., & Straus, M. A. (2000). *Handbook of family measurement techniques.* Thousand Oaks, CA: Sage.

Uruk, A. C., Sayger, T. V., & Cogdal, P. A. (2007). Examining the influence of family cohesion and adaptability on trauma symptoms and psychological well-being. *Journal of College Student Psychotherapy, 22,* 51–63.

Watzlawick, P., Bavelas, J. B., & Jackson, D. D. (2011). *Pragmatics of human communication: A study of interactional patterns, pathologies and paradoxes.* New York: W. W. Norton & Co.

Whaley, A. L., & Davis, K. E. (2007). Cultural competence and evidence-based practice in mental health services: a complementary perspective. *American Psychologist, 62*(6), 563–574.

CHAPTER 8

Families Who Are Multistressed

Catheleen Jordan, Vikki Vandiver, Hannah Szlyk, Julieann Nagoshi, and Craig Nagoshi

INTRODUCTION

This chapter addresses families involved with oppressive situations, multiple systems and environmental stress. Families reviewed here include families of lesbian, gay, bisexual, and transgender (LGBT) persons, as well as families with child maltreatment issues and caregivers of family members experiencing mental health problems. Commonalities between these seemingly diverse populations include external stressors that impinge on individuals and their families; this chapter summarizes the issues and external stressors. We also describe specific assessment methods that a practitioner can use when working with these groups, and conclude with a case study and study questions.

GAY AND LESBIAN FAMILIES

The University of California at Berkeley, Gender Equity Resource Center (2014) defines terms for family for the gay and lesbian community:

> Family: Colloquial term used to identify other LGBTIQ [lesbian, gay, bisexual, transgender, intersex, queer] community members. For example, an LGBTIQ person saying, "that person is family" often means that the person they are referring to is LGBTIQ as well.
>
> Family of Choice: Persons or group of people an individual sees as significant in their life. It may include none, all, or some members of their family of origin (the family you grew up in). In addition, it may include individuals such as significant others, domestic partners, friends, and coworkers. In this chapter, we will refer to family of choice and family of origin when we see a need to differentiate.

This section discusses relationship, legal, social stigma, and child issues for gay and lesbian families. Following sections provide tools for assessing potential problems in these areas.

Relationships

Relationship issues are discussed here in terms of same-sex/family relationships, legalities, couples, and disclosures.

Same-Sex Friendships and Family Relationships.   While some gay men and lesbians have strong and supportive family of origin ties that are a valuable source of aid and comfort in times of need, other lesbians and gay men have negative relations with their families of origin, ranging from grudging acceptance to outright rejection of them and/or their partner. Compared with heterosexuals, lesbians and gay men in general perceive less social support from their family of origin (Elizur & Mintzer, 2003; Kurdek, 2004, 2006). Greater social support from relatives is associated not only with greater personal well-being but also with greater relationship satisfaction in same-sex couples (Kurdek 1988, 1995), while the lack of such support helps to undermine relationship satisfaction. Distinctive types of social support may be of special relevance to lesbians and gay men. For example, support for a woman's lesbian identity may be particularly important to psychological well-being (Beals & Peplau, 2005).

Outside families of their origin and extended families, gay and lesbian individuals create families from friends, partners, and people within the LGBT community. These families, also called chosen families or families of choice (Morrow & Messinger, 2006), develop through voluntary choice and love. Families of choice typically provide similar benefits as benefits provided by families of origin: protection, socialization, belongingness, a source for self-esteem, and a sense of identity (Matthews & Lease, 2000). Lesbians and gay men may compensate for lower levels of family of origin support by establishing closer ties with friends. Such families of choice are a network of friends who provide love and support, celebrate holidays and rituals, share leisure activities, and offer assistance in time of need (Carrington, 1999). Such flexible family networks and the fictive kinship patterns, the result of choosing kin, have commonalities with practices in African American and Latino communities (Levitt, Horne, Puckett, Sweeney, & Hampton, 2014; Oswald, 2002). Further research on sources of stress and support for same-sex couples is needed, along with explicit analyses of how models of minority stress may apply to same-sex couples. One study looked at minority lesbian and gay populations and micro-oppression with the goal of measuring multiple minority stress and described the difficulties in measuring these types of stress (Balsam, Molina, Beadnell, Simoni, & Walters, 2011).

Same-Sex Couples: Love and Satisfaction.   Studies that have compared the qualities that lesbians, gay men, and heterosexuals seek in romantic partners (Peplau & Fingerhut, 2007; Peplau & Spalding, 2000) find that most individuals, regardless of sexual orientation, value affection, dependability, shared interests, and similarity of religious beliefs. Regardless of sexual orientation, men are more likely to emphasize a partner's physical attractiveness, while women give greater emphasis to personality characteristics (Peplau & Fingerhut, 2007). Studies have also reported no differences between lesbian and gay couples versus heterosexual couples in quality of closeness, affection, adjustments, love, and relationship satisfaction (Kurdek 2001, 2004, 2006; Peplau and Fingerhut, 2007; Roisman, Clausell, Holland, Fortuna, & Elieff, 2008; Rothblum, 2009). LGBT couples on average function at least as well as heterosexual couples (Pachankis & Goldfried, 2013), and it has been suggested that LGBT couples are at least as cohesive, flexible, and equal in terms of gender roles and at least as satisfied with their relationships as heterosexual couples (Green, Bettinger, & Zacks, 1996). A recent study suggests that same-sex couples tend to be more egalitarian than are heterosexual couples (Schechory & Ziv, 2007). Satisfaction and stability in gay and lesbian relationships are related to similar emotional qualities as those that operate in heterosexual relationships (Gottman et al., 2003).

The boundaries between friendship and romantic or sexual relationships for lesbians and gay men, however, may be more complex than for heterosexual relationships (e.g., Diamond & Dube, 2002; Nardi, 1999), with lesbians and gay men reporting more awareness of the transition from friendship to romance and more concerns about maintaining friendships after romances end. Like heterosexual couples, though, three general factors contribute to partners' psychological commitment to each other and to the longevity of lesbians' and gay men's relationships (Beals, Impett, & Peplau, 2002; Kurdek, 2000; Peplau & Spalding, 2000). These three factors are, first, positive attraction forces, such as love and satisfaction, which make partners want to stay together versus the availability of alternatives to the current relationship, most often a more desirable partner. Second, partners are less likely to leave a relationship if they perceive few alternative available partners. The third factor is about barriers that make it difficult for a person to leave a relationship, including investments that increase the psychological, emotional, or financial costs of ending a relationship, as well as moral or religious feelings of obligation or duty to one's partner.

Disclosures: Parent's Sexual Orientation.   Because of the fear of losing custody of children and of other potential harms, gay and lesbian parents may keep their sexual orientation secret (Patterson & Chan, 1996). Parents want to protect their children as well from possible discrimination because they have parents with a same-sex orientation. Yet secrecy can be a stressor and contribute to relationship difficulties, especially if partners disagree about the need for secrecy. It can limit support from others and leave a family with no one with whom to share celebrations

(Matthews & Lease, 2000). Research also suggests an association between psychological health and openness regarding one's sexual orientation. Jordan and Deluty (2000) found that increased outness for lesbian couples correlated with increased relationship satisfaction, and differing degrees of outness decreased relationship satisfaction.

Parents can decide to come out or hide their sexual orientation from their children. Parents may be waiting for the right age for children to learn about their sexual orientation. Parents also may find it important to consider their children's reactions to the disclosures, and to control from whom the information comes (Goldberg, 2007; Lynch & Murray, 2000). Parents' motivations can include their desire for their children to understand their personal and social worlds, the level of difficulty in keeping the sexual orientation a secret, and the fear of losing custody of the children to their former spouses.

Partners who wish to disclose their relationship to children may have to negotiate how and when to do it (Breshears & Beer, 2014). When they do make the disclosure, it is a complex and delicate task, because it may entail discussing the children's origins. If a partner enters a family where the other partner already has children, the role and meaning of the new same-sex partner also require explanation. Many gay, lesbian, and bisexual parents who do not live with or have custody of their biological children may also face disclosure issues, such as tempering the reactions of the custodial parent or members of the child's extended family, who can have an influence on the continuation of contact with the child (Shapiro, 2013). Parents also have to decide if they will disclose to a variety of people involved in a child's life, such as medical staff, child-care workers, school officials, and the children's peers and the parents of their peers.

Parents can receive a wide range of reactions when disclosing their homosexuality to their children, including anger, joking, thanks for being honest, denial, and refusal to talk about it (Breshears & Beer, 2014). Barrett and Tasker (2001) reported that daughters responded more sympathetically to their parents' disclosures than did their sons. Furthermore, researchers have found that younger children have the least difficulty accepting their parents' sexual orientation, while adolescents have the most difficulty (Lynch & Murray, 2000).

Legalities

Legal issues addressed in this section include legalities of same-sex relationships and legalities of same-sex parenting.

Legalizing Same-Sex Relationships: Marriage, and Domestic Partnerships.   For heterosexual couples, marriage represents both a public sign of commitment and a legal status affecting many aspects of life. In

2004 a report from the General Accounting Office estimated that marriage affects 1,138 federal rights, including taxes, Social Security, and veterans' benefits (General Accountability Office, 2004). Not surprisingly, lesbians and gay men have actively sought to make legal recognition of their relationships a reality. A Kaiser Family Foundation (2001) survey showed that 74 percent of lesbians and gay men at that time said that if they could legally marry someone of the same sex, they would like to do so someday. According to the American Community Survey, there were 214,773 male-male and 222,607 female-female reported unmarried partners and 695,222 male-male and 98,570 female-female reported married couples in the United States (U.S. Census Bureau, 2011).

The past ten years have seen major changes in the provision of marriage rights to same-sex couples. In 2004 Massachusetts became the first state to legalize same-sex marriages. At the time of this writing, eleven years later, thirty-seven states have granted or been enjoined by the courts to recognize same-sex marriages, with the Supreme Court set to rule this year on the issue for the entire country. In 2011 the Census reported that there are 168,092 same-sex married couples in the United States (U.S. Census Bureau, 2011). In contrast, thirteen states retained bans on same-sex marriage prior to June 26, 2015 (ProCon.org, 2015). Prior to the legalizing of same-sex marriages, increasing numbers of employers provided domestic partner benefits, such as health insurance, to same-sex partners, and today such benefits are provided in some municipal governments in states that do not recognize same-sex marriage (Sammer & Miller, 2013). The substantial social and legal benefits and protections accorded to legally married couples by state and federal laws are thus increasingly available to most same-sex partners in the United States and may soon be available to all same-sex partners who choose to marry. Such benefits also help to hold marriages together, based on the third relationship factor noted above about barriers that make it difficult for a person to leave a relationship, such as community properties and religious commitments. Lambda Legal is a Web site that summarizes the legal protections for LGBT people and their families, state by state (Lambda Legal, n.d.). Interestingly, after controlling for marriage and marriage-like commitments, the break-up rate for same-sex couples has been found to be comparable to the break-up rate for heterosexual couples (Rosenfeld, 2014).

In June, 2015, same sex marriage became legal in the entire United States after a Supreme Court ruling striking down state marriage bans (Freedom to Marry, 2015). States where gay marriage was previously banned have been noted to participate in various levels of disobedience toward the new law (BallotPedia, 2015). For example, the Texas Attorney General and top state health official were ordered to appear before a federal judge to assess if they will be held in contempt of court for violating or obstructing the law (Statesman, 2015).

Social Stigma

This section discusses the issue of societal stigma from two perspectives: (a) prejudice/discrimination against individuals and (b) prejudice/discrimination against family.

Societal Stigma: Prejudice and Discrimination against Individuals. The stigma of homosexuality affects lesbians, gay men, and their relationships in many ways. Lesbians and gay men who experience greater levels of discrimination have been consistently shown to be at greater risk for poor psychological adjustment and stress-related psychological disorders (e.g., Mays & Cochran 2001; Meyer, 2003).

Personal experiences of rejection and discrimination are common. The Kaiser Family Foundation's (2001) national survey found that 74 percent of lesbians and gay men reported experiencing discrimination based on sexual orientation, with 23 percent reporting that discrimination occurred "a lot." Additionally, 34 percent reported that their family or a family member had refused to accept them because of their sexual orientation. Discrimination and its resulting stress often come in the form of constantly experienced minor hassles, such as derogatory remarks, including jokes; comments based on stereotypes; hostile or threatening comments; comments expressing general dislike of gay men and lesbians (Swim, 2004); or poor service that is perceived to be due to the individual's sexual orientation. Gay-related stressors specific to lesbians and gay men include rejection, lack of support, or the individual's family ignoring the person's sexual orientation. Another set of gay-related stressors include the need to hide one's sexual orientation, fear of being exposed as homosexual, violence and harassment, lack of societal acceptance, and discrimination (Lewis, Derlega, Berndt, Morris, & Rose, 2001).

Discrimination based on sexual orientation also places strains on relationship functioning in gay and lesbian couples (Otis, Rostosky, Riggle & Hamrin, 2006). Todosijevic, Rothblum, & Solomon's (2005) study of same-sex couples in civil unions found that greater reports of more gay-specific stressors was associated with lower relationship satisfaction for lesbian couples but not for gay male couples. The effects of gay-related stress may directly affect couples' functioning, for example, through limited access to important resources such as jobs and housing, or rejection of the couple or their children by family, neighbors, or peers at work or school. Indirect effects of discrimination on couples' functioning include diminishing the self-esteem or mental health of the partners or their ability to function effectively in a relationship.

Societal Stigma: Prejudice, Discrimination, and Family Functioning. Although lesbian and gay couples experience many issues that heterosexual couples experience when pursuing options to have children, they also face stressors because of their sexual orientation. To bear and rear children, gay and lesbian persons must overcome many obstacles, the overriding obstacle being heterosexism. Gay and lesbian persons experience no validation from their families of origin because of disapproval of their sexual orientation and coupling. They face beliefs that they should have no association with children and that they are unfit to raise children. Furthermore, some believe that their children, if they do raise them, will be psychologically and socially maladjusted, will suffer social stigmatization (Matthews & Lease, 2000), will be negatively affected in the development of their gender identity, or will turn out as gay or lesbian themselves. On a practical and economic level, the parents often cannot procure insurance or file income tax as a family, and their children cannot receive social security benefits from both parents. In many states, lesbian and gay sexual partners violate laws and are highly vulnerable to negative outcomes in courts if there is a challenge to the custody of their children (Shapiro, 2013). Because of these and many other outcomes of the heterosexist ideology, gay and lesbian persons may come to believe that they are not fit for parenting (Matthews & Lease, 2000).

Also their family of origin may be less supportive when same-sex couples decide to have children. Even when one's family of origin is somewhat accepting or tolerant of one's sexual orientation and the couple's relationship, reactions may change if the couple decides to raise children. Members of one's family of origin might act on the myths about psychological and social difficulties the children may experience (Manning, Fettro, & Lamidi, 2014; Matthews & Lease, 2000). Gay and lesbian parents also face many health-care, legal, financial, social, and emotional hurdles, including lack of support from formalized support systems that assist heterosexual couples during parenthood (Shapiro, 2013).

Child

Lesbian and Gay Couples with Children.   Many lesbian and gay persons create and maintain a family life with children. According to the 2000 U.S. Census data, among adults aged twenty-two to fifty-five, 34 percent of lesbian couples and 22 percent of gay male couples who live together are raising children (U.S. Census Bureau, 2000).

Gay- and lesbian-headed families are created in a variety of ways. Gay or lesbian parents may have children in heterosexual unions. Currently, it is unclear how many lesbians and gay men are having children within the context of a same-sex relationship versus a heterosexual marriage or by insemination; research has not focused on the issue categorizing gay parents as single (Livingston, 2014). According to a national poll by the Kaiser Family Foundation (2011), 49 percent of gay men and lesbians who were not parents said they would like to have or adopt children of their own.

Same-sex couples have numerous options for parenthood, each affecting the biological ties of the child to the parents. First is surrogacy. Lesbian couples may use donor insemination, so that the woman who carries the child is biologically related to the child. Other lesbian couples use in vitro fertilization so that one woman contributes the egg while the other woman is the birth mother. Gay male couples may contribute sperm to a female donor who carries the child. Couples may adopt or go through foster care, in which case neither parent is biologically related to the child. Agencies such as My Fertility Choices (n.d.) advise LGBT singles or couples of their options and help them with decision making.

Same-Sex Parenting Style.   Studies to date have found that lesbian and gay persons function just as well as parents as do their heterosexual counterparts (Farr & Patterson, 2013). It should be noted that a well-advertised study by Mark Regnerus, associate professor of sociology at the University of Texas at Austin, has been used to claim that children of gay and lesbian parents do not do as well as children in heterosexual parented families. However, the study has been strongly criticized for its poor methodology, suspect peer-review and publication process, and ideologically motivated secret funders (Human Rights Campaign, 2013). Research that is more credible shows that lesbian and gay couples often report dividing child-care labor relatively evenly (Goldberg, 2010). Additional findings from Goldberg include the following:

- Lesbian and gay couples reported more sharing of child care, whereas heterosexual couples reported more specialization (i.e., mothers did more child care than fathers).
- Lesbian and gay parents participated more equally than heterosexual parents during family interactions.
- Lesbian couples showed the most supportive and least undermining behavior, whereas gay male couples showed the least supportive behavior, and heterosexual couples the most undermining behavior.
- Compared with heterosexual relationships, same-sex couples are as knowledgeable about effective parenting skills and demonstrate equal abilities to identify critical issues in child-care situations and to formulate suitable solutions to the problems encountered with their children (Goldberg, 2010).

Impact on Children.   Research documents that same-sex couples' children are comparable to children of heterosexual parents on measures of self-esteem, psychological well-being, cognitive abilities, and peer relations (Patterson, 2003; Tasker, 2005). In a recent review of child well-being in same-sex parent families, Manning et al. (2014) concluded that there is a clear consensus in the social science literature indicating that American children living in households with same-sex parents fare just as well as those children residing in households with different-sex parents over a wide array of well-being measures: academic performance, cognitive development, social development, psychological health, early sexual activity, and substance abuse. Rather, the authors found that the differences that exist in child well-being are largely due to socioeconomic circumstances and family stability. A recent meta-analysis by Fedewa, Black, and Ahn (2015) found that children in households with same-sex parent actually scored better on parent-child relationships, psychological adjustment, and adherence to more traditional gender roles and play than did children in households with opposite-sex parents, with no differences found for cognitive development, sexual orientation, or gender identity. Whereas adolescents may experience a difficult adjustment to their parents' sexual orientation, on the whole the children of gay and lesbian parents do not experience the expected downfalls that heterosexist beliefs suggest.

Assessment Tools for Families of Gay and Lesbian Persons

As the current knowledge focuses on couples' friendship and on lesbian and gay couples with children, assessment techniques may be specified for each area. Appropriate measures for this population evaluate individual issues and characteristics, as well as measures of the quality of family relationship and satisfaction. See table 8.1 for examples of measures to be used for assessing couples' friendships, parenting styles, internalized homophobia for individuals and families of gay and lesbian persons.

Assessment: Couples' Friendship.   Social workers can use ecomaps to assess the community in which the individual or couple lives. Social support may be of particular interest. Measures of individual functioning include depression, loneliness, or low self-esteem; social workers may also assess couples with a relationship measure such as Hudson's Index of Marital Satisfaction (Corcoran & Fischer, 2013; Hudson, 2011). All of these measures are available in the sourcebook of measures by Corcoran and Fischer (2013).

Table 8.1   Assessment Tools for Families of Gay and Lesbian Persons

Measures for Individuals	Measures for Couples and Families
Index of self-esteem	Index of marital satisfaction
Social support inventory	Index of family relationships
Loneliness inventory	Child/parent attitude

Assessment: Parenting Styles of Lesbian and Gay Couples.   Bigner and Jacobsen (1992) found no differences between gay and heterosexual fathers' parenting styles as measured with standardized parenting inventories. These inventories can be used with different populations; one example is the Parenting Styles Inventory II (Darling & Steinberg, 1993). A measure of the child's attitude toward the parent and the parent's attitude toward the child, along with other parenting inventories, can be found in Corcoran and Fischer (2013).

Assessment: Internalized Homophobia.   The Lesbian Internalized Homophobia Scale contains fifty-two items; its subscales measure unique aspects of internalized homophobia including (a) connection with the lesbian community, (b) public identification as a lesbian, (c) personal feelings about being a lesbian, (d) moral and religious attitudes toward lesbianism, and (e) attitudes toward other lesbians (Szymanski & Chung, 2001). The Internalized Homonegativity Inventory measures internalized homonegativity in gay men. Forty-two items were initially generated and three subscales explore Personal Homonegativity, Gay Affirmation, and Morality of Homosexuality (Mayfield, 2001).

CHILD MALTREATMENT IN FAMILIES

Child maltreatment is a pervasive problem in our society experienced by families of all races, income status, beliefs, and structures. The federal government defines child abuse and neglect as "any recent act or failure to act on the part of a parent or caretaker, which results in death, serious physical or emotional harm, sexual abuse, or exploitation, or an act or failure to act which presents an imminent risk of serious harm" (Child Abuse Prevention and Treatment Act [CAPTA] Reauthorization Act of 2010. Causal indicators include individual characteristics of parents and children, familial factors, community environment, culture, and societal values (Centers for Disease Control and Prevention [CDC], 2015; Pecora, Whittaker, Maluccio, & Barth, 2000). In 2012 state and local child protective services (CPS) received approximately 3 million referrals for child abuse or neglect, with 1,640 children dying from maltreatment that same year (U.S. Department of Health and Human Services, Administration for Children and Families, Administration on Children, Youth and Families, Children's Bureau [Children's Bureau], 2013). A recent non-CPS study estimated that "1 in 4 children in the United States will experience child maltreatment in his or her lifetime" (Finkelhor, Turner, Ormond, & Hamby, 2013). The prevention and/or early intervention of child maltreatment is key, considering that various studies have documented the link between childhood maltreatment and poor physical and mental health outcomes in adulthood (Gilbert et al., 2009; Herrenkohl, Hong, Klika, Herrenkohl, & Russo, 2013; Jonson-Reid, Kohl, & Drake, 2012).

Childhood maltreatment and adverse events have been shown to contribute to child mortality and child morbidity, and later substance and alcohol abuse, suicide risk, obesity, and related health issues (Dube et al., 2001; Gilbert et al., 2009; Springer, Sheridan, Kuo, & Carnes, 2007). Toxic levels of stress in children have been shown to affect brain circuitry and development, and to impair the body's immune response, neurocognitive functioning and life-long response to adverse events (Doom, Cicchetti, Rogosch, & Dackis, 2013; Middlebrooks & Audage, 2008). This section reviews types of maltreatment, assessment methods for child maltreatment and risk assessment, the *Diagnostic and Statistical Manual of Mental Disorders*, fifth edition (DSM-5; American Psychiatric Association [APA], 2013) diagnosis and child maltreatment assessment, and cultural sensitivity in child assessment.

Types of Maltreatment

The four major types of familial child maltreatment are (a) physical abuse, (b) sexual abuse, (c) psychological abuse, and (d) neglect (CDC, 2015). Although states have varying definitions of specific categories of child maltreatment, the universal definition is found in CAPTA (2010). As mentioned above, child maltreatment is a complex phenomenon requiring a multidimensional assessment to determine appropriate interventions. Singularly, the various perspectives individually fail to adequately address the cause of child maltreatment. Within the family unit, several parent and child traits have been shown to be strongly associated with the predisposition for child maltreatment (table 8.2) (Gilbert et al., 2009; Saewyc et al., 2006; Sidebotham & Heron, 2003). The more contemporary theoretical framework of assessment is based on an ecological perspective that views the causes of child maltreatment as multifaceted and fluid. The risks of maltreatment are cumulative and can derive from individual and

Table 8.2   At-Risk Parent and Child Profiles

Parent	*Child*
Poverty	Age and size of the child
Mental health problems	Infancy
Low educational attainment	Gender
Alcohol and drug misuse	Girls sexual abuse, neglect
Maltreatment as a child	Boys physical abuse
Parenting stress	Chronic illness
Social isolation	Disability
Marital discord	Externalizing behaviors
	Internalizing behaviors
	Sexual orientation/sexual identity

familial traits and relationships, as well as from the community and social culture, and be related to the stage of development of the child (Kotch & Lee, 2011).

Families experiencing child maltreatment typically come to the attention of CPS agencies via mandated reporters or referrals. DePanfilis & Costello (2014) review the process. If the report of alleged abuse or neglect is determined to warrant intervention, an initial assessment will be conducted with individuals who would have information concerned the alleged maltreatment. Decisions related to the initial include determining whether the maltreatment fits the definition set by state law, whether the child's immediate safety is jeopardized and if immediate intervention is needed, if future maltreatment is imminent, and if continued agency services are needed to ensure safety for the family. If child maltreatment is determined, then CPS staff will also conduct a family assessment to coordinate goals for intervention and care.

The primary mandate of CPS agencies is to ensure no further harm to children who are reported as alleged victims of child abuse and neglect. CPS agencies use a systematic collection of data to determine the degree of potential harm to a child at some future point in time (Doueck, English, DePanfilis, & Moote, 1993). Across the nation the prevailing approach is to combine practice wisdom and risk assessment instruments to create a risk assessment model and framework for case assessment, documentation, and case planning and service delivery (Firkins & Candlin, 2011; Shlonsky & Wagner, 2005). In addition to predicting risk of potential maltreatment, such models assist in prioritizing cases (English & Pecora, 1994; Fanshel, Finch, & Grundy, 1994; Jaganathan & Camasso, 1996) and in developing individualized treatment plans based on individual case levels of risk (English & Pecora, 1994).

An increasingly prominent method to child protection is differential response, which allows for more than one method in reporting child abuse neglect, depending on the severity of the alleged maltreatment (Child Welfare Information Gateway, 2014). Differential response has been used across the nation and has been found to be a cost-effective and effective approach to increase services to children and families, ensure child safety, and promote increased satisfaction among both family members and coworkers (National Quality Improvement Center on Differential Response in Child Protective Services, 2011; Siegel, 2012).

Assessment Methods for Child Maltreatment and Risk Assessment

The assessment of risk and safety is important for child maltreatment. Although several evaluative studies have been conducted on various types of risk assessment models, debate continues regarding their accuracy, validity, and predictability. This leads to debates on the formulation of the assessments used, on whether they should be actuarial (empirically identified through studying cases), consensus (instruments with items selected by experts), or blended (both consensus-based and empirically based) (Ryan, Wiles, Cash, & Siebert, 2004). Table 8.3 provides a list of well-established risk assessment tools.

Many CPS agencies have developed a safety assessment to determine the appropriate intervention for those children and families who have been identified as needing services. The safety assessment identifies the strengths of individuals and of the family as a whole that may help protect the child from future harm (Cash, 2001). In addition, the safety assessment determines areas in which supportive services are needed to ensure continued safety of the child. In partnership with the U.S. Department of Health and Human Services, the Administration for Children & Families, and the U.S. Children's Bureau, the Child Welfare Information Gateway (2014) is a publically accessible online source. This site not only

Table 8.3 List of Well-Established Risk Assessment Tools

Authors	Measure	Description
Abidin, R. R. (2012)	Parenting Stress Index (3rd ed.). Odessa, FL: Psychological Assessment Resources.	Covers parent and child domains of stress vs. general life stress
Magura, S., Moses, B. S., & Jones, M. J. (1987)	Assessing risk and measuring change in families: The Family Risk Scales. Washington, DC: Child Welfare League of America.	A standardized measure of a child's risk of entering substitute care, consisting of 26 individual scales that apply to a full range of risk situations that brings families into the child welfare system
Magura, S., & Moses, B. S. (1986)	Outcome measures for child welfare services. Washington, DC: Child Welfare League of America.	Provides several instruments for assessing individuals and families dealing with child abuse and neglect
Milner, J. S. (1986)	The Child Abuse Potential Inventory: Manual (2nd ed.). Webster, NC: Psytec.	A 160-item self-report instrument designed to identify an individual's potential for physical abuse
Ondersma, S. J., Chaffin, M. J., Mullins, S. M., & LeBreton, J. M. (2005)	The Brief Child Abuse Potential Inventory, Journal of Child and Adolescent Psychology, 35(4), 598 (2006).	A shortened form of the CAP consisting of 24 abuse and 9 validity items
Straus, M. A., Hamby, S. L., Finkelhor, D., Moore, D. W., & Runyan, D. (1998)	The Conflict Tactic Scale Parent-Child. Durham, NH: Family Research Laboratory.	A brief parent self-report measure to assess for potential child maltreatment

offers information for child welfare professionals on resources for additional help on the state and national levels, but also provides information on screenings for child maltreatment and tools for provider, program, and case evaluation.

DSM-5 Diagnosis and Child Maltreatment Assessment

Practice and research definitions of child maltreatment have influenced changes to the DSM-5 (APA, 2013). DSM-5 includes four different child maltreatment categories in a section called "Other Conditions That May Be a Focus of Clinical Attention." In this section, the International of Classification of Diseases, tenth revision, Clinical Modification (ICD-10-CM; World Health Organization, 2010) T codes and V codes are used, so that the clinician can communicate child abuse issues: child physical abuse, psychological abuse, sexual abuse, and neglect (APA, 2013). The criteria were added with the intention to better assist providers in screening for, identifying, and addressing child maltreatment in various practice settings (Slep, Heyman, & Foran, 2015).

Other V codes in the DSM-5 may also be important for clinicians to apply when their assessment suggests psychosocial problems that may be associated with child abuse. For example, the V code V61.8 is for "upbringing away from parents" and may apply to children that have been removed from the home and placed in foster care. Several other codes are used for spouse and partner abuse, housing and economic problems, and other social problems that may co-occur with child abuse and neglect.

Furthermore, more-accurate definitions; and greater accountability, evaluation, and results in the child welfare system's response to child maltreatment are needed (Gelles, 2014). To meet these demands, it is crucial that the system develop an effective, valid, reliable, and culturally sensitive assessment framework for interventions with families experiencing child maltreatment (Cash, 2001).

Cultural Sensitivity in Child Assessment

Considering the ever-evolving cultural demographic of the United States, cultural sensitivity is an important yet challenging element of any comprehensive assessment package (Raman & Hodes, 2012). According to Lewis-Fernández and Kleinman (1995), culture should be viewed as a dynamic process influenced by differences in gender, ethnicity, age, class, and race. Building on this definition, Canino and Spurlock (2000) make a cogent plea for the "in-depth understanding of patients' lives, their family myths, and cultural mores—essential if we hope to help troubled children and adolescents" (p. viii).

Although children and families of color have always been disproportionately represented in reports of child maltreatment, Caucasians dominate the CPS workforce. Canino and Spurlock (2000) suggest ways to address cultural sensitivity. It is essential that Caucasian practitioners in particular have a keen cultural self-awareness, awareness of non-Caucasian cultures, and the burden of related external and internal stressors. A culturally sensitive assessment of families experiencing child maltreatment should take into account cultural influences on the following areas: expectations of child development and behavior, attitudes toward health practices, child-rearing practices (sex education, sex roles and expectations, discipline, and social skills development), and family history (role of the extended family, family values, level of acculturation and adaptation to the community, and religion).

A comprehensive, culturally sensitive assessment is crucial to conduct appropriate interventions and positive outcomes for families experiencing child maltreatment. Practitioners in all fields of practice who provide services to abused and neglected children and their families should be familiar with and have access to a cadre of empirically tested assessment tools. Although a number of such tools are currently available in the field of child protection, there is great need for improved assessment instruments and models. To combat the dearth of culturally sensitive assessment instruments and models, practitioners should research the latest effective strategies in working with diverse families and have an understanding of the psychosocial stressors that families encounter, such as poverty, immigration, and single-parent households (Phillips & Paumgarten, 2009). More and more research demonstrates the long-term negative impact of immigration stressors, including impermanent residency, not only on the parent-child relationship, but on the emotional and cognitive development of the child (Perez & Fortuna, 2005; Potochnick & Perreira, 2010). For example, immigrant Latino families would greatly benefit from interventions addressing positive parenting and family cohesion (Leidy, Guerra, & Torro, 2010). In summary, mental health providers need to take into account the role of culture when determining the appropriate assessments and interventions for diverse families.

FAMILY OR CAREGIVER STRESS AND MENTAL ILLNESS

Caring for a relative with mental illness creates special stressors for family members and/or caregivers. Many issues involve control and independence, conflicting family roles, caregivers' emotional over-involvement, culture clashes with ethnically diverse families, and psychiatric illnesses experienced by more than one family member (Leff, 2005). In addition, providers who are treating an ill person do not always recognize that person's family and caregivers as a resource. The result is that many family members feel isolated and multistressed. The following section overviews stressors that affect families who care for loved one with mental illness, followed by discussions of suicide bereavement, assessment instruments for families and caregivers of people with mental illness, and assessment of caregivers.

Family Stress

Research has identified three key areas of societal and/or environmental stress that is experienced by family members and caregivers who have a mentally ill relative in treatment: (a) stigma, (b) lack of provider respect, and (c) organizational cultural competence, along with caregiver lack of experience or knowledge and issues of the relationship of the caregiver (sibling, adult child, or spouse) (Cloutterbuck & Mahoney, 2003; Magaña, Ramirez Garcia, Hernández, & Cortez, 2007; Perlick et al., 2007).

Stigma.   Stigma is a cluster of negative attitudes and prejudicial beliefs (World Health Organization, 2001), a reality for people with mental illness and their families, and a leading factor in discouraging both from getting the services they need (Warner, 2005). Family members report difficulties with accessing mental health services, either on behalf of their family member who has a mental illness or because of their own need, such as respite from the freedom of caregiving for a parent, child, or sibling with a mental illness (Drapalski et al., 2008). Some parents, for example, report having been forced to relinquish custody to obtain needed mental health services for their children (Substance Abuse and Mental Health Service Administration, Annual Survey, 2013). Others describe experiences in which they perceive mental health workers as blaming them for family problems and refusing to deal with their own grief issues (New Freedom Commission on Mental Health, 2003).

Stigma also plays a role in the underuse of mental health services by family members from ethnic communities. Recent immigrants are often reluctant to use mainstream health, mental health, or social services because of stigma-related concerns, including feelings of personal shame about mental illness and social embarrassment for one's family or community. Peer-based interventions have been found to reduce self-stigma and increase resources for coping and for mental health knowledge for families (Perlick et al., 2011; Smith et al., 2014).

Provider Respect.   Family members often play a dominant role in health-seeking behaviors and compliance with treatment. Despite providing information and playing a pivotal role in guiding their family members' health-care decisions, family members describe feeling disrespected when providers exclude them from sessions that involve the family member who has the mental illness (Vandiver, Jordan, Keopraseuth, &

Yu, 1995). Multifamily groups have been shown to increase patient out-come, effectively include loved ones, and culturally tailor the treatment process (Kopelowicz et al., 2012). Providers should also consider the impact of caregiving on the caregiver(s), and how stress and even mental health concerns may manifest in the caregivers and family members across cultural groups (Cloutterbuck & Mahoney, 2003; Magaña et al., 2007; Northouse, Williams, Given, & McCorkle, 2012).

Organizational Cultural Competence.   An additional concern of family members has to do with the cultural competence of providers and organizations. Health-care and social service providers often refer family members from ethnically diverse communities to mainstream mental health settings. However, the referred clients perceive many of the avail-able services as inadequate or inappropriate. Family members from non-English-speaking communities report difficulty with mental health organizations that rely heavily on English-only versions of health-care information (Institute of Medicine, 2002). It is essential that the provider conduct a cultural assessment of the patient and family to understand how family members expect to be involved in their loved one's care, the family's perception of care, and if outside resources will be needed (i.e., housing services, employment assistance, pastoral and/or religious refer-rals) (Barrio, 2000; Magaña et al., 2007).

Family Experience of Caring for Mentally Ill Relative

Here we look closer at some of the differential issues associated with fam-ily and caregiver stress: the family experience of parents, siblings' rela-tionships, children caring for adult parents with mental illness, and spouses caring for spouses. These distinctions are important, particularly in trying to set up targeted programs based on the needs and role of the family member or caregiver. Understanding these distinctions can also assist in the development of mental health promotion strategies that are unique to the life stage and role of the caregiver.

Family Members' Lack of Experience and Knowledge.   Research into the experiences of family members or caregivers who have a relative with mental illness report that families often provide care with little to no information or training about mental illness, problem-solving strategies, how to cope with the ongoing physical and emotional stressors of caring for an ill relative, and resources for social service, health benefits, or psychiatric services. In terms of parental caregivers, research suggests that mothers tend to take on most caregiving responsibilities; mothers report that they often feel unsupported and unprepared to care for their ill relative (Pickett-Schenk, 2003). Lefley (1996) has written extensively on the challenge of parents providing care to an adult child with mental illness. These burdens include the stressors of providing continuous instrumental support (e.g., financial assistance, transportation, housing) and subjective feelings of guilt, depression, anger, grief, and stigmatization (Judge, 1994). When education and support programs are offered for families, most participants are women (51 to 96 percent) who report caring for an adult male relative (57 to 90 percent) (Pickett-Schenk, 2003).

Sibling Caregivers.   Siblings' relationship also plays a role in caregiving. Studies have found that non-ill adult sisters are more likely to report greater feelings of stigma, to have frequent contact, and to offer emotional, caregiving, and direct support to their mentally ill sibling than are non-ill adult brothers. Sister siblings were also more likely to assume future care for an ill sister but not for a brother (Greenburg, Kim, & Greenley, 1997; Greenburg, Seltzer, Krauss, & Kim, 1999). One study on adults with schizophrenia found that feelings of reciprocity with the non-ill sibling and expectation of the ill sibling's future mental health struggles were predictors of greater sibling involvement in caregiving (Smith, Greenberg, & Mailick Seltzer, 2007).

Overarching themes in the sibling caregiver experience include mourning the loss of innocence as a child or young adult due to the sibling's illness, complex emotions related to being a caregiver and a healthier sibling, complicated dynamics with other family members about caregiving responsibilities, and positive emotions related to having external supports and to creating a closer bond with family members (Judge, 1994; Lukens, Thorning, & Lohrer, 2004).

Adult Children Caregivers.   With regard to adult children caring for a mentally ill parent, they report a variety of psychological experiences, ranging from low self-esteem, resentment, sense of robbed childhood, fear of intimacy, difficulty with attachment and trust, unresolved grief, and increased levels of compassion and empathy (Marsh et al., 1993; Murphy, Peters, Jackson, & Wilkes, 2011). The impact of the parental illness is related to the length of the illness and its timing during the adult child's development. It is important that the adult caregiver receive information on how to care for the parent, as well as resources and services that will assist the adult caregiver in addressing his or her well-being and mental health concerns (Judge, 1994; Murphy et al., 2011).

Spouse Caregivers.   Spouses experience distress in much the same way that parents do, except that issues of loss and grieving are more for the loss of the adult and romantic relationship. Common sources of stressors are economic, as when the primary wage earner becomes ill, or, in contrast, when the primary wage earner has to assume full care for an ill spouse or partner. The marital relationship is even more distressed when one spouse initiates court-ordered hospitalization proceedings for the ill spouse to receive needed help. Monin, Schulz, and Feeney (2014) suggest that compassionate love and identification of positive aspects of caregiving can mediate negative feelings related to caregiver burden and possible onset of depression. Spouses need assistance not only in how to care for their partner, but also in how to continue to manage their family and find resources for personal support outside of the nuclear family (Judge, 1994).

In summary, as research suggests, family stress is quite extensive for family members who care for an ill relative. The stress is experienced not only in the social environment (i.e., via stigma, provider relationships, and organizational issues) but also through multiple layers of family roles (i.e., from parents to siblings to spouses). By providing a thorough assessment of the societal, environmental, and differential issues affecting families and caregivers, social workers can identify interventions that reduce stressors.

Suicide Bereavement

Unfortunately, it is not uncommon for individuals struggling with mental illness to die by suicide. These deaths affect peers, friends, and family, especially those who were involved in the care of the person. It is believed that between 48 and 500 million people experience suicide bereavement each year (Pitman, Osborn, King, & Erlangsen, 2014). Not only does the death increase the risk of suicide and mental health symptoms among family members, but also a loved one's death by suicide may intensify preexisting feelings of shame and stigma due to the cause of death (Pitman et al., 2014). Considering that suicide bereavement is different from other types of losses (Jordan, 2001), it is critical that providers remain engaged with the loved ones during the postvention or post-death process. As mentioned earlier, the practitioner should assess and monitor loved ones for the development of suicidal ideation and depressive symptoms, and should provide psychoeducation on the nature of suicide and the loved ones' own bereavement process. Due to the shame and stigma related to suicide, loved ones may also need assistance connecting with their social network and maintaining communication and connection within the family unit (Jordan, 2001).

Assessment Instruments for Families and Caregivers of People with Mental Illness

Appropriate measures for families and caregivers of people with mental illness include those that assess personal stress.

Assessment of Stress. Measures of perceived stress (Cohen & Williamson, 1988) are helpful in determining the level of stress that the family or caregiver is experiencing, and other potential factors placing the family unit's wellness at risk. Many such measures have been

Table 8.4   Assessment Measures for Caregiver Stress

Measures	Sources
Caregiver Strain Index	Robinson, 1983
Caregiver Strain Questionnaire: Short Form 7	Brannan, Athay, & Andrade, 2012
Family Crisis Oriented Personal Evaluation Scales	McCubbin et al., 1991
Perceived Stress Scale	Cohen & Williamson, 1988

assessed across diverse cultural samples (Andreou et al., 2011; Lee, Chung, Suh, & Jung, 2014) and age groups (Kavazis & Wadsworth, 2014; White et al., 2014). A list of resources for assessment measures for caregiver stress is presented in table 8.4. Other assessment measures for acute stress and posttraumatic stress and childhood trauma are found at U.S. Department of Veterans Affairs, National Center for PTSD (n.d.).

Assessment of Caregivers. Studies support the link between patient mental illness and increased caregiver stress (Hastrup, Van Den Berg, & Gyrd-Hansen, 2011), yet few standardized measures have been designed to assess the impact of caregiving on loved ones and family members. Available measures determine the positive and negative consequences of informally caring for ill loved ones who suffer from physical and or/mental illness and range in age from adolescence to older adulthood (Brannan et al., 2012; Robinson, 1983).

CASE STUDY ESTEBAN: MOVING FROM ASSESSMENT TO INTERVENTION

The following case study illustrates caregiver stress and a situation where possible child maltreatment might occur.

Client Identifying Information

Name: Esteban Gonzalez
Date of Birth: 2/16/2000
Ethnicity: Mexican American
Address: 1901 Crocket Street Apt. C, Austin, Texas

Family Members Living in the Home

Esteban Garcia	Client	15 y.o.	
Maria Cisneros	Mother	35 y.o.	Administrative assistant
Miguel Garcia	Brother	5 y.o.	
Luis Garcia	Brother	3 y.o.	

Family Background.   Esteban has lived with his mother since the age of three. His biological father, Antonio, lives in Austin and occasionally sees Esteban on weekends; Mr. Garcia works for a construction company. Ms. Cisneros is remarried but is estranged from her current husband, who provides monetary support for the two younger boys. Ms. Cisneros works full time as an administrative assistant for the local health and human services office. The mother and three sons live together in a two-bedroom apartment on the east side of the city, not far from Esteban's new high school, an alternative high school that works with students that are at-risk for school failure and dropout.

Presenting Problem.   Esteban is a fifteen-year old student at an alternative high school. Esteban has been attending this school for only three months, after recently transferring from another local high school due to problems with inconsistent attendance and poor grades. Since enrolling in the alternative high school, his grades have been improving and his attendance has been consistent. Esteban is soft-spoken but liked by both his teachers and his peers. He is involved in the school documentary project this semester.

One day, Esteban asks to speak with the guidance counselor about his class schedule for the next term. Since the counselor is out of the school for the day, he is referred to speak with the school principal. Esteban appears to be uncomfortable and his appearance is disheveled. He also has trouble maintaining eye contact with the principal. Instead of mentioning his class schedule, he begins to talk to the principal about his concerns for his health and safety. He describes nonstop shooting pains in his body and fear that he will be "jumped" by drug dealers at his bus stop after school. He shows the principal his toe, which he believes is oozing pus due to an infection; the principal does not observe an infection, however. Seeing that Esteban's thoughts are not grounded in reality, a school social worker is brought into the office to speak with him and provide a mental health assessment.

Social Work Interview.   Esteban confides that he has been taking various substances for the past year, including marijuana, "spice," and cocaine, as a way to manage symptoms of depression, anxiety, and inattention. He adds that he feels guilty for causing his mother to feel stressed, since she is starting a new job and cannot take him to the doctor to address his toe and bodily pains. He also feels guilty for using drugs and not being a better role model for his little brothers at home.

When asked about previous mental health treatment, Esteban says that he has never talked to a doctor or specialist about his drug use or feelings of depression and anxiety. He is afraid that his mother will have to miss work to take him to appointments or that she will have to pay for his care. Esteban does mention that his biological and step-father both have histories of alcoholism and substance abuse, and he knows that his use will only further disappoint his mother. He fears that he will end up like these two men as well. When asked, Esteban denies any previous experiences of physical or sexual abuse and states that he has no thoughts of harming himself or others.

Monitoring. Esteban says that he wants to return to class and states that he does not want to tell the social worker anything else, in fear that he will get his mother in trouble. When asked about this statement, Esteban says that he fears his mother will be called by CPS because he is doing drugs and feels unwell, and that his brothers will be taken away to other families. The social worker educates Esteban on how CPS works and that a parent is not to be blamed if his or her child has a mental health problem, but that it is a parent's responsibility to get their child help. She adds that she only asks questions to learn more about him and his family and that she and the principal will work with him and his mother to get Esteban help. Esteban returns to class; the social worker tells him to come see her if he feels worse that day. Only staff that are in direct contact with Esteban are informed about his symptoms in order to contain his feelings of paranoia.

The social worker is considering several different diagnoses as she interviews Esteban and gains more facts about this case. She sees the need to determine an accurate DSM-5 diagnosis so that the proper treatment can be provided for Esteban. Foremost on the mind of the social worker is that Esteban shows signs of psychosis such as delusions and paranoia. The social worker is also concerned about the substance use and wonders if the symptoms are substance-induced psychosis or if Esteban may be experiencing a serious depressive episode with psychotic features or even may be showing signs of schizophrenia. The school setting, however, is not the best place for these determinations to be made: the social worker believes that it is imperative that the mother become involved and that Esteban receive a psychiatric evaluation.

Family Involvement and Psychoeducation. Despite Esteban's concerns of irritating his mother, the social worker contacts Ms. Cisneros to inform her of the school's concern for her son. Ms. Cisneros sounds exacerbated on the phone and is frustrated with Esteban's continuing "moods." She says that Esteban is often "down" and requires much of her attention when he is upset and wants rides to and from school. She also mentions that he only sits inside at home and does not want to help her with chores or with taking care of his brothers. The social worker reflects the mother's experiences and empathizes with the stress of caring for

Esteban's needs, as well as her two other sons. She does emphasize that if Esteban is really suffering from mental health concerns, which is common within his age group, his symptoms may get worse over time if left unaddressed. The social worker suggests that Ms. Cisneros pick Esteban up from school and bring him to a psychiatrist or psychiatric emergency room for an evaluation, with the guidance of the school staff. Ms. Cisneros at first refuses to meet, but finally agrees to come to the school office at the end of the day.

Parent and Staff Meeting.   With Esteban's knowledge, the social worker and principal inform Ms. Cisneros that, based on her clinical assessment this afternoon, her son may be experiencing psychotic symptoms either related to substance use or to a psychotic break. Ms. Cisneros asks if Esteban may be trying to seek attention from her and the staff. The social worker explains that her son presents as paranoid and fearful and that these symptoms are more severe than depressive or anxious emotions. Ms. Cisneros says that she will wait until next week to take Esteban to the doctor. The social worker asks Ms. Cisneros about her understanding of mental health services and if she has had previous experience seeing a psychiatrist or therapist. The mother shares how her estranged husband had seen counselors for alcoholism and it was unsuccessful. The social worker acknowledges her frustration with her partner's experience, but adds that it is important to try to help her son now. She also suggests that Esteban's symptoms may worsen over the course of the weekend and it would be better for the whole family if he receives help as soon as possible. She also reminds his mother that, as his guardian, it is her responsibility to get him the needed care immediately. The mother agrees to bring him to the hospital emergency room that day. The social worker provides her with referrals.

Caregiver Support.   The social worker provides the mother with the school's after-hours hotline and her work contacts if Ms. Cisneros needs extra support with receiving services. She adds that the counselors and staff at the high school will continue to support Esteban once he has been formally evaluated. Both parties agree to be in contact the following business day. The social worker asks Ms. Cisneros to have release-of-information signed with Esteban's providers for continuity of care purposes. Esteban is called to the office and the social worker walks with both Ms. Cisneros and Esteban to the school exit. Ms. Cisneros later leaves a voice message stating that Esteban has received a brief evaluation and will be seen by a hospital staff psychiatrist later that evening. In the case that the family did not follow through with the staff recommendations for a psychiatric evaluation and refuses to do so, an investigation of child neglect may be warranted.

Follow-Up.   The next school day the social worker met with Esteban individually and talked with him about his evaluation; Esteban gave her information about his psychiatric providers. Ms. Cisneros also contacted the social worker and discussed further her stresses associated with parenting Esteban. The social worker asks the mother to fill out the Caregiver Strain Questionnaire: Short Form 7 that provides a measure of the extent that the mother may experience additional demands, responsibilities, and difficulties resulting from caring for a child with emotional or behavioral disorders. In addition, the questionnaire assesses the subjective feelings of the caregiving function. At the time of the interview the social worker complimented the mother for getting her son the help he needed and empathized with how stressed and tired the mother appeared to be from managing the crisis with her son. The social worker further used the responses the mother gave on the measurement instrument to discuss the mother's strain and subjective feelings of distress that she experienced from caring for Esteban. The social worker also provided referrals for caregiver support services, noting that the mother may benefit from other support and education to be able to care for her son.

SUMMARY

This chapter discussed families who are multistressed by external sources such as stigma, oppression, and environmental and family stresses. Three different groups in particular were covered: gay and lesbian families, families experiencing child maltreatment, and caregivers of a family member with mental illness. For gay and lesbian families, the couple's friendship and couples with children were the two assessment areas reviewed. Families experiencing child maltreatment have been categorized according to type of maltreatment: physical, sexual, or emotional maltreatment; or neglect. Important areas for evaluation for this group include risk and safety assessment and cultural sensitivity. Finally, we discussed caregiver stress in families with a member diagnosed with mental illness and reviewed advantages of standardized assessments and areas for intervention.

We further suggested assessment techniques for each of the three areas. Measurement is similar for these families as for families described in preceding chapters. Finally, we presented a case study illustrating how to assess caregiver stress and how to assess and support a family going through an acute mental health crisis with an adolescent son.

STUDY QUESTIONS

1. Discuss the assessment issues for the multistressed family populations presented in this chapter. What are the similarities and differences in assessment method for each of the three groups presented here?

2. Consider the case study of Esteban presented at the end of this chapter. How might child assessment and family psychoeducation differ across diverse cultural and social groups?

3. Choose a family you know that is experiencing one of the problems described in the chapter and write an assessment using the Integrative Skills Assessment Protocol. Design a comprehensive measurement and treatment plan. Describe any difficulties you have encountered thus far.

REFERENCES

American Psychiatric Association (APA). (2013). *Diagnostic and statistical manual of mental disorders* (5th ed.; DSM-5). Washington, DC: Author.

Andreou, E., Alexopoulos, E. C., Lionis, C., Varvogli, L., Gnardellis, C., Chrousos, G. P., & Darviri, C. (2011). Perceived stress scale: Reliability and validity study in Greece. *International Journal of Environmental Research and Public Health, 8*(8), 3287–3298.

BallotPedia. (2015). *Local government responses to Obergefll v. Hodges.* Retrieved from http://ballotpedia.org/Local_government_responses_to_Obergefell_v._Hodges

Balsam, K. F., Molina, Y., Beadnell, B., Simoni, J., & Walters, K. (2011). Measuring multiple minority stress: The LGBT people of color microaggressions scale. *Cultural Diversity and Ethnic Minority Pychology, 17*(2), 163–174.

Barrett, H. B., & Tasker, F. (2001). Growing up with a gay parent: Views of 101 gay fathers on their sons' and daughters' experiences. *Educational and Child Psychology, 18,* 62–77.

Barrio, C. (2000). The cultural relevance of community support programs. *Psychiatric Services, 51*(7), 879–884.

Beals, K. P., Impett, E. A, & Peplau, L. A. (2002). Lesbians in love: Why some relationships endure and others end. *Journal of Lesbian Studies, 6,* 53–63.

Beals, K. P., & Peplau, L. A. (2005). Identity support, identity devaluation, and well-being among lesbians. *Psychology of Women Quarterly, 29,* 140–148.

Bigner, J., & Jacobsen, R. B. (1992). Adult responses to child behavior and attitudes toward fathering: Gay and nongay fathers. *Journal of Homosexuality, 23,* 99–112.

Brannan, A. M., Athay, M. M., & Andrade, A. R. V. (2012). Measurement quality of the Caregiver Strain Questionnaire-Short Form 7 (CGSQ-SF7). *Administration and Policy in Mental Health and Mental Health Services Research, 39*(1–2), 51–59.

Breshears, D., & Beer, C. L.-D. (2014). A qualitative analysis of adult children's advice for parents coming out to their children. *Professional Psychology and Research and Practice, 45,* 231–238.

Canino, I. A., & Spurlock, J. (2000). *Culturally diverse children and adolescents: Assessment, diagnosis, and treatment* (2nd ed.). New York: Guilford Press.

Carrington, C. (1999). *No place like home: Relationships and family life among lesbians and gay men.* London: University of Chicago Press.

Cash, S. J. (2001). Risk assessment in child welfare: The art and science. *Children and Youth Services Review, 23*(11), 811–830.

Centers for Disease Control and Prevention (CDC). (2015). *Injury prevention & control: Division of Violence Prevention: Child maltreatment.* Retrieved from http://www.cdc.gov/violenceprevention/childmaltreatment/

Child Abuse Prevention and Treatment Act (CAPTA) Reauthorization Act of 2010. Pub. L. 111-320 (2010). Retrieved from http://www.gpo.gov/fdsys/pkg/BILLS-111s3817enr/pdf/BILLS-111s3817enr.pdf

Child Welfare Information Gateway. (2014). *Differential response to reports of child abuse and neglect.* Washington, DC: U.S. Department of Health and Human Services, Administration for Children and Families, Administration on Children, Youth and Families, Children's Bureau.

Cloutterbuck, J., & Mahoney, D. F. (2003). African American dementia caregivers: The duality of respect. *Dementia, 2*(2), 221–243.

Cohen, S., & Williamson, G. (1988). Perceived stress in a probability sample of the United States. In S. Spacapan & S. Oskamp (Eds.), *The social psychology of health: Claremont symposium on applied social psychology* (n.p.). Newbury Park, CA: Sage.

Corcoran, K., & Fischer, J. (Eds.). (2013). *Measures for clinical practice: A sourcebook* (3rd ed.; Vols. 1 & 2). New York: Oxford University Press.

Darling, N., & Steinberg, L. (1993). Parenting style as context: An integrative model. *Psychological Bulletin, 113*, 487–496.

DePanfilis, D., & Costello, T. (2014). Child protective services. In G. P. Mallon & P. M. Hess (Eds.), *Child welfare for the twenty-first century: A handbook of practices, policies, & programs* (pp. 236–252). New York: Columbia University Press.

Diamond, L. M., & Dube, E. M. (2002). Friendship and attachment among heterosexual and sexual minority youths. *Journal of Youth in Adolescence, 31*, 155–166.

Doom, J. R., Cicchetti, D., Rogosch, F. A., & Dackis, M. N. (2013). Child maltreatment and gender interactions as predictors of differential neuroendocrine profiles. *Psychoneuroendocrinology, 38*(8), 1442–1454.

Doueck, H. J., English D. J., DePanfilis, D., & Moote, G. T. (1993). Decision-making in child protective services. *Social Service Review, 65*, 112–132.

Drapalski, A., Marshall, T., Seybolt, D., Medoff, D., Peer, J., Leith, J., & Dixon, L. (2008). Unmet needs of families of adults with mental illness and preferences regarding family services. *Psychiatric Services, 59*, 655–662.

Dube, S. R., Anda, R. F., Felitti, V. J., Chapman, D. P., Williamson, D. F., & Giles, W.H. (2001). Childhood abuse, household dysfunction, and the risk of attempted suicide throughout the life span: Findings from the Adverse Childhood Experiences Study. *Journal of American Medical Association, 286*(24), 3089–3096. doi: 10.1001/jama.286.24.3089

Elizur, Y., & Mintzer, A. (2003). Gay males intimate relationship quality: The roles of attachment security, gay identity, social support, and income. *Personal Relationships, 10*, 411–436.

English, D. J., & Pecora, P. J. (1994). Risk assessment as a practice method in child protective services. *Child Welfare, 73*, 451–473.

Fanshel, D., Finch, S. J., & Grundy, J. F. (1994). Testing the measurement properties of risk assessment instruments in child protective services. *Child Abuse and Neglect, 18*, 1073–1084.

Farr, R. H., & Patterson, C. J. (2013). Coparenting among lesbian, gay, and heterosexual couples: Associations with adopted children's outcomes. *Child Development, 84*, 1226–1240.

Fedewa, A. L., Black, W. W., & Ahn, S. (2015). Children and adolescents with same-gender parents: A meta-analytic approach in assessing outcomes. *Journal of GLBT Family Studies, 11*, 1–34.

Finkelhor, D., Turner, H., Ormond, R., Hamby, S., & Kracke, K. (2013). Children's exposure to violence: Indicators on children and youth. Child Trends Data Bank. Retrieved from http://www.childtrends.org/wp-content/uploads/2012/07/118_Exposure_to_Violence.pdf

Firkins, A. S., & Candlin, C. N. (2011). 'She is not coping': Risk assessment and claims of deficit in social work. In C. N. Candlin & J. Crichton (Eds.), *Palgrave studies in professional and organizational discourse* (pp. 81–98). New York: Palgrave Macmillan.

Freedom to Marry. (2015). *History and timeline of the freedom to marry in the United States.* Retrieved from http://www.freedomtomarry.org/pages/history-and-timeline-of-marriage

Gelles, R. J. (2014). How evaluation research can help reform and improve the child welfare system. *Program Evaluation and Family Violence Research, 4*(1), 7–28.

General Accountability Office (GAO). (2004). *Defense of marriage act: An update to prior report.* Retrieved from http://www.gao.gov/products/GAO-04-353R

Gilbert, R., Widom, C. S., Browne, K., Fergusson, D., Webb, E., & Janson, S. (2009). Burden and consequences of child maltreatment in high-income countries. *The Lancet, 373*(9657), 68–81.

Goldberg, A. E. (2007). Talking about family: Disclosure practices of adults raised by lesbian, gay, and bisexual parents. *Journal of Family Issues, 28*, 100–131.

Goldberg, A. E. (2010). *Lesbian and gay parents and their children: Research on the family life cycle.* Washington, DC: American Psychological Association.

Gottman, J. M., Levenson, R. W., Gross, J., Fredrickson, B. L., McCoy, K., Rosenthal, L., . . . & Yoshimoto, D. (2003). Correlates of gay and lesbian couples' relationship satisfaction and relationship dissolution. *Journal of Homosexuality, 45*, 23–44.

Green, R. J., Bettinger, M., & Zacks, E. (1996). Are lesbian couples fused and gay male couples disengaged? In J. Laird & R. J. Green (Eds.), *Lesbian and gays in couples and families* (pp. 185–230). San Francisco: Jossey Bass.

Greenburg, J. S., Kim, H. W., & Greenley, J. R. (1997). Factors associated with subjective burden in siblings of adults with severe mental illness. *American Journal of Orthopsychiatry, 67*, 231–241.

Greenburg, J. S., Seltzer, M. M., Krauss, M. W., & Kim, H. (1999). Siblings of adults with mental illness or mental retardation: Current involvement and expectation of future caregiving. *Psychiatric Services, 50*, 1214–1219.

Hastrup, L. H., Van Den Berg, B., & Gyrd-Hansen, D. (2011). Do informal caregivers in mental illness feel more burdened? A comparative study of mental versus somatic illnesses. *Scandinavian Journal of Public Health, 39*(6), 598–607.

Herrenkohl, T. I., Hong, S., Klika, J. B., Herrenkohl, R. C., & Russo, M. J. (2013). Developmental impacts of child abuse and neglect related to adult mental health, substance use, and physical health. *Journal of Family Violence, 28*(2), 191–199.

Hudson, W. W. (2001). *Index of marital satisfaction.* Retrieved from http://www .therapyinla.com/psych/psych0101.html

Human Rights Campaign. (2013). *The Regnerus fallout.* Retrieved from http://www.regnerusfallout.org/frequently-asked-questions

Institute of Medicine. (2002). *Speaking of health: Assessing health communication strategies for diverse populations.* Washington, DC: National Academy Press.

Jagannathan, R., & Camasso, M. J. (1996). Risk assessment in child protective services: A canonical analysis of the case management function. *Child Abuse and Neglect, 20,* 599–612.

Jonson-Reid, M., Kohl, P. L., & Drake, B. (2012). Child and adult outcomes of chronic child maltreatment. *Pediatrics, 129*(5), 839–845.

Jordan, J. R. (2001). Is suicide bereavement different? A reassessment of the literature. *Suicide and Life-Threatening Behavior, 31*(1), 91–102.

Jordan, K. M., & Deluty, R. H. (2000). Social support, coming out, and relationship satisfaction in lesbian couples. *Journal of Lesbian Studies, 4,* 145–164.

Judge, K. (1994). Serving children, siblings, and spouses: Understanding the needs of other family members. In H. P. Lefley & M. Wasow (Eds.), *Helping families cope with mental illness: Vol. 2. Chronic Mental Illness* (pp. 161–194). Chur, Switzerland: Harwood Academic Publishers.

Kaiser Family Foundation. (2001). *Inside-out: A report on the experiences of lesbians, gays and bisexuals in America and the public's view on issues and policies related to sexual orientation.* Menlo Park, CA: Author.

Kavazis, A. N., & Wadsworth, D. D. (2014). Changes in body composition and perceived stress scale-10 in National Collegiate Athletic Association Division I Female Volleyball Players. *Archives of Exercise in Health and Disease, 4*(3), 320–325.

Kopelowicz, A., Zarate, R., Wallace, C. J., Liberman, R. P., Lopez, S. R., & Mintz, J. (2012). The ability of multifamily groups to improve treatment adherence in Mexican Americans with schizophrenia. *Archives of General Psychiatry, 69*(3), 265–273.

Kurdek, L. A. (1988). Perceived social support in gays and lesbians in cohabiting relationships. *Journal of Personality and Social Psychology, 54,* 504–509.

Kurdek, L. A. (1995). Developing changes in relationship quality in gay and lesbian cohabiting couples. *Developmental Psychology, 31,* 86–94.

Kurdek, L. A. (2000). Attractions and constraints as determinants of relationship commitment: longitudinal evidence from gay, lesbian, and heterosexual couples. *Personal Relationships, 7,* 245–262.

Kurdek, L. A. (2001). Differences between heterosexual-nonparent couples and gay, lesbian, and heterosexual-parent couples. *Journal of Family Issues, 22,* 728–755.

Kurdek, L. A. (2004). Are gay and lesbian cohabiting couples really different from heterosexual married couples? *Journal of Marriage and Family, 66,* 880–900.

Kurdek, L. A. (2006). Differences between partners from heterosexual, gay, and lesbian cohabiting couples. *Journal of Marriage and Family, 68,* 509–528.

Lambda Legal. (n.d.). *In your state.* Retrieved from http://www.lambdalegal.org/states-regions?gclid=CjwKEAjws5CrBRD8ze702_2dyjYSJAAAJK9yFxUF3 YELIhFBdngT7pWdSUseK875dxkhfjSQB50EWhoCkvXw_wcB

Lee, E. H., Chung, B. Y., Suh, C. H., & Jung, J. Y. (2014). Korean versions of the Perceived Stress Scale (PSS-14, 10 and 4): Psychometric evaluation in patients with chronic disease. *Scandinavian Journal of Caring Sciences, 29*(1), 183–192.

Leff, J. (2005). *Advanced family work for schizophrenia: An evidence-based approach.* London: Gaskell.

Lefley, H. (1996). *Family caregiving in mental illness.* Thousand Oaks, CA: Sage.

Leidy, M. S., Guerra, N. G., & Toro, R. I. (2010). Positive parenting, family cohesion, and child social competence among immigrant Latino families. *Journal of Family Psychology: Journal of the Division of Family Psychology of the American Psychological Association (Division 43), 24*(3), 3–13.

Levitt, H. M., Horne, S. G., Puckett, J., Sweeney, K. K., & Hampton, M. L. (2014). Gay families: Challenging racial and sexual/gender minority stressors through social support. *Journal of GLBT Family Studies,* published online.

Lewis, R. J., Derlega, V. J., Berndt, A., Morris, L. M., & Rose, S. (2001). An empirical analysis of stressors for gay men and lesbians. *Journal of Homosexuality, 42,* 63–88.

Lewis-Fernández, R., & Kleinman, A. (1995). Cultural psychiatry: Theoretical, clinical and research issues. *Psychiatric Clinics of North America, 18*(3), 433–448.

Livingston, G. (2014). Less than half of U.S. kids today live in a "traditional" family. Pew Research Center Online Publication. Retrieved from http://www.pew research.org/fact-tank/2014/12/22/less-than-half-of-u-s-kids-today-live-in-a-traditional-family/

Lukens, E. P., Thorning, H., & Lohrer, S. (2004). Sibling perspectives on severe mental illness: Reflections on self and family. *American Journal of Orthopsychiatry, 74*(4), 489.

Lynch, J. M., & Murray, K. (2000). For the love of the children: The coming out process for lesbian and gay parents and stepparents. *Journal of Homosexuality, 39,* 1–24.

Magaña, S. M., Ramirez Garcia, J. I., Hernández, M. G., & Cortez, R. (2007). Psychological distress among Latino family caregivers of adults with schizophrenia: The roles of burden and stigma. *Psychiatric Services, 58*(3), 378–384.

Manning, W. D., Fettro, M. N., & Lamidi, E. (2014). Child well-being in same-sex parent families: Review of research prepared for American Sociological Association Amicus Brief. *Population Research and Policy Review, 33,* 485–502.

Marsh, D. T., Dickens, R. M., Koeske, R. D., Yackovich, N. S., Wilson, J. M., & Leichliter, J. S. (1993). Troubled journey: Siblings and children of people with mental illness. *Innovations and Research, 2*(2), 13–23.

Matthews, C. R., & Lease, S. H. (2000). Focus on lesbian, gay, and bisexual families. In R. M. Perez, K. A. DeBord, & K. J. Bieschke (Eds.), *Handbook of counseling and psychotherapy with lesbian, gay, and bisexual clients* (pp. 249–273). Washington, DC: American Psychological Association.

Mayfield, W. (2001). The development of an internalized homonegativity inventory for gay men. *Journal of Homosexuality, 41*, 53–76.

Mays, V. M., & Cochran, S. D. (2001). Mental health correlates of perceived discrimination among lesbian, gay, and bisexual adults in the United States. *American Journal of Public Health, 91*, 1869–1876.

McCubbin, H., & Thompson. A. (Eds.). (1991). *Family assessment inventories for research and practice* (2nd ed.). Madison: University of Wisconsin.

Meyer, I. H. (2003). Prejudice, social stress, and mental health in lesbian, gay, and bisexual populations: Conceptual issues and research evidence. *Psychology Bulletin, 129*, 674–697.

Middlebrooks, J. S., & Audage N. C. (2008). *The effects of childhood stress on health across the lifespan*. Atlanta, GA: Centers for Disease Control and Prevention, National Center for Injury Prevention and Control.

Monin, J. K., Schulz, R., & Feeney, B. C. (2014). Compassionate love in individuals with Alzheimer's disease and their spousal caregivers: Associations with caregivers' psychological health. *Gerontologist,* February.

Morrow, D. F., & Messinger, L. (2006). *Sexual orientation & gender expression in social work practice*. New York: Columbia University Press.

Murphy, G., Peters, K., Jackson, D., & Wilkes, L. (2011). A qualitative meta-synthesis of adult children of parents with a mental illness. *Journal of Clinical Nursing, 20*(23–24), 3430–3442.

My Fertility Choices. (n.d.). *Fertility information.* Retrieved from http://myfertility choices.com/fertility-information/lgbt-options/

Nardi, P. M. (1999). *Gay men's friendships: Invincible communities.* Chicago: University of Chicago Press.

National Quality Improvement Center on Differential Response in Child Protective Services (QIC-DR). (2011). Differential response in child protective services: A literature review. Version 2. Englewood, CO: Author.

New Freedom Commission on Mental Health. (2003). Achieving the promise: Transforming mental health care in America: Final report (DHHS Publication No. SMA-03-3832). Rockville, MD: U.S. Department of Health and Human Services.

Northouse, L., Williams, A. L., Given, B., & McCorkle, R. (2012). Psychosocial care for family caregivers of patients with cancer. *Journal of Clinical Oncology, 30*(11), 1227–1234

Oswald, R. F. (2002). Resilience within the family networks of lesbians and gay men: Intentionality and redefinition. *Journal of Marriage and Family, 64*(2), 374–383.

Otis, M. D., Rostosky S. S., Riggle E. D. B., & Hamrin, R. (2006). Stress and relationship quality in same-sex couples. *Journal Social Personality Relationships, 23*, 81–99.

Pachankis, J. E., & Goldfried, M. R. (2013). Clinical issues in working with lesbian, gay, and bisexual clients. *Psychology of Sexual Orientation and Gender Diversity, 1,* 45–48.

Patterson, C. J. (2003). Children of lesbian and gay parents. In L. D. Garnets & D. C. Kimmel (Eds.), *Psychological perspectives on lesbian, gay, and bisexual experiences* (2nd ed., pp. 497–548). New York: Columbia University Press.

Patterson, C. J., & Chan, R. W. (1996). Gay fathers and their children. In R. P. Cabaj & T. S. Stein (Eds.), *Textbook of homosexuality and mental health* (pp. 371–393). Washington, DC: American Psychiatric Press.

Pecora, P. J., Whittaker, J. K., Maluccio, A. N., & Barth, R. P. (2000). *The child welfare challenge* (2nd ed.). New York: Aldine de Gruyter.

Peplau, L. A., & Fingerhut, A. W. (2007). The close relationships of lesbians and gay men. *Annual Review of Psychology, 58,* 405–424.

Peplau, L. A., & Spalding, L. R. (2000). The close relationships of lesbians, gay men and bisexuals. In C. Hendrick & S. S. Hendrick (Eds.), *Close relationships: A sourcebook* (pp. 111–124). Thousand Oaks, CA: Sage.

Perez, M. C., & Fortuna, L. (2005). Chapter 6. Psychosocial Stressors, Psychiatric Diagnoses and Utilization of Mental Health Services Among Undocumented Immigrant Latinos. *Journal of Immigrant & Refugee Services, 3*(1–2), 107–123.

Perlick, D. A., Miklowitz, D. J., Link, B. G., Struening, E., Kaczynski, R., Gonzalez, J., Manning, L. N., Wolff, N., & Rosenheck, R. A. (2007). Perceived stigma and depression among caregivers of patients with bipolar disorder. *The British Journal of Psychiatry: the Journal of Mental Science, 190,* 535–536.

Perlick, D. A., Miklowitz, D. J., Struening, E., Kaczynski, R., Gonzalez, J., Manning, L. N., Wolff, N., & Rosenheck, R. A. (2007). Perceived stigma and depression among caregivers of patients with bipolar disorder. *British Journal of Psychiatry, 190,* 535–536.

Perlick, D. A., Nelson, A. H., Mattias, K., Selzer, J., Kalvin, C., Wilber, C. H., Huntington, B., Holman, C. S., & Corrigan, P. W. (2011). In our own voice-family companion: Reducing self-stigma of family members of persons with serious mental illness. *Psychiatric Services, 62*(12), 1456–1462.

Phillips, M. H., & Paumgarten, A. C. (2009). Hispanic caregiver perceptions of preventive service. *Child Welfare, 88*(3), 27–55.

Pickett-Schenk, S. (2003). Family education and support: Just for women only? *Psychiatric Rehabilitation Journal, 27,* 131–139.

Pitman, A., Osborn, D., King, M., & Erlangsen, A. (2014). Effects of suicide bereavement on mental health and suicide risk. *The Lancet Psychiatry, 1*(1), 86–94.

Potochnick, S. R., & Perreira, K. M. (2010). Depression and anxiety among first-generation immigrant Latino youth: key correlates and implications for future research. *Journal of Nervous and Mental Disease, 198*(7), 470–477.

ProCon.org. (2015). 50 states have legal same-sex marriage. Retrieved from http://gaymarriage.procon.org/view.resource.php?resourceID=004857

Raman, S., & Hodes, D. (2012). Cultural issues in child maltreatment. *Journal of Paediatrics and Child Health, 48*(1), 30–37.

Robinson, B. C. (1983). Validation of a caregiver strain index. *Journal of Gerontology, 38*(3), 344–348.

Roisman, G. I., Clausell, E., Holland, A., Fortuna, K., & Elieff, C. (2008). Adult romantic relationships as contexts of human development: A multimethod comparison of same-sex couples with opposite-sex dating, engaged, and married dyads. *Developmental Psychology, 44,* 91–101.

Rosenfeld, M. J. (2014). Couple longevitiy in the era of same-sex marriage in the United States. *Journal of Marriage and Family, 76,* 905–918.

Rothblum, E. D. (2009). An overview of same-sex couples in relationships: A research area still at sea. In D. A. Hope (Ed.), *Contemporary perspectives on lesbian, gay, and bisexual identities* (pp. 113–139). New York: Springer.

Ryan, S., Wiles, D., Cash, S., & Siebert, C. (2005). Risk assessments: Empirically supported or values driven?. *Children and Youth Services Review, 27*(2), 213–225.

Saewyc, E. M., Skay, C. L., Pettingell, S. L., Reis, E. A., Bearinger, L., Resnick, M., . . . Combs, L. (2006). Hazards of stigma: The sexual and physical abuse of gay, lesbian, and bisexual adolescents in the United States and Canada. *Child Welfare, 85*(2), 192–213.

Schechory, M., & Ziv, R. (2007). Relationships between gender role attitudes, role division and perception of equity among herterosexual, gay and lesbian couples. *Sex Roles, 56,* 629–638.

Shapiro, J. (2013). The law governing LGBT-parent families. *LGBT Families,* 291–304.

Shlonsky, A., & Wagner, D. (2005). The next step: Integrating actuarial risk assessment and clinical judgment into an evidence-based practice framework in CPS case management. *Children and Youth Services Review, 27*(4), 409–427.

Sidebotham, P., & Heron, J. (2003). Child maltreatment in the "Children of the Nineties": The role of the child. *Child Abuse and Neglect, 27,* 337–352.

Siegel, G. (2012). Worth the investment? Analysis of costs in a differential response program. *Protecting Children, 26*(3), 94–103.

Slep, A. M. S., Heyman, R. E., & Foran, H. M. (2015). Child maltreatment in DSM-5 and ICD-11. *Family Process.* doi: 10.1111/famp.12131

Smith, M. J., Greenberg, J. S., & Mailick Seltzer, M. (2007). Siblings of adults with schizophrenia: Expectations about future caregiving roles. *American Journal of Orthopsychiatry, 77*(1), 29.

Smith, M. E., Lindsay, M. A., Williams, C. D., Medoff, D. R., Lucksted, A., Fang, L. J., Schiffman, J., Lewis-Fernández, R., & Dixon, L. B. (2014). Race-related differences in the experiences of family members of persons with mental illness participating in the NAMI Family to Family Education Program. *American Journal of Community Psychology, 54*(3–4), 316–327.

Sammer, J., & Miller, S. (2013). *The future of domestic partner benefits: Society for Human Resource Management.* Retrieved from http://www.shrm.org/hrdisciplines/benefits/articles/pages/domestic-partner-benefits.aspx

Springer, K. W., Sheridan, J., Kuo, D., & Carnes, M. (2007). Long-term physical and mental health consequences of childhood physical abuse: Results from a large population-based sample of men and women. *Child Abuse & Neglect, 31*(5), 517–530.

Statesman. (2015). *In new legal woe, Paxton faces contempt of court.* Retrieved from http://www.statesman.com/news/news/in-new-legal-woe-paxton-faces-contempt-of-court/nnDWN/

Substance Abuse and Mental Health Service Administration (SAMHSA). (2013). *Results from the 2013 National Survey on Drug Use and Health: Summary of national findings.* Retrieved from http://www.samhsa.gov/data/sites/default/files/NSDUHresultsPDFWHTML2013/Web/NSDUHresults2013.pdf

Swim, J. K. (2004). Day to day experiences with heterosexism: Heterosexist hassles as daily stressors. Department of Psychology Presentation, Penn State University, University Park, State College.

Szymanski, D. M., & Chung, B. Y. (2001). The lesbian internalized homophobia scale. *Journal of Homosexuality, 41,* 37–52.

Tasker, F. (2005). Lesbian mothers, gay fathers, and their children: A review. *Journal of Developmental Behavioral Pediatrics, 26,* 224–240.

Todosijevic J., Rothblum, E. D., & Solomon, S. E. (2005). Relationship satisfaction, affectivity, and gay specific stressors in same-sex couples joined in civil unions. *Psychology of Women Quartely, 29,* 158–1.

University of California at Berkeley, Gender Equity Resource Center. (2014). *Definition of terms* (updated July 2013). Retrieved from http://geneq.berkeley.edu/lgbt_resources_definiton_of_terms#family_of_choice

U.S. Census Bureau. (2000). *Census 2000 data for the United States.* Retrieved from https://www.census.gov/census2000/states/us.html

U.S. Census Bureau. (2011). *American Community Survey.* Retrieved from http://www.census.gov/hhes/samesex/files/SScplfactsheet_final.pdf

U.S. Department of Health and Human Services, Administration for Children and Families, Administration on Children, Youth and Families, Children's Bureau. (2013). *Child maltreatment.* Retrieved from http://www.acf.hhs.gov/programs/cb/resource/child-maltreatment-2013

U.S. Department of Veterans Affairs, National Center for PTSD. (n.d.). *List of all measures.* Retrieved from http://www.ptsd.va.gov/professional/assessment/all_measures.asp

Vandiver, V., Jordan, C., Keopraseuth, K., & Yu, M. (1995). Family as educator: Cross-cultural approaches for integrating family knowledge with psychosocial rehabilitation programs. *Journal of Psychosocial Rehabilitation, 19*(1), 47–54.

Warner, R. (2005). Local projects of the World Psychiatric Association to reduce stigma and discrimination. *Psychiatric Services, 56,* 570–575.

White, R. S., Jiang, J., Hall, C. B., Katz, M. J., Zimmerman, M. E., Sliwinski, M., & Lipton, R. B. (2014). Higher perceived stress scale scores are associated with higher pain intensity and pain interference levels in older adults. *Journal of the American Geriatrics Society, 62*(12), 2350–2356.

World Health Organization. (2001). *Mental health, new understanding, new hope.* Retrieved from http://www.who.int/whr/2001/en/index.html

World Health Organization. (2010). *International classification of diseases* (10th rev.; ICD-10). Retrieved from http://www.who.int/classifications/icd/en/

CHAPTER 9

Multicultural Assessment

Dorie J. Gilbert

INTRODUCTION

In our increasingly multicultural society, social work practitioners are challenged to demonstrate an understanding of how factors like race or ethnicity, gender, sexual orientation, age, and different physical and mental abilities affect our practice and assessment strategies with clients. This chapter focuses on the influence of race/ethnicity or ethno-cultural factors on a client's assessment. Standardized measures and clinical diagnostic categories for multicultural assessment have been brought into question in numerous critiques of standardized assessment practices (Dana, 2000, 2005). Furthermore, ethnocentrism of the U.S. majority culture has resulted in assessment procedures and measurement instruments that do not fully consider culturally based ways of thinking, feeling, and behaving that fall outside of the majority (Eurocentric) perspective. The historical misdiagnosis and distortion of ethnic and racial populations based solely on a Euro American worldview has been called "cultural malpractice" (Hall, 1997) that "occurs as a result of unintentional, often unconscious, but unremitting bias from a variety of sources" (Dana, 2000, p. xiii). The goal of multicultural assessment training is to increase the practitioner's ability to conduct assessments using culturally congruent techniques, methods, and clinical conceptions, without which the most well-intentioned practitioners act unethically.

Toward this goal, this chapter covers the limitations of standardized assessment methods and ethnic-sensitive assessment strategies for four groups: (a) American Indians and Alaska Natives, (b) African Americans and blacks, (c) Hispanics and Latinos, and (d) Asian and Pacific Islander Americans. These groups have been historically overrepresented in receiving inaccurate and culturally biased assessments, diagnoses, and interventions. This chapter includes a guide for identifying examples of specific measures, by ethnicity, recommended for use with specific clients (see table 9.1). A case study illustrates a culturally grounded assessment approach.

BACKGROUND ON ETHNIC-MINORITY CLIENTS

By the year 2050 racial and ethnic minorities in the United States will represent nearly 53 percent of the population (U.S. Census Bureau, 2014). At the same time, many whites are starting to gain increased understanding of their own ethnic ancestry and heritages (e.g., Italian or Irish) and thereby are creating a new entity in the history of American ethnic groups, referred to as Euro Americans. Ethnic groups who are able to blend into the Euro American–dominated society of Anglo-Saxon and European groups have successfully assimilated into the mainstream of American society and power (Lum, 2004). However, the color factor has been a barrier to African Americans, Latinos, Asian Americans, and Native Americans. Thus, groups of color, while increasing in numbers, remain a minority because of a lack of economic, political, and social power (Feagin & Feagin, 2003; Lum, 2004). The social construction of race in our society means that most ethnic-minority individuals continue to contend with societal stigma and negative outcomes perpetuated by the inherent bias in a majority-minority culture context. This chapter outlines the basic demographic, sociocultural experiences of the four groups and briefly discusses relevant group-related factors that may influence a client's clinical presentation during the assessment process. A comprehensive description of each group is beyond the scope of this chapter; practitioners are advised to consult other works for further details.

American Indians and Alaska Natives

The terms "Native Americans" or "Native peoples" refer to all descendants of the pre-Columbian inhabitants of North America, including American Indian, Alaska Native, and First Nations, Inuit, and Mexican Indian people (Paniagua, 2005). Today's 4.1 million Native Americans account for 1.5 percent of the U.S. population, and this percent is growing as a result of increased birthrates, decreased infant mortality, and increased willingness to report American Indian ancestry (U.S. Census Bureau, 2014). There are more than 550 federally recognized American Indian tribes and Alaska Native village groups nationally (Russell, 2006).

The land, language, religion, and culture of Native peoples were nearly destroyed by the colonialization practice of the Europeans; today Native peoples remain one of the most disadvantaged groups in the nation. Their strengths are grounded in Native cultural values including but not limited to a fluid sense of time, with the view of being ruled by a clock as unhealthy and unnatural; a sense of spirituality that incorporates guidelines for behavior; a collective identity strongly linked to family, clan, and nation; a deep respect for elders' knowledge and wisdom;

leaders' willingness to sacrifice on behalf of the communities; and the view of children as the future of Native nations (Weaver, 2008).

Mental health is a leading health problem among Native populations, and they primarily seek professional psychological services for substance abuse, anxiety, depression, and adjustment-related problems, which can be associated with a historical trauma response to the genocide of Native peoples and the population's unresolved grief from this trauma (Brave Heart, 2001).

African Americans and Blacks

African Americans make up 13 percent of the U.S. population. The more than 33 million individuals constituting this group include people with roots in Africa and the African diaspora, including the West Indies, South America, and the Caribbean (Feagin & Feagin, 2003). In addition, the number of immigrants from African countries is increasing, with large numbers of immigrants from Nigeria, Ghana, and Ethiopia (Dhooper & Moore, 2001).

Afrocentric values and traditions include unity (striving for unity in family, community, and race), self-determination (defining, naming, and creating for ourselves), collective work and responsibility (building and maintaining community and solving problems together), cooperative economics (building and maintaining an economic base of community), purpose (restoring people to their original traditional greatness), creativity (enhancing the beauty and benefits of self and community), and faith (belief in righteousness of the black struggle). Although African Americans are diverse and vary in terms of the extent to which they endorse these principles, these values reinforce positive mental and physical health (Gilbert, Harvey, & Belgrave, 2009).

African Americans lead the nation across a number of mental health and health disparities. The Office of Minority Health and Health Disparities (2008) reports that African Americans experience disproportionately high death rates from preventable diseases and mental health concerns, including depression, substance abuse, and suicide. Similar to Native Americans, many current problems of African Americans can be traced to their historical trauma experience of slavery and genocide.

Hispanics and Latinos

The term "Hispanic" is an ethnocultural label for a heterogeneous constituency of people of Mexican, Dominican, Puerto Rican, and Cuban descent, as well as of individuals from other Central and South American countries. However, many in the group prefer the term "Latino." Mexican Americans, who reside primarily in the western and southwestern

United States, comprise almost two-thirds of Latinos. The actual number of Latinos in the United States is probably greater than official data indicate as a result of undocumented immigrants being missed by the census. Although they are the largest racial and ethnic minority in the United States, Latinos face multiple challenges that continue to affect quality of life (National Council of La Raza, 2010).

Latino values include the important role of godparenthood (*compadres*), a deep sense of family obligation (*familismo*), social engagement and avoidance of interpersonal conflict (*simpatía*), and emphasis on spiritual beliefs, as well as the Spanish language, which helps preserve cultural identity (Dhooper & Moore, 2001).

Findings show that Hispanics have similar rates of psychiatric disorders as non-Hispanic Euro Americans, but as a group they underuse the mental health–care system, which may be partly because of the lack of bilingual and bicultural professionals. Among Hispanic Americans with a mental health disorder, fewer than one in eleven contacts mental health specialists (U.S. Department of Health and Human Services, Office of the Surgeon General [DHHS], 2008).

Asian and Pacific Islander Americans

Asian Americans and Pacific Islanders place a high value on harmony in relationships, mutual dependency rather than individual dependency, and important cultural values (Chow, 2001). These values include filial piety, modesty, respect for authority, and communal responsibility. Similar to other ethnic-minority groups, Asian Americans and Pacific Islanders are more group oriented than self oriented and have histories of discrimination and continued oppression in this country.

The myth that Asian Americans are a monolithic model minority creates the belief that they have their own resources to succeed and overcome discrimination and prejudice, which denies their vulnerability and need for mental health services and masks the struggles among subgroups (Dhooper & Moore, 2001). As a group, Asian Americans are 25 percent as likely as Euro Americans and 50 percent as likely as African Americans and Hispanics to seek outpatient mental health care and less likely than Euro Americans to receive inpatient care. When they do seek care, they are more likely to be diagnosed as "problem free" (Suicide Prevention Resource Center, n.d.).

CONSIDERATIONS IN ASSESSING ETHNIC-MINORITY CLIENTS

The concepts of emic and etic functioning underlie the notion of culturally competent assessment practice. Some aspects of functioning are unique to the client's culture (emic), and others are common across many cultures (etic). Eurocentric (or majority) culture assumes an etic position, which is detrimental for members of ethnic minority groups. When practitioners approach assessment from the assumption that all individuals should be treated the same (e.g., with the same assessment instruments, the same assumptions about mental health), they are likely to misdiagnose clients who do not identify with mainstream culture. Inasmuch as the initial assessment phase determines the course of treatment, it is important that practitioners avoid the tendency to gloss over cultural components when assessing clients (Draguns, 2002). Flawed culturally competent assessments usually occur for three main reasons: (a) practitioners' bias and/or lack of awareness of cultural differences, (b) reliance on stereotypes or overgeneralizations for assessment strategies, and (c) culturally biased measurement and assessment instruments.

Practitioners' Bias and/or Lack of Awareness of Cultural Differences

The literature contains numerous examples of misdiagnoses and differential assessment outcomes for ethnic-minority clients. For example, research over the decades has documented that African Americans receive more-severe diagnostic labels than Euro Americans and have higher-than-expected rates of diagnosed schizophrenia and lower rates of diagnosed affective disorders. In addition, diagnostic testing is used less frequently with African American clients even when they have insurance (Snowden, 2003). When African Americans do seek mental health care, they often are prescribed higher doses of psychiatric medication, which may result in increased side effects and decreased medication compliance (Office of Minority Health and Health Disparities, 2008). These differences point to ways in which clinicians can be biased in the course of routine practice; they also point to practitioners' attitudes, communication with persons of color, and lack of cultural competence and cultural humility (Tervalon & Murray-García, 1998) are factors not only in maintaining these disparities but also in exacerbating them (Smedley, Stith, & Nelson, 2003).

Lack of awareness of culture-based symptoms can also result in misdiagnosis. Latino and other clients who believe in the supernatural and believe that fate or a deceased person is in control of their lives may be diagnosed as psychotic. Hispanics may experience *ataque de nervios* (attack of nerves) with such symptoms as screaming uncontrollably, crying, trembling, verbal and physical aggression, dissociative experiences, fainting episodes, and suicidal behaviors (DHHS, 2008). Another example is the common practice of ancestor veneration (Grills, 2002), the practice of some people of African-descent who call on ancestors as part of a coping strategy, whereas the majority culture might misdiagnose some-one who "talks" to ancestors as hallucinating and psychotic.

For practitioners to be aware of the cultural differences that can affect the assessment process, they must first be aware of their own cultural orientation to understand how they may potentially impose their own values or worldviews on others. Social workers—of all racial/ethnic backgrounds—should self-assess themselves to determine if their own cultural orientation and values may interfere with effective assessment of their clients. Pedersen and Ivey (1993) sagely remind us that ignoring the influence of our own and others' culturally learned assumptions "is a little like speeding in a car down a busy street without having your hands on the steering wheel" (p. 1).

Reliance on Stereotypes or Overgeneralizations for Assessment Strategies

A common mistake practitioners make in their attempt to master culturally sensitive assessment is to apply stereotypes and overgeneralizations about a client's racial/ethnic group during the assessment process. A practitioner conducting an assessment with an Asian American female client may notice the client's quiet, withdrawn behavior and assume that this is a normal demeanor of Asian American women. The practitioner therefore may not explore other reasons for the observed behavior or investigate the specific beliefs and norms of the client's subgroup (e.g., Chinese, Filipino). An erroneous assumption that some practitioners make in assessing ethnic-minority clients is that racial/ethnic status is the equivalent construct of culture. The extent to which a person conforms to any particular culture—that is, those group-based attitudes, beliefs, and behaviors—depends on both cultural identity and the level of identification with that culture.

Cultural identity is a person's affiliation with a specific group—for example, a person's membership in an ethnic group. In contrast, cultural identification is a personal trait; it is the extent to which individuals view themselves as involved with an identifiable group along with their investment or stake in that particular culture. Thus, it is critical to determine a client's ethnic-group schematicity, or the extent to which the client's culture derives from his or her ethnic group. Cultural orientations vary within each of the ethnic-minority groups addressed here, particularly as an increasing number of people identify with multiple ethnicities or choose not to define themselves by racial/ethnic categories at all. A good example is the use of the term "Hispanic" to describe a person from a large, ethnically diverse group of people who differ from each other regarding a number of demographic variables. In addition to cultural orientation that centers around racial/ethnic status, individuals in any group differ with regard to a number of other variables (e.g., class, gender, age, religion, immigration status, sexual orientation, educational level), all of which challenges the myopic notion of the monolithic group. Each client is unique and must be encountered without prejudgment and assumptions. Ethnic identity is one component of our sense of self. The Multigroup Ethnic Identity Measure (Phinney, 1992) measures attitudes, behaviors, practices, and belongingness to assess the concept we have of ourselves as a member of a racial/ethnic group. Practitioners should first determine a client's ethnic group orientation and identity by asking the client before proceeding to administer assessment instruments.

Culturally Biased Measurement and Assessment Instruments

Standardized measures are usually the first choice for social work practitioners in conducting assessments; however, most of these measures have been constructed on the basis of the majority culture and with little attention to the values, attitudes, and life experiences of individuals from non-mainstream cultures. Dana (2005) uses the term "imposed etics" to describe the way in which all instruments in the United States "are still assumed to be etic in nature, or universal, rather than emic" (n.p.). Although standardized measures may pass the test of high reliability and stability, they can be culturally biased when used with ethnic-minority groups (Aponte & Crouch, 2000). In some instances, important emic-assumed mental health–related concepts lack true equivalents in languages other than English, and in cultural interpretations other than Euro American. When faced with standardized assessment procedures, for example, some Asian Americans approach the very task of responding differently from the developers of the procedures (Snowden, 2003). Other research suggests that African Caribbean women's experiences and management of emotional distress differ from the Westernized constructs of distress (Sisley, Hutton, Louise Godbody, & Brown, 2011).

Paniagua (2005) ranked measurement instruments on the basis of the level of cultural bias. Highly biased instruments include clinical interviews (e.g., the mental status examination), trait measures, self-report psychopathology measures (e.g., Minnesota Multiphasic Personality Inventory, referred to as MMPI and MMPI-2; Beck Depression Inventory; and the Rorschach test) (as reported in Paniagua, 2005). For example, compared to the Beck Depression Inventory, the Center for Epidemiologic Studies Depression (CES-D) scale contained a number of items that were more likely to be endorsed by Chinese Americans regardless of their level of depression.

The DSM Culture and Assessment.   Most social worker will rely on the *Diagnostic and Statistical Manual of Mental Disorders,* fifth edition

(DSM-5; American Psychiatric Association [APA], 2013) for assessment. The DSM has been criticized for lack of contextualization of disorders resulting from oppression (e.g., racism as a trauma) and oppression-induced conditions; it remains a subject of debate (Frances, First, Pincus, Kutchins, & Kirk, 2005). However, major improvements have been made to incorporate cultural considerations and strategies for taking ethnicity into account for assessment. Among the more innovative features of the DSM-IV (APA, 2000) is the inclusion of explicit considerations of culture (Mezzich et al., 2008). Section III of the DSM-5, "Emerging Measures and Models," states, "Understanding the cultural context of illness experience is essential for effective diagnostic assessment and clinician management," and further delineates that "there is evidence that racism can exacerbate many psychiatric disorders, contributing to poor outcomes, and that racial biases can affect diagnostic assessment" (APA, 2013, p. 749).

The DSM-5 also updates the "Outline for Cultural Formulation." The updated "Outline" now calls for systemic assessment of

- Cultural identity of the individual (racial, ethnic, or cultural reference group, acculturation, language, religion, socioeconomic status, place of birth, migrant status, sexual orientation);
- Cultural conceptualization of distress (cultural constructs; the level of severity and meaning of syndromes that should be assessed in relation to the norms of the individual's cultural reference groups);
- Psychosocial stressors and cultural features of vulnerability and resilience (stressors that vary within cultural interpretation);
- Cultural features of the relationship between the individual and the clinician (language barriers, racism, social status, trust, and safety); and
- Overall cultural assessment (summary of the implications of the components of cultural formulation).

Furthermore, the DSM-5's introductory section (APA, 2013, pp. 14–15) notes, "Culture provides interpretive frameworks that shape the experience and expression of the symptoms, signs and behaviors that are criteria for diagnosis" and explains three cultural concepts:

- Cultural syndrome: Cluster of co-occurring symptoms found in a specific cultural group, community or context (e.g., *ataque de nervios*)
- Cultural idiom of distress: Linguistic term, phrase, or way of talking about suffering that is specific to a cultural group
- Cultural explanation or perceived cause: Explanatory model among a cultural group for causes of symptoms, illness, or distress

Finally, the DSM-5 glossary (APA, 2013, p. 833) includes culture-specific concepts of distress, including

- *Ataque de nervios:* Intense emotional upset (Latino);
- *Dhat* syndrome: anxiety, fatigue, weakness, weight loss, impotence (South Asia);
- *Khyal* cap: panic attack (Cambodians);
- *Kufungisisa:* range of psychopathology (Zimbabwe);
- *Maladi moun:* range of medical and psychiatric disorders (Haiti);
- *Nervios:* state of vulnerability and stressful life experiences (Latino);
- *Shenjing shuairuo:* weakness, worry, insomnia (China);
- *Susto:* distress and misfortune (Latino);
- *Taijin kyofusho:* anxiety and avoidance of interpersonal situations (Japan)

Practitioners should be familiar with and make use of these advances presented in the DSM-5 (APA, 2013). Along with use of culturally grounded techniques presented in the DSM, the literature points to four alternative or mixed models of assessment with ethnic-minority clients' use of revised tests, assessment of identity and acculturation, use of thematic apperception tests, and qualitative assessments.

FOUR RECOMMENDED ASSESSMENT STRATEGIES FOR MULTICULTURAL PRACTICE

Table 9.1 includes a selected list of measures for the four ethnic groups covered in this chapter, along with information on how to obtain those measures. The measures presented reflect the four recommended alternatives introduced above and discussed below.

Alternative 1: Use of Revised Tests and Newly Devised Ethnic-Specific Tests

Revised tests are instruments that have been developed and validated to tap the emic-based cultural contexts of mental health issues; they include translations of commonly used tests. Examples include the Chinese version of the Quick Inventory of Depressive Symptomatology, Clinician Rated and Self-Report (Yeung et al., 2012) and the Vietnamese adaptation of the Depression Anxiety and Stress Scale (Tran, Tran, & Fisher, 2013). Whenever possible, practitioners should use tests that have been normed on the client's ethnic population in assessments; however, such tests are rare, and their development lags behind revisions of the original test.

In contrast, some researchers question whether the areas of needed assessment are the same for Euro Americans as they are for ethnic-minority groups. For example, racial socialization or the impact of societal

Table 9.1 Selected List of Measures for Four Ethnic Groups and Cross-Cultural Measures for Ethnic Minority Children and Families

Racial/Ethnic Group	Measure	Measure Characteristics	Reliability/Validity	Where to obtain
American Indians/ Alaska Natives	Cultural Involvement and Detachment Anxiety Scale (CIDAQ). Promising measure for examining culturally related anxiety in American Indian and Alaska Natives, particularly in college counseling and behavioral health-care centers.	Scale contains three factors measuring anxiety: (1) social involvement w/Native American and cultural knowledge, (2) economic issues, and (3) social involvement with majority culture.	High levels of item-total reliability, internal consistency, and convergent and divergent validity. Cronbach's alpha .92 for total scale.	Daniel W. McNeil Dept. of Psychology West Virginia University Anxiety, Psychophysiology, and Pain Research Laboratory P.O. Box 6040 Morgantown, WV, 26506-6040 Email: dmmcneil@wvu.edu
	Native American Addictions Severity Index (ASI). Adult version customized for Native Americans. Assesses chemical dependency and behavioral health concerns.	The ASI (developed by S. M. Manson) is a comprehensive survey-type questionnaire that assesses a range of areas that could be affected by a respondent's substance abuse (or legal status, employment, family and social relationships, etc.).	The ASI has been found to be reliable and valid over the past 12 years across various populations. The Native American version is available for both adults and adolescents.	Computerized programs: Accurate Assessments 823 Harney St., Suite 101 Omaha, NE 68102 (402) 341-8880 (800) 324-7966

Table 9.1 Selected List of Measures for Four Ethnic Groups and Cross-Cultural Measures for Ethnic Minority Children and Families—*(continued)*

Racial/Ethnic Group	Measure	Measure Characteristics	Reliability/Validity	Where to obtain
	Tribe-specific Thematic Apperception Type (TAT). Tests developed by Dana (1982) to assess emotional themes, conflicts, and concerns unique to Lakota culture.	Tests use picture story techniques. Assessors and interpreters should be familiar with specific culture, history, philosophy, healing practices, and language of the population.	In the absence of adequate validity research for most standardized instruments with Native American/Alaska Natives, local adaptations of TAT tests can provide valuable emic-based alternatives (Allen, 1998).	Richard H. Dana, Ph.D. Regional Research Institute Portland State University P. O. Box 751 Portland, OR 97207 (503) 725-4040
African Americans	Optimal Extended Self-Esteem Scales (OESES). Instruments for assessing the extended self concepts for African Americans' racial/cultural identity and values based on Afrocentric principles.	Separate scales are developed for children, adolescents, and adults. Items on each scale vary according to developmental level.	Cronbach alpha coefficients were .82 and .76 for the OESES-Adolescent and the Rosenberg Self-Esteem, respectively (n = 95 males and 95 females adolescents).	Seward E. Hamilton Jr. Ph.D. Gore Education Complex-Building–C, #305 Dept. of Psychology Florida A & M University Tallahassee, FL 32307

Table 9.1   Selected List of Measures for Four Ethnic Groups and Cross-Cultural Measures for Ethnic Minority Children and Families—*(continued)*

Racial/Ethnic Group	Measure	Measure Characteristics	Reliability/Validity	Where to obtain
	Index of Psychological Well-Being among African Americans. A 23-item index constructed from 40 items in the National Survey of black Americans interview schedule.	Factors analysis revealed 7 factors: happiness, self-esteem (positive), blame for bad job, self-esteem (negative), economic well-being, role performance, and interpersonal relations.	Reliability coefficients for the scale range from .59 to .70.	Anderson Franklin, Ph.D. Psychology Dept. The City College of New York Convent Ave. @ 138th Street New York, NY 10031 Ajfcc@cunyvn.cuny.edu
	The Perceived Racial Stress and Coping Apperception Test (PRSCAT) (Johnson, 1996). Designed to elicit child and adult conceptualizations of race-related stressors and the racial coping strategies available to cope with those stressors.	The PRSCAT consists of 5 picture cards for which the respondent tells a story and offers an explanation of what he or she would do. Responses are coded from 0 to 4 depending on the intensity of the racial conflict expressed by the respondent.	Interrater reliability coefficients for racial conflict ratings and racial coping strategies were .83 and .75, respectively.	Deborah J. Johnson, Ph.D. Dept. of Child and Family Studies 1430 Linden Drive University of Wisconsin-Madison Madison, WI 53706 (608) 263-4066

Table 9.1   Selected List of Measures for Four Ethnic Groups and Cross-Cultural Measures for Ethnic Minority Children and Families—*(continued)*

Racial/Ethnic Group	Measure	Measure Characteristics	Reliability/Validity	Where to obtain
	Scale for Racial Socialization for Adolescents (SORS-A) (Stevenson, 1994). A 45-item scale designed to assess the degree of acceptance of racial-socialization attitudes and race-related messages of childrearing within African American culture.	The SORS-A has 4 subscales: spiritual and religious coping, extended family caring, cultural pride reinforcement, and racism awareness teaching.	Initially normed with 236 inner-city African American adolescents, the SORS-A has fair reliability with an alpha of .75 for the total scale. Factors analyses suggest racial socialization has 2 dimensions: (a) protective and (b) proactive, regarding adolescents' perceptions of racial socialization.	Dr. Howard C. Stevenson, Jr. University of Pennsylvania Division of Applied Psychology and Human Development 3700 Walnut St. Philadelphia, PA 19104
Hispanic/ Latino Americans	Children's Health Locus of Control. A 20-item measure that has been suggested as appropriate for cross-cultural use with Mexican American youth.	Scale determines the extent to which respondent believes that one has control over the status of one's health, ranging from belief in self-control (Internal), control by someone more powerful (Powerful Other), or uncontrollable factors (Chance).	Two studies by Guinn (1998) using the scale with Mexican American youth reported alpha reliabilities of .76 for Internal, .72 for Powerful Others, and .80 for Chance (Study 1, 1997) and .78 for Internal, .75 for Powerful Others, and .81 for Chance (Study 2, 1998).	Parcel (1978). Center for Health Prevention Research, University of Texas Health Science Center at Houston, 7000 Fannin Street, Houston, TX 77030

Table 9.1   Selected List of Measures for Four Ethnic Groups and Cross-Cultural Measures for Ethnic Minority Children and Families—*(continued)*

Racial/Ethnic Group	Measure	Measure Characteristics	Reliability/Validity	Where to obtain
	Spanish version of Expectations About Counseling Questionnaire (EAC-B). Based on research documenting the relationship between ethnicity and counseling expectations and Hispanics' unmet expectations of counselors and the counseling process.	Questionnaire is composed of 53 items constituting 17 scales grouped into 4 general expectance factors: personal commitment, facilitative conditions, counselor expertise, and nurturance.	All scales correlated above .60, the criterion proposed for translated instruments. Results suggest that the Spanish version of the EAC-B is a reliable and valid translation for students and nonstudents from a variety of Hispanic populations.	Robin A. Buhrke School of Education 312 Merrick University of Miami Coral Gables, FL 33124
	Simpatía Scale (SS). The SS is a 17-item scale developed to measure the concept of simpatía, the Hispanic cultural script that denotes the general tendency to avoid interpersonal conflict.	The concept of *simpatía* is often cited as potentially important for Hispanics in drug treatment.	SS has good construct validity and good internal consistency with alpha of .80 for the overall scale.	Dr. James D. Griffith Institute of Behavioral Research Texas Christian College Fort Worth, TX 76129

Table 9.1 Selected List of Measures for Four Ethnic Groups and Cross-Cultural Measures for Ethnic Minority Children and Families—*(continued)*

Racial/Ethnic Group	Measure	Measure Characteristics	Reliability/Validity	Where to obtain
Asian Americans/ Pacific Islander Americans	Hawaiian Culture Scale–Adolescent Version This scale is used to assess the degree to which adolescents know of, believe in, value, and practice elements of traditional Hawaiian culture, and to delineate the biological (i.e., blood quantum) and sociocultural factors shaping ethnic identification.	The 50-item inventory (7 subscales) measures the source of learning the Hawaiian way of life, how much the maintaining of Hawaiian beliefs is valued, Hawaiian blood quantum, and specific cultural traditions.	Cronbach alpha ranged from .82 to .96 for Hawaiian adolescents and from .76 to .96 for non-Hawaiian adolescents. These coefficients indicate satisfactory internal consistency.	Earl S. Hishinuma Dept. of Psychiatry Native Hawaiian Mental Health Research Development Program 1356 Lusitana St., 4th Floor John A Burns School of Medicine University of Hawaii at Manoa Honolulu, HI 96813 earlhish@aol.com
	Suinn-Lew Asian Self-Identity Acculturation Scale (SL-ASIAS) This scale is used to assess self-identity and level of acculturation among Asian Americans.	Scale has been used in conjunction with MMPI-2 with Asian Americans. Less-acculturated Asian Americans scored in the most disturbed direction on MMPI-2.	Researcher reported Cronbach's alpha for internal consistency of .88 and .91 from two studies. Scale has been widely used in the past 10 years in spite of limited research.	Suinn, Rikard-Figueroa, Lew, & Vigil (1987).

Table 9.1   Selected List of Measures for Four Ethnic Groups and Cross-Cultural Measures for Ethnic Minority Children and Families—*(continued)*

Racial/Ethnic Group	Measure	Measure Characteristics	Reliability/Validity	Where to obtain
Cross-cultural Measures for Ethnic Minority Children and Families	Kaufman Assessment Battery for Children (K-ABC) (Kaufman & Kaufman, 1983). Kaufman Adolescent and Adult Intelligence Test (KAIT) (Kaufman & Kaufman, 1993). This is a culturally sensitive IQ test.	K-ABC is an individually administered assessment battery that measures achievement and intelligence in children. The KAIT is designed to assess cognitive functioning and may be useful when working with culturally diverse persons aged 11–85 (Russo & Lewis, 1999).	Research suggests that the measure is useful for Mexican American assessment and may be useful for general cross-cultural assessment. Scales are currently undergoing revisions and norming with widely diverse populations.	American Guidance Service 4201 Woodland Rd. Circle Pines, MN 55014-1796 800-328-2560
	The Dominic (Valla, Bergeron, Berube, & Gaudet, 1994; Valla, Bergeron, Bidaut-Russell, St. Georges, & Gaudet, 1997) is a cartoon-based questionnaire designed to study the mental health status of children age 6 to 11.	Drawings convey situations based on symptoms of 7 more prevalent diagnoses in the DSM-III-R Axis I (1980 attention deficit hyperactivity disorder, conduct disorder, oppositional defiant disorder, major depressive disorder/dysthymia, separation anxiety disorder, over-anxious disorder, and simple phobia).	The Dominic character was designed to be interpreted as either a boy or a girl. It includes racially appropriate pictures of the characters. Internal consistency for each of the subscales ranged from .62 to .88 (Valla et al., 1994).	Jean-Pierre Valla, Ph.D. Hôpital Rivière-des-Prairies 7070 Boulevard Perras Montreal, Quebec H1E, 1A4 Canada (514) 323-7260, ext. 2281 Fax (514) 323-4163 Jpvalla@sympatico.ca

Table 9.1   Selected List of Measures for Four Ethnic Groups and Cross-Cultural Measures for Ethnic Minority Children and Families—*(continued)*

Racial/Ethnic Group	Measure	Measure Characteristics	Reliability/Validity	Where to obtain
	Family Pressures Scale-Ethnic (FPRES-E) (McCubbin, Thompson, & Elver, 2000). This scale is a 64-item measure designed to be inclusive of pressures related to the life experiences of families of color.	Adapted from the Family Inventory of Life Events and Changes, this scale obtains an index of the severity of culturally sensitive pressure in the family system, especially in Native American families, including families of Hawaiian descent.	The FPRES-E has excellent internal consistency with an alpha of .92. Scale was normed on 174 families of Native Hawaiian ancestry and was found to be the strongest predictor of family distress among this study population.	McCubbin, Thompson, & McCubbin (1996, 227–236) provides instructions for permission to use the instrument.
	Multigroup Ethnic Identity Measure (MEIM) (Phinney, 1992). Designed to measure ethnic identity, particularly among adolescents across multiple ethnic groups.		The MEIM has good internal consistency with alphas above .80 for subscales across a range of ethnic groups. There is evidence of some degree of concurrent validity between the MEIM and the Rosenberg Self-Esteem Inventory. for Minority Students.	Jean S. Phinney, Ph.D. Department of Psychology California State University Los Angeles, CA 90032

oppression on psychological functioning of African American teens is assessed by the Scale for Racial Socialization for Adolescents. Another example of culture-specific constructs for assessment included in table 9.1 is the Simpatía Scale. This was developed to measure the concept of *simpatía*, the Hispanic cultural script that denotes the general tendency to avoid interpersonal conflict.

Alternative 2: Assessment of Cultural and Ethnic Identity, Acculturation, and Acculturative Stress as Moderators of Standardized Tests

In discussing the development of the Hawaiian Culture Scale, Hishinum et al. (2000) note that the first step in discerning the role of ethnicity is to develop valid measures, and the second step is to determine the association of ethnic constructs in indicators of psychological adjustment. There is some evidence that ethnic-identity measures offer some assistance in interpreting problematic standardized instruments. As such, practitioners should assess the client's cultural identity as a moderator variable and administer appropriate measures as part of the assessment interview with the client. Measures used to examine the client's culture self can provide critical information about the client's cultural identity, which may be a precondition for mental, physical, and spiritual well-being (Dana, 2005). For example, Constantine, Alleyne, Wallace, and Franklin-Jackson (2006) found that African American adolescent girls who had stronger Afrocentric cultural orientation were likely to have higher levels of both self-esteem and perceived social support satisfaction.

Acculturation (low to high) has been studied extensively among ethnic-minority populations and has mental health implications. For example, acculturation has been linked to anxiety responding in American Indian and Alaska Natives; the Native American Cultural Involvement and Detachment Anxiety Questionnaire (CIDAQ) was developed by McNeil, Porter, Zvolensky, Chaney, and Kee (2000) to assess acculturation anxiety in American Indian and Alaska Natives. Moreover, a growing body of assessment research focuses on the inclusion of acculturative stress and racism-based trauma as part of a holistic assessment procedure with ethnic-minority clients, given their exposure to racism and discrimination (Bryant-Davis & Ocampo, 2005). An example is the Social, Attitudinal, Familial, and Environmental Acculturative Stress Scale (Padilla, Wagatsuma, & Lindholm, 1985). In general, practitioners should understand the relationship among identity, acculturation, acculturative stress, discrimination, and mental health among racial/ethnic minorities. For Latina girls, the relationship between acculturation and depressive symptoms can be explained by the level of perceived discrimination (Lorenzo-Blanco, Unger, Ritt-Olson, Soto, & Baezconde-Garbanati, 2011); lower self-esteem and increased depressive symptoms have been linked to Latina adolescents who reported experiencing more discrimination (Umaña-Taylor & Updegraff, 2013).

For more information on some cultural-specific rapid assessment instruments in the area of cultural identity, acculturation and acculturative stress, Corcoran and Fischer's (2013) volumes of *Measures for Clinical Practice and Research: A Sourcebook* contain new scales and material, including the Acculturation Rating Scale for Mexican Americans–II, the Scale of Racial Socialization–Adolescent Version, the Orthogonal Cultural Identification Scale, and the Multigroup Ethnic Identity Scale.

Alternative 3: Use of Thematic Apperception-Type Tests

Increasingly, debates exists about whether projective measures are inherently based on Eurocentric assumptions and should thus be summarily dismissed with ethnic-minority clients, or whether there is some value in emic-based adaptations (Dana, 2000). Several picture story tests have been developed over the years targeting various populations. The Tell-Me-a-Story (TEMAS) test is the only comprehensive assessment instrument constructed for ethnic minority and nonminority children and adolescents with established reliable and valid scoring systems for the emic-based picture story techniques with Hispanic, African American, Asian American, and Euro American children (Constantino, Dana, & Malgady, 2007).

Also, Murphy et al. (2000) report that the pictorial approach (using the Dominic mental health assessment measure; Valla et al., 1994) may be more effective than a written version in assessing anxiety and depression in children. The Dominic is a cartoon-based questionnaire designed to study the mental health status of children aged six to eleven. The drawings convey situations based on symptoms of the seven prevalent diagnoses in the DSM axis I: attention deficit/hyperactivity disorder (ADHD), conduct disorder (CD), oppositional defiant disorder (ODD), major depressive disorder/dysthymia (MDD), separation anxiety disorder (SAD), overanxious disorder (OAD), and simple phobia (SPh). The Dominic/Dominique character was designed to be interpreted as either a boy or a girl and also includes racially appropriate pictures of the characters.

Alternative 4: Qualitative Assessment and Triangulated Assessment Approaches

Paniagua (2005) suggests that the least-biased assessment approaches involve self-monitoring (e.g., client's own records of thoughts, behaviors, feelings) and self-report individualized rating scales, which can accurately capture a client's interpretations and beliefs about behavior. Culture-specific measures, such as life histories and interviews, can be used to elicit assessment information.

In addition, whenever possible the practitioner should use more than one assessment strategy. Often this requires combining qualitative and quantitative assessment techniques or using multiple standardized instruments. For example, practitioners working with a Native population at the Eagle Lodge Behavioral Health Treatment Center use extensive psychosocial qualitative assessment interviews in conjunction with the Traumatic Symptoms Inventory Index.

Combining measures can also be useful when assessing mental health in ethnic-minority groups. Multiple screenings were used to determine that the Center for Epidemiologic Studies—Depression scale, a ten-item scale that takes about two minutes to administer, and is a useful tool with Puerto Rican patients to identify those in need of in-depth mental health evaluation in a primary care setting. To assess convergent validity, Robison, Gruman, Gaztambide, and Blank (2002) compared multiple versions of four depression screening tools (CES-D, Geriatric Depression Scale, Yale one-question screen, and Primary Care Evaluation of Mental Disorders two-question screen) to the Composite International Diagnostic Interview (CIDI), the World Health Organization's diagnostic interview, which has been validated in adult Latino populations. The study involved 303 Puerto Rican primary care patients age fifty and older who completed all screens and the CIDI in a face-to-face interview. Between 34 and 61 percent of patients screened positive for depression, depending on the measure, with 12 percent meeting DSM criteria for major depression.

In addition to the recommended alternatives, social work practitioners are encouraged to use Jordan and Franklin's Integrative Skills Assessment Protocol, a detailed guide for conducting a comprehensive assessment framework (see chapter 1). This protocol focuses on assessing the client in an environmental context and uses an integrative assessment approach that borrows from several assessment models. General guidelines from this protocol are used in presenting the following case study and in discussing how the assessment guided the intervention.

CASE STUDY JANET: MOVING FROM ASSESSMENT TO INTERVENTION

Client Identifying Information. Janet is a nineteen-year-old African American female attending a small community college in a large, predominantly Euro American area about an hour away from her hometown community, an inner-city urban environment.

Family and Social History. Janet is from a lower-middle-class, urban background. Janet's parents divorced when she was thirteen, and she and her brother lived with her mother but had regular contact with their father. Janet's parents argued often, with a major conflict centering around the father's bouts with unemployment as a security guard. Janet's mother is a nurse. After the divorce, Janet's brother, Derek, began having problems at home and at school. He became defiant with his mother, started skipping school, and has spent some time in jail for possession of marijuana. Over the past year, Janet has drifted away from her family. Janet says she was extremely frustrated with "not being able to get through" to her brother. Janet's parents are also very concerned about Derek, but, as Janet put it, "They are caught up in their own problems" from the divorce. For the past seven months Janet has worked part-time at a popular chain restaurant, which is where she met Sam, her boyfriend whom she has been dating for five months. Sam is an African American student who was born and raised in an upper-middle-class, predominantly Euro American environment. Sam is supportive but says he feels that Janet's recent problems with her schoolwork will pass and that she is "trying too hard to prove herself" in her new college environment. Janet has not made many friends at her college. At first she believed that she was going to be fine and fit in, but once she started to develop her social life, Janet became distressed in the predominantly Euro American university environment.

Nature of Presenting Problem. Although Janet had a successful first semester in the community college, during the beginning of her second semester she began to have difficulty passing her exams and says she feels that she is "falling apart." Janet has experienced increased anxiety about school and her surroundings. She describes herself as "just moving on" with her life, which she defines as getting an education and getting away from her inner-city upbringing.

Racial and Ethnic Considerations. Janet comes from an inner-city neighborhood, but she has not been part of that community for nearly a year. Janet came from a predominantly African American community and has not had very much exposure to a large, predominantly Euro American metropolitan school or community. Considering her ethnicity and non-Eurocentric background, it is necessary to assess Janet's racial/ethnic identity and cultural orientation.

Measurement

As recommended in this chapter, the first step in multicultural assessment strategy is to access the cultural orientation of clients and their level of acculturation by identifying client's attitudes.

Measure: Multigroup Ethnic Identity Measure. The Multigroup Ethnic Identity Measure (MEIM) (Phinney, 1992) is a fourteen-item ethnic identity scale that measures ethnic attitudes, behaviors, practices, and belongingness, particularly among adolescents across multiple ethnic groups. It is a public domain questionnaire, meaning that no permission is needed to use it.

The scale has also differentiated two unique types of bicultural adolescents (i.e., blended and alternating) and a third group of predominantly African American adolescents who were not bicultural (i.e., separated) and had a strong sense of African American identity (Phinney & Devich-Navarro, 1997). Janet's score indicated she is strongly centered in her ethnic group identity and has a more separated than bicultural identity.

Next, two standardized clinical scales were used to assess Janet's anxiety level and her degree of psychological splitting.

Measure: Clinical Anxiety Scale (Thyer, 1992). This twenty-five-item scale measures the amount, degree, or severity of clinical anxiety. Sample scale items are "I feel afraid without good reason" and "I feel generally anxious." Janet scored 40, which exceeds the clinical cutoff score of 30, thus indicating that that she is experiencing anxiety in the clinical range.

Measure: Splitting Scale (Gerson, 1984). This fourteen-item scale assesses symptoms of splitting, the psychological defense mechanism used to keep ambivalence at bay. This scale has been normed on female and male psychology students, as well as on a sample from an urban health clinic; it has moderate to good reliability and validity. Sample scale items are, "When I'm with someone really terrific, I feel dumb" and "I often feel I can't put the different parts of my personality together so that there is one 'me.'" Janet scored 60, reflecting moderately high characterological use of splitting.

Next, an ethnic specific test was employed to assess Janet's behavior in the context of her cultural orientation.

Measure: Social, Attitudinal, Familial, and Environmental Acculturative Stress Scale (Padilla et al., 1985). This is a twenty-four-item scale that assesses acculturative stress in social, attitudinal, and familial and environmental contexts, including perceived discrimination, perceived barriers to adaptation, negative reactions of family members to one's desire to adapt, feelings of isolation, and difficulties in communication. Participants rate each item on a scale of 1 (not stressful) to 5 (extremely stressful). Reasonable reliability of the scale has been established with a diverse sample, including African American college students on both predominantly Euro American and historically African American college campuses (Joiner & Walker, 2002). Janet scored well above the mean score for samples on which the scale was normed.

How the Assessment Guided the Intervention Plans

The intervention selected for Janet should address each of the concerns identified in the assessment, with specific attention to the presence of acculturative stress, anxiety, and splitting. Given Janet's ethnic consider-ations and the timing of the onset of her anxiety, it appears that accultur-ative stress plays a substantial role in her presenting problem. Culture-based assessments provide valuable information not always evident in standardized measures. For example, studies on acculturative stress show that recent immigrants have stronger acculturative stress than the children and grandchildren of immigrants, and African Americans on a predominantly Euro American campus have higher acculturative stress than those in a predominantly African American college setting (Joiner & Walker, 2002). Treatment would include interventions to reduce accultur-ative stress. Practitioners should be knowledgeable about how risks to the psychosocial well-being of people of color are often rooted in collec-tive and historical disenfranchisement and contemporary challenges associated with loss of traditional culture and identity. Strong family and community bonds, wisdom and guidance of elders, and positive cultural practices, traditions, and strong ethnic identity are among the recognized strengths and buffers that should be incorporated into culturally congru-ent interventions for youths and adolescents of color. For example, infu-sion of Afrocentric values has been associated with decreased depression, lowered anxiety, and increased competitiveness in academic achievement (Constantine, Alleyne, & Wallace, 2006). Reduction in acculturative stress should reduce clinical anxiety and characterological splitting and allow Janet to concentrate on her schooling and career plans.

SUMMARY

Evidence-based, culturally sensitive assessment practices are still in development. In ensuring a do-no-harm assessment approach, social work practitioners are encouraged to probe, question, and make changes in any cases where there is a possibility that standardized assessment techniques may not be culturally appropriate for a client assessment. Once an individual is labeled with an invalid assessment or inaccurate pathological diagnosis, intervention and evaluation of the client's progress are no longer valid. This chapter has discussed in detail several alternative assessment approaches for use in multicultural assessment and encouraged practitioners to adopt those into practice.

STUDY QUESTIONS

1. How has the ethnocentrism of the U.S. culture affected assessment procedures and measurement instruments for nonmajority (i.e., ethnic-minority) clients?

2. The special concerns about assessing ethnic minority clients center around three main issues. List and define those three issues.

3. What are some of the criticisms about the DSM with respect to assessing ethnic minority clients? What are some of the updates found in the DSM-5 related to ethnicity and culture?

4. What are the four recommended alternative or mixed models for multicultural assessment? How can practitioners combine these methods with the DSM-5 updates? List alternative models applied in the case study?

WEB SITES

Assessments.com, www.assessments.com/default.asp
Multicultural Family Institute, www.multiculturalfamily.org
National Center for Cultural Competence, http://nccc.georgetown.edu/
    resources/assessments.html

REFERENCES

Allen, J. (1998). Personality assessment with American Indian and Alaska Natives: Instrument considerations and service delivery style. *Journal of Personality Assessment, 70,* 17–42.

American Psychiatric Association (APA). (1980). *Diagnostic and statistical manual of mental disorders* (3rd ed.; DSM-III). Washington, DC: Author.

American Psychiatric Association (APA). (2000). *Diagnostic and statistical manual of mental disorders* (4th ed.; DSM-IV). Washington, DC: Author.

American Psychiatric Association (APA). (2013). *Diagnostic and statistical manual of mental disorders* (5th ed.; DSM-5). Washington, DC: Author.

Aponte, J. F., & Crouch, R. T. (2000). The changing ethnic profile of the United States. In J. F. Aponte, R. Y. Rivers, & J. Wohl (2nd ed.), *Psychological interventions and cultural diversity* (pp. 1–17). Boston: Allyn and Bacon.

Brave Heart, M. Y. H. (2001). Clinical social work assessment with Native clients. In R. Fong & S. Furuto (Eds.), *Culturally competent practice: Skills, interventions, and evaluations* (pp. 163–195). Boston: Allyn and Bacon.

Bryant-Davis, T., & Ocampo, C. (2005). Racist incident-based trauma. *Counseling Psychologist, 33,* 479–500.

Chow, J. C. (2001). Assessment of Asian American/Pacific Islander organizations and communities. In R. Fong & S. Furuto (Eds.), *Culturally competent practice: Skills, interventions, and evaluations* (pp. 211–224). Boston: Allyn and Bacon.

Constantine, M. G., Alleyne, V. L., Wallace, B. C., & Franklin-Jackson, D. C. (2006). Africentric cultural values: Their relation to positive mental health in African American adolescent girls. *Journal of Black Psychology, 32*(2), 141–154.

Constantino, G., Dana, R. H., & Malgady, R. G. (2007). *TEMAS (Tell-Me-a-Story) assessment in multicultural societies.* Mahwah, NJ: Erlbaum.

Corcoran, K., & Fischer, J. (2013). *Measures for clinical practice and research: A sourcebook:* Vol. 1. *Couples, families, and children.* New York: Oxford University Press.

Dana, R. H. (1982). *Picture-story cards for Sioux/Plains Indians.* Fayetteville: University of Arkansas.

Dana, R. (Ed.). (2000). *Handbook of cross-cultural and multicultural personality assessment.* Mahwah, NJ: Erlbaum.

Dana, R. H. (2005). *Multicultural assessment principles, applications, and examples.* Mahwah, NJ: Erlbaum.

Dhooper, S. S., & Moore, S. E. (2001). *Social work practice with culturally diverse people.* Thousand Oaks, CA: Sage.

Draguns, J. G. (2002). Universal and cultural aspects of counseling and psychotherapy. In P. B. Pedersen, J. G. Draguns, W. L. Lonner, & J. E. Trimble (Eds.), *Counseling across cultures* (pp. 29–50). Thousand Oaks, CA: Sage.

Feagin, J. R., & Feagin, C. B. (2003). *Racial and ethnic relations* (7th ed.). Upper Saddle River, NJ: Prentice Hall.

Frances, A., First, M. B., Pincus, H. A., Kutchins, H., & Kirk, S. A. (2005). Issue 1: Is the DSM-IV a useful classification system? *Taking sides: Clashing views on controversial issues in abnormal psychology* (3rd. ed., pp. 2–13). New York: McGraw-Hill.

Gerson, M. J. (1984). Splitting: The development of a measure. *Journal of Clinical Psychology, 40,* 157–162.

Gilbert, D. J., Harvey, A. R., & Belgrave, F. Z. (2009). Advancing the Africentric paradigm shift discourse: Evidence-based Africentric interventions in social work practice with African Americans. *Social Work, 54*(3), 243–252.

Grills, C. (2002). African-centered psychology: Basic principles. In T. A Parham (Ed.), *Counseling persons of African descent* (pp. 10–24). Thousand Oaks, CA: Sage.

Guinn, C. I., & Montoya, R. J. (1998). Natural language processing in virtual reality. *Modern Simulation & Training, 6,* 44–45.

Hall, C. I. J. (1997). Cultural malpractice: The growing obsolescence of psychology with the changing U.S. population. *American Psychologist, 52,* 642–651.

Hishinuma, E. S., Andrade, N. N., Johnson, R. C., McArdle, J. J., Miyamoto, R. H., Nahulu, L., . . . Yates, A. (2000). Psychometric properties of the Hawaiian Culture Scale-Adolescent Version. *Psychological Assessment, 12,* 140–157.

Johnson, D. J. (1996). The perceived racial stress and coping apperception test. In R. L. Jones (Ed.), *Handbook of tests and measurements for Black populations* (pp. 231–244). Hampton, VA: Cobb and Henry.

Joiner, T. E., & Walker, R. L. (2002). Construct validity of a measure of acculturative stress in African Americans. *Psychological Assessment, 14*(94), 462–466.

Kaufman, A. S., & Kaufman, N. L. (1983). Kaufman Assessment Battery for Children. Circle Pines, MN: American Guidance Service.

Kaufman, A. S., & Kaufman, N. L. (1993). *Kaufman Adolescent and Adult Intelligence Test (KAIT)*. Circle Pines, MN: American Guidance Service.

Lorenzo-Blanco, E. I., Unger, J. B., Ritt-Olson, A., Soto, D., & Baezconde-Garbanati, L. (2011). Acculturation, gender, depression, and cigarette smoking among U.S. Hispanic youth: The mediating role of perceived discrimination. *Journal of Youth and Adolescence, 40*(11), 1519–1533.

Lum, D. (2004). *Social work practice and people of color: A process-stage approach* (5th ed.). Belmont, CA: Brooks/Cole.

McCubbin, H. I., Thompson, A. I., & McCubbin, M. A. (1996). *Family assessment: Resiliency, coping, and adaptation: Inventories for research and practice*. Madison: University of Wisconsin.

McNeil, D. W., Porter, C. A., Zvolensky, M. J., Chaney, J. M., & Kee, M. (2000). Assessment of culturally related anxiety in American Indian and Alaska Natives. *Behavior Therapy, 31*, 301–325.

Mezzich, J. E., Kirmayer, L. J., Kleinman, A., Fabrega, H., Parron, D. L., Good, B. J., . . . Manson, S. M. (2008). The place of culture in DSM-IV. In J. E. Mezzich & G. Caracci (Eds.), *Cultural formulation: A reader for psychiatric diagnosis* (pp. 167–181). Lanham, MD, US: Jason Aronson.

Murphy, D. A., Cantwell, C., Jordan, D. D., Lee, M., Cooley-Quille, M. R., & Lahey, B. B. (2000). Test-retest reliability of Dominic anxiety and depression items among young children. *Journal of Psychopathology and Behavioral Assessment, 22*, 257–270.

National Council of La Raza (2010). *America's future: Latino child well-being in numbers and trends*. Washington, DC: Author.

Office of Minority Health and Health Disparities. (2008). *Eliminate disparities in mental health*. Retrieved from http://www.cdc.gov/omhd/

Padilla, A. M., Wagatsuma, Y., & Lindholm, K. J. (1985). Acculturation and personality as predictors of stress in Japanese and Japanese-Americans. *Journal of Social Psychology, 125*(3), 295–305.

Paniagua, F. A. (2005). *Assessing and treating culturally diverse clients: A practical guide* (3rd ed.). Thousand Oaks, CA: Sage.

Parcel, G., & Meyer, M. (1978). Development of an instrument to measure children's health locus of control. *Health Education Monographs, 6*, 149–159.

Pedersen, P. B., & Ivey, A. (1993). *Culture-centered counseling and interviewing skills: A practical guide*. Westport, CT: Praeger.

Phinney, J. S. (1992). The multigroup ethnic identity measure: A new scale for use with diverse groups. *Journal of Adolescent Research, 7*, 156–176.

Phinney, J. S., & Devich-Navarro, M. (1997). Variations in bicultural identification among African American and Mexican American adolescents. *Journal of Research on Adolescence, 7*, 3–32.

Robison, J., Gruman, C., Gaztambide, S., & Blank, K. (2002). Screening for depression in middle-aged and older Puerto Rican primary care patients. *Journals of Gerontology, 57A*, M308–M314.

Russell, C. (2006). *Racial and ethnic diversity: Asians, Blacks, Hispanics, Native Americans, and Whites* (5th ed.). Ithaca, NY: New Strategist.

Russo, S., & Lewis, J. (1999). The cross-cultural applications of the KAIT: Case studies with three differentially acculturated women. *Cultural Diversity and Ethnic Minority Psychology, 5*(1), 76–85.

Sisley, E. J., Hutton, J. M., Louise Goodbody, C., & Brown, J. S. L. (2011). An interpretative phenomenological analysis of African Caribbean women's experiences and management of emotional distress. *Health & Social Care in the Community, 19*(4), 392–402.

Smedley, B. D., Stith, A. Y., & Nelson, A. R. (Eds.). (2003). *Unequal treatment: Confronting racial and ethnic disparities in healthcare.* Washington, DC: National Academic Press.

Snowden, L. R. (2003). Bias in mental health assessment and intervention: Theory and evidence. *American Journal of Public Health, 93,* 239–243.

Stevenson, H. (1994). Validation of the scale of racial socialization for African American adolescents: Steps toward multidimensionality. *Journal of Black Psychology, 20,* 445–468.

Suicide Prevention Resource Center (SPRC). (n.d.). *Suicide among Asian Americans/ Pacific Islanders.* Retrieved from http://www.sprc.org/sites/sprc.org/files/ library/asian.pi.facts.pdf

Suinn, R. M., Rikard-Figueroa, K., Lew, S., & Vigil, P. (1987) The Suinn-Lew Self-Identity Acculturation Scale: Concurrent and factorial validation. *Educational and Psychological Measurement, 52,* 1041–1046.

Tervalon, M., & Murray-García, J. (1998). Cultural humility versus cultural competence: A critical distinction in defining physician training outcomes in multicultural education. *Journal of Health Care for the Poor and Underserved, 9*(2), 117–125.

Thyer, B. A. (1992). Clinical Anxiety Scale (CAS). In W. W. Hudson (Ed.), *The Walmyr Assessment Scale scoring manual.* Temple, AZ: Walmyr.

Tran, T. D., Tran, T., & Fisher, J. (2013). Validation of the Depression Anxiety Stress Scales (DASS) 21 as a screening instrument for depression and anxiety in a rural community-based cohort of northern Vietnamese women. *BioMed Central Psychiatry, 13.*

U.S. Census Bureau. (2014). 2014 National population projections: Summary tables; Table 11, percent distribution of the projected population by Hispanic origin and race for the United States, 2015 to 2060. Retrieved from http://www.census .gov/population/projections/data/national/2014/summarytables.html

U.S. Department of Health and Human Services, Office of the Surgeon General (DHHS). (2008). *Surgeon General's Report: Fact sheet for Latinos/Hispanic Americans.* Retrieved from http://mentalhealth.samhsa.gov/cre/fact3/asp

Umaña-Taylor, A. J., Zeiders, K. H., & Updegraff, K. A. (2013). Family ethnic socialization and ethnic identity: A family-driven, youth-driven, or reciprocal process? *Journal of Family Psychology, 27*(1), 137–146.

Valla, J. P., Bergeron, L., Berube, H., & Gaudet, N. (1994). A structured pictorial questionnaire to assess DSM-III-R based diagnoses in children (6–11): Development, validity and reliability. *Journal of Child Psychology, 22,* 404–423.

Valla, J., Bergeron, L., Bidaut-Russell, M., St. Georges, M. & Gaudet, N. (1997). Reliability of the Dominic-R: A young child mental health questionnaire combing visual and auditory stimuli. *Journal of Child Psychology and Psychiatry and Allied Disciplines, 38*(6), 717–724.

Weaver, H. (2008). Native Americans. In G. C. Gamst, A. Der-Karabetian, & R. Dana (Eds.), *Readings in multicultural practice* (pp. 217–239). Thousand Oaks, CA: Sage.

Yeung, A., Feldman, G., Pedrelli, P., Hails, K., Fava, M., Reyes, T., & Mundt, J. C. (2012). The Quick Inventory of Depressive Symptomatology, Clinician Rated and Self-Report: A psychometric assessment in Chinese Americans with major depressive disorder. *Journal of Nervous and Mental Disease, 200*(8), 712–715.

PART IV

Assessing Outcomes

The last section of the book covers an important area of assessment that was briefly discussed in chapter 1, and that is the importance of monitoring and evaluating the outcomes of interventions being delivered to clients. Chapter 10, "Linking Assessment to Outcome Evaluation: Using Single-System and Group Research Designs," emphasizes the importance of clinical social workers systematically appraising the outcomes of their own practice and integrates the long-standing tradition of practice evaluation in social work with the newer emphasis on evidence-based practice (EBP) that was also discussed in previous chapters. Specifically, this chapter provides more-detailed information on how to use measures and research designs to determine if clients are improving and illustrates specific methods demonstrating how to move from the initial assessment phases to interventions. The chapter further provides several resources for identifying interventions that are grounded in research evidence.

CHAPTER 10

Linking Assessment to Outcome Evaluation: Using Single-System and Group Research Designs

Bruce A. Thyer and Laura L. Myers

INTRODUCTION

The social work profession has long paid attention to the importance of conducting evaluations on the outcomes of clinical services; this ongoing evaluation is an integral part of empirical, clinical assessment. For example, more than ninety years ago one of the founders of social casework, Mary Richmond (1917/1935), claimed, "Special efforts should be made to ascertain whether abnormal manifestations are increasing or decreasing in number and intensity, as this often has a practical bearing on the management of the case" (p. 435). Individual clinical social workers are concerned with evaluating the outcomes of their own practice with clients, not only to help build on the evidence-based foundations of social work knowledge but also to use feedback in continuing work with clients, small groups, couples, or families. This is why, for example, the Code of Ethics of the National Association of Social Workers (NASW) mandates that "social workers should monitor and evaluate policies, the implementation of programs, and practice interventions. Social workers should promote and facilitate evaluation and research to contribute to the development of knowledge. Social workers should . . . fully use evaluation and research evidence in their professional practice" (NASW, 1999, section 5.02).

It is a particular strength of the clinical social work profession, which is the largest provider of mental health services in the United States, that the bulk of practitioners are engaged in agency-based practice in public or not-for-profit private agencies. Thus, we are ideally positioned to collaborate with other disciplines in the design and conduct of effectiveness research. According to Mullen (1995), "Social work has no more important use of research methods than assessment of the consequences of practice and policy choices. . . . Small scale, agency-based studies are worthwhile if they succeed in placing interest in effectiveness at the center of agency practice and when they create a critical alliance between practitioners and researchers" (pp. 282–283). Katherine Ell (1996), past executive director of the Institute for the Advancement of Social Work and Research, similarly pointed out, "Studies are needed on the effectiveness of psychosocial intervention, including interventions previously tested under ideal controlled conditions, in real-world health care systems" (p. 589). And as early as 1965, the late Harold Lewis commented on the importance of agency-based research being conducted by social workers: "Some would reject agency-based research as inconsequential because it is directed to immediate practice ends rather than on development of theory. Others deny the value of agency-based research in helping clarify and add to significant problems encountered in day-to-day practice. Both represent attitudes that can, and often do, prove the costliness of all causes of 'waste' in the utilization of the efforts of the research worker" (p. 24).

Evaluation of the outcomes of clinical social work generally makes use of two major forms of inquiry: (a) single-system designs and (b) group research designs. Both rely on certain fundamental prerequisites. First, the clinical social worker must have available a practical, reliable, inexpensive, and valid outcome measure for use in evaluating results. Second, it must be possible for the social worker to administer the outcome measure with clients on at least two, and ideally more, occasions. If social workers can accomplish the foregoing, with some modest efforts, they are well on their way to designing empirical evaluations of the results of clinical social work practice. This may include practice conducted on a variety of levels, such as one-to-one therapy, group work, marital or family counseling, or the treatment of couples. In principle and in fact, these methods also can be used in the design and conduct of social work outcome studies of organizational, community, and policy practice as well, but such endeavors are outside the scope of the present chapter.

We now review the basic principles of the design and conduct of single-system designs, as used in the evaluation of clinical social work. We then explain group research designs for the same purpose.

THE DESIGN AND CONDUCT OF SINGLE-SYSTEM DESIGNS

Other chapters in this text have reviewed the factors involved in selecting reliable and valid quantitative and qualitative outcome measures for use in clinical assessment. The distinction between assessment and screening measures that are suitable for arriving at, perhaps, a formal diagnosis of a mental disorder or other baseline or pretreatment assessment of client status or functioning has also been made. Throughout the text, readers have been encouraged to use measures that are sensitive to the types of important changes in client functioning that may occur during clinical social work. Please note that the application of the methods of single-system designs (SSDs) may be undertaken in the context of virtually any model of social work assessment and treatment.

In the context of SSDs, clinical social workers attempt to empirically measure client functioning repeatedly over time. This can be done before, during, and/or after intervention. Measures taken before formal treatment begins are the baseline of client functioning. How many measures are enough to constitute a credible baseline? There is no simple answer to this. One is better than none, two are better than one, at least three are necessary to ascertain a real trend in the data (because any two data points can be linked to form a straight line), four are better than three, and so forth. Ideally, baseline data, when graphed, should appear relatively stable to you and stable means that one would answer no to the questions, "Are the data clearly increasing?" and "Are the data clearly decreasing?" This is a rather conservative test because fairly unambiguous trends in the data are required for visual detection.

Data can also be gathered during the course of actual clinical social work intervention (in the treatment phase), or after treatment has been discontinued (in the follow-up phase). The experimental logic behind SSDs is relatively simple: The baseline data phase is an operational manifestation of the hoary (but most certainly valid) social work precept, "Begin where the client is at." If you carefully select your outcome measure to be reliable and valid, you may be able to augment your clinical judgment that the client is getting worse, getting better, or staying the same during the assessment process. You may, therefore, be able to go to your supervisor or managed-care utilization reviewer, and, in addition to your personal and professional powers of persuasion, display a graph justifying the need for intervention.

Next, continue the process of assessment/measurement during treatment using the same methods and measures you employed during the baseline. If you get immediate and dramatic improvements, this too is good and is consistent with the hypothesis that your intervention caused the improvements. Note the careful wording here: "Consistent with the hypothesis that treatment caused the improvements." This is a more cautious and conservative interpretation than "My services caused the client to improve." In most circumstances, your clinical assessment of outcomes may justify the former conclusion, but it is a very rare practice situation indeed that enables you to embrace the latter. We use some examples of the use of SSDs to evaluate the outcome of clinical social work to illustrate the scope and flexibility of these evaluation methods.

The A-B Design

The A-B design is among the simplest forms of SSD and involves the social worker taking a baseline measure of client functioning before and during intervention. One master of social work (MSW), Barker, used this approach in her practicum setting at a vocational rehabilitation program for persons with disabilities. A client, "John," was a twenty-three-year-old African American man with moderate mental retardation and a seizure disorder. While in the program, John displayed numerous inappropriate behaviors such as taunting peers, throwing objects, threatening violence, demonstrating physical aggression against staff and peers, and making inappropriate sexual advances. The severity and frequency of John's inappropriate behavior were placing him in danger of imminent discharge from the vocational rehabilitation program.

Barker developed a way to reliably observe and count John's inappropriate behavior; she did this for five consecutive workdays. She then implemented a simple reward program wherein John could earn reinforcers (augmented opportunities for socialization) based on appropriate behavior. She used the plan over the following seven days, and it seemed to result in a considerable reduction in John's inappropriate behavior (see figure 10.1). The data in figure 10.1 suggest but do not prove that the reward program Barker developed caused the improvements in John's behavior—there are too many other explanations that could account for the changes. However, the data certainly suggest, and at the very least reveal, that the plan did not seem to result in any exacerbation of inappropriate behavior. The agency staff were very impressed with the appar-

Figure 10.1   Daily Number of Aggressive Behaviors Displayed by John

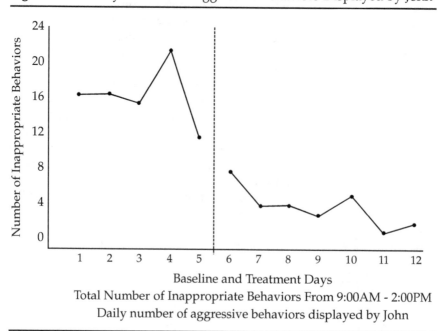

Baseline and Treatment Days
Total Number of Inappropriate Behaviors From 9:00AM - 2:00PM
Daily number of aggressive behaviors displayed by John

ent results of the student's program, which, it should be noted, focused on strengthening positive behaviors via rewards and made no use of punishment. Barker and Thyer (2000) provide addition details about this case.

The A-B design, like all SSDs, is a theory-free approach (in that it can be applied to evaluate the outcomes of practice using diverse interventive models) that is relatively simple, and is widely used.

The A-B-A Design

The A-B-A design involves the continued collection of data after the discontinuation of the social work intervention. Another MSW student used this approach at a senior citizens' center that served a hot meal at lunchtime every day. In Florida in the late 1980s, there was no law requiring safety-belt use among automobile drivers, and the student wanted to see whether she could get senior citizens to use their safety belts more frequently. She developed a reliable method of using independent observers stationed outside the senior citizens' center parking lot to record the over-the-shoulder use of safety belts by exiting drivers. This was baselined for seven consecutive days (the first A phase). The intervention consisted of having an MSW student stand at the exit to the parking lot after lunch and display to the departing elderly drivers a printed sign reading "Please Buckle Up—I Care" on one side and "Thanks for Buckling Up!" on the other side. The observer displayed the first side to unbuckled exiting drivers, and flipped the sign over if the observer saw them buckling up. The second side was displayed if the driver was already buckled as he or she left. Independent observers collected data on safety-belt use during the two-week implementation of the intervention (the B phase). Use of the sign was then halted, but data continued to be collected for another six consecutive days (the second A phase). (See figure 10.2.)

Figure 10.2 depicts the data from this A-B-A study (see also Thyer, Thyer, & Massa, 1991). The baseline data showed that, on average, about 42 percent of exiting drivers were using their safety belts. This increased to about 60 percent during the intervention phase and dropped to about 48 percent during the second A phase. Data from the first A phase are fairly stable, and the magnitude of the change between the first A phase and the B phase suggests that a real change occurred—certainly an 18 percent increase in safety-belt use is a meaningful one. The immediate decline in belt use after the intervention favors the hypothesis that the display of the sign actually caused more-frequent safety-belt use. Furthermore, because there are two changes in the outcome measure corresponding to the introduction and removal of the intervention, the A-B-A design can be a methodologically stronger SSD than the A-B design alone, which allows for only one such possible shift in the data. Therein is the experimental logic behind the stronger SSDs—that is, those that may permit causal inferences.

Figure 10.2   Daily Percentages of Observed Safety Belt Use

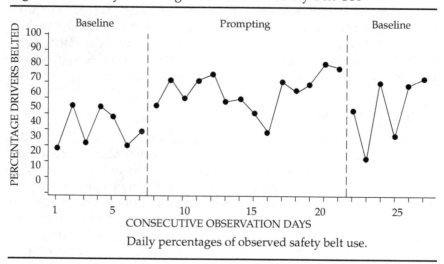

Daily percentages of observed safety belt use.

SOURCE: Reproduced from Thyer, Thyer, and Massa (1991, p. 128) with permission.

Faced with an A-B design like the one described earlier, the skeptic could claim that something else may have happened at the same time treatment was implemented and that the observed changes were due to that other factor, not to the introduction of social work intervention. Indeed, the skeptic is correct to raise this reasonable caveat. However, with the results of the A-B-A design used to evaluate safety belt use, the skeptic would have to argue for two successive, coincidental changes—one that happened to occur when treatment began and the second that happened to occur when treatment was halted! Here one's skepticism must weaken. Perhaps, just perhaps, social work intervention really did cause the observed changes. What seems more plausible? Either there is a real functional relationship between social work and outcomes, or there is no such relationship and it is merely a coincidence. Of course, such a judgment needs to take into account the nature of the client problem or situation, its duration and severity, and the quality and magnitude of any observed changes. Nevertheless, you can appreciate the logic at work. You will appreciate it even more in the next design.

The A-B-A-B Design

By now you have figured out where this is going. The A-B-A-B design involves the collection of reliable and valid data over a first baseline phase, then during an initial treatment phase, then over a second baseline phase during which treatment is halted, and then during a second treatment phase when treatment is reinstated. A clear example of this type of design was used at an elementary school to evaluate a simple intervention designed to reduce school violence (Murphy, Hutchison, & Bailey, 1983). Before the school opened at 8:45 A.M., arriving children went to a playground for free play. One to three teachers' aides monitored the playground, and there were more than 220 children at play. Playground violence was common—interpersonal physical aggression, property abuse, and so forth. A reliable and valid way to measure violent acts was developed, and baseline assessments were gathered for twelve mornings (first A phase). The first intervention period involved the introduction of organized games that the teachers' aides mediated and had a brief timeout contingency for particularly dangerous behaviors; this was implemented for seven days (first B phase). Four days of baseline conditions (second A phase) followed, and then six days of the same intervention (second B phase; see figure 10.3). The average number of violent acts observed during the first A phase was 212; during the first B phase, 91; during the second A phase, 191; and during the second B phase, 97. The clarity of the data argue strongly in favor of the hypothesis that introducing structured

Figure 10.3   Frequency of Incidents Recorded during the Twenty-Minute Morning Observation Periods in the Play Group

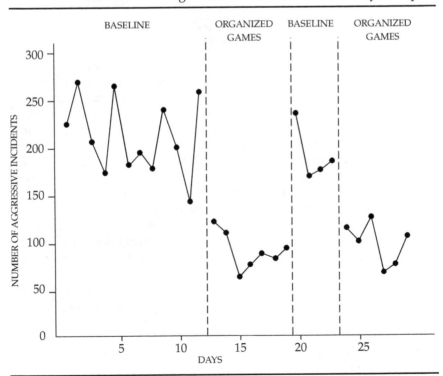

SOURCE: Reproduced from Murphy, Hutchison, and Bailey (1983, p. 33) with permission.

games actually caused the observed reductions in violence and aggression. The skeptic would be hard pressed to argue that anything except the psychosocial intervention was causally responsible for the changes, because there are three consecutive alterations in the data clearly associated with the introduction or removal of the intervention. This is quite compelling visually, so much so that there is no need to use inferential statistics to help the reader draw a conclusion. The data almost hit you between the eyes. Given the paucity of intervention research that tries to reduce school violence (as opposed to simply studying it using descriptive or correlational methods), this study by Murphy et al. (1983) is all the more compelling, despite the elegant simplicity of its research design.

Social workers have used single-system research designs to evaluate their practice since the late 1960s, and examples of clinical assessment and evaluation using these methods have been published in every major social work journal (see Thyer & Thyer, 1992). Mainstream social work research textbooks include these methods as a viable and practical approach to clinical assessment (e.g., Grinnell & Unrau, 2008; Royse, Thyer, & Padgett, 2015; Rubin & Babbie, 2014; Thyer, 2010); SSDs can be creatively employed in the evaluation of social work practice that is derived from all theoretical orientations.

THE DESIGN AND CONDUCT OF GROUP RESEARCH DESIGNS

You have undoubtedly been exposed to the general principles behind the design and conduct of group research designs, also called "nomothetic research designs." Rather than relying on many consecutive measurements taken from one or a small number of clients (as in SSDs), group designs typically rely on few (usually two or three) repetitions of measurement on larger groups of clients.

Group designs typically use inferential statistics such as t-tests, analysis of variance, or chi-square assessments to aid the practitioner-researcher in making reliable judgements as to whether change has really occurred. SSDs usually rely on the visual inspection of graphically presented data to infer the existence of reliable changes in client functioning. Each approach has its strengths and limitations, indications, and contraindications. If you are employed in an agency where relatively few clients with a particular problem seek assistance, it will be very difficult to conduct a credible group research design to evaluate the outcomes of social work services. In such circumstances, SSDs may be applicable. If, however, you have access to large numbers of clients and/or multiple repeated measurement of client functioning is not possible, then a nomothetic approach is the way to go. It is definitely not the case that one method is intrinsically superior to the other.

Nomothetic designs used in evaluation research can be hierarchically ranked in terms of their strength or potential for yielding internally valid conclusions. A common system is to categorize them as preexperimental, quasi-experimental, and truly experimental (see Royse et al., 2015; Thyer, 2010, 2013; Thyer & Myers, 2007); we follow this convention here.

Preexperimental Group Research Designs

Perhaps the simplest outcome study used in clinical assessment is the posttest-only group design, wherein a group of clients is formally assessed after having received a social work intervention. Myers and Rittner (1999, 2001) provide a realistic example of the X-O design; they used a convenience sample of about one hundred adults who had been raised in a traditional, old-fashioned orphanage. Many years after these people had left the orphanage, Myers and Rittner contacted them and asked them to complete some standardized assessments about their psychosocial functioning, including such issues as family and interpersonal relationships, educational attainment, employment history, emotional or mental disorders, quality of life, life satisfaction, and so on. In this way, the social workers were able to determine that adults who had been raised in an orphanage enjoyed fairly positive lives, with generally good incomes, interpersonal relationships, life satisfaction, educational attainment, and quality of life.

A stronger form of preexperimental group design systematically assesses client functioning before social work intervention, and then again using similar methods after treatment. This design can be diagrammed as an O-X-O design. An example of this design in the evaluation of clinical practice was conducted by an MSW Schwartz while interning at a psychiatric hospital in Atlanta. The student was assigned to a partial hospitalization program wherein depressed or substance-abusing clients spend time from 9:00 A.M. to 3:00 P.M., Monday through Friday, in a structured hospital setting, receiving psychotherapy, group work, family therapy, vocational services, and other interventions. Partial hospitalization is much less expensive than inpatient treatment. The student found that there were few studies that had examined the outcomes of partial hospitalization services. She was able to work with her field instructor and hospital administrators to administer to all newly admitted depressed patients a rapid assessment instrument, the Generalized Contentment Scale (GCS), which is a measure of depression. Then, just before discharge, the student asked the patients to complete the GCS again. During the course of her internship, the student obtained admission and discharge GCS scores from a total of nine clients; the mean score at admission was about 60, and the discharge score averaged 43.

A t-test found this reduction (lower scores mean less depression) to be statistically significantly different. Did Schwartz show that partial hospitalization caused the clients to improve? By no means. There are too many alternative explanations for the improved scores to permit her to draw such a conclusion. However, the data are consistent with the hypothesis that the program is effective; the data are also consistent with the hypothesis that the clients are not getting worse. Most psychiatric programs lack even this minimal level of evaluation data, and in this limited sense, Schwartz's study was a useful undertaking in programmatic assessment. More details can be found in Schwartz and Thyer (2000).

Quasi-Experimental Group Research Designs

Quasi-experimental group research designs are characterized by their use of some sort of control group—that is, a number of people who receive no social work treatment, alternative social work or other treatment method, or (more rarely) placebo social work treatment. The logic being that if improvements are seen in a group of clients who receive an active social work intervention and no changes or only small effects are seen in the control group, then there is tentative evidence (evidence consistent with the hypothesis) that social work caused improvements.

A school social worker helped conduct a quasi-experimental evaluation of alternative schooling provided to disruptive middle and high school youths. The school administrators wanted to compare the results of a standard alternative school (AS) program to the regular AS combined with an intensive family intervention component. In lieu of complete suspension (with its deleterious academic effects), behaviorally disruptive youths are placed in ASs that provide a much more structured and disciplined school environment. The standard AS program was provided to 95 youths during the 1994–95 school year, and the same AS program plus a program of intensive family involvement was provided to 120 youths during the 1995–1996 school year. The school staff wanted to test the hypothesis that augmenting AS with intensive family work (largely provided by the AS school social worker) would help the students make greater academic and disciplinary gains than those achieved through the standard AS program. Outcome measures included standardized measures of self-esteem, depression, locus of control (all assessed before and after AS), academic grades, and school attendance achieved. These areas were assessed in the home school during the terms before and during the terms after placement in the AS. This design is a bit more complicated to diagram and looks like this:

	1994–95	1995–96
Year 1 (standard AS program)	O-X-O	
- -		
Year 2 (standard AS with intensive family involvement)		O-Y-O

The X refers to the standard program, and the Y refers to the standard program plus intensive family involvement. The dashed line separating the two groups means that they were not constructed using random assignment; more on this later. Obviously, the school administration could not preselect or randomly assign school-aged children to the AS in given years—hence the mandated use of a nonrandom comparison group. Inferential statistics were used to look at group scores both before and after the youths' entry into the AS program (within-group changes) and between the two groups at the beginning and end of the program (between-group changes). Although the overall results were mixed, students who received the AS program with added family involvement demonstrated greater improvements in locus-of-control, grades, and attendance; a smaller proportion of kids dropped out of school as well. Aeby, Manning, Thyer, and Carpenter-Aeby (1999) can be consulted to learn more details about this quasi-experimental study.

A licensed clinical social worker (LCSW) used a similar design to compare the clinical outcomes at a student counseling center. The social worker was employed at this center and arranged for all college students seeking counseling services to complete the Symptom Checklist 90 (SCL 90), a rapid assessment instrument that measures multiple psychiatric symptoms like anxiety and depression. In the normal course of the center's operation, not all students seeking counseling could be immediately accommodated and were instead placed on a waiting list. Some time later they were recontacted, readministered the SCL 90, and scheduled for counseling. All clients were then readministered the SCL 90 at the termination of counseling. This structure lent itself to the naturalistic construction of the following quasi-experimental group design:

Immediate Treatment Group ($N = 41$)   O-X-O

- - - - - - - - - - - - - - - - -

Delayed Treatment Group ($N = 14$)   O O-X-O

Here both groups of college students received the same treatment (counseling provided by licensed mental health professionals, including clinical social workers), but the second group received delayed treatment. This delay was noncontrived, having been dictated by the exigencies of agency resources and staff availability. Inferential statistics were used to examine pre- versus posttreatment mean scores on various psychiatric symptoms both within the groups over time and between the groups at pre- and posttreatment. On the initial assessment, the groups had essentially equivalent levels of symptoms. After counseling, the immediate treatment group's symptoms were greatly reduced. However, after a time, when the delayed treatment group was reassessed (without having had any formal treatment), their scores were found to have not changed. When the delayed treatment group subsequently received counseling, they improved to an extent similar to those seen among the immediate treatment group. This creative study produced data consistent with the hypothesis that the services at the counseling center were followed by symptomatic improvements among the students and that the improvements were unlikely to be due to the simple passage of time, because the delayed treatment group experienced no change between their first and second evaluations. Given the few published studies that empirically evaluate the clinical outcomes of college-based student counseling centers, this study was a very useful contribution to the literature. For more details, see Vonk and Thyer (1999).

Experimental Group Research Designs

True experiments involve the random assignment of clients to different conditions, to a new social work intervention, to standard care, to some other alternative service, to placebo treatment, or to no treatment whatsoever. There are considerably fewer opportunities to conduct genuine experimental group research designs to evaluate clinical social work practice, but occasionally circumstances do permit their use, perhaps to an extent that is underappreciated by the profession. Indeed, a recent bibliography covering the years 1949–2013 found that more than 700 experimental studies have been published by social workers (Thyer & Massie, 2015). True experiments have much higher levels of internal validity, allowing stronger inferences about whether social work treatment caused any observed improvements. This is why our research textbooks stress their value.

A school social worker was employed as an elementary school social worker, and a large number of behaviorally disruptive children were referred to him each year. He used a structured group-work treatment program using cognitive behavioral methods to try to help the children. The social worker could not always accommodate his referrals immediately, and he had to place some children on a waiting list before he could place them in a new group. To be fair to all the children, the social worker tossed a coin to determine which children entered group intervention immediately and which began group work later. This process naturally generated a genuinely random waiting list comparison group and enabled him to develop the following experimental design:

Immediate Treatment Group ($N = 31$)	R O-X-O-O
Delayed Treatment Group ($N = 21$)	R-O-O-X-O

The prefix R before each group indicates that random assignment was used to create the two groups. The O indicates some type of standardized assessment, and X stands for receiving the cognitive behavioral group therapy. The outcome measures included student self-control, self-esteem, and reliable assessments of in-class behavior, and the data were examined using inferential statistics. The results provided answers to the following questions: "Did children who entered group work have improved self-esteem, self-control, and behavior?" Yes. "Were these improvements due to simply being assessed?" No. "Were the improvements caused by the group work?" Yes. "Were the improvements maintained over a fairly long period after the social work intervention was completed?" Yes. The clinical social worker who can provide data-based answers to such questions is indeed in an enviable position. Larkin and Thyer (1999) provide more details about this experimental evaluation of clinical social work practice.

If you can use random assignment to create sufficiently large groups (more than twenty), a pretreatment assessment is not necessary to be fairly sure that the groups are equivalent. Some genuine experiments make use of the approach of posttest-only control-group design to evaluate the outcomes of social work. A MSW student did this to determine whether he could promote voting behavior among low-income African American residents of a small Georgia community. A few months before the presidential election of 1988, the student went to the voting office and obtained the names and addresses on mailing labels for all registered voters in the poorest voting precinct in his town. This precinct contained a large number of public housing projects and was more than 90 percent African American. The student randomly picked four hundred voters from the list of 2,500 names and randomly assigned each to one of four different experimental conditions. Those assigned to Group 1 received a letter signed by the local chairs of the Democratic and Republican parties urging the citizen to be sure to vote in the upcoming presidential election. They received the letter about three days before the election. Those assigned to Group 2 received the same letter twice: about a week before and again about three days before the election. Those assigned to Group 3 received the letter three times: two weeks, one week, and a few days before the election. Voters randomly assigned to Group 4 received no reminder letters.

The student hypothesized that a higher proportion of those receiving the letter would vote, relative to those who did not get the letter, and that the more letters a voter received, the more likely a voter would be to vote. After the election, the student went back to the voting registrar's office for a printout of who among his four hundred voters actually voted. This information did not reflect how they voted but simply whether they actually cast a ballot (this is publically available information). He was able to use simple inferential statistics to determine whether the groups reliably differed in terms of the proportion that voted. This experimental strategy can be diagrammed as follows:

Group 1 (1 letter)	R	W	O
Group 2 (2 letters)	R	X	O
Group 3 (3 letters)	R	Y	O
Group 4 (no letter)	R		O

Again, R indicates that the group was formed on the basis of random assignment; W, X, and Y refer to the experimental treatment condition; and the gap in Group 4's diagram signifies no intervention. (For the results, see Canady & Thyer, 1990.)

As demonstrated in the preceding examples, clinical social workers have a wide array of preexperimental (making use of a single group of clients), quasi-experimental (using two or more nonrandomly assigned groups of clients), and experimental (with groups created using true random assignment methods) designs that they can use to evaluate practice outcomes. Practicality and internal validity are almost inversely proportional. The designs that are easiest to implement in real-life practice are usually the weakest ones. Those with the highest levels of internal validity may be too difficult to implement in agency-based or private practice settings.

WHAT ABOUT EXTERNAL VALIDITY?

No doubt you have been exposed to the concept of external validity, which refers to the extent that a researcher (or reader of a research study) can generalize the findings of a given study to similar clients or groups. There are two basic methods for demonstrating the external validity of a given study. The first approach (the most widely taught but all too rarely employed) involves obtaining a sample of clients that is genuinely representative of the larger universe of individuals with similar problems. The method used to approximate a representative sample involves randomly choosing a subset of clients to participate from the larger sample of such persons. A randomly chosen sample can be confidently viewed as legitimately representative of the larger group from which they were chosen. Therefore, a finding from a truly randomly selected sample of clients can be legitimately generalizable. For example, consider the problem of determining the average age of all clients, about four thousand of them, currently receiving services at a large agency. You could manually extract the information from every chart. However, this would be a lot of unnecessary work because you can obtain virtually the same result by randomly sampling a much small subset of charts from your entire set of patient records, perhaps as few as a few hundred records. There are some handy tables in some research books (e.g., Royse et al., 2015) and Web sites that tell you what size sample you need to randomly select from a given population to have a fairly accurate estimate of the real statistic you are interested in. Using the same statistical logic following elementary probability theory a suitably rigorous research design from a randomly selected sample of clients who genuinely benefited much more from Treatment A than from Treatment B, then you can infer that Treatment A is very likely better than Treatment B for the others in the universe of clients sampled. Thus, all things being equal (e.g., cost, social validity, ethical appropriateness), Treatment A should be offered in lieu of Treatment B to members of that group. So far so good, but here is where we come up abruptly against the practical realities of agency-based clinical research: we can almost never obtain a randomly chosen sample of clients from the larger universe of clients we wish to generalize to.

The truth is that field research usually employs convenience samples of clients—that is, persons chosen on the basis of their availability, ability, and willingness to provide informed consent, among other variables. Even client groups obtained through some approximation of random sampling are usually compromised because of patient mortality (dropping out of the study), inability to locate clients posttreatment or at follow-up, clients' refusal to continue participation in the study, or other detrimental developments. As soon as any of the initially randomly selected clients begin dropping out of your study for any reason, the representativeness of your sample is compromised and external validity becomes suspect.

Therefore, our advice to clinical social workers evaluating their own practice and to novice program evaluators valiantly trying to determine whether clients are getting better is simply this: accept from the outset that your findings may well end up not being generalizable and that you are not capable of conducting a study with strong external validity. This is unfortunate when measuring your study against the idealized canons of ivory-tower science, but it need not be a source of embarrassment, so long as you are modest in your initial goals. Do not claim that you will determine whether assertive community treatment for persons with bipolar disorder is better than, say, interpersonal psychotherapy for such persons, as a general rule. You would be ill advised to try to conduct such a study to yield generalizable knowledge applicable to all persons meeting the *Diagnostic and Statistical Manual of Mental Disorders,* fifth edition (DSM-5; APA, 2013) criteria for bipolar disorder. Instead, be more modest in your aspirations: "Do the clients at our agency do better with assertive community treatment than those clients receiving interpersonal psychotherapy?" Note the subtle distinction. You can accomplish the latter goal at your agency, whereas it is extremely unlikely that with modest resources you would be able to satisfactorily answer the question. It is perfectly legitimate and desirable to find out whether your clients are getting better and to leave the development of generalizable knowledge to others better equipped to do so via training and resources. It is unfortunate that many clinical social workers, imbued with the mistaken notion that the only scientifically acceptable finding is one obtained from a randomly selected sample, abandon any efforts at empirically evaluating the outcomes of their work because the findings may not be generalizable. Remember that evaluation studies that are small scale, locally conducted, unfunded, and with imperfect design are an exceedingly valuable undertaking and should not be dismissed.

But how will the profession ever develop generalizable knowledge? The answer is replication. Replication can be accomplished in many ways. Let's say that Professor Faust at the Holistic Healing Center made the following finding: drug-abusing clients randomly assigned to receive reinforcers, contingent on submitting drug-free urine screens, were more drug abstinent than clients who submitted similar urine specimens but did not receive reinforcement for abstinence. Faust can replicate this finding at the same agency at a later time with a different group of similar clients. If the same result emerges, then our confidence in this approach to treating drug abusers is somewhat strengthened. Or, Faust can try to replicate his study at another agency with similar clients. Or, other researchers at different agencies (perhaps in different parts of the country), independent of Faust, can use this approach to see whether they obtain similar outcomes. Or, other independent researchers at different agencies in other parts of the country can try to replicate Faust's findings with different clients. If the effect was first obtained using samples of only men, then researchers could see if it holds up with samples of women. If it was first demonstrated with Euro American clients, researchers could look for similar in samples of African American or Hispanic clients.

You can see the value in this approach—"science via creeping incrementalism," it could be called. Rather than conducting one massive study that controls for all possible threats to internal and external validity, more-limited investigations can approach solving a given problem in a more piecemeal manner. Such lofty aspirations are out of reach for most agency-based clinical social workers, who are concerned not with building the edifice of scientific knowledge but with obtaining credible data regarding the outcome of their own efforts. This, too, is a noble endeavor and should not be dismissed as trivial. Indeed, it can be argued that localized efforts by clinical social workers are more relevant to practice and evaluation concerns than are grandiose megastudies.

Linking Assessment to Outcome

The primary value of undertaking assessment in social work practice is to promote our efforts to improve client well-being and functioning. The achievement of enhanced client functioning is greatly facilitated by systematically assessing client behavior and reports of affect and thoughts prior to, after, and sometimes during the intervention process. Lacking such a systematic approach, we must rely solely on impressionistic reports, reports much more subject to misinterpretation than more objective, but admittedly still imperfect methods. It is to this end that both SSDs and group research designs can and should be undertaken as a routine part of practice evaluation. The term "intervention validity" has been given to the "extent to which assessment results can be used to guide the selection of interventions and evaluation of outcomes" (Elliott, Gresham, Frank, & Beddow, 2008, p. 15). The applications of SSDs and group designs to evaluating outcomes is obvious because they used research designs to evaluate the outcomes of practice. The linkage between assessment results and intervention is perhaps less obvious but is equally important because a part of the evidence-based practice process is to be able to use the empirical assessment information to select interventions. Here are three distinctive but nonexclusive ways in which this linkage can be undertaken; nosological diagnostic approach, symptomatic treatment, and functional assessment of behavior. The authors point out distinct advantages and limitations of these.

1. Nosological Diagnostic. The nosological diagnostic approach that was first described in chapter 1 employs some formal system of classifying client functioning and bases the selection of interventions on the client's diagnosis. This is perhaps most widely recognized in the approach promoted in the mid-1990s by the psychology profession, which developed the model called "empirically validated treatments," later transformed to empirically supported treatments, and more recently titled research-supported treatments. These are all terms for the same model. In this approach, given a particular diagnosis, the social worker consults some resource to learn what treatments enjoy the highest levels of research support, and, ideally, offers one or more of these research-supported treatments to the client. The following section of this chapter describes some resources where such research-supported treatments can be located. Many, but by no mean all, research-supported treatments are focused on mental disorders, as defined in the *Diagnostic and Statistical Manual of Mental Disorders*. This diagnostic approach is a relatively blunt integration of research and practice and has many shortcomings (see https://www.div12.org/psychological-treatments/; Nathan & Gorman, 2007).

2. Symptomatic Treatment. Another approach can be labeled "symptomatic treatment." Formal diagnoses are eschewed except in cases involving evident organic pathology, and instead the various behavioral, intellectual, and affective features troubling the client are approached piecemeal. Someone exposed to severe trauma and who subsequently experiences nightmares, fear, and avoidance to situations resembling the traumatic event, and who has an exaggerated startle response, is treated with therapies that credible research has shown to alleviate nightmares, behavioral fear, avoidance responses, and excessive flinching. This can all be done, and effectively accomplished, without recourse to giving a formal diagnosis of posttraumatic stress disorder (PTSD), a condition that undeniably exists, but not clearly as a coherent disease, mental or physical. As the various problems troubling the client are resolved, the condition, in effect, evaporates. But there is no effort to locate a panacea-like pill or psychotherapy which, if applied, alleviates everything as the underlying mental illness is said to be treated. Using simple SSDs recording various client problems (e.g., number and intensity of nightmares, fears and avoidance, severity of flinching) a close integration of assessment, treatment, and clinical evaluation can be accomplished.

   3. Functional Assessment of Behavior.   A third approach to linking assessment to outcome, one perhaps most closely congruent with social work's person-in-environment perspective, is called "functional assessment of behavior," also sometimes called "functional behavioral assessment." In this method, formal diagnoses are not pertinent, except perhaps in true diseases with an evident organic etiology. Instead, the social worker develops operational definitions of the client's functioning and uses direct observation, client reports, reports of caregivers and significant others, and other methods of objective assessment to help determine the environment circumstances in which the target behaviors are more or less likely to occur. From this information, provisional hypotheses are crafted speculating on presumptive links between one set of environmental conditions or client circumstances, and the enhancement or reduction of a given behavior. One focuses on the possible function a behavior is serving. Is it followed by reinforcing events being presented, or unpleasant circumstanced being removed? If such a regularity is observed, perhaps the (ultimately) dysfunctional behavior is being inadvertently maintained by its consequences, or perhaps the target behavior is associated with boredom, sleep deprivation, hunger, or thirst. Such hypotheses can be empirically tested. Alter the consequences following the behavior or the antecedent events preceding it. Does behavior change in the predicted direction? If so, you have provisionally corroborated your etiological hypothesis. If not, you need to come up with alternative ideas. Client aggression, for example, could be maintained by positive reinforcement, negative reinforcement, a deprivation state (thirst or hunger), or some discomfiting condition, such as a severe headache, hemorrhoids, or arthritis, for example. School avoidance could be maintained by parental reinforcement for staying home, avoiding something fear-evoking at school (e.g., a bully), or the desire to preserve mother from being beaten by father. These are quite different causes for a problem, and appears superficially similar. Functional assessment of behavior requires the use of a single-subject design in order to be effectively undertaken and represents a truly genuine person-in-environment approach that integrates assessment, treatment planning, and evaluation of outcomes. Functional assessment of behavior has not yet penetrated the social work literature to any great extent, but a few disciplinary resources are available (e.g., Filter & Alvarez, 2012; Filter & Horner, 2009; Cipani, 2014; School Social Work Association of America, 2001; Thyer, 2015) as well as a considerable body of work available in the field of behavior analysis.

Finding Research-Supported Interventions

Clinical social workers now have a wide array of resources they may consult to learn about psychosocial interventions with credible research support, and chapters 1 and 3 introduced some of these resources. Among the most credible sites are the systematic reviews of the Cochrane (www.cochrane.org) and Campbell (www.campbellcollaboration.org) collaborations. These are international organizations whose primary purpose is commissioning and publishing high-quality systematic reviews in the broad areas of health care and social welfare, education, criminal justice and international development. Many of these reviews address the overall evidence pertaining to the effectiveness of interventions, while others deal with the reliability and validity of assessment measures for use in practice. It is fair to say that the systematic reviews by these two entities reflect the most stringent attempts to assess all the relevant evidence and to summarize this in as transparent and bias-free manner as possible.

The Society of Clinical Psychology of the American Psychological Association supports a Web site (www.div12.org). The site contains information on effective interventions for over a dozen major disorders found in the DSM-5 (APA, 2013), with each treatment being supported by at least two well-designed randomized experimental studies that demonstrate that the treatment under consideration was at least equivalent to an existing accepted treatment, and was superior to either no treatment or to a credible placebo therapy. This resource, while a good starting place, is handicapped in that an intervention may be designated as research-supported if it meets the standard of having at least two supported studies but ignores the possible presence of studies that fail to support the intervention's value. Apart from this Web site, the Society of Clinical Psychology has helped produce a textbook, *A Guide to Treatments That Work* (Nathan & Gorman, 2007), which is similarly focused on DSM-defined conditions and contains two parallel chapters on each disorder: one addressing psychosocial treatments, and the other psychopharmacological ones. This is a very valuable, albeit somewhat dated, resource.

The U.S. Substance Abuse and Mental Health Services Administration supports a National Registry of Evidence-based Programs and Practices (NREPP; http://www.nrepp.samhsa.gov/) that lists several hundred individual, group, couple, and family-based psychotherapies, as well as a large number of community-based interventions, which meet some modest standards of research support. Some of these practices have been elaborated on in the form of extensive toolkits dealing with specific psychosocial issues or problems (e.g., depression, chronic mental illnesses, supported employment, supported housing, etc.). These toolkits contain information on starting one of these programs, including not only treatment manuals but also information on valid assessment measures, advertising brochures, PowerPoint presentations, creating an advisory board, assessing program fidelity, and so on. Myers and Wodarski (2014) describe how these toolkits can be used in social work education practice classes in a soup-to-nuts package aimed at teaching students about these research-supported programs.

The California Evidence-Based Clearing House for Child Welfare (http://www.cebc4cw.org/home/) supports a searchable database on programs and practices specific to child welfare which possess varying levels of research support, as assessed using a scientific merit rating system. However about 40 percent of the practices listed on this Web site actually lack credible research support, so mere inclusion of a given practice on this Web site does not automatically imply that it actually is scientifically based. However, like the NREPP, this clearinghouse is an excellent resource to begin one's search for research-supported interventions.

SUMMARY

The social work profession has a long history of recognizing the importance of clinical practice evaluation. The two major forms of inquiry for evaluating social work outcomes are SSDs and group designs. Both of these methods match well with the evaluative aspects of clinical assessment and help practitioners determine the effectiveness of their interventions. With SSDs, the clinician measures a single client's (or small group's) functioning before, during, and after intervention; with group designs, social workers use inferential statistics to look at outcomes on larger groups of clients. This chapter reviewed different models of each design and the issues of external validity, as well as generalizability of results. Finally, this chapter discussed broad but distinct approaches for moving from assessment to intervention and provides resources for finding research-based clinical interventions.

STUDY QUESTIONS

1. Think of a client you have seen in your field placement. Design a single-system study to evaluate client outcomes. Include problem, measurement, and goal/objective. Present your expected findings on a graph.

2. Now consider your field placement agency. Design a group study to help the agency look at its client outcomes. What design would be best? What measures? What would you expect to find?

3. Considering Questions 1 and 2, speak to the issue of generalizability (external validity). How could you improve the external validity of your designs?

REFERENCES

Aeby, V. G., Manning, B. H., Thyer, B. A., & Carpenter-Aeby, T. (1999). Comparing outcomes of an alternative school program offered with and without intensive family involvement. *School Community Journal, 9*, 17–32.

American Psychiatric Association (APA). (2013). *Diagnostic and statistical manual of mental disorders* (5th ed.; DSM-5). Washington, DC: Author.

Barker, K. L., & Thyer, B. A. (2000). Differential reinforcement of other behavior in the treatment of inappropriate behavior and aggression in an adult with mental retardation at a vocational center. *Scandinavian Journal of Behaviour Therapy, 29*, 37–42.

Canady, K., & Thyer, B. A. (1990). Promoting voting behavior among low-income Black voters using reminder letters: An experimental investigation. *Journal of Sociology and Social Welfare, 17*(4), 109–116.

Cipani, E. (2014). Comorbidity in DSM childhood disorders: A functional perspective. *Research on Social Work Practice, 24*, 78–85.

Ell, K. (1996). Social work research and health care policy and practice: A psychosocial research agenda. *Social Work, 41*, 583–592.

Elliott, S. N., Gresham, F. M., Frank, J. L., & Beddow, P. A. (2008). Intervention validity of social behavior rating scales: Features of assessments that link results to treatment plans. *Assessment for Effective Intervention, 34*, 15–24.

Filter, K. J., & Alvarez, M. E. (2012). *Functional behavioral assessment*. New York: Oxford University Press.

Filter, K. J., & Horner, R. H. (2009). Function-based academic interventions for problem behavior. *Education and Treatment of Children, 31*(2), 1–19.

Grinnell, R. M., & Unrau, Y. A. (2008). *Social work research and evaluation: Foundations of evidence-based practice*. New York: Oxford University Press.

Larkin, R., & Thyer, B. A. (1999). Evaluating cognitive-behavioral group counseling to improve elementary school students' self-esteem, self-control, and classroom behavior. *Behavioral Interventions, 14*, 147–161.

Lewis, H. (1965). The use and place of research in the administration of the social agency. *Child Welfare, 44*, 21–25.

Mullen, E. J. (1995). A review of *Research Methods for Generalist Social Work. Social Work, 40*, 282–283.

Murphy, H. A., Hutchison, J. M., & Bailey, J. S. (1983). Behavioral school psychology goes outdoors: The effect of organized games on playground aggression. *Journal of Applied Behavior Analysis, 16*, 29–35.

Myers, L. L., & Rittner, B. (1999). Family functioning and satisfaction of former residents of a non-therapeutic residential care facility: An exploratory study. *Journal of Family Social Work, 3*(3), 53–68.

Myers, L. L., & Rittner, B. (2001). Adult psychosocial functioning of children raised in an orphanage. *Residential Treatment for Children and Youth, 18*(4), 3–21.

Myers, L. L., & Wodarski, J. S. (2014). Using the Substance Abuse and Mental Health Services Administration (SAMHSA) evidence-based practice kits in social work education. *Research on Social Work Education, 24,* 705–714.

Nathan, P. E., & Gorman, J. M. (Eds.). (2007). *A guide to treatments that work* (3rd ed.). New York: Oxford University Press.

National Association of Social Workers (NASW). (1999). *Code of ethics.* Washington, DC: Author.

Richmond, M. (1935). *Social diagnosis.* New York: Russell Sage Foundation. (Original published in 1917).

Royse, D., Thyer, B. A., & Padgett, D. K. (2015). *Program evaluation: An introduction* (6th ed.). Belmont, CA: Brooks/Cole.

Rubin, A., & Babbie, E. (2014). *Research methods for social work* (8th ed.). Pacific Grove, CA: Brooks/Cole.

School Social Work Association of America. (2001). *School Social Work Association of America resolution statement: School social work services.* Retrieved from http://c.ymcdn.com/sites/www.sswaa.org/resource/resmgr/imported/School%20Social%20Work%20Services.pdf

Schwartz, W. L., & Thyer, B. A. (2000). Partial hospitalization treatment for clinical depression: A pilot evaluation. *Journal of Human Behavior in the Social Environment, 3*(2), 13–21.

Thyer, B. A. (2013). *Quasi-experimental research designs.* New York: Oxford.

Thyer, B. A. (2015). The DSM-5 definition of mental disorder: Critique and alternatives. In B. Probst (Ed.), *Critical thinking in clinical thinking and diagnosis* (pp. 45–68). New York: Springer.

Thyer, B. A. (Ed.). (2010). *Handbook of social work research methods* (2nd ed.). Thousand Oaks, CA: Sage.

Thyer, B. A., & Massie, K. (2015). *A bibliography of randomized experiments in social work, 1949–2013.* Unpublished manuscript.

Thyer, B. A., & Myers, L. L. (2007). *A social worker's guide to evaluatng practice outcomes.* Alexandria, VA: Council on Social Work Education.

Thyer, B. A., & Thyer, K. B. (1992). Single system research designs in social work practice: A bibliography from 1965–1990. *Research on Social Work Practice, 2,* 99–116.

Thyer, B. A., Thyer, K. B., & Massa, S. (1991). Behavioral analysis and therapy in the field of gerontology. In P. K. H. Kim (Ed.), *Serving the elderly: Skills for practice* (pp. 117–135). New York: Aldine de Gruyter.

Vonk, E. M., & Thyer, B. A. (1999). Evaluating the effectiveness of short-term treatment at a university counseling center. *Journal of Clinical Psychology, 55,* 1095–1106.

APPENDIX 2A

Patient Health Questionnaire-9 (PHQ-9)

Over the last 2 weeks, how often have you been bothered by any of the following problems?	Not at all	Several days	More than half the days	Nearly every day
1. Little interest or pleasure in doing things	0	1	2	3
2. Feeling down, depressed, or hopeless	0	1	2	3
3. Trouble falling or staying asleep, or sleeping too much	0	1	2	3
4. Feeling tired or having little energy	0	1	2	3
5. Poor appetite or overeating	0	1	2	3
6. Feeling bad about yourself, or that you are a failure or have let yourself or your family down	0	1	2	3
7. Trouble concentrating on things, such as reading the newspaper or watching television	0	1	2	3
8. Moving or speaking so slowly that other people could have noticed, or the opposite—being so fidgety or restless that you have been moving around a lot more than usual	0	1	2	3
9. Thoughts that you would be better off dead or of hurting yourself in some way	0	1	2	3

For score coding: _____ + _____ + _____ + _____

Total score:

If you checked off any problems, how difficult have these problems made it for you to do your work, take care of things at home, or get along with other people?

Not Difficult at all	Somewhat difficult	Very difficult	Extremely difficult
☐	☐	☐	☐

Scoring Instruction

1	4	5	9	10	14	15	19	20	27
Minimal		Mild		Moderate		Mod. Severe		Severe	

APPENDIX 2B

Sample Clinician Report for the Youth Outcome Questionnaire 2.0 (YOQ)

Assessment: Clinician Report

DOB: 1/1/1992
Date of Assessment: 1/8/2008

Gender: Female
Date Report Created: 8/7/2008

Youth Outcome Questionnaire 2.0 (YOQ)

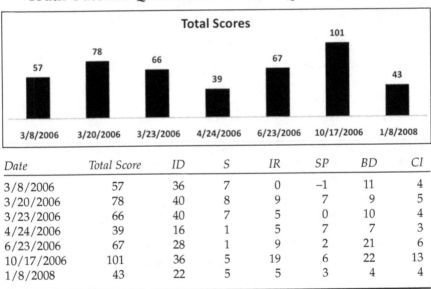

Date	Total Score	ID	S	IR	SP	BD	CI
3/8/2006	57	36	7	0	−1	11	4
3/20/2006	78	40	8	9	7	9	5
3/23/2006	66	40	7	5	0	10	4
4/24/2006	39	16	1	5	7	7	3
6/23/2006	67	28	1	9	2	21	6
10/17/2006	101	36	5	19	6	22	13
1/8/2008	43	22	5	5	3	4	4

Item Analysis

Item	Response	Comments
1. Wants to be alone more than other children of the same age	Never or almost never (0)	
2. Complains of dizziness or headaches	Rarely (1)	
3. Doesn't participate in activities that were previously enjoyable	Never or almost never (0)	

4. Argues or is verbally disrespectful	Rarely (1)	
5. Is more fearful than other children of the same age	Sometimes (2)	
6. Cuts school or is truant	Rarely (1)	
7. Cooperates with rules and expectations	Sometimes (0)	(R) Relative strength
8. Has difficulty completing assignments, or completes them carelessly	Rarely (1)	
9. Complains or whines about things being unfair	Sometimes (2)	
10. Experiences trouble with bowels, such as constipation or diarrhea	Rarely (1)	
11. Gets into physical fights with peers or family members	Rarely (1)	
12. Worries and can't get certain ideas off his or friends, family members, or other adults her mind	Never or almost never (0)	
13. Steals or lies	Never or almost never (0)	
14. Is fidgety, restless or hyperactive	Rarely (1)	
15. Seems anxious or nervous	Rarely (1)	
16. Communicates in a pleasant and appropriate manner	Rarely (1)	(R)
17. Seems tense, easily startled	Sometimes (2)	
18. Soils or wets self	Rarely (1)	
19. Is aggressive toward adults	Rarely (1)	
20. Sees, hears, or believes things that are not real	Rarely (1)	Critical item endorsed
21. Has participated in self-harm (e.g., cutting or scratching self, attempting suicide)	Never or almost never (0)	
22. Uses alcohol or drugs	Sometimes (2)	
23. Seems unable to get organized	Rarely (1)	
24. Enjoys relationships with family and friends	Sometimes (0)	(R) Relative strength
25. Appears sad or unhappy	Rarely (1)	
26. Experiences pain or weakness in muscles or joints	Rarely (1)	
27. Has a negative, disrespectful attitude toward	Rarely (1)	
28. Believes that others are trying to hurt him or her even when they are not	Rarely (1)	Critical item endorsed
29. Threatens to or has run away from home	Never or almost never (0)	
30. Experiences rapidly changing and strong emotions	Never or almost never (0)	
31. Deliberately breaks rules, laws, or expectations	Never or almost never (0)	
32. Appears happy with her- or himself	Sometimes (0)	(R) Relative strength

33. Sulks, pouts, or cries more than other children of the same age	Sometimes (2)	
34. Pulls away from family or friends	Sometimes (2)	
35. Complains of stomach pain or feeling sick more than other children of the same age	Never or almost never (0)	
36. Doesn't have or keep friends	Never or almost never (0)	
37. Has friends of whom I don't approve	Never or almost never (0)	
38. Believes that others can hear his or her thoughts or that she or he can hear the thoughts of others	Never or almost never (0)	
39. Engages in inappropriate sexual behavior (e.g., sexually active, exhibits self, sexual abuse towards family members or others)	Never or almost never (0)	
40. Has difficulty waiting his or her turn in activities or conversations	Rarely (1)	
41. Thinks about suicide, says she or he would be better off if dead	Never or almost never (0)	
42. Complains of nightmares, difficulty getting to sleep, oversleeping, or waking up from sleep too early	Never or almost never (0)	
43. Complains about or challenges rules, expectations, or responsibilities	Never or almost never (0)	
44. Has times of unusual happiness or excessive energy	Rarely (1)	Critical item endorsed
45. Handles frustration or boredom appropriately	Frequently (–1)	(R) Relative strength
46. Has fears of going crazy	Never or almost never (0)	
47. Feels appropriate guilt for wrongdoing	Sometimes (0)	(R) Relative strength
48. Is unusually demanding	Never or almost never (0)	
49. Is irritable	Rarely (1)	
50. Vomits or is nauseous more than other children of the same age	Rarely (1)	
51. Becomes angry enough to be threatening to others	Rarely (1)	Critical item endorsed
52. Seems to stir up trouble when bored	Rarely (1)	
53. Is appropriately hopeful and optimistic	Rarely (1)	(R)
54. Experiences twitching muscles or jerking movements in face, arms, or body	Never or almost never (0)	
55. Has deliberately destroyed property	Never or almost never (0)	
56. Has difficulty concentrating, thinking clearly, or attending to tasks	Never or almost never (0)	

57. Talks negatively, as though bad things are all his or her fault	Rarely (1)	
58. Has lost significant amounts of weight without medical reason	Never or almost never (0)	
59. Acts impulsively, without thinking of the consequences	Never or almost never (0)	
60. Is usually calm	Sometimes (0)	(R) Relative strength
61. Will not forgive her- or himself for past mistakes	Sometimes (2)	
62. Lacks energy	Sometimes (2)	
63. Feels that he or she doesn't have any friends, or that no likes him or her	Sometimes (2)	
64. Gets frustrated and gives up, or gets upset easily	Rarely (1)	

General Interpretation Guidelines

Cutoff. Total scores of 46 or more are in the clinical range.
Reliable Change Index (RCI). A difference of thirteen points or more (RCI) between two total scores is clinically significant.

Youth Outcome Questionnaire 2.0 (YOQ), 1/8/2008

Total score is the total of the following six subscales. High scores reflect endorsement of a large number of items, indicating distress in the intrapersonal, somatic, interpersonal, social, and behavioral domains. Scores equal to or greater than 46 are in the clinical range:

- Intrapersonal distress assesses emotional distress, including anxiety, fearfulness, hopelessness, and thoughts of self-harm. Scores equal to or greater than 16 are in the clinical range.

- Somatic assesses somatic distress, including symptoms typical in emotionally disturbed children and adolescents, such as headaches, dizziness, stomachaches, nausea, bowel difficulties, and pain or joint weakness. Scores equal to or greater than 5 are in the clinical range.

- Interpersonal relations assesses issues relevant to relationships with parents, other adults, and peers. Items cover attitude toward others, communication and interaction with friends, cooperativeness, aggressiveness, arguing, and defiance. Scores equal to or greater than 4 are in the clinical range.

- Social problems assesses problematic behaviors that are socially related, including truancy, sexual problems, running away, destruction of property, and substance abuse. Similar to the interpersonal relations subscale, this subscale also addresses aggressiveness. However, the aggressive content found here is more severe, typically involving the breaking of social mores. Scores equal to or greater than 3 are in the clinical range.

- Behavioral dysfunction assesses the ability to organize tasks, complete assignments, and concentrate. It measures inattention, hyperactivity, and impulsivity. Scores equal to or greater than 12 are in the clinical range.
- Critical items assess paranoia, obsessive-compulsive behaviors, hallucinations, delusions, suicidal ideation, mania, and eating disorders. Scores equal to or greater than 5 are in the clinical range.

Note

An automated screening is not a substitute for a complete evaluation or clinical judgment but can contribute to formulation of a diagnosis and planning treatment. Alert reports assess the significance of clinical change. They are derived from statistical comparison of individual patient's progress with normative groups of patients with similar levels of initial severity. Progress expectations and predictions for any particular patient must be based on the totality of clinical and psychometric data available.

APPENDIX 4A

Ethnographic Assessment Case Study

Eighteen-year-old Erica, a first-year college student, had grown up in Korea. Although she was newly arrived in the United States, as the daughter of a North American father and a Korean mother, she considered herself bicultural. In our first meeting, through her Americanized dress and her unaccented, fluent English, Erica appeared perfectly adapted to life in the United States. It soon became apparent, however, that this was not the case.

Erica entered treatment voluntarily, seeking relief from the intensifying loneliness and anxiety that had troubled her since she had come to college. Yet, Erica seemed to feel ill at ease when I asked her to describe her family history and her current concerns. The first few sessions were characterized by Erica's reluctance to speak of personal and emotional matters with me.

It was clear that Erica was resistant to treatment, and given her international background, I suspected that some of her resistances were cultural. Her quietness in sessions suggested that she was not used to putting her worries and her feelings into words, and I wondered whether Korean norms surrounding emotional expression contributed to her silence. To better grasp the nature of Erica's cultural resistance to treatment, I began to explore the norms governing these aspects of language use in Korea. In the next session I told Erica that I had noticed that she felt uncomfortable talking about herself in treatment with me, and I asked her how she would describe her difficulties if she were in a Korean setting. Erica responded that in Korea, as a rule, people did not convey their problems to others directly; that to do so would be considered selfish and antisocial. Keeping in mind that Erica might feel this way about her own participation in treatment, I told her that there seemed to be different rules about disclosing personal issues in Korea and in New York. Erica agreed, and we spent the rest of the session, as well as the next, identifying these rules in general terms.

Following this ethnographic line of inquiry into Korean norms of discussing personal issues, Erica became interested in understanding how these norms applied to her. Although her family was bicultural, in Korea she had learned to talk about herself sparingly and modestly and to voice her opinions indirectly. When she behaved this way at college, her roommates found her passive and meek. They urged her to be more assertive and vocal, but Erica felt uncomfortable speaking in ways that would have marked her as brash, egocentric, and aggressive in Korea. In addition, in Korea Erica had learned that it was unacceptable to express emotions such as sadness and anger openly. In Korea she had received emotional nourishment from others who were attuned to her needs and who responded to them without her having to verbalize them. Failing the responsiveness of others, Erica had learned that these emotions were to be silently endured.

As a consequence of our discussions, Erica began to understand that these Korean norms of emotional expression were at odds with those of other students on campus, who freely complained of their moods and their problems. Erica realized that she could not expect other students to be attuned to her sentiments and needs and that unless she learned to communicate her emotions to them, her isolation would grow. Erica used our final sessions to practice verbalizing her emotional states, and together we addressed the feelings of selfishness and aggression this evoked in her. By the end of the treatment, Erica had become more aware of the conflicting cultural norms surrounding emotional expression and had become more adept at expressing her feelings to others.

SOURCE: Seeley, K. M. (2004). Short-term intercultural psychotherapy: Ethnographic inquiry. *Social Work*, 49(1), 126–127. Reproduced by permission of Oxford University Press and the National Association of Social Workers.

APPENDIX 4B

Use of Qualitative Methods to Determine the Ecological Validity of Neuropsychological Testing

STEPS IN ECOLOGICAL VALIDITY ASSESSMENT

Step 1: Getting to Know the Participant

This critical step makes use of the initial time spent getting to know the individual at their service site, by getting to know the individual's routines through the gathering of basic demographic, symptom, and psychosocial data (the quantitative data; see Gioia & Brekke, 2009). This step occurs after consent to participate in the study has been obtained. During this rapport-building phase, a plan for the researcher to join the individual in their community is cocreated; this is not a simple process and might be taxing for the participant. Carlsson, Paterson, Scott-Findlay, Ehnfors, and Ehrenberg (2007) discuss multiple strategies for interviewing participants who have communication and cognitive difficulties (e.g., recognizing fatigue). The researcher needs to take ample notes as the potential participant describes what they will be doing over the next few days. If there is a generic activity that the researcher wants to observe with each person (e.g., money management), and the person has not mentioned this activity, these areas will be raised to see when this activity might next come up for them (e.g., when their monthly check arrives). Observations should be scheduled in the least obtrusive way possible. Evidence for rapport-building would be demonstrated by the participant's trust in the initial process and by their adequate communication skills. There is no formal measure for this kind of engagement. Exclusion would be based on high levels of psychiatric symptoms that interfere with rapport (e.g., manic or highly anxious behavior, extreme paranoia). In this initial visit it is also critical to have the researcher ask the individual how he or she wants to introduce the researcher to others as he or she accompanies them in the community. The introduction might take one form for close personal friends and family, and another for neighbors and mental health professionals. Rehearsing these introductions might be helpful.

Step 2: Utilizing Prolonged Engagement with Participants

To create credible findings for ecological validity of NP assessments, one needs to spend ample time with each individual to allow for opportunities to view a range of community activities, some of them repeatedly. The method employed here is somewhere between rapid ethnographic assessment and a full ethnography.

The method presented here calls for a period of initial immersion (9 to 15 hours over 3 consecutive days, approximately 3 to 5 hours per day; weekends and evenings are possible) viewing participant-led activities, and most importantly, homing in on specific tasks that are part of instrumental activities of daily living (IADLs; Lawton & Brody, 1969). IADLs are activities such as using the telephone, getting to places beyond walking distance (use of transportation), grocery shopping, meal preparation, household chores, laundry, taking medications, and managing money. The IADLs form the foundation of observation for all populations with cognitive decline, and thus serve as a baseline of common tasks for analysis. In addition, each individual has her or his own interests (e.g., using computers, crafts and model making, attending church), which provide additional opportunities to view a wide range of complex tasks beyond IADLs. Every opportunity should be made to attend these additional activities, even though some might be out of the immediate community in which the participant lives. Activities that cannot be viewed in the initial 3 consecutive days, or those needing additional observation, will be scheduled with the participant when they naturally occur.

Step 3: Encouraging Participant-Led Activities with Opportunity for Reflection

Once the observation of the participant begins there are many opportunities to use questions during the task or after the completion of a complex task—such as ordering a meal in a restaurant—to probe some of the specific task components. For example, one individual in the study ordered a meal in a fast food restaurant and chose a milkshake that he did not like, which created a dilemma for him. Questions posed by the researcher at the moment of the event offered the individual a chance to think aloud with the researcher listening, and decide what to do next (e.g., keep the shake or request a new one). This example of an event offered a distinct opportunity to view problem solving as it unfolded. The technique is similar to that used in cognitive interviewing when individuals are commenting on the development of a measure (Willis, 2005). By observing events in real time, there is an increased opportunity to discover how the person creates a plan of action around the various tasks, to witness their emotional state while doing the task, as well as to examine their decision making about the particular action. Metacognitive processes are often called "thoughts about thinking," and can enhance the observed experience in ways not tapped by observation or tests alone (Lysaker et al., 2005). Obtaining reflection from the participant serves as a clarification about what the interviewer observed and also serves as a validity check of the method.

Questions about awareness of deficits in thought or action can be asked. Enough information needs to be solicited to determine whether any struggles observed are because of a social emotional context (anxiety, fear) or whether it was difficult for the individual to conceptualize the skills necessary to negotiate the task (e.g., talking with a waiter about returning an incorrect order). The model presented here captures both the strengths and difficulties of the individual with neurocognitive deficits in the community context.

Step 4: Taking Field Notes

The least obtrusive way to collect data about everyday activities is through the use of field observation and notes. Wolcott (1995), in *The Art of Fieldwork*, provided suggestions to help the researcher "be there" in the field. He does not recommend that the observer be aloof, but rather that the observer constantly challenge him- or herself about the observed behavior, which is a great fit for observing and understanding cognitive deficits. The strategies of field work are mainly nondirective, but there is a flow between asking direct questions and asking no questions at all, which feeds into the art of this procedure.

As soon as possible after the observation is completed, the observer should write up notes that describe the events in abundant detail, which will refresh your memory when you return to the notes. The write-up should occur prior to the next scheduled observation; otherwise events will blur and crucial details might be lost. Observed events directly related to NP should be listed and taken with the researcher back to the field, to assist in understanding whether the observation was isolated or more frequently occurring. Consultation with a neuropsychologist is useful in this stage, as well as in the ongoing data analysis. Digital audio recorders used post interview can help to get main thoughts down quickly, and details can be added when doing the full write-up of the observation.

Step 5: Having Contact with Significant Others and Community Members

During the observation it is likely that the individual will have social contact with others in her or his community, which is an important area of functioning to observe. Mental health professionals might be included in these community contacts. The additional information from these significant others could prove useful as collaborative information, especially in understanding their role in helping the individual with daily tasks. These persons can serve as primary resources for the individual completing their daily routine tasks. They can provide an additional source of data to triangulate; however, this would require a separate set of permission/consent forms. It is important to negotiate with the individual in the study how these transactions should be made.

Step 6: Coding and Categorizing Observed Behaviors and Strategies

One key use of ecological validity is as an assessment tool, because the integrated data collected can be used to make determinations or predictions about functional outcomes. One rubric for analysis is to use predominant behavioral strategies as used in IADLs for describing observed tasks. In this study, in developing the ecological validity method, four types of strategies were used: (a) instrumental, (b) rote, (c) social facilitative, and (d) social independent. Although there is overlap in these strategies, the analysis called for making an overall judgment about the predominating behavioral style.

Rote activities enable basic community living (such as doing chores), but are largely characterized by repetitious or scripted behavior that is often, but not always, demonstrated and guided by others. Instrumental tasks are most aligned with multiple activities of daily living—self-care, shopping and other activities related to food, making and keeping appointments, keeping clothes clean—and are generally more complex, goal-oriented, and a bit more self-directed. Facilitative social activities are social connections formed with people to facilitate daily functioning, usually of the more complex instrumental tasks (e.g., asking someone to help with budgeting, with transportation, or advice about decisions). Independent social activities are social connections and interactions that are actively cultivated by the individual and that enrich work, school, living, community, and family tasks, but the individual is not largely dependent on others for completion of tasks or for direction (Gioia & Brekke, 2009). Other rubrics or templates for analysis are likely to be developed with the addition of more individual observations.

Step 7: Employing Intercoder Agreement as a Means to Strengthen Validity of the Data

Participant profiles are created from the descriptions of tasks in the field notes as a means to reduce the data into a document that can be read, coded, and rated by multiple coders. These are basically summary narratives of daily activities created by the researcher for rating purposes; summary narratives were created in the current study of 10 individuals (Gioia & Brekke, 2009). After the initial coding was completed by the author, instructions were given to a second coder to make judgments about the fit or lack of fit with the behavioral styles mentioned above. This analytic task effectively quantitized the qualitative data into categories that could be compared across coders. Using this approach, Gioia and Brekke (2009) found that having two coders independently make inferences from the text was a useful approach for achieving credibility of the data.

Step 8: Using the Cocreated Results

Results should optimally be cocreated and checked with the participant living in the community. In other words, validating that the strategy used to offset the neurocognitive deficit was one that was agreed on by both the researcher and the participant. Fully employing a participatory action research (PAR) model into the eight steps would render the findings clinically useful as a means to educate, empower, and engage the individual, their support network, the researcher, and the research audience about the challenges to perform daily tasks in the community when one has a disorder that affects cognition (Kidd & Kral, 2005). Persons with neurocognitive impairment are typically cut off from PAR engagement because of stigma and other beliefs about their ability to participate. However, this research method of ecological validity could be ideal for consciousness raising for stakeholders, and contributes an essential understanding of the notions of ecological validity in these NP disorders.

SOURCE: Gioia, D. *Qualitative Health Research* (vol. 19, no. 10), pp. 1495–1503. Copyright © 2009 by SAGE Publications. Reprinted by permission of SAGE Publications, Inc.

APPENDIX 5A

Psychological Testing Instruments for Children and Adolescents

INFANT DEVELOPMENT SCALES

Brazelton Neonatal Behavioral Assessment Scales

1. Neurological intactness
2. Interactive behavior
   (a) Motor control (putting thumb in mouth)
   (b) Remaining calm and alert in response to stimuli (bell or light)
3. Responsiveness to the examiner and need for stimulation

Bayley Scales of Infant Development

1. Mental abilities (memory, learning, problem solving)
2. Motor skills
3. Social behaviors (social orientation, fearfulness, and cooperation)

Gesell Development Schedules

1. Fine and gross motor behavior
2. Language behavior
3. Adaptive behavior (eye-hand coordination, imitation, and object recovery)
4. Personal-social behavior (reaction to persons, initiative, independence, play responses)

Denver Developmental Screening Test

(Can be administered by a person with limited training, screening test to indicate if more in-depth testing is needed.)

1. Developmental delays
2. Problems in personal/social, fine motor/adaptive, language, and gross motor skills

INTELLIGENCE TESTS FOR PRESCHOOL AND SCHOOL-AGE CHILDREN

Stanford-Binet

(Used with both preschool and school-age, usually administered to children between 2-8 years old. Disadvantage is that it gives only an overall score, doesn't address specific strengths and weaknesses. May not be good for bilingual/bicultural children.)

1. Vision
2. Eye-hand coordination
3. Hearing
4. Speech

Wechsler Scales Consist of:

Wechsler Preschool and Primary Scale of Intelligence (WPPSI) and Wechsler Intelligence Scale for Children-Revised (WISC-R). Most widely used to test cognitive functioning of school-age children. These scales include six verbal and six performance subtests.

System of Multicultural Pluralistic Assessment (SOMPA)

This test is based on the WISC-R and takes into account a child's handicapping condition and sociocultural background.

SPECIAL ABILITIES TESTS

Bender Visual Motor Gestalt Test

1. Visual perceptual skills
2. Eye-hand coordination

Peabody Picture Vocabulary Test

(Originally designed to be used with persons who are nonverbal, mentally retarded, and/or have cerebral palsy.)

Detroit Test of Learning Aptitude

1. Auditory and visual memory
2. Concentration

TESTING FOR MENTAL RETARDATION

(An IQ score below 70 indicates that a client may be mentally retarded. However, a low IQ score by itself is not sufficient for diagnosis. The client's adaptive score must also be measured. The following three instruments measure adaptive behavior.)

- Vineland Social Maturity Scale
- American Association on Mental Deficiencies (AAMD) Adaptive Behavior Scales
- Adaptive Behavior Inventory for Children

PERSONALITY TESTS

I. Objective tests, designed to determine predominant personality traits or behavior:

Minnesota Multiphasic Personality Inventory (MMPI) (can be used with adults and adolescents)

Personality Inventory for Children (PIC)

II. Projective tests give clients a stimulus, such as a picture to respond to—responses indicate problem areas.

Rorschach Test

Holtzman Inkblot Technique Thematic Apperception Test (TAT)

Children's Apperception Test (CAT)

Michigan Picture Test

Task of Emotional Development Test

Blacky Pictures

Make-a-picture-story Test

SOURCE: Shaefor, B., Horejsi, C., & Horejsi, G. (1988). *Techniques and guidelines for social work practice* (1st ed.). Copyright © 1988. Reprinted by permission of Pearson Education, Inc., New York, NY.

APPENDIX 6A

The Scales of Minnesota Multiphasic Personality Inventory-2, Restructured Form (MMPI-2-RF)

Validity Indicators

CNS: Cannot Say
VRIN-r: Variable Response Inconsistency
TRIN-r: True Response Inconsistency
F-r: Infrequent Responses
Fp-r: Infrequent Psychopathology
  Responses
Fs: Infrequent Somatic Responses
FBS-r: Symptom Validity
RBS: Response Bias
L-r: Uncommon Virtues
K-r: Adjustment Validity

Somatic/Cognitive Scales

MLS: Malaise
GIC: Gastro-Intestinal Complaints
HPC: Head Pain Complaints
NUC: Neurological Complaints
COG: Cognitive Complaints

Externalizing Scales

JCP: Juvenile Conduct Problems
SUB: Substance Abuse
AGG: Aggression
ACT: Activation

Interpersonal Scale

FML: Family Problems
IPP: Interpersonal Passivity
SAV: Social Avoidance
SHY: Shyness
DSF: Disaffiliativeness

PSY-5 (Personality Psychopathology Five) Scales, Revised

AGGR-r: Aggressiveness-Revised
INTR-r: Introversion/Low Positive
  Emotionality: Revised
DISC-r: Disconstraint-Revised

Higher Order (H-O) Scales

EID: Emotional/Internalizing Dysfunction
THD: Thought Dysfunction
BXD: Behavioral/Externalizing
  Dysfunction

Restructured Clinical (RC) Scales

RCd-(dem): Demoralization
RC1-(som): Somatic Complaints
RC2-(lpe): Low Positive Emotions
RC3-(cyn): Cynicism
RC4-(asb): Antisocial Behavior
RC6-(per): Ideas of Persecution
RC7-(dne): Dysfunctional Negative
  Emotions
RC8-(abx): Aberrant Experiences
RC9-(hpm): Hypomanic Activation

Internalizing Scales

SUI: Suicidal/Death Ideation
HLP: Helplessness/Hopelessness
SFD: Self-Doubt
NFC: Inefficacy
STW: Stress/Worry
AXY: Anxiety
ANP: Anger Proneness
BRF: Behavior-Restricting Fears
MSF: Multiple Specific Fears

Interest Scales

AES: Aesthetic-Literary Interests
MEC: Mechanical-Physical Interests
PSYC-r: Psychoticism-Revised
NEGE-r: Negative Emotionality/
  Neuroticism-Revised

Michigan Alcohol Screening Test (MAST Revised)

The MAST is a simple test that helps assess if you have a drinking problem.

1. Do you feel you are a normal drinker? ("normal"— drink as much or less than most other people)
   Circle Answer: Yes No

2. Have you ever awakened the morning after some drinking the night before and found that you could not remember a part of the evening?
   Circle Answer: Yes No

3. Does any near relative or close friend ever worry or complain about your drinking?
   Circle Answer: Yes No

4. Can you stop drinking without difficulty after one or two drinks?
   Circle Answer: Yes No

5. Do you ever feel guilty about your drinking?
   Circle Answer: Yes No

6. Have you ever attended a meeting of Alcoholics Anonymous (AA)?
   Circle Answer: Yes No

7. Have you ever gotten into physical fights when drinking?
   Circle Answer: Yes No

8. Has drinking ever created problems between you and a near relative or close friend?
   Circle Answer: Yes No

9. Has any family member or close friend gone to anyone for help about your drinking?
   Circle Answer: Yes No

10. Have you ever lost friends because of your drinking?
    Circle Answer: Yes No

11. Have you ever gotten into trouble at work because of drinking?
    Circle Answer: Yes No

12. Have you ever lost a job because of drinking?
    Circle Answer: Yes No

13. Have you ever neglected your obligations, your family, or your work for two or more days in a row because you were drinking?
    Circle Answer: Yes No

14. Do you drink before noon fairly often?
    Circle Answer: Yes No

15. Have you ever been told you have liver trouble such as cirrhosis?
    Circle Answer: Yes No

16. After heavy drinking have you ever had delirium tremens (d.t.'s), severe shaking, visual or auditory (hearing) hallucinations?
    Circle Answer: Yes No

17. Have you ever gone to anyone for help about your drinking?
    Circle Answer: Yes No

18. Have you ever been hospitalized because of drinking?
    Circle Answer: Yes No

19. Has your drinking ever resulted in your being hospitalized in a psychiatric ward?
    Circle Answer: Yes No

20. Have you ever gone to any doctor, social worker, clergyman, or mental health clinic for help with any emotional problem in which drinking was part of the problem?
    Circle Answer: Yes No

21. Have you been arrested more than once for driving under the influence of alcohol?
    Circle Answer: Yes No

22. Have you ever been arrested, even for a few hours because of other behavior while drinking?
    Circle Answer: Yes No

    (If yes, how many times _____)

Scoring for the MAST: Please score one point if you answered the following

1. No

2. Yes

3. Yes

4. No

5. Yes

6. Yes

7–22: Yes

Add up the scores and compare to the following:

> 0–2: No apparent problem
> 3–5: Early or middle problem drinker
> 6 or more: problem drinker

APPENDIX 7A

Examples of Circular Questions

I. Problem: Definition

Questions: Whenever possible, ask for a description of the specific behaviors which are perceived to be problematic.

A. *Present*
   - What is the problem in the family now?
   - What concerns bring you into therapy now? or: What concerns bring you here now?
   - What is the main concern of the family now?
   - What problems do the other children have?
   - For children: What changes would you like in your family?

   1. Difference
      - How is this different than before?
      - Has this always been true?

   2. Agreement/Disagreement
      - Who agrees with you that this is the problem?

   3. Explanation/Meaning
      - What is your explanation for that?
      - What does his behavior mean to you?

B. *Past*
   - What was the problem in the family then?

   1. Difference
      - How is that different from now?

   2. Agreement/Disagreement
      - How is that different from now?
      - Who agrees with Dad that this was the major concern of the family then?

   3. Explanation/Meaning
      - What is your explanation for that?
      - What do you believe was the significance of that?

SOURCE: Fleuridas, C., Nelson, T. S., and Rosenthal, D. M. (1986). The evolution of circular questions: Training family therapists. *Journal of Marital and Family Therapy, 23,* 113–127. Copyright © 1986 John Wiley and Sons. Reproduced with permission of Blackwell Publishing Ltd.

C. *Future/Hypothetical*
  - What would be the problem in the family if things were to continue as they are?

1. Difference
  - How would that be different than it is now?

2. Agreement/Disagreement
  - Do you agree, Mom?

3. Explanation/Meaning
  - If this were to happen, how would you explain it?
  - What purpose would that serve?

II. Sequence-of-Interaction Questions: Focus on interactional behaviors.

General Examples	Specific Examples
A. Present	
• Who does what when? • Then what happens? • What next? • Where is she when this happens? • What does she do? • Then what do they do? • Who notices first? • What does he respond? • When he does not do that (problem definition), what happens?	• Ask Daughter: When Mom tries to get Sister to eat (to solve or prevent the presenting problem) and she refuses, what does Dad do? Then what does Mom do? What does Brother do? And what does Sister do? Then what happens? • When Mom and Brother are fighting, what does Dad do? • Does Dad get involved in that fight or stay out of it? Describe what happens. • When Dad doesn't get involved in their fights, what happens? How does Mom react when Dad doesn't get involved?
1. Difference	
• Has it always been this way?	• Has Brother always behaved in this manner?
2. Agreement/Disagreement	
• Who agrees with you that this is how it happens?	• Who agrees with you that Mom yells at Dad every time he stomps out of the house?
3. Explanation/Meaning	
• What is your explanation for this? • What does this mean to you?	• How do you explain Dad's tendency to leave home often? • What does Dad's behavior mean to you?

General Examples	Specific Examples
B. Past	
• Who did what then?	• What did Dad do on those days when Brother used to push Mom around?
• What solutions were tried?	
1. Difference	
• How was it different?	• How was Dad's behavior different? Describe what he used to do
• When was it different?	
• What else was different then?	
• How does that differ from how it is now?	• When did he do this? How often?
• Was it then more or less than it is now?	• When did he change?
	• How did Dad respond to the earlier situation? Then what happened?
	• How does that differ from how he responds now?
	• Was he gone more or less often then he is now?
2. Agreement/Disagreement	
• Who agrees with you?	• Who agrees with Mom that Dad is more involved in the fights now?
3. Explanation/Meaning	
• How do you explain this change?	• How do you explain this recent involvement?
• What does this change (or lack of change) mean to you?	• What does it mean to you that day after day, year after year, things between the two of you have not changed?
C. Future/Hypothetical	
• What would she do differently if he did (not) do this?	• What do you think Mom would do if Dad were to ignore Brother?
	• What will Dad do with Brother when Mom begins to work nights?
1. Difference	
• How would it be different if he were to do this?	• How would your parents' relationship be different if Mom were to return to school?
2. Agreement/Disagreement	
• Who would agree with you that this is probably what would happen?	• Do you think Mom would agree that they would probably get a divorce if she were to return to school?

General Examples	Specific Examples
3. Explanation/Meaning • Tell me why you believe this would happen. • How do you think your wife would explain it? • What would this mean to you?	• Dad, why do you think your daughter and wife both agree that a divorce is likely should your wife return to work? • What would a divorce between your parents mean to you?

APPENDIX 7B

Mediator's Assessment of Safety Issues and Concerns (MASIC)

Date: _____ Case Name(s): _____ Case Number: _____ Circle: Mother / Father

MEDIATOR'S ASSESSMENT OF SAFETY ISSUES AND CONCERNS
PRACTITIONER VERSION 2 (MASIC-2P) [i]

(ADMINISTERED VERBALLY BY THE MEDIATOR IN FAMILY LAW CASES WITH CHILDREN)

The authors of this instrument recommend that, if possible, the mediator should (a) obtain any court or police records that might address parties' violent or abusive conduct before completing this Assessment, (b) complete this Assessment in intake session(s) separate from negotiation session(s), and (c) complete this Assessment with each party privately (i.e., separately from the other party).

[Read introduction and questions to each party:] In mediation, parents work together to try to make decisions in their children's best interests outside of court. Mediators do not take sides and do not decide for the parents how to settle their case. Rather, mediators assist both parents in exploring ways to resolve any disagreements in this confidential settlement process. Before the parents start negotiations, we do an intake where we explain the mediation process and ask parents to give us some background information and complete a confidential intake form.[ii] You may wonder about some of the questions, but it is helpful to think of this like a visit to the doctor's office. There, you are often asked questions that may not seem important to you, but are important to the doctor. The questions we ask are important to us in deciding what would work best for you and the other parent. So please answer the following questions to the best of your ability, knowing that we will keep your answers to these questions private and confidential from the court and the other parent.

Section 1

1. What is your age: _____ What is the other parent's age: _____

2. Are you employed? ☐ Yes ☐ No Is the other parent employed? ☐ Yes ☐ No

3. If you have ever lived/stayed with the other parent, when was the last time that you lived or stayed together?

   [Focus here on whether the parents are currently living or staying together.] _____

4. If you have ever lived/stayed with the other parent, for how long did you live/stay together? _____

5. Which parent left the relationship? ☐ You ☐ The other parent ☐ Both parents decided to end relationship

6. Why did [you/the other parent] leave the relationship? _____

   _____

7. Do you have any children from another marriage or relationship who live with you? ☐ Yes ☐ No

---

[i] Amy Holtzworth-Munroe, Connie J.A. Beck, and Amy G. Applegate, Mediator's Assessment of Safety Issues and Concerns Practitioner Version 2 (MASIC-2P) (2012). The questions in Section 2 of this assessment have been adapted from Marshall L.L., Development of the Severity of Violence Against Women Scale; Sullivan CM, Parisian JA, Davidson WS, Index of Psychological Abuse; and Tjaden P, Thoennes N, National Violence Against Women Survey. The Marshall, Sullivan, and Tjaden screens, in their entirety, have been validated. In addition, initial reliability and validity data for Section 2 of the MASIC is available and can be obtained from the authors upon request (Holtzworth-Munroe, Pokman, Rossi, Beck, and Applegate, June 2012, Association of Family and Conciliation Courts conference). The authors wish to acknowledge their law and psychology students who assisted, directly and indirectly, in the development of this Assessment.
[ii] To obtain a copy of the Confidential Intake Form used by mediators in the Viola J. Taliaferro Family and Children Mediation Clinic at the IU Maurer School of Law, contact Professor Amy G. Applegate at aga@indiana.edu.

1

Date: _____ Case Name(s): _____ Case Number: _____ Circle: Mother / Father

8. If yes, how does the other parent get along with your other child or children? _____

_____

9. Are you comfortable mediating with the other parent? ☐ Yes   ☐ No

10. If not, what makes you uncomfortable? _____

_____

11. What, if anything, would make you feel more comfortable? _____

_____

12. Do you think there is any reason why you should not participate in this mediation? ☐ Yes   ☐ No

13. If yes, please explain: _____

_____

14. Everyone fights or argues with family members and friends now and then. What happened when you fought or argued with the other parent involved in this mediation?

_____

_____

15. Which of the following statements most correctly describes how you and the other parent have made decisions in the past twelve (12) months? [If parents ask what kind of decisions, break out question into child/ren's care / finances / other kinds of decisions – ask them to clarify.]

____ You have made almost all decisions
____ You have made the majority of the decisions
____ You and the other parent have shared equally in making decisions
____ The other parent has made the majority of the decisions
____ The other parent has made almost all of the decisions

16. How satisfied are you with your role in influencing and making decisions about your child/ren's care?

____ Very satisfied
____ Satisfied
____ Neutral / it varies
____ Unsatisfied
____ Very unsatisfied

17. Do you have any of the following concerns about the other parent?

____ Overuse of alcohol or prescription medications
____ Illegal drug use
____ Mental health problems
____ Child abuse and/or neglect concerns
____ Any criminal history

2

Date: _____ Case Name(s): _____ Case Number: _____ Circle: Mother / Father

If yes, please tell me about your concerns: _____

_____

18. Do you think the other parent will say that s/he has any of the following concerns about you?

      ___ Overuse of alcohol or prescription medications
      ___ Illegal drug use
      ___ Mental health problems
      ___ Child abuse and/or neglect concerns
      ___ Any criminal history

19. Have either you or the other parent ever been involved with the Department of Child Services (Child Protective Services)?   ☐ Yes ☐ No

20. If yes, please explain: _____

_____

21. During the mediation, would you prefer to sit in the same room with the other parent or in a different room?
      ☐ Same room   ☐ Different room   ☐ No preference

22. If in a different room, why? _____

23. If in the same room, why? _____

24. Are there any current or past protective orders, restraining orders, or orders of protection issued against the other parent in this case?   ☐ Yes   ☐ No

25. If yes, please explain: _____

_____

26. Does the other parent own or have access to any weapons? ☐ Yes ☐ No

27. If yes, what kind(s) of weapons?_____

28. Do you own or have access to any weapons? ☐ Yes ☐ No

29. If yes, what kind(s) of weapons?_____

30. If the Court ordered mediation, why do you believe that the Court ordered this matter to mediation?

_____

_____

31. What parenting plan or arrangements do you think would work best for your family?

_____

_____

Date: _____ Case Name(s): _____ Case Number: _____ Circle: Mother / Father

Section 2

Now, I am going to ask you a series of questions about your relationship with NAME [the other parent]. I am interested in things that [NAME] may have done during a conflict, disagreement, fight, or in anger, or to scare you or hurt you.

First, I will ask if something ever happened, and you should answer yes or no.

Second, if you answer yes, then I will ask if it happened within the past 12 months.

	A. Did the other parent ever (whether living together or not)		B. Did that happen in the past 12 months?	
1.	Call you names?	Yes No	Yes No	
2.	Insult you or make you feel bad in front of others?	Yes No	Yes No	
3.	Yell or scream at you?	Yes No	Yes No	
4.	Forbid you to go out without him/her?	Yes No	Yes No	
5.	Try to control how much money you had or spent?	Yes No	Yes No	
6.	Try to control your activities in or outside the home?	Yes No	Yes No	
7.	Try to control your contact with family and friends?	Yes No	Yes No	
8.	Act extremely jealous, or frequently check up on where you've been or who you've been with?	Yes No	Yes No	
9.	Demand that you obey him/her?	Yes No	Yes No	
10.	Physically abuse or threaten to abuse pets to scare or hurt you, or when angry at you?	Yes No	Yes No	
11.	Punish or deprive the children because he/she was angry at you?	Yes No	Yes No	
12.	Make threatening gestures or faces at you or shake a fist at you?	Yes No	Yes No	
13.	Threaten to take or have the children taken away from you?	Yes No	Yes No	
14.	Destroy property, for example, hit or kick a wall, door, or furniture or throw, smash, or break an object?	Yes No	Yes No	
15.	Drive dangerously to scare you, or when angry at you?	Yes No	Yes No	
16.	Throw an object at you to scare or hurt you, or when angry at you?	Yes No	Yes No	
17.	Destroy or harm something you care about?	Yes No	Yes No	
18.	Threaten to hurt someone you care about?* (If yes, ask for details and write them here)	Yes No	Yes No	
19.	Threaten to hurt you?* (If yes, ask for details and write them here)	Yes No	Yes No	
20.	Threaten to kill him/herself?* (If yes, ask for details and write them here)	Yes No	Yes No	
21.	Threaten to kill you?* (If yes, ask for details and write them here)	Yes No	Yes No	

4

Date: _____ Case Name(s): _____ Case Number: _____ Circle: Mother / Father

22.	Threaten you with a weapon or something like a weapon?* (If yes, ask for details, including, what kind(s) of weapon(s) or object(s); write details here)	Yes	No	Yes	No

I want to remind you that all my questions concern things that [NAME] may have done during a conflict, disagreement, or fight, or in anger, or to scare or hurt you.

23.	Hold you down, pinning you in place?	Yes	No	Yes	No
24.	Push, shove, shake or grab you?	Yes	No	Yes	No
25.	Scratch you, or pull your hair, or twist your arm, or bite you?	Yes	No	Yes	No
26.	Slap you?	Yes	No	Yes	No
27.	Hit or punch you?	Yes	No	Yes	No
28.	Kick or stomp on you?	Yes	No	Yes	No
29.	Choke or strangle you?	Yes	No	Yes	No
30.	Burn you with something?	Yes	No	Yes	No
31.	Use a weapon or something like a weapon against you? If yes, what kind(s) of weapon(s) or object(s)?	Yes	No	Yes	No
32.	Demand or insist that you engage in sexual activities against your will?	Yes	No	Yes	No
33.	Physically force you to engage in sexual activities against your will?	Yes	No	Yes	No
34.	Follow or spy on you in a way that made you feel frightened or harassed?	Yes	No	Yes	No
35.	Try to contact you against your will or in a way that made you feel frightened or harassed, for example, by unwanted phone calls, mail, text messages, or Facebook contacts?	Yes	No	Yes	No
36.	Stand outside your home, school, workplace, or other places where he/she had no business being, and in a way that made you feel frightened or harassed?	Yes	No	Yes	No
37.	Leave items for you to find in a way that made you feel frightened or harassed?	Yes	No	Yes	No
38.	Do anything else similar to the kinds of behaviors we've been discussing? If yes, what kind(s) of behavior(s)?	Yes	No	Yes	No

Now consider the things we've been discussing or similar kinds of things:

39.	As a result of the other parent's behaviors, did you ever feel fearful, scared or afraid of physical harm to yourself or to others?	Yes	No	Yes	No

5

Date: _____ Case Name(s): _____ Case Number: _____ Circle: Mother / Father

	As a result of the other parent's behaviors, have you ever received any of the following types of physical injury?				
40.	Scratch, small bruise, swelling, or other mild injury?	Yes	No	Yes	No
41.	Fracture, small burn, cut, large bruise, or other moderate Injury?	Yes	No	Yes	No
42.	Major wound, severe bleeding or burn, being knocked out, or other severe injury? Notes:	Yes	No	Yes	No
43.	Blindness, loss of hearing, disfigurement, chronic pain, or other permanent damage? Notes:	Yes	No	Yes	No
44.	Did you seek, or should you have sought medical attention For any injury caused by the other parent?	Yes	No	Yes	No
45.	As a result of the other parent's behaviors, did you or someone else ever call the police? Who called the police? When and what specifically prompted the call?	Yes	No	Yes	No

Section 3

1. [*If the parent endorsed any of items 22-31 and 33 above*]: You said that [NAME] [*insert applicable behaviors, e.g., has slapped you and choked you*] in the past 12 months. Have these types of behaviors been happening more often recently?   ☐ Yes ☐ No

2. [*If the parent endorsed any of items 22-31 and 33 above*]: Have these types of behaviors been getting worse or more serious recently?   ☐ Yes ☐ No

For **ALL** parties, regardless of whether or not they endorsed items 22-31 and 33, ask the following questions:

3. Are you afraid that the other parent will harm you during the mediation or after you leave because of what you say or do in mediation?   ☐ Yes ☐ No

4. If yes, please explain: _____

5. Do you believe that you are in danger at this time? ☐ Yes ☐ No

6. If yes, please explain: _____

7. Is there anything else you would like to share with me/us [the mediator(s)]?

_____

8. Is there anything else you think I/we [the mediator(s)] should know?

_____

ANSWER KEY

When responding to the questions, please use these choices for your answers about whether something EVER happened:

YES or NO

When responding to the questions, please use these choices for your answers about the PAST 12 MONTHS:

YES or NO

Index

About the Editors

Catheleen Jordan, Ph.D.
Cheryl Milkes Moore Professorship in Mental Health
School of Social Work, The University of Texas at Arlington

Catheleen Jordan is professor and holder of the Cheryl Milkes Moore Professorship in Mental Health at The University of Texas at Arlington, School of Social Work, where she has taught since 1985. She received the Lifetime Achievement Award from the National Association of Social Workers–Texas, where she was president from 2007 to 2009.

Professor Jordan has more than 100 publications, including *Introduction to Family Social Work*, fourth edition (with Don Collins and Heather Coleman of the University of Calgary). Her areas of expertise include family social work assessment and intervention, particularly in the areas of family violence. She is codirector of the Youth Offender Diversion Alternative Project (YODA) with Peter Lehmann and is editor for two journals: *Children in Schools* and *Journal of Social Work Education*.

Professor Jordan previously directed the Community Service Clinic and the Ph.D. program at the School of Social Work, where she was also chair of the Direct Practice Sequence. Prior to academia, Professor Jordan worked with Child Protective Services in Texas and with Court Appointed Special Advocates in California, and received her Ph.D. at the University of California Berkeley in 1986.

Cynthia G. S. Franklin, Ph.D.
Assistant Dean for Doctoral Education and Stiernberg/
Spencer Family Professor in Mental Health

Professor Franklin is Stiernberg/Spencer Family Professor in Mental Health and Assistant Dean for the Ph.D. program in the School of Social Work at the University of Texas at Austin. Professor Franklin also holds a faculty fellow appointment at the Meadows Center for Preventing Educational Risk in the Department of Special Education.

Professor Franklin has more than 150 publications in the professional literature and is a world-renowned scholar in school mental health. Her research examines the practice and effectiveness of solution-focused brief therapy with children and adolescents. She is the current editor-in chief for the *Encyclopedia of Social Work* and is the author of several books, including *The School Services Sourcebook: A Guide for School-based Professionals* (Oxford University Press) and *Solution Focused Brief Therapy: A Handbook of Evidence-base Practice* (Oxford University Press).

Over the past twenty-five years, Professor Franklin has worked as a therapist, consultant, trainer, and researcher for schools and mental health agencies. She is a clinical fellow of the American Association of Marriage and Family Therapy and holds practice licenses in clinical social work (LCSW) and marriage and family therapy (LMFT).

CPSIA information can be obtained
at www.ICGtesting.com
Printed in the USA
BVHW09s2014200718
522149BV00005B/17/P